THE UNTIMELY PRESENT

POST-CONTEMPORARY INTERVENTIONS

Series Editors: Stanley Fish and Fredric Jameson

THE UNTIMELY PRESENT

Postdictatorial Latin American Fiction

and the Task of Mourning

IDELBER AVELAR

Duke University Press   Durham and London   1999

00-665

© 1999 Duke University Press

All rights reserved

Printed in the United States of America on acid-free paper ∞

Typeset in Weiss by Tseng Information Systems, Inc.

Library of Congress Cataloging-in-Publication Data appear

on the last printed page of this book.

CONTENTS

Acknowledgments ix

Introduction: Allegory and Mourning in Postdictatorship 1

1. OEDIPUS IN POST-AURATIC TIMES
Modernization and Mourning in the Spanish American Boom 22

2. THE GENEALOGY OF A DEFEAT
Latin American Culture under Dictatorship 39

3. COUNTERTRADITIONS
The Allegorical Rewriting of the Past 86

4. ENCRYPTING RESTITUTION
A Detective Story in the City of the Dead 107

5. PASTICHE, REPETITION, AND THE ANGEL
OF HISTORY'S FORGED SIGNATURE 136

6. OVERCODIFICATION OF THE MARGINS
Figures of the Eternal Return and the Apocalypse 164

7. BILDUNGSROMAN AT A STANDSTILL, OR
THE WEAKENING OF STORYTELLING 186

8. THE UNMOURNED DEAD AND THE PROMISE
OF RESTITUTION 210

Afterword: Postdictatorship and Postmodernity 230

Notes 235

Works Cited 271

Index 287

A BRECHTIAN MAXIM:

DO NOT BUILD ON THE GOOD OLD DAYS,

BUT ON THE BAD NEW ONES.

—Walter Benjamin, *Reflections*

ACKNOWLEDGMENTS

How is restitution possible or conceivable when that which is to be restituted belongs in the order of *affect*? The one who expresses heartfelt gratitude in this sense resembles the mourner: both are engaged in a restitutive task perceived to be imperative and impossible, ineluctable yet necessarily failed. Both are involved in ritualized practices that exceed, and are exceeded by, the affect they attempt to translate and express. As a requisite for the very writing of their books, the thankful have to conjure and actively forget the proper names they now bring back to presence and remember in their notes of acknowledgment. The mournful, in their turn, bring the other back into presence as part of a labor the ultimate horizon of which is active forgetting itself. Across that dialectic between reminiscence and oblivion all work of mourning and all gestures of gratitude find their conditions of possibility and their limit. This book will have the opportunity to ask whether there is anything accidental about this convergence between mourning and gratitude, between remembering-to-forget and forgetting-to-remember, between the impossibility of properly thanking these proper names and the impossibility of properly mourning the proper names we Latin Americans lost under dictatorship.

The possibility of posing these problems would not exist were it not for the interlocution with and friendship of Alberto Moreiras and George Yúdice throughout virtually all of the past decade. Alberto Moreiras wrote the first theoretical exploration of postdictatorship as a concept in 1993, and his dialogue, guidance, and generosity in the early stages of this project helped not only get it off the ground but provided it with its tentative but growing coherence. From Hegel to Piglia, from Gadamer to Borges, we covered quite a bit of ground together, and to him I owe sincere thanks. George Yúdice has been a dear friend for almost a decade, in New York, Rio, Belo Horizonte, Buenos Aires, Italy, Durham, and Champaign. He has contributed in a most cosmopolitan fashion not only to this book but to a good many events in my career. I owe to his intelligence, breadth, and verve more than the traditional academic mechanisms of quotes and references could ever express. From Fredric Jameson I received the precious feedback and generous exchanges by now as legendary among his students as the superb lectures on anything from third world film to Brecht and Marx, Proust and Barthes. From Walter Mignolo I learned not only what I know about Latin American coloniality and postcoloniality but also whatever ethic of listening I may have been able to craft for myself. True gratitude is owed to him as well. With Teresa Vilarós I shared hypotheses on the Latin American and Spanish postdictatorships, and her rigorous reading of an early stage of this book was decisive for me. Michael Hardt offered me invaluable responses to my writing on postdictatorship, as well as learned guidance through Deleuze, Blanchot, Bataille, and Klossowski.

Nelly Richard not only has made possible for me to establish a dialogue with theoretical and artistic scenes in Chile. Her intense and experimental writing, her friendship, and the pioneering *Revista de Crítica Cultural* she edits have indeed been conditions of possibility for my work. Willy Thayer, who to my mind has produced some of the most rigorous and inventive readings of Marx in recent decades, has been a dear friend for years. His dialogue and proper name have a presence that is beyond the restitutable in this book's notes as well. To Diamela Eltit I owe not only the unpayable gift of having been able to read her work, to which I hope to have made justice in chapter 6. Her generosity in receiving me several times in her house, to discuss Chilean literature and her own labor of writing, was instrumental for this book. In Santiago I have also enjoyed the friendship and hospitality of poet Sergio Parra and critic Raquel Olea, who both helped me with the research on recent Chilean fiction. To Marina Arrate gratitude is due for making available to me her impeccable analysis of Diamela Eltit's *Por la patria*. I have had the joy and privilege of meeting Pablo Oyarzún in Santiago, and his work too has been more inspiring than what can be made immediately visible. I have also dialogued in Chile with the voices and texts of Carlos Pérez Villalobos, Sergio Rojas, and Federico Galende. Of their truly philosophical intelligence I will always have great remembrances.

In the United States several people have read portions of the manuscript, or dialogued with me in ways that have informed it. Julio Ramos is the author of the Latin American book of criticism I admire the most, the text I truly would like to have written. Having become his friend and interlocutor in recent years has indeed been a joy, and his contribution to whatever merits this book might have is immeasurable. John Beverley offered me a generous reading of a chapter, and to him I owe sincere thanks as well. John Kraniauskas offered invaluable input on chapter 2 and the interlocution without which much of the rest of the book could not have been written. At Duke I am indebted to Mark Healey, Horacio Legrás, Juan Poblete, Tatjana Gajic, and Jon Beasley-Murray for brilliant readings of parts of the book. In Argentina, Ricardo Piglia read an earlier version of what later became chapters 3 and 4, and his positive response meant much for the development of this project. I hope to have done justice to his work as well. Noé Jitrik, one of the most important Latin American intellectuals and a key critic of Argentine literature, generously hosted me and provided me with precious avenues of research in Buenos Aires. Above all I must thank Tununa Mercado, for existing, for sharing so generously, and for writing the most radical postdictatorial prose I know. If I have not conveyed the singularity of her work in chapter 8 this book will have failed, for her rethinking of writing in the light of mourning indeed provides me with the conceptual backbone for what I have attempted here.

The two Brazilian authors I have analyzed in this book, Silviano Santiago and João Gilberto Noll, met with me to discuss Brazilian literature as well as their fictional (in the case of Silviano Santiago also critical-theoretical) work, and I thank them for their attention and comments. In Brazil and in the United States Ana Lúcia Gazolla has provided more energy and continuing support than I deserve, and she has made this book possible in more ways than we might know ourselves. Gratitude is due also to a number of former colleagues and teachers from the Federal University of Minas Gerais, especially to Julio Pinto. At the University of North Carolina, Chapel Hill, I must thank Fred Clark for two years of great dialogue. At the University of Illinois, Urbana-Champaign, I have found the collegial and friendly atmosphere so essential for any intellectual project. Ronald W. Sousa has supported and believed in my work from the beginning. I am grateful to him and to the entire team he leads in the Department of Spanish, Italian, and Portuguese, in the case of this book specifically to Elena Delgado and Paul Borgeson for offering their views on some of the theses presented here. The dialogue with my colleagues in the Unit for Criticism and Interpretive Theory has been most enlightening as well. Peter Garrett invited me to speak on post-dictatorial mourning at the unit; Michael Bérubé and Janet Lyon have continually supported the encounter between Latin America and critical theory; and Joe Valente offered me an insightful critique of an earlier version of chapter 8. For conversations on Brazilian music and literature, I will be forever indebted to Christopher Dunn. The undergraduate Spanish majors and graduate students in Spanish and comparative literature at Illinois have left their marks on this book or on books yet to come. To all of them, too numerous to mention, I owe heartfelt thanks. I have also profited from comments made to me at Illinois, Duke, Yale, De Paul, Dickinson College, and Tulane in the United States; the Minas Gerais, Rio de Janeiro, Santa Catarina, and Fluminense Federal Universities in Brazil; the Catholic University in Quito; and ARCIS University in Santiago, all during round tables or lectures related to this book. Gratitude is also due to J. Reynolds Smith, Sharon P. Torian, and Patricia Mickelberry for their superb editorial job.

I would also like to acknowledge permissions to reprint previously published material: parts of chapter 2 appeared in *Journal of Latin American Cultural Studies* as "Dictatorship and Immanence"; parts of chapters 3 and 4 appeared in Spanish as "Cómo respiran los ausentes: la narrativa de Ricardo Piglia" in *Modern Language Notes* 110 (1995): 416–32; chapter 5 has been slightly modified since its appearance in *Modern Fiction Studies* 44, no. 1 (1998): 184–214, as "The Angel of History's Forged Signature"; article versions of chapters 6 and 8 are forthcoming respectively as "Restitution and Mourning in Latin American Post-dictatorship," in *boundary 2* 26 (1999), and "An Anatomy of Marginality: Figures of the Eternal Return and the Apocalypse in Chilean Post-dictatorial Fiction," in *Studies in Twentieth-Century Literature* (1999).

As a reminder of how much affect exceeds the attempt at restitution, let it be said that without Nara and Alexandre none of this would have been possible, or mattered in the first place. I could never imagine I would have to mourn my mom-in-law, Leila Palhares (1940–98), before I could send her a copy of this. This book is dedicated to her memory.

INTRODUCTION Allegory and Mourning in Postdictatorship

The *possible*, which enters into *reality* as that *reality itself dissolves,* is operative and effects the sense of dissolution as well as the remembrance of that which has been dissolved. . . . In the perspective of ideal recollection, then, dissolution as a necessity becomes as such the ideal object of the newly developed life, a glance back on the path that had to be taken, from the beginning of dissolution up to that moment when, in the new life, there can occur a recollection of the dissolved. —FRIEDRICH HÖLDERLIN, *Essays and Letters on Theory*

At the most basic level a book on postdictatorial fiction is expected to deal with the theme of memory, and this will indeed be the case here. The literature produced in the aftermath of the recent Latin American dictatorships, however, confronts not only the need to come to terms with the past but also to define its position in the new present ushered in by the military regimes: a global market in which every corner of social life has been commodified. This book thus proceeds with two parallel goals in mind, on the one hand attempting to assess how and under what conditions of possibility contemporary postdictatorial literature and culture engage the past, and on the other interrogating the status of the literary in a time when literature no longer occupies the privileged position it once did. In fact, my effort is to think both questions simultaneously. If the dictatorships' raison d'être was the physical and symbolic elimination of all resistance to the implementation of market logic, how has the triumph of such a project informed Latin America's cultural and literary memory? How can one pose the task of mourning —which is always, in a sense, the task of *actively forgetting* —when all is immersed in *passive* forgetting, that brand of oblivion that ignores itself as such, not suspecting that it is the product of a powerful repressive operation? If the neoliber-alism implemented in the aftermath of the dictatorships is founded upon the passive forgetting of its barbaric origin, how can one, to use Wal-ter Benjamin's expression, seize hold of a reminiscence as it flashes up in a moment of danger, such danger being represented today by a com-modification of material and cultural life that seems to preclude the very existence of memory? Can literature still play any role in this mnemonic and political task?

Growing commodification negates memory because new commodi-ties must always replace previous commodities, send them to the dustbin of history. The free market established by the Latin American dictator-ships must, therefore, impose forgetting not only because it needs to erase the reminiscence of its barbaric origins but also because it is proper to the market to live in a perpetual present. The erasure of the past as past is the cornerstone of all commodification, even when the past becomes yet another commodity for sale in the present. The market operates ac-cording to a substitutive, metaphorical logic in which the past must be relegated to obsolescence. The past is to be forgotten because the market demands that the new replace the old without leaving a remainder. The task of the oppositional intellectual would be to point out the residue left by every substitution, thereby showing that the past is never simply erased by the latest novelty. The anachronistic, obsolete commodity, the recycled gadget, the museum piece, are all forms of survival of what has been replaced in the market. These images of ruins are crucial for postdictatorial memory work, for they offer anchors through which a connection with the past can be reestablished. In incessantly producing the new and discarding the old, the market also creates an array of left-overs that point toward the past, as if demanding restitution for what has been lost and forgotten. The texts I examine here insistently confront the ruins left by the dictatorships and extract from them a strongly alle-gorical meaning. Whereas the hegemonic political discourses in Latin America would like to "put a final stop" to "the fixation in the past," the vanquished, those who were defeated so that today's market could be implemented, cannot afford to have their tradition relegated to oblivion. In different forms the texts analyzed here bear witness to this will to reminisce, by drawing the present's attention to everything that was left unaccomplished and mournful in the past. In the very market that submits the past to the immediacy of the present, mournful literature will search for those fragments and ruins—remainders of the market's substitutive operation—that can trigger the untimely eruption of the past.

The imperative to mourn is the postdictatorial imperative par excellence. The literature I address in this book engages a mournful memory that attempts to overcome the trauma represented by the dictatorships. My focus will be those postdictatorial texts that remind the present that it is the product of a past catastrophe; these texts thus carry the seeds of a messianic energy, which, like the Benjaminian angel of history, looks back at the pile of debris, ruins, and defeats of the past in an effort to redeem them, being at the same time pushed forward by the forces of "progress" and "modernization." There is a *belatedness* proper to this endeavor, for it establishes a salvific relation with an object irrevocably lost. This is an engagement that cannot but be perpetually catching up with its own inadequacy, aware that all witnessing is a retrospective construction that must elaborate its legitimacy discursively, in the midst of a war in which the most powerful voice threatens to be that of forgetfulness. In the conceptual repertoire of modern criticism one particular notion will be crucial to understanding the nature of this engagement with the past, namely, the notion of *allegory*: "Whereas in the symbol destruction is idealized and the transfigured face of nature is fleetingly revealed in the light of redemption, in allegory the observer is confronted with the *facies hippocratica* of history as a petrified, primordial landscape. Everything about history that, from the very beginning, has been untimely, sorrowful, unsuccessful, is expressed in a face—or rather in a death's head."[1]

One of Benjamin's greatest contributions to the theory of the allegorical is to have shown the irreducible link that binds allegory and mourning. In much Baroque drama the final condensation of meaning around a corpse imposes upon the audience a pressing consciousness of its own transitoriness and mortality. Allegory thus entertains a close connection with the awareness of death: "The allegorization of the physis can only be carried through in all its vigor in respect of the corpse. And the characters of the *Trauerspiel* [tragic drama, literally, "mourning play"] die, because it is only thus, as corpses, that they can enter the homeland of allegory."[2] Allegory elevates corpses to the status of epochal emblems. The corpse embodies the allegorical object because *mourning lies at the very origin of allegory*. The mournful subject who confronts the loss of a loved being displays a special sensibility toward objects, articles of clothing, former possessions, anything that might trigger the memory of the one who died. The mournful self, much like a collector (two figures Benjamin often saw as akin to one another), makes a rescuing operation of the act of remembrance. His/her mute and melancholy stare upon an object detaches it from all connections, turns it into an emblem of what has been lost, an allegorically charged monad.

Allegory maintains a fundamental relationship with time. Whereas the symbol privileges timeless, eternalized images, allegory, by virtue of being a ruin, is necessarily a temporalized trope, bearing within itself the marks of its time of production. If mourning is in a fundamental sense a confrontation with time and its passing, allegory, as the trope that voices mourning, cannot but bear in itself unmistakable temporal marks. Paul de Man once noted that in the symbol the relationship between image and substance is one of simultaneity, where the intervention of time is merely a contingent matter, "whereas, in the world of allegory, time is the originary constitutive category."[3] If postdictatorial texts cannot, by definition, obviate their temporal predicament, if their thrust is to come to terms with a past catastrophe, it is expectable that they will display that pressing awareness of time proper to allegory. As opposed to the market's perpetual present, where the past must incessantly be turned into a tabula rasa to be replaced and discarded with the arrival of new commodities, the allegorical temporality of mourning clings to the past in order to save it, even as it attempts ultimately to produce an active forgetting of it.

To recall the famous Marxian dichotomy, mourning does not deal with use values. There is no "use" for an epitaph or a memorial—they dwell outside all utility. The work of mourning includes, as well, a moment of suspension of exchange value, for the mourner will always perceive his/her object as unique, resistant to any transaction, substitution, or exchange.[4] To be sure, mourning's ultimate horizon is itself a relationship of exchange: as the libido reinvests a new object, the "accomplished mourning work" will be the one that manages to carry out that metaphorical operation whereby the lost object is subsumed under a newly found object of affection. The horizon of completion for mourning is thus a metaphorics not unlike that of the market. However, what is most proper to mourning is to resist its own accomplishment, to oppose its own conclusion: "this is what mourning is, the history of its refusal."[5]

The mourner is by definition engaged in a task that s/he does not want to conclude. Therefore, even if the goal of a successful mourning work turns out to be an act of substitution in its own right—in the sense that the completion of mourning work entails the discharge of libido into a surrogate object—this substitution never fully erases the past, which is to say that mourning is never simply completed. It is in this sense, then, that one speaks of the interminability of mourning work: mourning necessarily poses itself an unrealizable task. Unlike the replacement of old by new commodities, the substitution proper to the work of mourning always includes the persistence of an únmourned, unresolved remainder, which is the very index of the interminability of mourning. That is, the exchange implied in mourning includes an acknowledgment of the limits of exchange. If the mourner does not achieve true introjection of the lost object, no healing of the loss will ever take effect without leaving behind an unassimilable residue, and mourning work will always preserve a dimension irreducible to the metaphorical operation proper to the market. What cannot be replaced, what lingers on as a residue of memory, is precisely the allegorically charged ruin—hence the contention that mourning suspends exchange value to posit a third dimension, irreducible to use and exchange, and not contemplated by Marx's opposition: that of *memory value*, a paradoxical kind of value, to be sure, because what is most proper to it is to resist any exchange. It is due to that insistence of memory, of the survival of the past as a ruin in the present, that mourning displays a necessarily allegorical structure.

The attempt to define the concept of allegory runs into many obstacles, not the least of which is an entrenched romantic prejudice that, continuing the neoclassical reaction against baroque "exaggeration," saw in allegory nothing more than a didactic and quasi-religious catechism. The classical-romantic reading of allegory coalesces in Johann Wolfgang von Goethe, according to whom the true nature of poetry consists in creating symbols, that is, in seeing the general in the particular, whereas in allegory "the particular serves only as an instance or example of the general."[6] Likewise, Georg Hegel identifies in allegory a "frostiness," which consists in its being

> the abstraction of a universal idea which acquires only the empty
> form of subjectivity and is to be called a subject only, as it were, in

a grammatical sense. An allegorical being, however much it may be given a human shape, does not achieve the individuality of a Greek god or of a saint or of some other actual person, because, in order that there may be congruity between subjectivity and the abstract meaning which it has, the allegorical being must make subjectivity so hollow that all specific individuality vanishes from it.[7]

This is the view that led to an understanding of allegory as an aberrant, pathological deviation from the organic, disinterested, translucent ideal of symbolic poetic language. In Hegel's view of allegory the conceptual element, the realm of meaning, "dominates" and subsumes under itself a "specific externality [that] is only a sign."[8] The symbol avoids this subsumption by rounding up a closed totality in which image and meaning, sign and concept are indistinguishably unified. In the symbol, Hegel argues, the reabsorption of the conceptual element into its aesthetic actualization is such that the separation between the two, proper to allegory, is bridged. If "digestion is for Hegel the assimilation and appropriation of an outer into an inner, and as such a figure for dialectic in general,"[9] it is the sublative, ascending mediation of the symbol, not the abrupt, undialectical discontinuity of allegory, that must be privileged. The symbol is thus affirmed as the aesthetic ambassador of the dialectic, the trope capable of appropriating the outer into the inner and carrying out the successful digestion that is itself the privileged gastronomic symbol of dialectic thought.

In England it was up to Samuel Taylor Coleridge, who assumed the task of directing enraged attacks at allegory as a "mechanic" form, to which he opposed the "organic," "natural," "transparent" quality of the symbol.[10] There was thus an element of untimeliness to allegory in the nineteenth century. Benjamin notes in the *Passagen-Werk* that only Charles-Pierre Baudelaire's poetry articulates a full response to the primacy of the symbol: "as an allegorist, Baudelaire was isolated."[11] Goethe, Hegel, and Coleridge agreed in seeing in allegory a degeneration in which the particular is only a sheer externality in which the conceptual-universal lodges itself. It is as though in allegory singularities referred back too quickly to the universalities for which they stand. What Goethe, Hegel, and Coleridge condemned in allegory was the *lack of mediation*. The abrupt, dizzying manner in which allegory alludes to its object made it unfit for the romantic project, which tended to privilege the progressive ascension of meaning into a well-rounded totality. As the symbol was designated the mode of signification par excellence, allegory was reduced to a "mere mode of designation."[12]

A revealing passage by Benedetto Croce chastises allegory for submitting spirit to the materiality of writing: "allegory is not a direct mode of spiritual manifestation, but a kind of cryptography or writing."[13] In Croce's idealist aesthetics this represented, to be sure, a shortcoming. Beyond the value judgment, however, Croce captures a fundamental component of the problem, namely, the link between allegory and writing, more specifically between allegory and crypt. In its origins, in medieval iconography and baroque emblem books, allegory took the form of a relationship established across an image and its caption. Karl Giehlow, an instrumental figure in the early twentieth-century rehabilitation of allegory, postulated a relationship between the sixteenth-century reemergence of allegory and the then newly initiated deciphering of Egyptian hieroglyphs. The importance accorded by the baroque to the physical arrangement of print upon the page is certainly well known. Croce is thus right in noting the link between allegory and inscription, for in baroque allegory all interiority is evacuated into the exteriority of the page: "[In] allegorical personification . . . there is not the faintest glimmer of any spiritualization of the physical. The whole of nature is personalized, not so as to be made more inward, but on the contrary—so as to be deprived of soul."[14] Allegory thus maintains a relationship with the divine, but with a fallen, incomprehensible, Babelic, written divinity. Allegory flourishes in a world abandoned by the gods, one that preserves, however, a trace of memory of such abandonment and therefore has not been eaten away by oblivion quite yet. My job here will be, then, to track down the cryptic manifestation of this allegorical trace in the corpus of postdictatorial literature.

Revisiting one of Freud's most illustrious cases, that of the Wolf Man, Nicolas Abraham and Maria Torok have developed the notion of *cryptonymy* to allude to the organized system of partial synonymies incorporated into the ego as a sign of the impossibility of naming the traumatic word. The crypt, for Abraham and Torok, is a figure for the paralysis that maintains mourning at a standstill.[15] In the now classic Freudian distinction between mourning and melancholia, itself elaborated under the impact of the Wolf Man case,[16] mourning designates a process of over-coming loss in which the separation between the ego and the lost object can still be effected, whereas in melancholia the identification with the lost object reaches an extreme in which the ego is engulfed and be-comes itself part of the loss. Cutting across this distinction, Abraham and Torok differentiate between introjection and incorporation as two modalities of internalization of loss. Introjection designates the horizon of a successful completion of mourning work, whereby the lost object is dialectically absorbed and expelled, internalized in such a way that the libido can now be discharged into a surrogate object. Introjection thus secures a relation to the deceased at the same time as it compensates for the loss.[17] In incorporation, on the other hand, the traumatic object remains lodged within the ego as a foreign body, "invisible yet omnipres-ent,"[18] unnameable except through partial synonyms. Needless to say, as long as this object resists introjection it will manifest itself in distorted and cryptic form. Expressing a "refusal to reclaim as our own the part of ourselves that we placed in what we lost,"[19] incorporation erects an intra-psychic tomb where the loss is denied and the lost object is buried alive, as it were. For Freud art and literature constitute, along with dreams and parapraxias, a privileged mode of manifestation of this unresolved trauma and loss. What Abraham and Torok name *crypt* will be here understood, in all its manifestations, whether in literature or in cultural and political practices, as *allegorical crypt*, that is to say, the remainder that names the phantasmic persistence of unresolved mourning work. And it is here that the allegorical nature proper to all ruins forces us to reflect anew on the specificity of postdictatorial mourning.

If postdictatorial mourning manifests itself in certain semiotic prac-tices as allegory, then it is the possible link between the crypt of a love object buried alive within the ego—the insistence of incorpora-tion, or the refusal to mourn—and the structure of allegory that must be pursued. For in allegory too the sign undergoes resistance to figuration, or the usage preemptive of the very figurative capability of signs seen by Abraham and Torok as characteristic of incorporation. The establish-ment of an intrapsychic tomb implies a use of words that reduces them to phantasmic doubles of the object itself, fantasized materializations of the word's unnameable traumatic referent. Melancholia thus emerges as a reaction against a threat to the protective crypt, because the subject begins to identify with the love object as a way of protecting him/her from the possibility of being mourned. Much like the allegorical tradition of hieroglyphs and baroque emblems—where the very materiality of the object takes over the image and its epigraph—the incorporative refusal to mourn becomes manifest in the subject as a subsumption of all metaphoricity under a brute literalness identified with the object itself. As writer Tununa Mercado has explored extensively in *En estado de memoria*—highly fragmented and reflexive memoirs analyzed later in this book—the labor of mourning has much to do with the erection of an *exterior* tomb where the brutal literalization of the internal tomb can be metaphorized. Such attempt to crystallize the recognition of Antigone, to install the irreducibility of mourning in the polis (and have that irreducibility acknowledged by the state), counters the putative takeover of melancholia. This attempt is itself mediated, however, by allegorical structures. As Mercado writes her way through melancholia into mourning work, her very text becomes a mediating force between the ghost of a becoming-universal of allegory (the melancholic's abyss where the gaze can only find allegories) and the Antigonal struggle to erect civic symbols where the imperative to mourn can be sanctioned in the polis. This struggle itself faces not only psychic obstacles, of course, as a transnational political and economic order repeatedly reaffirms its interest in blocking the advance of postdictatorial mourning work—as the digging of the past may stand in the way of the accumulation of capital in the present.

   In spite of the fact that allegory has occupied a major space in the Southern Cone's aesthetic and cultural debates, the whole complex that links allegory to memory, experience, and writing qua inscription is still virtually unthought, often explained away in more or less sophisticated versions of a specular reflexivism: in times of censorship, writers are forced to resort to "indirect ways," "metaphors," and "allegories" to "express" what is invariably thought to be a self-identical content that could remain so inside another rhetorical cloak in times of "free expression." More thinking than this into allegory can be drawn from Ricardo Piglia's brief anecdote of how right after his trip abroad and return to the country in 1977, the Argentine dictatorship had renamed bus stops as "zones of detention."[20] In the very slippage of *detención* through its wide spectrum of meanings—detain, stop, incarcerate—and the expansion of those zones to bus stops across the entire city, the inscription lent itself to be read allegorically and reconnected with collective history. The image and its caption experimented under dictatorship a becoming-allegory, for they condensed the significance of an experience lived throughout the polis. If the dictatorships have resignified every corner of the city, if the catastrophe is blocked from public memory by the absence of monuments to the dead, postdictatorial literature depicts the urban space as an allegorical ruin. It is through these ruins that postcatastrophe literature reactivates the hope of providing an entrance into a traumatic experience that has seemingly been condemned to silence and oblivion.

To the melancholy gaze, history is inevitably spatialized, only redeemed in a freezing gesture that captures the past as an allegorical monad. Such salvific relation with memory must petrify the past as image and sever it from all cushioning associations, thus making of "memory not an instrument for exploring the past but its theater."[21] This brings us to one of the major discontinuities between Benjamin and the more orthodox Hegelian tradition that culminates in György Lukács: whereas the Hegelian tradition could only privilege the sublative, progressive flow of becoming, Benjamin, more schooled in the teachings conveyed by catastrophes, made of the recollecting act an interruptive machine, much like Bertolt Brecht sought to present his scenes as independent shots juxtaposing and contrasting separate situations. The metaphor of memory-as-theater, as opposed to memory-as-instrument, makes the remembered image condense in itself, as a scene, the entire failure of the past, as an emblem rescued out of oblivion. Trapped between the imperative of memory and a general inability to imagine an alternative future, postdictatorial fiction maintains an estranged, denaturalized relation with its present. Pressed by the demand to bear a certain remembrance, it attempts to respond to an unprecedented atrophy in our memories, epitomized in our incapacity to synthesize the past as a coherent totality. The demand that literature become the reserve of memory is, to a great extent, an impossible demand, and it is in this impossibility, as an expression of it, that allegory emerges.

In an article that is more often attacked than actually read, Fredric Jameson connects third world literary production with the primacy of the allegorical. I do not rehearse Jameson's arguments again here, but I draw on one of his observations about the relevance of allegory for postcolonial situations: "It was not difficult to identify an adversary who spoke another language and wore the visible signs of colonial occupation. When those are replaced by your own people, the connections to external control are much more difficult to represent."[22] The impossibility of representing the totality is one of the sources of allegory, because allegory is a trope that thrives on breaks and discontinuities, as opposed to the unfractured wholeness presupposed by the symbol. What Jameson describes as the predicament of postcolonial societies is, mutatis mutandis, also the dilemma of postdictatorship. When the enemy has disappeared, or at least become much more difficult to locate, literature will *allos-agoreuein* (speak otherwise). In *Hotel Atlântico*, by the Brazilian João Gilberto Noll, the protagonist goes into a bookstore and leafs through a book in which "a British Catholic spy walks into a church to thank God for the grace of living in an age when there is clearly an enemy, someone against whom to fight."[23] This stands in ironic counterpart to Noll's texts, where this enemy is nowhere to be found, invisible amidst a postcatastrophe scenario. The enemy has become invisible or unrepresentable, of course, because his victory has been so resounding. If "resistance" was once the banner under which a certain Latin American literature was written, the advent of allegory in postdictatorship certifies that resistance has become a rather modest agenda. If resistance was the axis that connected individual and collective experiences under dictatorship, now this connection must be established otherwise. How to reestablish that connection is, then, one of the major threads I will pursue in the analysis of postdictatorial literature.

Because my theoretical argument presupposes, to a great extent, a historical framework, I take as my starting point not the dictatorships themselves, but the period immediately preceding them. My underlying hypothesis is that the dictatorships, as ushers of an epochal transition from State to Market, represented the crisis of a specific form of cultural politics proper to the boom of Latin American literature in the 1960s. I will attempt to make clear why I take the boom to represent an aestheticization of politics, or more precisely a *substitution of aesthetics for politics*. Thus the first chapter flash backs to the ways in which Emir Rodríguez Monegal, Mario Vargas Llosa, Julio Cortázar, Octavio Paz, Carlos Fuentes, and Alejo Carpentier all converged, despite their many differences, in presenting Latin American literature's extraordinary achievements not only as detached from the continent's social backwardness but also as an effective surrogate for it. The boomers' notorious disavowal of any links with the tradition and their insistence on the foundational, almost Adamic role played by their generation are interpreted in the context of this rhetorical operation. The discarding of the past was part of the portrayal of their own writing as a resolute catching up with history, an Oedipal assassination of the European father that finally integrated Latin America into the universal movement of modern literature. Monegal's diatribes against a "backward" rurality and Cortázar's proclamations of the boom as a moment of illumination and consciousness of the Latin American people, as well as Fuentes's insistent announcements that "now, for the first time we . . . ," were all different instances of this sacralizing of a writing that appeared to have achieved transparent coincidence with its contemporaneity. Such sacralizing had its fictional counterpart in several novels that depicted symbolic figures of demiurge-founders encoded in their writers' alter egos: Mario Vargas Llosa's *La casa verde*, Alejo Carpentier's *Los pasos perdidos*, Gabriel García Márquez's *Cien años de soledad*, and so on. All in all, the boom found in this surrogate politics — this compensatory role for literary writing — its historical vocation.

This would not have been paradoxical had it not entailed a reestablishment of the very auratic, premodern, quasi-religious quality that these fully modern narrative projects strove to eliminate. The traditional aura of the *letrado* [man of letters] thus had a dubious status in the boom. On the one hand, it appeared to have been driven away by what undoubtedly was a modernizing, updating, secular, and forward-looking enterprise. On the other, it reemerged in the form of foundational literary figures who installed their writing as the primordial, inaugural moment in which contradictions of a social, political, and economic nature could definitively be resolved. The lettered religion sneaked cult value back in by the side door. What I will attempt to analyze as the *compensatory* vocation of the boom takes shape in this restoration of the aura in a postauratic historical moment.

I look at the experience of the dictatorships against the background of this epochal paradox — the paradox of an auratic, quasi-religious form of cultural modernization — because the dictatorships, by making modernization the inescapable horizon for Latin America, by voiding such modernization of all liberating, progressive illusions (after the dictatorships, after all, modernization irrevocably came to spell integration into global capital as minor partners), preempted the compensatory operation proper to the boom. After the thorough technification imposed by the dictatorships, the magisterial and regulative role assigned to literature by the boom was bound to meet its historical limit. Whereas the boom had attempted to reconcile a modernizing thrust with the compensatory reestablishment of the auratic in the postauratic, such reconciliation was now all but impossible, preempted by a new hegemony that reproduced itself by relentlessly annihilating the aura of the literary, unveiling that aura as a remnant of a moment still incomplete in the unfolding of capital; hence my argument that the date of the decline of the boom, consensually located around 1972 to 1973, was (and not gratuitously) coincident with the fall of the great alternative social project to emerge in Latin America at that moment: Salvador Allende's Popular Unity. Thus in the same sense that Peter Blake proposed 15 July 1972 as the date of the end of modernism (when several functionalist-style apartments built in St. Louis in the 1950s had to be dynamited because they had become uninhabitable) I follow John Beverley in proposing 11 September 1973 as the allegorical date of the decline of the boom.

The second chapter maps out this new hegemony of the technical such as it manifested itself in the social-scientific theory of authoritarianism as well as in the transformations undergone by the university. In the latter I observe what can roughly be described as the passage from the humanist university, set up to form ideologues to administrate the executive, juridical, and ideological apparatuses, to a new university whose main function is to produce technicians. I argue that whereas the former could nurture within itself a contradiction that allowed *intellectuals* to emerge and compete with ideologues for space, the latter bears witness to the decline of intellectuals, now defeated by the figure of the technical expert. The rift separating technicians and intellectuals, although uncertain and mobile, is argued to be essentially irreducible, for while the former intervene only insofar as they are legitimated by the normativity of a specific field, the latter interrogate the *previous* slicing up of knowledge, which is the requisite for the very constitution of particular fields. Whereas technicians instrumentalize a certain expertise in order to understand a given object, intellectuals forcibly think the *totality* that makes possible the emergence of particular objects, which is to say that intellectual reflection necessarily addresses the ultimate foundation, the fundamental principle, the ground not grounded by anything other than itself. The task of intellectuals is thus understood to be coextensive with the site assigned by Immanuel Kant to the Faculty of Philosophy, that of reflecting upon the ultimate conditions of possibility of all knowledge. With the thorough technification of the social body—carried out by the dictatorships as part of the epochal transition from State to Market— the possibility of such reflection is argued to have definitively dissolved.

A dramatic instance of this blocking out of the visibility of the ulti-mate ground is offered in my critique of José Joaquín Brunner's and Fer-nando Henrique Cardoso's social-scientific theories of authoritarianism. In these hegemonic accounts of the nature of the recent Southern Cone regimes, the dictatorships are equated with authoritarianism in such a way that liberal democracy emerges as their universal antithesis. Thus, in Brunner's work the identification of age-old authoritarian elements in Chilean culture was to prove that liberal and democratic values had not been continuous in the country, in a naturalization of the opposi-tion that precluded, for example, any investigation of a possible com-plicity between the two. This line of analysis led Brunner to associate the intellectuals' loss of status not to the epochal transition from State to Market—with the correlative transition from intellectual to techni-cian—but rather, and most astoundingly, to democratization as such. An analogous, and ideologically more serious, operation takes place in Car-doso's work, where the Brazilian and Spanish American dictatorships are repeatedly explained as products of bureaucratic clusters somehow not reducible to, and mysteriously contradictory with, capitalist class inter-est. Because a bureaucracy, unlike a ruling social class, can be unseated without any transformation ensuing in the economic model, Cardoso's positing of the dictatorships as a result of aberrant bureaucratization laid the ground for a "transition to democracy" strongly hegemonized by neoliberal-conservative forces. The social-scientific theory of authori-tarianism is then argued, on the basis of this analysis, to be itself a *symp-tom* of the technification ushered in by the dictatorships, a *product* of the epochal transition rather than a theory of it.

Such generalized immanentization or detranscendentalization—the blocking out of the visibility of the ultimate ground—is subsequently studied in some of the allegorical literature written under dictatorships.

In the grand allegorical machines devised in the Brazilian J. J. Veiga's *A Hora dos Ruminantes,* the Chilean José Donoso's *Casa de campo,* and the Argentine Daniel Moyano's *El vuelo del tigre,* I observe the waning of the earlier magical-realist or fantastic contrasting of opposing logics. Whereas in magical realism a premodern cosmogony was invariably mobilized (and tamed) by the dominant modernist narrative machinery, in a process that entailed a demonization of the indigenous or precapitalist logic, in these allegorical fables the entire text is subsumed under the logic proper to the tyrannies portrayed. All coexistence of modes of production (and their respective logics) having been eliminated, the ultimate foundation underlying such tyrannies or catastrophes becomes invisible to characters, narrator, and reader alike, most often appearing unascribable to the will or action of any subject. The strict spatiotemporal circumscription common in these texts is analyzed within this frame, as they display the petrification of history characteristic of all allegory. Allegory is thus shown to have nothing to do with a mere encoding of a self-identical content that masks itself in order to escape censorship (the notion of allegory hitherto hegemonic in the criticism of the literature produced under dictatorships). In contrast to such an instrumentalist view, I contend that the turn toward allegory spelled an epochal transmutation, parallel to and coextensive with a fundamental impossibility to represent the ultimate ground, a constitutive failure that installed the object of representation as a lost object.

The general framework developed in the two first chapters, despite the seemingly chaotic mixture of references—the boom, the role of the intellectual and the university, the social-scientific theory of authoritarianism, and the renewed relevance of the allegorical—has a unifying thread: it delineates, so to speak, a *topology of defeat.* By showing the impact of historical defeat upon these practices (many of which merely were symptoms of it), I lay the ground for an analysis of postdictatorial texts. The leap is not only a temporal but also a qualitative one, insofar as postdictatorship is taken not only to allude to these texts' posteriority in relation to the military regimes (one of the novels analyzed, Diamela Eltit's *Lumpérica,* was actually written and published at the height of the Pinochet regime), but also and most important their reflexive incorporation of said defeat into their system of determinations. Thus, in a way similar to the definition of the postmodern as the critical and denaturalizing moment of the modern, postdictatorship comes to signify, in the context of this endeavor, not so much the epoch posterior to defeat but rather the moment in which defeat is unapologetically accepted as the irreducible determination upon literary writing in the subcontinent. In this framework, I analyze five of the finest novelists writing in Latin America today: the Argentines Ricardo Piglia and Tununa Mercado, the Brazilians Silviano Santiago and João Gilberto Noll, and the Chilean Diamela Eltit.

After a brief third chapter in which I address Ricardo Piglia's highly original interpretation of the Argentine literary tradition, my fourth chapter analyzes Piglia's futurist/cyberpunk detective story *La ciudad ausente*. The novel confronts the reader with the image of a storytelling machine constructed by the early-twentieth-century avant-garde writer Macedonio Fernández; the machine is based on the recombination of narrative nuclei that it develops from the first story fed into it: Edgar Allan Poe's "William Wilson." In a moment in which the past has been blocked from memory, in a postdictatorial city corroded by oblivion, the machine represents the survival of the possibility of circulating narratives. Macedonio's machine has a fundamental connection with mourning: it is as an attempt to mourn the death of his beloved Elena that Macedonio invents this mechanical and political device for preserving the past. Junior, a sort of alter ego of Piglia's, attempts to track down this unsettling machine that progressively emerges as the very image of counterhegemonic memory. The painful dissociation between literature and experience is countered with a strategy made possible by the machine: the recombination of stories allows for the appropriation, dissemination, and desubjectivation of proper names. Narrative becomes a way of producing apocryphal experience. A rich arsenal of embedded narratives maps out Argentina's past and present, climaxing in the story of a Joycean island where no document ever remains because its inhabitants periodically wake up speaking a different language, and *Finnegans Wake* is the only text that remains legible in all of them. For Piglia, storytelling can reconstitute memory because experience can be made apocryphal, that is, narrated under false names, as if it belonged to another. Hence the titles of some of his books—*Nombre falso, Respiración artificial*—combine a noun that designates the sphere of the proper, of the unique, of the absolutely and irreducibly personal, with an adjective that makes it false, artificial, apocryphal. In *La ciudad ausente,* that combination of the personal and the apocryphal produces a utopian allegory in which memory has both an individual and collective, affective and political dimension.

My fifth chapter addresses Silviano Santiago's rewriting of 1930s Brazilian novelist Graciliano Ramos in *Em Liberdade*. As a counterpoint to G. Ramos's *Memórias do Cárcere*, the classic memoirs of his incarceration in 1936 to 1937 by Getúlio Vargas's regime, Santiago's *Em Liberdade* invents a diary of G. Ramos's first days "in freedom," a period marked no longer by a victimization ultimately recoverable by a voyeuristic, compassionate empathy with suffering (the pity and commiseration that *Memórias do Cárcere*, throughout its 600-plus pages, is very Nietzscheanly at pains to ward off), but rather by a new predicament: the sheer absence of events, the anguish of the blank page, the "post" moment in which not even heroicization and martyrdom are possible or desirable options. Taking on G. Ramos's self, writing his imaginary diary by using his name and fabricating a whole narrative according to which the diary's originals had been handed by G. Ramos to a friend with the request that they be published only twenty-five years after his death—a narrative only disavowed by the subtitle on the cover, which reads "Fiction by Silviano Santiago"—*Em Liberdade* shuffles proper names to the point of creating hilarious misunderstandings among some critics, who went to great lengths to show how Santiago had performed a superb "editorial" job with G. Ramos's "manuscript." The pastiche is replicated *en abyme* in the diary, when G. Ramos projects a story in which he would speak through the voice of eighteenth-century poet and republican insurgent Cláudio Manuel da Costa, in a reinterpretation of the 1792 anticolonial and antimonarchic insurrection in Minas Gerais. The story imagined by G. Ramos, in its turn, displays several coincidences with the assassination of reporter Wladimir Herzog by the Brazilian dictatorship in 1975, in a dizzying proliferation of replicas that encodes a true philosophy of history after political defeats. As in *La ciudad ausente*'s appropriation of Macedonio Fernández, the rewriting of the past is never tainted by any ironic will; never does any parodic distance emerge between the novel's writing self and G. Ramos's historical voice. Unlike in *La ciudad ausente*, however, in *Em Liberdade* there is no room for utopia. One of the goals of my analysis is to show that instead of mobilizing the past for an affirmative present project, Santiago pushes the present back, making of the unaccomplished past the very allegory of a present in crisis.

My sixth chapter begins with an analysis of Diamela Eltit's *Lumpérica*, published at the height of the Pinochet regime and connected with a remarkable resurgence of visual and performing arts in Chile. In *Lumpérica* the protagonist's communion with the destitute bodies of beggars at the public square imagines a politics and a sexuality alternative to the terror that hovers over the city. The encounter between the protagonist and the lumpen collective is, however, filtered by the phallic violence that emanates from spotlights located above the square. It is in the conflict between the anonymity made possible by the night and the unbearable reality of "lights and proper names" that the drama narrated by *Lumpérica* takes place. The dominant trope in Eltit's text is prosopopoeia, for L. Iluminada's voice is the only instance whereby the inarticulate, voiceless lumpen can inscribe their plight on the metropolitan concrete. Woman, lumpen, and America meet in the word *Lumpérica*, and Eltit's black mass comes to represent a marginal, utopian space that nevertheless does not survive the morning light, although it is announced again for the following night. Subversion is thus foregrounded but voided in a narrative structure modeled after the eternal return. In *Los vigilantes*, a postdictatorial and mournful novel published eleven years later, Eltit becomes remarkably more redemptive: the protagonist is now isolated as the only uncontaminated reservoir in a polis completely eaten away by oblivion. *Lumpérica*'s destitute collective now fades into the background, dimly envisioned, at best, as a chased, victimized, and powerless mass, all in all reliant on the protagonist's charitable philanthropy. The Christian motif, present in *Lumpérica* but submitted to a heretic, atheistic eternal return, takes a position of dominance in *Los vigilantes*. This change is also expressed in the temporality that organizes the novel, which takes leave from the eternal return to embrace *the apocalyptic*. My reading explores the leap from *Lumpérica*'s temporality of the eternal return to *Los vigilantes*'s temporality of the last day, interpreting that shift as emblematic of the trajectory of postdictatorial literature.

My analysis of João Gilberto Noll's texts in the seventh chapter contrasts Noll with Piglia and Santiago, because for Noll the void emerging from the divorce between literature and experience is not to be filled but rather embraced and radicalized. Noting how Noll's characters and narrators dramatize an impossibility of telling stories, an atrophy in memory, and a fundamental incapacity to synthesize experience, I contrast

Piglia's and Santiago's apocryphal saturation to Noll's strategy of rarefaction. The proper name no longer circulates apocryphally, but fades away as an index of a crisis in the subject. Depicting failed, jobless, nameless forty-year-olds whose attempts to learn from experience meet with a paralyzing inability to organize lived moments in a rounded-up narrative, Noll undoes the dialectical model of the bildungsroman so central to the modern novel. In *Bandoleiros*, a trip to the United States during the Reagan years provides a rather disquieting look at this privileged source of learning represented by the genre of travel literature. Unlike Wim Wenders's early cinema or Jean Baudrillard's U.S. diary, Noll's travel through American mythology no longer provides any true encounter with otherness or any alternative source of narratives: mass-cultural banality has preempted all hopes of encountering the virgin, uncontaminated reality popularized by European travel narratives in America. Noll's characters recall the Baudelairean flâneur, but the cities through which they drift no longer offer any epiphanic moment that could raise experience above the brute succession of events, the tired repetition of its own facticity. Noll's is thus a literature that starkly refuses to affirm anything and remains cynically suspicious of all restitution. As opposed to Piglia's and Santiago's projects, in which there is still room for an affirmative role for literature—utopian in Piglia, critical in Santiago—Noll produces a purely corrosive, negative picture of the voiding of memory and impoverishment of experience after catastrophes. This negativity is emblematized in the dissolution of the proper name, which becomes, in Noll's fiction, an allegory of the impossibility of living personal, individual stories.

Finally, in my eighth chapter I tackle Tununa Mercado's *En estado de memoria*, a text that provides the most radical and uncompromising reflection on the nature of postdictatorial trauma. Narrated in first person, *En estado de memoria* relates a series of events in the protagonist's life from her exile in France (1967–70) and Mexico (1974–86) to the return to Argentina after the restoration of democracy. Working through the ruins of historical failure, the experience of exile, an intense engagement with psychoanalysis, and, most decisively, a reflection on the abyssal status of her writing—a Herculean labor permeated by a confrontation with Hegel's *Phenomenology of Spirit*—*En estado de memoria* will accept no compensation, no facile imaginary healing, no eluding of mourning. Mercado delves into various postdictatorial phenomena (the spurious attempts to cling to national identity in exile, the oblivion of the catastrophe afterward, the weight of the memory of the dead), without accepting any substitutive mechanisms. In the laborious process of personal and political reconstruction engaged in by the protagonist, her confrontation with the imperative to write becomes the major axis through which the work of mourning begins to be carried out. Mercado's is, then, a postdictatorial novel par excellence in that it accepts the inheritance of the trauma and is written as an attempt to come to terms with that trauma.

The differences among these writers emerge, it should be noted, out of a common terrain, namely, the defeat of the political practices that could have offered an alternative to the military regimes. Piglia, Santiago, Eltit, Noll, and Mercado share the will not to elude that defeat. For all of them, the epochal defeat represented by the dictatorial transition from State to Market binds two parallel phenomena: the imperative to mourn and the decline of storytelling. Mourning and storytelling are, even at the most superficial level, coextensive with one another: the accomplishment of mourning work presupposes above all the telling of a tale about the past. Conversely, only by ignoring the imperative to mourn, only by repressing it into neurotic oblivion, can one proceed to narrate today without confronting the epochal crisis of storytelling and the decline in the transmissibility of experience. This has been, of course, the hegemonic strategy, the victorious version. Had I chosen to study the current dominant forms of literary prose in the subcontinent I would have of necessity had to turn elsewhere, for example, to casual, experimentation-free, "pop" best-selling postmodernism, or to demagogic-populist, phalogocentric mythifications of national or continental "identity" in magical or regionalist key, or yet naive realisms and testimonialisms of various kinds, neomystical prose bordering on self-help, and so on. The representative is by definition the dominant, the doxic, that which is in accord with its present. In contrast, I would submit that the authors treated here, along with a few others, have in common that *untimeliness* that makes them foreign to their present. *Unzeitgemäß*—the untimely in the strong Nietzschean sense—alludes to that which runs against the grain of the present, "acting counter to our time and thereby acting on our time and, let us hope, for the benefit of a time to come."[24] The untimely takes distance from the present, estranges itself from it by carrying and caring for the seeds of time. An untimely reading of the present will, then, at the same time rescue past defeats out of oblivion and remain open to an as yet unimaginable future.[25]

This untimeliness is, today, in times of defeat, the very essence, the very constitutive quality of the literary. Indeed, literature seems today, to us as well as to many outside literary circles, an untimely enterprise. This may be the sole justification to tarry with it, without making any concessions to aestheticist-reactive defenses of the literary institution against challenges coming from culturalism. For if literature can no longer be the surrogate redemption that the optimistic, positive ontology of the boom wished to make of it, it may also be, on the other hand, a little too early to give in to the apocalyptic, pronounce death sentences over the literary, and start searching for surrogate objects upon which to apply the same positive optimism. For these would remain, in spite of all euphoria, just that: objects of a compulsive substitution, that is, of a neurosis still ignorant of itself. They would simply instrumentalize, once again, the will to elude the defeat, the unwillingness to accept it and think through it, which was for Benjamin the most horrifying crime you could commit against the memory of the dead. Against culturalist optimism, this book accepts the defeat of the literary coextensive with the advent of the telematic moment of global capital (implemented in Latin America, as we know, over the corpses of so many). Such acceptance is *precisely the reason why it tarries with it*: so that the recollection of the dissolved can begin, as Hölderlin, writing at the threshold of madness, seems to have understood.

1. OEDIPUS IN POST-AURATIC TIMES

Modernization and Mourning in the Spanish American Boom

In 1997, as I write this study of contemporary fiction from Argentina, Brazil, and Chile, the "winds of democracy" and market euphoria have swept over the Spanish- and Portuguese-speaking Southern Cone. In Argentina, Carlos Menem is reconducted to presidency, anchored in a neoliberal version of a Peronism whose former popular component now finds itself tamed, turned into a docile appendix of global capital; in Brazil, the not unpredictable fate of once-oppositional dependency theory is embodied in sociologist Fernando Henrique Cardoso, reelected president by virtue of a solid alliance with rural oligarchies, business elites, and former heads of the military regime; in Chile, the posttransition pact joins the ultra-Right, Christian democrats, and renovated socialists in an indistinguishable praise of consensus, stability, and free market. A study of the present symbolic production of these countries from the standpoint of their postdictatorial condition bears the stamp of the untimely. Judging from the frailty of existing elaborations of experiential memory in official public spheres, one would never know that barely a decade (in the case of Chile, less than that) has evolved since the completion of one of the most brutal massacres known in Latin American history. Market logic absorbs even the documentation of disappearances and tortures as yet another piece of the past for sale, while the ever more domesticated social sciences take it upon themselves to instrumentalize information in the interest of a peaceful and responsible transition.

In this context, it may not be wise to entertain any illusions of uncooptability, but one thing that a philosophically informed reflection on literature can do is to foreground a certain reserve of meaning, shed light upon a certain area of experience alien to the imaginary of the democratic transitions. I would like to think of this area as mappable into a *topology of affects*. What I mean by that expression will hopefully be clarified as I move along. For now, suffice it to say that I take the word *affect* in a rather material sense. Affects—as opposed to feelings, sensations, emotions, that is, all the vocabulary inherited from a certain Romanticism—are not exhausted within the boundaries of ego psychology or any other narratives grounded on the primacy of interiority and the self.[1] As I will refer extensively to concepts such as mourning and memory, all the necessary precautions will be taken to desubjectivize them and delimit them as *immanent to the social field*, thereby doing with postdictatorial literature something entirely other than a "psychology of a nation." Such reduction of affects to an egological vocabulary has its own history in Latin America; it reappears in much of the rhetoric surrounding exile, as well as in that more general resurrection of confessional literature during the 1970s, such as the Brazilian marginal poetry or the various forms of testimonialism. That historical moment will be dealt with as an entrance to a social and cultural transformation coinciding with the crisis of the military regimes, the aftermath of which being the proper object of this endeavor.

The argument around affects and experience will often lead to an intervention in the ongoing debate over the status of literature in the rearrangement of Latin American civil societies. Several conclusions have recently been drawn about literature's relevance, political and otherwise, in this rearrangement. John Beverley has justified his shift from literature to *testimonio* on the grounds that "where literature in Latin America has been (mainly) a vehicle for engendering an adult, white, male, patriarchal, 'lettered' subject, testimonio allows for the emergence—albeit mediated—of subaltern female, gay, indigenous, proletarian, and other identities."[2] In the most consistent critique of literature's role in the continent, George Yúdice has opposed, on the one hand, art and literature as "the privileged conveyors of national identity . . . in the modern period" and "gatekeeper[s] permitting certain classes of individuals to establish standards of taste within the public sphere and excluding others" to, on the other hand, testimonio as the expression of a "liberated consciousness free of such elitism."[3] Alongside praise for testimonio, similar arguments have been made for shifting critical attention to indigenous pictography, popular artisanship, and mass media as objects now endowed with the social relevance literature once had. The growing consensus is that "literature seems to have ceded its critical position or become marginalized."[4] I will in many instances operate within this consensus, although hopefully displacing it as well. In a context where the written word comes under increasing critical attention and faces an unprecedented challenge from a predominantly audiovisual culture, one cannot simply go on with the business of reading and analyzing texts while ignoring the larger disciplinary problems faced by literary criticism.

One of the threads of the argument harks back to the 1970 decision by Cuba's Casa de las Américas to begin awarding a prize for testimonial texts. Cuban testimonialist Miguel Barnet would argue that as opposed to an "exotic, paternalistic, colonizing" literature, testimonio offered "the gaze from within, from the Latin American *I*, from the Latin American *we*."[5] In rather different manners Barnet, Beverley, and Yúdice were reacting against the privileged position enjoyed by that trend of modern Latin American literature known as the boom. Indeed, the struggle over the literary within Latin American studies today—as well as the discussion concerning modernity and postmodernity in the continent—hinges, to a great extent, on the stance one takes toward the legacy left by the boom. Revisiting these texts thus imposes itself as an urgent task, for their impact can be felt everywhere from the perception of Latin America abroad to the profile of arts and humanities curricula at schools and universities in and out of the continent.

One of the boom's fundamental features was a coupling of literary production with a self-descriptive, self-justifying critical practice, as in Carlos Fuentes's and Alejo Carpentier's essays, or Vargas Llosa's and Emir Rodríguez Monegal's critical activity. Such critical labor, nurtured by the stunning commercial achievements of their fiction, helped forge a solid hegemony upon what has been understood as literature in the continent. In his *La nueva novela hispanoamericana*, Carlos Fuentes, by then already an internationally acclaimed novelist, offers a narrative in which the boom emerges as the culmination of a maturing process in Latin American literature. His text displays one of the crucial discursive strategies of the period: the construction of a genealogy in which the present invariably takes the form of a successful overcoming of the past. The passage from Domingo Sarmiento to Rómulo Gallegos is described as "the transit from epic simplism to dialectical complexity, from the security of answers to the impugnation of questions."[6] History comes to be recounted through the organicist metaphors of progress, development, and growth, as civilization wages yet again its holy war against barbarism. The novel of the Mexican Revolution is said to have imposed a "first qualitative change" by eliminating "our primitive gallery of villains."[7] A progressively conquered complexity and gradual surmounting of earlier flaws constitutes the central tropes in this modernizing rhetoric centered on the "for the first time." The new narrative is argued to represent the moment when "for the first time, our novels knew how to laugh," while Julio Cortázar's characters are defined as the "first beings in the Latin American novel who simply exist, . . . without any discursive attachments to good or evil."[8]

Such euphoria reinforced the certainty of having resolved old problems and dichotomies. This is the discourse of inauguration, the Adamic face of the boom. Emir Rodríguez Monegal curiously recasts the age-old Latin American polarity between the urban and the rural by arguing that boom novels are proof that the conflict, now transcended for good, had been false from the beginning: "whereas in the old novels the city was usually an absence making its mysterious arbitrariness felt, in the new novelists' world the city is the pivot, the center, the place where all roads intersect."[9] Monegal's strategy goes further than asserting the obvious, quantitative literary shift from the rural to the urban (which accompanied a continental social process); it systematically associates the rural with simplism and preartistic primitivism: "The classic opposition between urban and rural novels has been dissolved at its base. . . . Those narratives of peasants and jungles, with two-dimensional characters and mechanical, documentary expositions are now long gone."[10] As the "mechanical and documentary" are progressively equated with the politically real, the new literature appears to represent the imaginary dissolution of conflicts. But if the thrust of Monegal's argument is to claim that one is dealing with a "false opposition," it is interesting to note that the "overcoming" of the dichotomy was conceived as the elimination of one of its terms. The assumption is that the elaborated and complex city has definitively discarded the mechanical and simple countryside. As Monegal balances his judgment by stating that "what is dead is not the rural novel, but rather the bad rural novel," any critical reader is immediately led to ask if such a thing as the "bad urban novel" would not exist also or if it could be forgotten other than by bad faith. At any rate, the important point is that the boom's reaction against the *novela de la tierra* is elaborated through a curious identification between the artistic and the urban, as opposed to a rurality which, with its stories of "peasants and jungles, . . . rarely achieves the purely literary plane."[11]

I believe that such association had less to do with preferences of scenario, characterization, or any strictly narratological matters. After all, several of the novels acclaimed by Monegal and his fellow boomers as paradigms of the "new narrative" are rural or semirural: *Cien años de soledad*, Juan Rulfo's *Pedro Páramo*, Guimarães Rosa's *Grande Sertão: Veredas*, and so on. The explanation is to be searched elsewhere, namely in the fact that within the boom's discursive imaginary, the urban became synonymous with the universal. By identifying rural literature with the past, one convinced oneself that the past was now dead, that we were all part of the same global village, and that the painful distinction between center and periphery had finally been erased. See how Monegal finishes his diatribe against the rural: "now, each Latin American big city . . . aspires to having its Balzac, its Galdós, its Proust, its Joyce, its Dos Passos, its Moravia, its Sartre."[12] One might be tempted to caricature the problem a little and say that within the discursive possibilities offered by the boom, Buenos Aires or Caracas might have their Balzac, but it was highly unlikely that Tucumán or Chiapas would ever have their Steinbeck. In the direct correlation of rurality equals naturalism, everything nonurban became unnarratable in the new fiction's revolutionary language, a conclusion that although deducible from Fuentes's and Monegal's arguments, remains unsaid in their texts. Instead, in Fuentes's work the flowery frontispiece reads, "we, Latin Americans, at last integrated into the march of universal literature:"

> The certainty as to the universality of language allows us rigorously to speak of the contemporaneity of the Latin American writer, who suddenly becomes part of a common cultural present. . . . Our writers can direct their questions not only to the Latin American present, but also to a future that will be increasingly common at the levels of culture and spiritual condition of all men, no matter how accentuated our technical isolation and deformation may be.[13]

In this rather coarse reading of some structuralist postulates, universal culture would supposedly emerge from linguistic universality, over and above social and economic differences, an assumption that permeated the boom's entire discursive spectrum, from the Right (e.g., Monegal and Paz) all the way to the Left (e.g., Carpentier and Cortázar). Hence the possibility of referring to the boom as a *discursive formation*:[14] certain necessary conditions presided over the archive of possible statements, regardless of the polemics and disagreements among its members. Alejo Carpentier presents the same conception of cultural modernization: "[Fuentes's *Terra Nostra*] has been made possible thanks to the evolution of the Latin American novelist toward the acquisition of an ever vaster, ever more ecumenical, ever more encyclopedic culture that has bloomed from the local to achieve the universal."[15] Universality is here understood as an integration into the Western canon, an accomplishment by which one eventually succeeded in surpassing the European masters:

> [W]hen they had Proust and Joyce, the Europeans were barely or not at all interested in Santos Chocano or Eustasio Rivera. Now, however, when they only have Robbe-Grillet, Nathalie Sarraute or Giorgio Bassani, how can they not turn their eyes and look beyond their borders for more interesting, less lethargic, more alive writers? Search, within recent European literature, for an author comparable to Julio Cortázar, a novel of the quality of *El siglo de las luces*, a profound and subversive poetic voice such as that of the Peruvian Carlos Germán Belli; they are not to be found anywhere.[16]

Vargas Llosa, author of the preceding quote, thus voices the boom's Oedipal thrust, complementary to and directly dependent on the Adamic gesture to which I alluded earlier. We murder the European father by outplaying him under his own rules; we show him his moribund body while he acknowledges that the crown has a new bearer. The victorious Oedipal narrative told the story of a dead father reading the books written by his son. As is the case with every triumphant Oedipus, however, not all accounts were settled; the father never dies as irreversibly as one imagines. There is always a restitutive moment in which the father's ghost, the specter once thought to be unequivocally conjured, returns to haunt the living. A genealogical reading must, above all, come to terms with the itinerary of this return.

What can be observed in the critical pieces by boom writers is a tendency to see literature as disproportionately "advanced," "ahead of its time" vis-à-vis the continent's economic and social backwardness.

Whether this was indeed so, that is, whether they were right in postulating a precocious maturity in Latin American literature, does not matter much. I would actually argue this is a false problem altogether. What has to be attended to is the rhetoric in which the diagnosis of a *dissymmetry* between the social and the literary came to be equated with the postulate of a *substitutive* operation whereby the latter was said to *compensate* for the former. "No matter how accentuated our technical isolation," we write the best literature in the world. The relationship between culture and economics then took a twisted form: they were so far apart that the development of the former bore no relationship to the backwardness of the latter; yet they were close enough that one could remedy, cure, function as a corrective of the other. This paradox has been constitutive of the evolution of contemporary Latin American literature and has a significant bearing on the current dilemmas faced by literary criticism in the continent.

Yet one should not think that the gestures observed in Fuentes, Monegal, Vargas Llosa, and Carpentier were somehow a product of a presumed naïveté on their part or simply mistakes that could have been avoided. It remains to be explained why the boom's close complicity with modernization theory was not an option among others, that is, why boom writers were not a group freely choosing the stance to be taken toward modernization. Besides the voluntarist reading of the Cuban Revolution—encouraged, it is true, by the Cuban leaders themselves, but a reading also appropriated in South America as a kamikaze, suicidal strategy—another factor was crucial in this process. As Angel Rama has argued, the boom represented the culminating moment in the professionalization of the Latin American writer.[17] For the first time in Latin America an entire generation of writers found their means of survival in literary writing through the autonomization of the literary sphere from state patronage. It was this becoming-autonomous that laid the ground for triumphant assertions of literature's consciousness-raising powers, such as this one by Julio Cortázar: "What is the boom if not the Latin American people's most extraordinary achievement of consciousness of its own identity? . . . Those who qualify it as a commercial maneuver forget that the boom was not brought about by publishers, but by the readers; and who are the readers if not the people of Latin America?"[18] Beatriz Sarlo has compellingly demonstrated how an "illusory continuity between aesthetics and politics" operated in Cortázar.[19] Such continuity —a *necessary, constitutive* one—took the form of an interesting paradox: progress and liberation were embodied by pre-Kantian, premodern free-thinking egos who chose what they wanted or did not want to read.

Whereas it is true, as Julio Ramos has shown in his now classic *Desencuentros de la modernidad en América Latina: Literatura y política en el siglo XIX*, that the first signs of aesthetic autonomization could already be observed in the nineteenth century with José Martí, it is also true that as late as the 1930s and 1940s Borges could avoid the "mortal shame" of being sold in bookstores and personally take care of the distribution of his 300-copy editions among Buenos Aires's circle of literati.[20] Compare that with the regular 100,000 yearly copies of *Cien años de soledad* released since 1968, and the dimension of the change becomes apparent. The notion of the book as a marketable object did not become unavoidable in Latin America until the transmutation of the 1960s. Despite the mass of material available on the boom, we still lack a serious study of the effects of fulfilled autonomization, that is, there is nothing comparable for the twentieth century to Julio Ramos's discursive mapping of Sarmiento, Andrés Bello, and Martí.[21] At any rate, it is certain that by becoming autonomous, the Latin American fictionist underwent a fundamental displacement: he was no longer primarily a state functionary, a career in which countless Latin American male writers had found their means of survival beginning long before the national independences. Their recent professionalization indicated an accomplished, if problematic and uneven, separation of social spheres. The aesthetic was now a sphere in itself, subject to market laws and pressures. In this context it became unthinkable to fantasize that literature was anything other than labor. No more Romantic bohemia, no more "inspiring muses." The Latin American writer's achievement was then also a *loss*: the price to be paid for social autonomy was the dissolution of the aura. At the very core of the dramatic need to cope with a sweeping modernization lay the loss of the auratic quality of the literary. Just as nineteenth-century art had sensed the threat unleashed by the advent of reproductive techniques such as photography and "reacted with the doctrine of *l'art pour l'art*, that is, with a theology of art,"[22] the boom perceived an analogous decay of the aura and responded with an aestheticization of politics or, more to the point, a substitution of aesthetics for politics. We are now moving toward the terrain on which the current polemic surrounding the status of the literary takes place. As can be seen through the preceding debate, the thematic of a crisis, or even death of literature, rather than arising from the subsequent emergence of an excluded subject presumably expressing itself in an epic narrative of liberation, testimonial or otherwise, was already delimiting the very conditions of possibility of the high-modernist boom itself.

In Latin America literature had hardly ever been secular and autonomous in the same sense that European literature had evolved into a separate sphere endowed with independent institutions, patterns of taste, a common rationality, and so on.[23] Writing, especially the one defined as literary, had always been in Latin America a sort of supplementary religion; the letrado, "owner of writing in an illiterate society, had proceeded to sacralize it."[24] The decline of the aura, brought about by the development of market forces and professionalization, marks the proper historical specificity of the boom. Such autonomization of literature would bring with itself a puzzling paradox: the very moment when literature became independent as an institution, the very moment when it completely realized itself and therefore radically became itself coincided with the total collapse of its historical raison d'être in the continent. Whereas it had traditionally flourished in the shadow of a precarious state apparatus, now an increasingly technocratic state could dispense with it; it had always been instrumental in forming a lettered and humanistic elite, but now that elite dumped it for more efficacious economic theories imported from Chicago; university departments of literature and humanities had been vital means of reproducing ideology, but now ideology wore the neutral mask of modern technology.

The developments just described support my contention that facile characterizations of the boom, so common today, as a draconian elite plot to construct fictions of national identity in order to dominate subaltern sectors are somehow misguided. The boom attempted to come to terms with an opposite predicament: a fundamental impossibility for the elites, by virtue of modernization itself, to instrumentalize literature for social control. *The boom was nothing but mourning for that impossibility,* which is to say mourning for the auratic. It was actually an incomplete mourning process, one that did not—could not, for structural reasons—go beyond what Freud calls the triumphant phase of mourning work.[25] Fuentes,

Monegal, and Cortázar offer several instances of a rhetoric delimited by the paradox just described: on the one hand Latin American fiction was regarded as being centuries "ahead" of an economically backward continent, but such precocious maturity could only blossom because literature, now autonomous and secular, had lost its functionality. Literature was ahead *because* it was behind. It was precocious *because* it was anachronistic vis-à-vis the continent's massive technologization. The celebratory tone of the period then sutured the fracture through a substitutive operation that attempted to compensate not only for social underdevelopment but also for the loss of the auratic status of the literary object.

The structure of compensation was thus determined by constraints emerging from a shift in literature's relationship to modernization. The compensatory mode, although more immediately visible in the critico-theoretical writings by boom authors, was not any less operative in their novels. I can't explore this possibility to the full here, but I refer the reader to Jean Franco's demonstration of how novels as dissimilar as Gabriel García Márquez's *Cien años de soledad*, Alejo Carpentier's *Los pasos perdidos*, and Mario Vargas Llosa's *La casa verde* all converge in systematically presenting "allegories of an 'author' doubled in the foundational character, who appear without predecessors and often operate outside the system of change, hierarchy, and power that has condemned Latin American countries to anachronism and dependency."[26] The demiurge who founds the polis through his writing: this is arguably the most fitting allegory for the boom, from Melquíades, the scribe in *Cien años de soledad*, to the narrator-protagonist of *Los pasos perdidos*, who returns to nature in search of the precultural, only to find the jungle of the always already written. It is not hard to see how these images of writer-founders offered a fictional counterpoint to self-representations put forth by boom authors in their critical pieces.

This denial of tradition, however, rather than a simple repetition of the early-twentieth-century avant-garde gesture, displayed a rather unique and complex dialectic. The image of the ultramodernist radically breaking with everything that preceded him/her was never valid for Latin America, a region where the persistence of tradition was so ineluctable that it could not possibly be disregarded. More than invent radical newness or "burn the museum," at stake was a return to the pristine moment when writing inaugurated history, when naming things amounted to bringing them into being: a vindication of literary writing within a galloping modernization that increasingly dispensed with it, an operation that included the search for a "literary vocation" in Latin American chronicles and historiography,[27] a decisive move, to be sure, in forging the hegemony of the literary within a certain institutional and educational imaginary in the continent, as well as in retrospectively establishing a genealogy for the boom. More than simply ignoring tradition, the boom "declared its own image as part of a whole represented by itself through an act of con-fusion. The 'new narrative' succeeded . . . in confusing itself with a tradition that it invented."[28]

One could thus show how González Echevarría's analysis of the temporality of *Cien años de soledad* uncovers an allegory of the boom itself: "Time is circular in the fiction but not in Melquíades' room. The Archive appears to be successive and teleological, while the plot of the novel is repetitive and mythical."[29] That is to say, the novel's anecdotal content (its vast appropriation of Latin American history as fictional material) submits to a syntax of reversals, repetitions, returns—in a word, to the law of iterability; but the "Archive," writing itself, somehow bypasses it and grounds myth and history in a timeless primordiality. The insistent thematization of writing by boom novels performed the task of carrying out that rhetoricopolitical operation. A writer-demiurge postulated a realm that could both account for (precede) and overcome (succeed) Latin America's unbearable cycle of political and social repetitions. Literature—and who is Melquíades if not the very image of the Latin American writer?[30]—became the privileged realm for such a substitution.

Whereas the thrust of the early modernist avant-garde had resided in the relentless annihilation of the aura, the Latin American boom strove to restore the auratic against the grain of a secular, modernized world. The impossibility of such restoration would trigger the economy of mourning. By the 1960s an ever tighter integration into the world market, the gradual elimination of precapitalist enclaves, the writer's growing professionalization, and the full autonomization of the literary were all strong reasons precluding the possibility of auratization of art in Latin America. However, the uneven and paradoxical character proper to modernization and autonomization in the continent maintained alive the *demand* for the aura. The aura was no longer possible, yet structurally it could not disappear. *Literature would be postulated as the depository of such phantasmatic aura.* Hence the boom writers' manifest irritation whenever the theme of their market success was brought to the fore: among other things, the book market stands for the anachronism of the aura, the dissolution of art's untainted uniqueness, and the ultimate equation between the industrial assembly line and the production of aesthetic objects.

It is thus tempting to hold up the impossibility of coincidence between the temporality of the anecdote and the temporality of writing in *Cien años de soledad* as an allegorical image for the distressing disjunction that defined the boom: the need for reconciliation between fables of identity and teleologies of modernization, the circular time of myth versus the linear, onward-flowing time of secular history. If developmentism had made modernization the total, inescapable horizon for Latin American countries, tendentially identity had to take a necessarily phantasmatic form. "Identity was never here";[31] it was always already that which one once had. Rather than a remnant of an earlier moment, the discourse on identity was a retrospective construction, a compensatory ideologization providing the fictional basis for the belief that once one truly was identical to oneself. The thought of identity became the reactive, resentful face of the triumphant assertions of universality, in a bizarre complicity between Caliban and Oedipus. Commenting on the Brazilian cultural scene of the 1960s, Roberto Schwarz sums up that predicament with a brilliant formula, *national by subtraction:* "Both [left and right-wing] nationalist tendencies hoped to fulfill their goals by the elimination of everything non-indigenous. The residue would be the essence of Brazil."[32] The expression of such paradox in the realm of economics came to be known, of course, as dependency theory, which insistently reduced class determination to macroeconomic (and from a philosophical point of view, extrinsic) factors, thereby reencountering its right-wing counterpart and disavowed accomplice: the Chicago-school modernization theories.[33]

In sum, there is no incompatibility between the boom-as-Latin-American-identity and the boom-as-triumphant-entrance-into-the-global-market. Identity, by definition, only becomes a pressing issue once one has lost it, or, more to the point, when one posits it as lost identity, thereby creating a narrative according to which one once in fact had it. As in the Freudian *Nachträglichkeit* (afterwardness), the memory of the trauma *is* the real trauma; there is no primary process other than the fiction retrospectively produced by the secondary.[34] Literature provided that retrospective fiction by combining high-modernist techniques with a decisive commitment to narrate the premodern realm prior to the originary fall. The examples are legion: "el lado de acá" and the ironically named Traveler, "who had never left Argentina"[35] in Cortázar's *Rayuela*, the indigenous communities destroyed by Fushía's arrival in Vargas Llosa's *La casa verde*, the idyllic world of the Venezuelan jungle in Carpentier's *Los pasos perdidos*, the Eden-like Macondo before the Banana Company in García Márquez's *Cien años de soledad*, and so forth. My own view is that such crossroads between tradition and modernity lend themselves to be conceptualized as a reinscription of the auratic in the age of technology, much in the sense in which Andreas Huyssen has argued that "the need for auratic objects . . . seems indisputably a key factor of our museumphilia."[36] The boom will then have operated as the moment when certain pre-Fall, pre-global "identity markers" made a definitive entrance into the museum.

My sketchy outline represents only an initial step toward the mapping of the terrain where the decline of the aura met the demand for compensation. The substitution of the structures of civil society by intellectuals, a traditional practice in Latin America, took a rather particular twist in the boom. Although the phenomenon has never been exclusive to literature, the boom transformed literary writing into the privileged realm for that substitution. The reasons for such privilege lay, not in the genius of a few talented novelists, as has been affirmed so many times; they are to be searched elsewhere, namely, in the historical convergence that made of literature the space where fables of identity and teleologies of modernization could coexist and be reconciled. No economic model available could harmonize them, yet "our" literature was irreducibly "Latin American" and at the same time "modern," "advanced," and on a par with the first world. It should come as no surprise, then, that the thick ideological layer underlying both the notions of identity and of modernization was never called into question by the criticism associated with the "new narrative." Jorge Luis Borges's encyclopedic culture and narrative self-awareness would earn him unlimited praises, but his radical dismantling of the identitarian fallacy would remain unexplored, especially in its political consequences; José María Arguedas, if ever mentioned, would be for his "authentic" portrayal of indigenous communities, not for his relentless suspicion of literature's very rhetorical apparatus in its complicity with a developmentist teleology.[37] Those operations, I insist, are not to be regarded as options among others, or mistakes otherwise avoidable by more skillful critics and novelists. They are rigorously determined by the economy of an incomplete, triumphant mourning work that could only come to terms with the loss of the aura in compensatory, that is, imaginary fashion. Therefore the boom, rather than being described as the moment when Latin American literature "found its identity" ("a continent finding its voice" was the phono-ethno-logocentric motto endlessly repeated at the time, the echoes of which still have not subsided), can more properly be defined as the moment when literature imaginarily compensated for the loss of an identity, which, by definition, only came into being retrospectively, that is, only existed as lost identity. The boom met its epochal horizon by necessarily reducing mourning for the aura to a pacifying substitution of culture for politics. Such reduction would no longer be possible after the dictatorships.

The paradoxes I have described did not simply disappear; they were violently "resolved." Facing increasing popular pressure, Latin American elites, at various moments and at different paces, decidedly abandoned any projects of self-sustained, nationalist development, in order to embrace once and for all multinational capital as minor partners. The victory of the Brazilian military in 1964 inaugurated that historical period, opening up a continental transition not to be fulfilled until 1976, the year of the Argentine coup. I take from John Beverley the suggestion that, within that cycle, one specific date was crucial to the literary camp.[38] Allegorically speaking, it could be argued that the boom ended on 11 September 1973, as the Chilean military ousted Salvador Allende's Popular Unity, thereby putting an end to the "peaceful road toward socialism." Most critics agree on 1972 to 1973 as the date range of the boom's final demise, but Beverley's insight allows us more directly to link the decline of the boom to the ground that made it possible in the first place: the uneven and contradictory modernization of Latin America.

The fall of Salvador Allende can be taken as allegorically pointing to the death sentence over the boom because the latter's historical vocation, namely, the tense reconciliation between modernization and identity, had now been preempted. After the Chilean Popular Unity's demise, all modernization in the Southern Cone came to spell integration into the global capitalist market. This was, let us make no mistake, the central role of the military regimes: to purge the social body of all elements that could offer some resistance to a generalized opening to multinational capital. The boom ended with the bombing of Allende's presidential palace, because in retrospect 11 September 1973 made irreversible the advent of a historical period in which the dictatorships would void modernization of all liberating content. The military regimes succeeded in defeating all populist and nationalist projects of self-sustained capitalism, en route to becoming the exclusive purveyors of modernization. In that context literature's substitutive function, in the forms that it took during the boom—that of literary writing as epic entrance into the first world and burial of a failed, backward past—was bound to vanish, subsisting at best in highly ideological versions. The substitution of aesthetics for politics, which had been expected to be temporary and ultimately wither away in the revolutionary politicization of aesthetics, indeed ended, but for different reasons, namely the dictatorships' well-nigh subsumption of politics into aesthetics—an aesthetics of the grotesque and the farcical.

During the boom a systematic intercommunication in the intellectual field, the unifying presence of Cuba, and the belief in a common Latin American cause were all factors pushing toward a continental canon. Although it could certainly be demonstrated that Vargas Llosa's novels responded to an unmistakably Peruvian dilemma, or that Cortázar's work was determined in its totality by an Argentine problematic, their interventions increasingly revolved around the signifier *Latin America*. At the level of the authors' critical and theoretical work, as well as in the formation of a reading public and in the emergence of new editorial policies, such Latin Americanism constituted the utopian facet of the boom. After the dictatorial experience, a generalized return to national canons begins to take place, not simply due to an epiphanic realization that the Latin America imagined by the boom bore the unequivocal marks of a handful of metropolises—Buenos Aires, Mexico City, Lima, and marginally Bogotá and Caracas—therefore not pertaining, unlike their rhetoric would have one believe, either to the Portuguese-speaking or to the non-criollo sectors of the continent, but also and more important because the dictatorships, by submitting unconditionally to *international* capital, turned the *nation* into the crucial battlefield for all political action.

The fundamental operation carried out by the dictatorships was, no doubt, an unprecedented homogenization of Latin America. However, those processes of homogenization were themselves national; that is, they confronted particular national situations, appealed to specific national myths, and triggered a resistance that, despite continental and worldwide solidarity, followed a fundamentally national dynamic. The more intellectuals had to leave their countries, in a diasporic phenomenon of considerable proportions, the more the nation acquired the obsessive status of lost object and utopian promise. For those who stayed, the history of the nation was the source to which the present could turn. Ricardo Piglia became an *Argentine* writer in a new sense:

> I don't think in terms of Latin American literature. If I had to think of a certain ordering, it might be one of cultural or linguistic areas. Say, of a Caribbean literature, a River Plate literature. . . . One could see the perspective of magical realism as a sort of dominant poetics in the sense of what Latin America is for the Europeans. It works as something like *lo latinoamericano* [the Latin American] seen from an external reading key. . . . I would rather think of regional traditions, understanding regions as linguistic crossroads, cultural knots where the weight of certain *historias* [stories/histories] can be found.[39]

Piglia's imperative to confront "the weight of certain *historias*" had as much to do with the evolution of his own thinking as it did with the passage from the boom's triumphant mourning work to a confrontation with a rather distinct imperative to mourn forced by the experience of the dictatorships. Recognizing the irreducibility of mourning implied, as we will see, the acknowledgment of a certain realm where the nation was also irreducible.

Such is the cluster of problems that one has to attend to when discussing the validity of the national referent for contemporary literature. In that spirit, I attempt to show how the novels of Chilean Diamela Eltit, Argentines Ricardo Piglia and Tununa Mercado, and Brazilians João Gilberto Noll and Silviano Santiago represent a complex reinscription of the national problematic in the postdictatorial moment of their respective countries, which evolved from socialist or populist experiments (Allende's Popular Front in Chile, the Brazilian *petebismo*, and the Argentine *peronismo*) to a violent integration into the world market. The ensuing crisis of central topoi of Latin American intellectual history—such as the narrative of "identity" in its umbilical relationship with a certain centrality of the literary institution—was determinant in my choice of authors: they represent some of the most radical and risk-taking responses to a postidentitarian horizon. Before proceeding to them, however, I would like to offer a brief introduction to some of the debates that shaped the Brazilian, Argentine, and Chilean intellectual fields and literary canons during the military regimes.

2. THE GENEALOGY OF A DEFEAT

Latin American Culture under Dictatorship

When the Brazilian military ousted João Goulart's populist government on 31 March 1964, the Left still held optimistic prospects for Latin America: the Cuban Revolution celebrated its fifth anniversary with repeated signs of vitality; in Chile Salvador Allende's popular coalition, although defeated in the elections by Christian Democrat Eduardo Frei, received an unprecedented 38.6 percent of the vote, laying the ground for the electoral victory of 1970; widespread occupations of factories by Argentine workers set the tone for what was perceived to be Perón's imminent return from exile; the armed struggle in Colombia and Venezuela achieved partial but significant victories. All these events contributed to strengthening within the Brazilian Left an interpretation of the coup that relied upon an old, narcotic belief in progress. The military regime, it was affirmed, would self-destruct. It could not detain the march of history. The Left paid dearly for such unshakable optimism, not only with exile, torture, and death, but also by hampering the comprehension of its own trajectory. Instead of a much needed critique of messianism and paternalism, the fragmented Brazilian Left embarked on a desperate attempt at an isolated armed confrontation, clearly doomed to failure, with the military regime. Granted, it is easy to pass this judgment retrospectively; but it is also true that several of the period's most lucid minds had already seen the dead-end street and warned against it. For the armed Left, however, recognizing it would have meant reexamining its entire mythology, including the Leninist notion of vanguard party. The suicidal recourse to militarism proved to be the least painful option.

It is useful to distinguish two periods in the evolution of the Brazilian dictatorship. From 1964 to 1968 (date of the so-called coup within the coup, marked by the promulgation of Institutional Act 5, which closed Congress, suppressed civil liberties, and gave almost unlimited power to the military), repression targeted basically two groups, forcing into exile the political leadership of the previous populist regime—João Goulart, Leonel Brizola, Celso Furtado, Miguel Arraes—and more important for the regime, destroying the vital working-class, peasant, and student movements of the early 1960s. I will not devote space here to relating the burning of student organizations, the depredation of peasant leagues and trade unions, because they are all exhaustively documented in a growing literature.[1] This first phase was characterized, at first sight paradoxically, by a remarkable cultural thriving that continued the legacy of the precoup days. Repression was highly selective, operating with a view to a clearly defined purpose. Speaking of the cultural scene between 1964 and 1968, Roberto Schwarz notes: "Tortured and jailed for a long time were only those who had organized the contact with workers, peasants, marines and soldiers. . . . Having severed the ties between cultural movements and masses, Castelo Branco's government did not prevent the theoretical and artistic circulation of the leftist ideals that, although in a restricted area, flourished extraordinarily."[2]

A quick look over the artistic production of the time confirms Schwarz's assessment: the Cinema Novo's "aesthetic of hunger" still generated films such as Gláuber Rocha's *Terra em Transe* (1966), where earlier beliefs in the revolutionary power of the image were rethought in the light of the defeat of 1964; popular music went through one of its most fertile moments, with the television *festivais* revealing names such as Chico Buarque de Hollanda, Edu Lobo, Caetano Veloso, and Gilberto Gil; the Arena theatrical group continued its productions of oppositional plays by Oduvaldo Vianna Filho and Gianfrancesco Guarnieri, as well as that more general tropicalization of Bertolt Brecht; 1964 marked the debut of the musical spectacle known as *Opinião*, in which Nara Leão, Zé Kéti, and João do Vale combined the politically committed stance of the populist era with avant-gardist performances that bridged formal experimentation and political utopia. By 1968 this effervescence had become a real threat to the generals. Student protests multiplied and antidictatorship rallies gathered multitudes, culminating in the massive demonstration known as passeata dos 100 mil. The regime responded with a ferocious counterattack. Again, Roberto Schwarz hits the mark: "Whereas in 1964 it had been possible for the Right to 'preserve' cultural production, since it sufficed to eliminate its contact with the working and peasant masses, in 1968, when students and the audience of the best films, theater, music and books already constituted a politically danger-ous mass, it was necessary to replace or censor professors, dramatists, writers, musicians, books, editors—in other words, it was necessary to liquidate the moment's very living culture."[3]

1968 inaugurated the period where "you really began to feel the pres-ence of a censor next to your typewriter."[4] The repressive apparatus annihilated the armed resistance of a student movement whose con-nections with the working class had already been severed. Meanwhile, the ideological machine operated at full force: television disseminated daily messages about how great things were, federal censorship tightly controlled the written press, and an economic boom, favored by the in-creased extraction of surplus value made possible by repression, contrib-uted to keep the middle class satisfied or immobilized. The oppositional art remaining within the country was progressively driven to a corner, as pornography took over national film and adultery became the dominant theme in theater. The attack on literate culture included the paramilitary bombing of one of the country's most important publishing houses, Civi-lização Brasileira. In 1973 the guerrilla's defeat in the midwestern county of Araguaia put an end to all hopes of a violent overthrow of the mili-tary. The regime triumphantly declared its victory against "subversion."

Yet it would be a mistake to limit the state's role in those days to one of repression. "Censorship was neither the only nor the most efficient strategy adopted by the military governments in the cultural field."[5] The state was never limited to negating its oppositional antithesis; it imposed a new positivity as well. However important it may be to denounce re-pressive policies, nothing has precluded a clear understanding of sym-bolic production under dictatorships more than the exclusive focus on censorship. Brazil witnessed not only suppressions, but also the emer-gence of a new ideology substantially different from everything reaction-ary thought had produced so far. Besides granting generous subsidies to megaconglomerates (TV Globo, Editora Abril, etc.), the state propelled a new tourism policy that fed on the mercantilization of popular culture. In the Northeast the Casas de Cultura Popular operated in close association with the tourism industry.[6] Through organs such as the Conselho Fed-eral de Cultura, the state made of "Culture for the People" its new motto. For the elaboration of such policies, the technocratic state resorted largely to traditional, conservative intellectuals left over from the old agroexporting society, now clustered mostly around Instituto Brasiliero de Geografia Estatística (IBGEs; Academies of Letters and the Histori-cal and Geographical Institutes). The contradiction lay in the fact that those intellectuals, as remnants from the latifundium, operated within a conservative humanism barely suitable for the modernizing technocracy.

The ideology of miscegenation, as Brazilian national ontology, was the major trace that subsisted in the passage from the *bacharelesca* (rhetoric-centered) culture of the old agroexporting state to the techni-fied imaginary of the military dictatorship. Both maintained a fundamen-tal appeal to an ontology that celebrated *mestiçagem* (miscegenation) as Brazil's achieved identity, a sort of bizarre utopia in which one was sup-posed to be living but which one didn't quite know yet. A solid grain of ideology was displaced from Gilberto Freyre's racial harmony theories, elaborated in the 1930s, to the dictatorship's well-nigh celebration of Bra-zilian miscegenation as proof of accomplished democracy. As the mass media were handed over to private capital, the state found its cultural function around the axes of preservation and patrimony, legitimating itself in a genealogy of the nation that excluded all ruptures and con-flicts. Pedro Demo, secretary of cultural affairs in 1979, exemplifies the official rhetoric: "This intellectualized culture, which finds it important to know names of French food or classical music, have good manners, go to the theater, appreciate hermetic films and protest songs, may well have its value, because it does no harm to appreciate literature, music, theater, ballet, etc. But it is necessary to note that this has nothing to do with the country's social problems."[7]

Such alien culture had its positive counterpart in the secretary's praise of the "*caboclo's* [backlands dweller] attachment to the Amazon jungle, folk singers, *literatura de cordel* [string literature], popular pharmacology."[8] This strange opposition shows how the state undertook the task of guard-ing national memory: it appropriated the very tropes of the national-popular Left. In the first enumeration the curious link connecting French food with classical or protest music lies in their nonbelonging in the lives of peaceful, docile citizens, that is, their exteriority to true Brazilian iden-tity. As pastime and entertainment, moderate doses of folklore and my-thology could do no harm, provided the social boundaries remained well drawn. Anti-intellectualism then took a perverse form in Brazil: instead of attacking the population's *lack of access* to literate culture or critiqu-ing the vices that said dissymmetry had produced in the intelligentsia, intellectual reflection as such was demonized. Here was another conver-gence between the military and the populist-reformist Left: a mythical valorization of the popular in opposition to an "inauthentic" or "non-national" culture. The discourse of identity allowed the regime to deny working and lower middle classes all rights to cultural goods, while stig-matizing those goods as elitist anyway. The regime then channeled class hatred into a realm where culture had become a harmless substitute for politics and accomplished that goal by appearing as an ally of the poor in its holy war against "French food and classical and protest music." As the regime intensified repression against oppositional cultural production, it also succeeded in isolating it from the poorer sectors, only, in a second move, to domesticate popular culture as folklore and ornamentation.

A certain populist rhetoric, originated within the nationalist or Stal-inist Left, was actively appropriated by the military regime and became part and parcel of its cultural policy. If the 1960s had witnessed the Left develop a populist ethos and nurture a profound suspicion of all intel-lectual activity, it was now the Right who took charge of protecting a national identity by definition alienated and doing it while selling out the country to multinational capital. Television, as well as state organs in charge of culture, were vital for this process: the former became the privileged vehicle for a certain abject and scandalous representation of the popular (especially through "reality shows," as a true obsession with "reality" swept Brazilian society in the 1970s, paralleling the hegemony of naturalism in the arts), while the state co-opted and absorbed that populist ethos en route to turning folklorism into a docile and com-pensatory appendix of technology. The evolution of Brazilian literature under dictatorship had much to do with this climate: naturalist repre-sentations of bombastic media scandals produced some of the period's best-selling books. Another instance of the populist Zeitgeist was the rather violent polemic against an enemy usually identified by the name of "theory," by which writers, journalists, and professors lamented, on the pages of some of the country's widest-circulating newspapers, that the unique and ethereal pleasure afforded by literature was in danger of disappearing thanks to methods alien to Brazilian identity and ruthless in their contempt for "personal"—read impressionistic—analyses. At that point structuralism became, due to its growing hegemony in humanities departments, virtually a metonymic synonym for theory as such, and while it has to be conceded that its legacy in Brazilian literary studies was far from inspiring, the furious reaction that it provoked indeed said much more about its detractors than about its particular fate in Brazil.[9]

The gradually escalating repression observed in the Brazilian case does not hold true for Chile. On the first days following the coup of 11 September 1973 Pinochet's machine of murder and torture was already working at full speed. Exile and incarceration of those connected with or vaguely suspected of sympathies for the Popular Unity government began to be carried out immediately afterward. The impact of exile upon Chilean culture was far greater than in Brazil; by the late 1970s tens of thousands of Chileans had been forced to or chosen—though in such circumstances this is a pointless distinction—to live abroad. The consequences for literary criticism become clear once one takes a quick look at its trajectory in Chile during the 1970s. The university reform of 1967 had coincided with a qualitative leap in Chilean literary criticism, as the university opened up to several theoretical approaches that challenged the dominance of impressionism or generational-biographical methods.[10] A strong sociohistorical school of criticism gradually came into being, as the dependency paradigm conquered hegemony, particularly at the University of Chile. Several prominent intellectuals (e.g., Pedro Lastra, Nelson Osorio, and Hernán Loyola) directed publishing series in presses such as Nascimento and Universitaria, introducing major Latin American names as well as new theoretical developments from Europe. The anguishing circle of specialized language and reduced public was tackled, as critics/writers of the caliber of Federico Schopf and Antonio Skármeta managed to expand their activity to mass circulation newspapers. All in all, writing literature and criticism was perceived as inseparable from building a new society. By the mid 1970s, most of that vibrant generation had gone into exile, and those who stayed were forced to work under the worst circumstances. The old predominance of impressionistic criticism associated with the official press was consolidated, most notoriously through the figure of Ignacio Valente, Chile's authorized reviewer for the ultra-conservative *El Mercurio*. In addition, university-based criticism was deprived of all major channels of publication, with the parallel proliferation of the marketing-oriented language of mass media reviews.[11]

New paradigms emerged within very restricted intellectual circles, as we will see, but some time passed before those could ground a new reflection on Chilean literature.

The cultural effervescence of the Allende years (1970–73) can barely be evoked in a few lines. More than 300 independent theatrical groups were active in playhouses and in the streets.[12] Decisive state investments in cinematography, music, and university-managed radio stations guaranteed circulation of symbolic goods not immediately subjected to market laws.[13] Most decisively, Chile witnessed the emergence of a new permeability between popular and erudite cultures—with mutual formal transits between them—as well as a concerted effort to incorporate the impact of such developments into mass culture.[14] Chile's editorial industry took a gigantic leap, as Quimantú press made available at low cost a vast number of titles of national and international literary classics, releasing editions that ranged from 50,000 to 100,000 copies and included everything from Mark Twain to Nikolay Gogol, Giovanni Boccaccio, Pablo Neruda, Gabriela Mistral, Fyodor Dostoyevsky, and so on. These books, sold not only in bookstores but also at kiosks in popular neighborhoods, revolutionized the experience of readership in Chile. In a country of fewer than 10 million, one single series of literary classics (Minilibros) accounted for 3.6 million books sold in one year, a phenomenon unheard of in Latin America, except maybe for Cuba. Following the coup a systematic demonization of the Popular Unity's literate legacy occupied much air time in the media. As Jaime Collyer points out, Chile was "one of the few countries where attested book burnings proliferated and editorial activity was reduced to a minimal expression."[15] The number of titles published in Chile grows consistently under Allende, peaking at 719 in 1972; after the coup, it would decline steadily year after year, reaching a record low of 244 in 1979.[16]

In Chile, "there was never an *official culture* like the one known in Franco's Spain or in fascist Italy."[17] Pinochet's regime never created any *organic intellectuals*, unless one considers as intellectuals the hysteric monologuists on God, family, and tradition. Not a single thinker, researcher, or writer of any relevance served Pinochet's dictatorship in decisive fashion. Needless to say, this is not necessarily the case in all dictatorships; besides the Spanish and Italian examples, one can mention Brazil, where the regime did count on intellectuals such as Roberto Campos or Gilberto

Freyre. The Chilean dictatorial state imposed a thorough privatization of public life, an obsession with individual success, and a horror for politics and collective initiative, as well as a passion for consumerism, all grounded on sheer fear, that is, a "culture of the superego," in José Joaquín Brunner's felicitous expression.[18] The policy entailed control for people, freedom for things, especially for capital and commodities. The discourse put forth by the regime fed off three basic sources: (1) the geopolitics of the Doctrine of National Security: Chilean society suffered from a disease and some body parts had to be "amputated" to cure it; (2) conservative Catholicism: Chile, in its "essence," belonged among Western Christian nations and social egalitarianism equaled blasphemous atheism; (3) nationalist populism: Chilean people were by nature peace-loving, quiet, and so on. Such ideology found its economic counterpart in monetarist neoliberalism: the freedom to restructure every corner of social life according to market logic.

The cultural sphere witnessed the state's withdrawal from its earlier role as a sponsor. Instead, private arts foundations operated with the purpose of improving the public image of their respective corporations by promoting awards and grants. The official ideological edifice, however, functioned primarily through the mass media. Beginning in 1973 with the bombing of the Popular Unity's radio stations and the army occupation of Televisión Nacional to the subsequent censorship and spectacularization of information, the Chilean dictatorship made of television the key axis of its cultural intervention.[19] This was part of a violent separation among an erudite culture directed at the wealthy (opera, classical theater, and so on), a stereotypical and paralyzing mass media culture geared toward larger sectors of the population, and both popular and avant-garde art, now ghettoized and forced to confront not only repression and censorship but also tight financial constraints in a context dominated by market-driven values. This rearrangement forced all nonofficial cultural production to debate between institutionalization and marginality, the need for political and symbolic rupture and the parallel need, oftentimes contradictory with the first, for social interlocution on a broader level.[20]

Political repression peaked in 1978 to 1979, paving the way for Pinochet's victory in the 1980 constitutional plebiscite (where space for dissent was virtually nonexistent) and the extension of his presidency until 1989. Parallel to this escalation, however, civil society slowly reemerged from defeat. The year 1983 marked a major break: exiles began to return, censorship of books was lifted, 200,000 mourners gathered in the streets to commemorate the tenth anniversary of Pablo Neruda's death, and a vigorous sequence of protests culminated in a general strike called by the Confederation of Copper Workers in May 1983. Until 1987 some twenty-odd day-long "journeys of protest" took place, mostly in Santiago.[21] Unlike the armed resistance to the Brazilian dictatorship in the early 1970s, this movement was fundamentally working-class based. Protests reached greater strength in the *poblaciones* (low-income neighborhoods, slums), where workers erected barricades and faced a violent repression, in an event later known as La Revuelta de los Pobladores. Still well into the decade, when democratization had largely been accomplished in the subcontinent, the poorer sectors of Chilean society faced a nightmarish routine of invasions, ransackings, and beatings. It was also in those sectors, undoubtedly, that the military dictatorship faced the fiercest struggles of resistance.

In the cultural field, opposition to the dictatorship also gained a firmer footing. In a context where Chilean folklore and popular culture had come to be closely associated with the memory of the Popular Unity, these manifestations had been violently repressed and its organizations only began to reemerge toward the late 1970s, with interventions centered on the past and oftentimes appealing to symbolic figures such as Pablo Neruda or Violeta Parra. Important moments in this trajectory were the birth of the Unión Nacional para la Cultura (UNAC; National Union for Culture) in 1978, the consolidation and success of popular theatrical groups such as ICTUS, and the reemergence of several bands that subscribed to different genres of the so-called new chilean song, also traditionally associated with the memory of the Popular Unity. The social sciences set out to evaluate the experience of the first years of authoritarianism in some rather innovative research produced through organizations such as Facultad Latinoamericana de Ciencias Sociales (FLACSO; Latin American Faculty of Social Sciences) and CENECA (Centro de Indagación y Expresión Cultural y Artística), which attest to a turn toward more localized objects of research, with special attention being devoted to "culture." A vigorous resurgence of plastic and literary arts got under way with groups such as Colectivo Acciones de Arte (CADA; Collective Artistic Actions) and a broad spectrum of practices known as *escena de avanzada*. I address these artistic practices later as an introduction to my analysis of Diamela Eltit's *Lumpérica*, for Eltit's literature arose in direct relationship with them. For now I want to stress that all this opposition succeeded in opening some fractures in the regime and forcing it to negotiate. The victory, however, was a partial one, because the military cannot be said ever to have lost its hegemony over the so-called democratic transition. Rather, the military ultimately managed to impose a highly paced and restrained return to democracy. The controlled and circumscribed passage to democracy marks another specificity of the Chilean evolution that sets it apart from, say, the abrupt fall of the Argentine generals.

In Argentina the left fringe of the intellectual field was decisively affected, throughout the 1960s and early 1970s, by the conjunction of an international phenomenon with a national one: the emergence of national-liberation and socialist movements in the third world (Algeria, Cuba, Vietnam, and so on) coincided with the proscription of Peronism in Argentina (1955–73) and the disillusionment with rather feeble periods of liberal democracy. The popular component of these liberation struggles, coupled with the rupture of the national alliance binding leftist intellectuals and significant portions of the liberal elite in the opposition to Perón (1946–55), contributed to a change noticeable everywhere in the Argentine Left: Peronism began to be reread "from the Left," that is, the Left entertained the possibility that Peronism might after all (be forced to) assume revolutionary positions. Many of the progressive intellectuals who had opposed Perón between 1946 and 1955 reoriented themselves, in an assortment of different manners, toward a reinterpretation that somehow allowed for a convergence with the populist leadership against liberalism and international capital. Most notably, for the Sartre-influenced group congregated around the magazine *Contorno* (Ismael and David Viñas, León Rozitchner, Juan José Sebreli), "it was a matter of making explicit the reasons for the tragic game of mirrors that had led them to oppose a regime that, in spite of everything, was becoming less questionable in their eyes in the light of subsequent political developments."[22] As the disillusionment with liberalism grew, a certain *essence* of Peronism as a social phenomenon began to be distinguished from all possible uses or actualizations of it, even by Perón himself. This perception was progressively reinforced as old predictions of a weakening or disappearance of Peronism after its removal from the state apparatus proved wrong in the 1960s and 1970s. An important part of this rearrangement was played by the group of intellectual activists expelled from the Communist Party who founded *Pasado y Presente,* a magazine that reevaluated Peronism by sending liberalism to the other side of the barricade as the common enemy. Incorporating new developments in the humanities and helping establish a Gramsci–inflected national-popular model in which Peronism was rethought approvingly, *Pasado y Presente* was in many senses paradigmatic of the Argentine Left's trajectory in that period.

The drama for much of that intelligentsia was not uniquely Argentine but was undoubtedly stronger there than anywhere else in Latin America: how to conceive of their own role in a populist movement characterized by its stark anti-intellectualism? As critiques of intellectual genealogies lent themselves to be read as allegorical self-critiques, most of the progressive sector moved toward the 1960s focal discussion—possible or desirable relations between intellectuals and masses—nurtured by a profound suspicion of "theoreticism" and willfully oblivious to a growing messianism on the Left that attempted to suture the contradiction between the theory of the organic intellectual and its insertion within a movement that seemed to negate all forms of intellectual mediation. What was invariable in both moments, before and after the turn toward Peronism of the progressive intelligentsia's itinerary, as Silvia Sigal has noted in her insightful analysis, was its reactive nature: "they passed . . . from a negative unity to another, from anti-Peronism to a rejection of [liberal Frondizi's] governmental anti-Peronism."[23] The approximation with Peronism entailed a growing refusal of all forms of democratic mediation: "Opposed in almost everything, revolutionary Left and third-worldist Peronism coincided, however, in a characterization of democratic institutionality as a formal one. From this adjective we derived the chain: formal-seemingly-deceiving-false,"[24] Beatriz Sarlo has reasoned retrospectively, in the same vein. There is a sense, of course, in which democratic institutionality *had* always been false in Argentina, if only because it was always on the verge of yet again being overthrown. It is admirable, nevertheless, how a large fraction of today's Left has undertaken a self-critique of its earlier positions. What remains to be seen is to what extent the retrospective repudiation of the 1970s militarization of politics will lead them to embrace liberal democracy as a goal in itself.

The aforementioned hyperpoliticization took place, one should not forget, while a literary boom conquered a certain Latin America that was in the process of being construed (in the North as well as in the South) largely in the image of that very literary boom. It is imperative to keep this complex dialectic in mind. In Argentina—well, actually in France, but no doubt writing from within the Argentine tradition—Cortázar became the link with the Latin Americanist dimension embodied by the boom. The right wing of the literary field in Argentina—say, the *Sur* journal group: Silvina Ocampo, Adolfo Bioy Casares, Manuel Mujica Láinez, all under the more universal shadow of Borges—never really laid down a bridge to the new Latin American literature. Many contrasted that to the ubiquitous presence of the boom in the Cuban *Casa de las Américas* in order to argue that a "Marxist takeover" had occurred in the continent's literature. This conservative reading certainly did not grasp the complexity of the boom's political legacy (how easy it would be if one's heritage were indeed so uncontaminated and unambiguous!), but it lent itself to be read as symptomatic in the Argentine context: the late 1950s to early 1960s witnessed *Sur's* definitive loss of hegemony in the cultural field, for not even in "strictly aesthetic matters," as the group liked to put it, were they any longer the cutting edge in what came from the first world, as the journal resigned itself to introducing minor names such as Graham Greene or Aldous Huxley, while the best Anglo-American modernism—Joyce, Faulkner, Fitzgerald—entered Argentina following other paths, the only exception to this rule being Borges's translation of Faulkner's *The Wild Palms*, done back when *Sur* was indeed the dominant branch within the aesthetic avant-garde. Within the national tradition the reevaluation of landmark writers despised by *Sur,* such as Roberto Arlt and Leopoldo Marechal, had been on the way for well over a decade, due mostly to the efforts of those assembled around *Contorno,* and literary professionalization in the 1960s made largely anachronistic the journal's old approach based on the creative genius. Ricardo Piglia was thus right when he suggested that Argentine literature ended up not obeying *Sur's* historical prognosis, as Leopoldo Marechal, Macedonio Fernández, and Roberto Arlt tend to gain more prominence than the constellation privileged by *Sur*.[25]

It has become a commonplace to refer to the turn of the 1970s in Argentina as a period of hyperpoliticization. After the *cordobazo* (popular rebellion in Córdoba) in 1969, a series of popular protests began to undermine the basis of the military dictatorship. Following Perón's return and victory in the presidential elections of 1973 the militarization of politics only grew in Argentina. The figure of the intellectual began to collapse into that of the grassroots guerrilla activist. In the literary field a deep suspicion of all theorization gained wider ground, as the Peronist Left received "that minuscule portion of power—culture—as a recompense for its services or as a trap in which it would ultimately fall."[26] As the cult of spontaneity and a populist empiricism gained ground, the figure of the "Europeanized intellectual" increasingly came under fire. For sectors of the literary sphere the strengthening of paternalism and messianism installed a Faustian dilemma: to specialize and professionalize literate culture while at the same time maintaining and radicalizing the political commitment that very specialization had made impossible or futile, at least in the populist forms it took. "Real" politics had been sent to the other side of the barricades, where obedient and grandiloquent militants screamed ever more loudly that a revolutionary had no use for books, only for weapons. By the time Cortázar wrote *El libro de Manuel* (1973), a novel about the predicament of expatriate activists in Paris and permeated with reproductions of newspapers attesting to the growing right-wing violence in Latin America, the split between literature and politics could be read in an allegorical key, physically on the pages. Whereas the plot of the novel bears witness to the privatization— that is, depoliticization—of revolutionary activity, politics as such found a home in the newspaper cutouts, the function of which oscillated between document and ornament. Cortázar often referred to what he perceived as the "flaws" of *El libro de Manuel*, arguing that they derived from the fact that the book had been written with a view to a political impact, not "literary quality."[27] The fundamental questions, however, remained unasked: What was the historical ground that caused those two things to be antinomical to each other? What was it that allowed politics to be reinscribed as naturalist ornament? Why could the political avant-garde no longer be the aesthetic avant-garde?

Be that as it may, as Cortázar returned to some form or other of realism, postcoup Argentine literature written both in and out of the country seemed to follow a different path. In fact, it would not be far-fetched to hypothesize that paralleling a crisis of populism in politics Argentina witnessed a crisis of realism in the arts, not so much in the sense that realist works were no longer being produced, but rather that the realist aesthetic congealed into a nostalgic, cliché-saturated form. At any rate, the history of Argentine culture during the dictatorship is still largely to be written. Much valuable material has nevertheless begun to formulate some hypotheses: Francine Masiello has shown how national rock music, in a context in which it was prohibitively dangerous to engage in any mass congregation of a political nature, became a means for the exercise of sociality and exchange of experience.[28] Likewise, Liliana Heker has reflected on how literary workshops provided some intellectual breathing room as well as a means of survival when the university found itself under violent scrutiny and repression.[29] Andrés Avellaneda has not only done a superb job of compiling the absurdities of censorship during the military regime but has also analyzed a number of the period's cultural manifestations to argue that realism could now only exist as "testimonial caricature or populist loudspeaker."[30] Reviewing a mass of narratives written during the dictatorship, Fernando Reati has compellingly shown how the need to represent what appears unrepresentable, coupled with the subsequent imperative to mourn the dead, brings about a deep crisis in the very structure of mimesis.[31]

Osvaldo Pellettieri and others have delved into the remarkable phenomenon of Teatro Abierto, a series of annual productions of plays by twenty-one of Argentina's best authors and collectively managed by professionals of theater for several years beginning in 1981, during the heyday of tyranny. Combining a politically committed stance with formal experimentalism and surviving terrorist attacks—including the burning of its headquarters a week after inauguration—Teatro Abierto was arguably the most massive cultural event to happen in Argentina during the dictatorial days.[32] As is so typical during dictatorships, cinema suffered more from internalized censorship and financial troubles, as it was initially dominated by pornography and slapstick, only reemerging with quality films in the early to mid-1980s. Adolfo Aristaráin's *Time for Revenge* inaugurated this rebirth in 1981 with a multilayered political allegory centered around a worker who simulates muteness after an accident in the copper mines and wins a civil suit against the corporation but finds himself unable or unwilling to return to normality after his victory. After the fall of the generals Argentina produced some of Latin America's best cinema, a good deal of which focused on different facets of the postdictatorial predicament, such as the return from exile (in Fernando Solanas's *Sur* or Alberto Fischerman's *The Days of June*), the inevitable burden of complicity and guilt (in Luis Puenzo's Oscar-winning *The Official Story*), and the emblematization of exclusion and silencing through the image of madness (in Eliseo Subiela's *Man Facing Southeast*).[33]

Several nationally specific debates stirred Argentine culture during and after the dictatorship. Unlike in Chile, home to a powerful socialist labor movement, in Argentina hegemony over the working class had been conquered by a personalist movement in which no function for the intellectual seemed visible; unlike in Brazil, the Argentine postdictatorship did not envision the constitution of a left-wing post-Stalinist mass party where the intelligentsia could reorient its political goals. The result is that much of the postdictatorial debate on the direction of intellectual politics has been polarized between the alternative represented by the former members of *Contorno*—say, David Viñas or León Rozitchner—who continue asserting the primacy of the model of militarized politics and view in the present configuration nothing more than an accommodation to the market or a generalized betrayal and, on the other hand, an assortment of progressive intellectuals who attempted to overcome isolation through an approximation with—and subsequent withdrawal from—Alfonsín's Radical Party government. This trajectory includes some of the cultural critics who began to edit *Punto de Vista* in 1978, during the heyday of political repression in Argentina. Initially directed by Beatriz Sarlo, Carlos Altamirano, and Ricardo Piglia, and later joined by María Teresa Gramuglio, Hugo Vezzetti, and others, *Punto de Vista* contributed to a slow and intricate recomposition of intellectual culture in Argentina. The scope of the magazine's intervention included bringing to the fore figures hitherto marginal to the Argentine left, such as Raymond Williams and Pierre Bourdieu, as it attempted to develop a materialist framework for the analysis of literature, and mass, popular, and erudite cultures. From the beginning it also included decisive allusions to the Argentine past, finding in historical reflection the possibility of posing themes related to the country's political reality in a context of ferocious repression over intellectual activity. Furthermore, its pages housed some of the first critical assessments of the new narrative produced in and out of Argentina after the coup by figures such as Ricardo Piglia, Juan José

Saer, Juan Carlos Martini, and Daniel Moyano. After the dictatorship the *Punto de Vista* group, along with a circle exiled in Mexico and known as Mesa Socialista (including Pancho Aricó, Juan Carlos Portantiero, and Oscar Terán), was instrumental in forming the Club de Cultura Socialista, where the new role of socialists and the intellectual-state relation would be some of the major themes. The literature I will discuss in this book in great measure foregrounds these themes, and some of the knots faced by these collectives will return in my analytical chapters.[34]

One or Two Things at Stake in the Theory of Authoritarianism

In Brazil and the Southern Cone the theory of authoritarianism has been the most widely accepted social-scientific account of the dictatorships. "The use of the terms *authoritarian* and *authoritarianism* imposed itself as legal currency to characterize the type of political regimes that came into being in Brazil and the Southern Cone during the past two decades."[35] In Brazil Fernando Henrique Cardoso's analyses of dependency began to incorporate the word *authoritarianism* to define the state instituted in 1964, in an evolution that culminated in *Autoritarismo e Democratização* (1975). Beginning in the early 1970s the Argentine Guillermo O'Donnell characterized the emerging regimes as "bureaucratic-authoritarian," showing how development and modernization in Latin America, far from entailing liberal forms of government, triggered technocratic military dictatorships.[36] In Chile José Joaquín Brunner produced a number of studies of Chilean society under the same rubric. Although there are obvious differences among these social scientists—Brunner's sociology focuses on culture, O'Donnell's political science privileges the study of state forms, and Cardoso's central concerns converge on economic formations—the recurrence of explanatory models based on some form or other of a theory of authoritarianism is noteworthy. Underneath the term's seemingly descriptive nature it is crucial to investigate the rhetoric in which it is embedded, especially in the two versions that grounded not only the conceptualization of the Chilean and Brazilian military regimes, but also the conservative redemocratizations that later ensued, that is, the sociological works of José Joaquín Brunner and Fernando Henrique Cardoso.

José Joaquín Brunner is the signatory of the most thorough anatomy of post-1973 state ideology, or "the authoritarian conception of the world," as he calls it. Arguing that the political transformation was part of a larger refoundation that relied on a value system fundamentally different from everything hitherto known by Chilean society, Brunner shows the imbrication between the doctrine of national security and the transnational market, between armed forces and internationalized bourgeoisie, between, in a word, political authoritarianism and capitalist class interest. What Brunner accomplishes in his first major study is a dissection of dictatorial ideology as a *totality*, that is, as a complex in which "authoritarianism is not simply added, but rather is an essential element of the new model, designed to make possible a reorganization of society on the basis of its disciplining."[37] Dispelling any illusions that one was facing an aberration, Brunner shows how authoritarianism performed the function of "maintaining the order adequate to the new model of capitalist development,"[38] thus being *organic* to the implementation of market values in Chile. Market ideology, military doctrine, and religious traditionalism—the three components of the "authoritarian conception of the world"—are demonstrated to form a coherent, unified ideology.

In a later study Brunner points out that postcoup Chilean social sciences witnessed a general trend to examine the roots of authoritarianism in Chilean history from the Leninist Left to conservative Catholicism. By unveiling said traces, "these studies showed that the liberal and democratic beliefs have not been continuous and their development not immune to contradictions in the past decades."[39] The text begins to set up a dichotomy whereby "liberal and democratic beliefs" appear as that which, *by definition*, opposes authoritarianism. The ubiquity of authoritarian positions is presented as coextensive with the fact that "liberal and democratic beliefs" have not been continuous. Regardless of how much room one makes for subsequent "contradictions"—instances in which "even" liberals were authoritarian—liberal democracy emerges as the remedy against authoritarianism. The self-evidence of the opposition is thus taken for granted. If the regimes are authoritarian, those who oppose them do it in the name of democracy, don't they? Again, underneath the seemingly obvious meaning of these terms, some rhetorical webs must be attended to. Taking the several authoritarian critiques of democracy voiced by conservative sectors after 1973 as a justification of the coup—done from a Catholic-traditionalist, neoliberal-mercantile or national-security point of view—Brunner argues, correctly in my opinion, that the capitalist refoundation of Chile could not be accomplished under a democratic regime. However, the opposition between authoritarianism and democracy seems to be naturalized to the point where the latter is seen as a form that "prevents the *full state expression* of a sole class, the dominant one."[40] From the fact that the installation of the transnational market demanded a military dictatorship, Brunner deduces the far more questionable claim that representative democracy by definition curbs class domination.

The dichotomy returns in an essay in which Brunner describes the practices that progressively undermined the military regime, noting the key role of *memory* in their struggle: "the symbolic experience of democracy becomes the central axis of a collective memory that resists disappearance."[41] The clash between the military regime and oppositional forces again appears as one between authoritarianism and democracy. Never considering the possibility that the popular memories alluded to might turn out to be *irreducible* to the notion of democracy (or force it to be reinterpreted in novel and unexpected ways), Brunner's text instead establishes an automatic identification between the two. The history of a "cultural tradition" is equated with the history of democracy as such. The stage is set for the aftermath of the dictatorships not to be imagined as anything other than a transition to democracy: "if the authoritarian order cannot . . . organize itself in the form of a complete culture . . . , neither can the democratic order emerge as a culture until there exist conditions to assure a transition to democracy as a political regime."[42] This sentence shows better than any other the naturalization of the signifying chain "popular resistance-democratic ethos-parliamentary democracy," as though each term followed organically from the previous one. Democracy as a popular practice or experience, once conflated with "democracy as political regime," leaves little room for transitional politics to be imagined as anything other than a return to parliamentary liberalism.

That the dichotomy observed in Brunner also operates in Cardoso is apparent in the very title of *Autoritarismo e Democratização*. What in Brunner is a subtle rhetorical operation takes the form, in Cardoso, of a careful dissociation of (multi)national corporate interests from the military regimes. The raison d'être of the Brazilian dictatorial state was to be found "less in the political interests of multinational corporations (which prefer forms of state control more permeable to their privatist interests) than in the political and social interests of bureaucratic layers (civil and military) that organize ever more in order to control the state sector of the productive apparatus."[43] The statement's ideological power relies on its subtle conflation of political authoritarianism and economic statism, as though the two always and necessarily went together. Cardoso's explanatory model presupposes that a dictatorial state is somehow not really "permeable to privatist interests." Systematically downplaying the complicity between dictatorship and multinational capital, glossing over the military regime's role in an unprecedented extraction of surplus value and concentration of wealth, Cardoso can manufacture the mirage of a bureaucracy acting on its own behalf, a "state bourgeoisie" with interests not coincident with those of multinational capital. This ideological fantasy would be instrumental in guaranteeing the hegemony of conservative liberalism in the postdictatorial redemocratization: after all the dictatorship, Cardoso makes us believe, never really acted in the interests of capital, but rather of an anachronistic state bureaucracy. While correctly critiquing the characterization of the military regimes, made by sectors of the Left, as "fascist"—those regimes, unlike fascism, did not rely on popular mobilization and did not make use of a party structure—Cardoso redefines the ruling elites under dictatorship as a state bureaucracy:

> There is no possible similarity between the associate-dependent bourgeoisies from Latin America and their counterparts in the U.S. and Europe. . . . The real shield of the local internationalized bourgeoisies, in this sense, is the multinational conglomerate, protected and allied with the state of matrix-societies. *On the contrary, the local states serve as a political support more for "functionaries," the military, fragments detached from the local bourgeoisie and not integrated to the internationalization of the market, rather than to the great internationalized bourgeois interests.*[44]

This is a solid piece of ideology: national and international free-marketeers became marginal factors in the dictatorial regime, as the regime was supposedly acting on behalf of a mysterious bureaucratic cluster somehow not reducible to capitalist class interest. It should be kept in mind that a state bureaucracy, unlike a social class, can be unseated without any change in the prevailing economic model. The definition of the dictatorship as "authoritarian state" made room for the next step, an oppositional class alliance hegemonized by neoliberal-conservative forces, leading to a redemocratization that never interrogated the economic model imposed by the military. After all, those in whose interests it had been sustained were carefully exempted from any responsibilities in the dictatorial barbarism. *The theory of authoritarianism was the ideological ground provided by the social sciences for the conservative hegemony in the so-called democratic transitions.* There is thus no contradiction between Cardoso-the-firm-opponent-of-the-military-regime in 1975 and Cardoso-the-implementer-of-neoliberal-policies in 1997. The former was actually the condition of possibility of the latter. No point, then, in wondering what was made of the valiant soldier of democracy. No betrayals have taken place. What was understood by "democracy" was already given in 1975.

According to Cardoso the success of the military's economic policies depended on the "state's capacity increasingly to become an entrepreneur and manager of companies. With this, instead of strengthening 'civil society'—the bourgeoisie—as economic-financial policies seemed to desire, the base of an expansionist, disciplinary and repressive state was reinforced."[45] Again, the conflation of the state's very real repressive action and the mirage of a statist "expansion," a nowhere-to-be-found state entrepreneurship, made possible what would become the cornerstone of the conservative hegemony in the so-called transition: to present the dictatorship as product of a few statist bureaucrats, opposed in everything to "civil society," the latter oddly equated with the bourgeoisie. Once the matter was posed in this fashion, political choices became inevitably limited to a two-item menu: democracy and authoritarianism. The liberal-conservative alliance that led Tancredo Neves-José Sarney to power could now appear as the embodiment of a universal yearning for democracy.

The critique of the theory of authoritarianism entails a terminological change: I will not designate the term *transition*, as do the social sciences, as the return to parliamentary democracy, free elections, and juridical institutionality. The end of the dictatorships cannot, from the perspective I advance here, be characterized as a transitional process. As was implicit in my critique, *the real transitions are the dictatorships themselves.* According to Willy Thayer, "Let us not take 'transition' as the postdictatorial process of redemocratization in Latin American societies, but rather more broadly, as the process of 'modernization' and transit from the modern national state to the transnational post-state market. In this sense, for us the transition is primordially the dictatorship. It was the dictatorship that made the transit from State to Market, a transit euphemistically designated as 'modernization.'"[46] This interpretation crucially shifts the emphasis from a derivative transition to an epochal one. The epochal transition was no doubt the dictatorship, not the return of civil rule that ensued once the real transition had been accomplished. In other words, the return of democracy in itself does not imply a *transit* to any place other than the one where the dictatorship left off. "Transition to democracy" meant nothing but the juridical-electoral legitimation of the successful transition carried out under the military, that is, the ultimate equation between political freedom for people and economic freedom for capital, as if the former depended upon the latter, or as if the latter had somehow been hampered by the generals. It should thus not be a cause for surprise that the category of "governability" has enjoyed such a central status in postdictatorial social sciences. No other word so succinctly summarizes the role of those disciplines in legitimating the epochal transition, for governability is a problem that, by definition, can only occupy the victorious. For those who have been defeated, it goes without saying that the question of governability does not pose itself. From the standpoint of the defeated, the very concept belies an irrevocable complicity with the victorious.

Something should be said, however, about the specificity of the Argentine experience regarding the meaning of the word *transition*. The Brazilian and Chilean epochal transitions from State to Market can be unequivocally observed to have taken place during the dictatorships themselves. Those were two-decade-long processes where even the return to democracy was highly controlled and ultimately hegemonized by the military regimes themselves. On the other hand, Argentina's seven-year-long *proceso*, in spite of doing what it could to dismantle the welfare state and deregulate the economy, cannot at first sight be said to have realized that epochal transition, at least not in so clear a fashion. It is well known that in 1983 the state was still responsible for a comparatively large portion of the Argentine economy. For a number of historical reasons the Argentine transition to the global market was far more unstable than that of its neighbors, the unspeakable absurdity and arbitrariness of its repressive system between 1976 and 1983 being another index of such instability. Although the possibility of significant resistance had been already eliminated by 1976, the Argentine generals confronted a working class whose degree of organization and unionization was unparalleled in the continent. In addition, Argentina, unlike Brazil, saw the phenomenon of armed urban guerrilla emerge *before* the coup; the period from 1973 to 1976 was one of generalized violence, on the Left and the Right, actually one that progressively took the form of a massacre of the former by the latter (mostly through the notorious Alianza Anticomunista Argentina— AAA; Argentine Anticommunist Alliance). The elimination of these barriers was evidently a condition sine qua non for the epochal transition. The Argentine generals performed that groundwork, so much so that today the task of deregulation and unrestricted privatization is being carried out by the very Peronism that once was—or was believed to be, such ambiguity being the mark of Peronism—the major obstacle to that task's full actualization.

Having fallen in a far more abrupt fashion, the Argentine generals' control over the return to democracy was far more problematic. The current insistence, by progressive Argentine intellectuals, on the need to defend and preserve institutional democracy as a value in itself is considerably more emphatic than in the rest of the region and is no doubt related to this specificity acquired by the expression *transition to democracy* for Argentines. The proceso's last, desperate attempt to regain legitimacy was the suicidal war against Great Britain, an obvious maneuver to conquer some popular basis—over and above, of course, the indisputable fact that the Falkland Islands rightly belong to Argentina. After the defeat in the South Atlantic, Argentines entered the affective terrain proper to postdictatorship: the experience of defeat, disillusionment, and destitution. A short period of euphoria would follow Raúl Alfonsín's election in 1983, only to see disenchantment take over again in the wake of Alfonsín's systematic concessions to the military concerning their crimes, as well as to the IMF concerning issues of economic policy. This displacement is emblematized in the trajectory of the word *impossible* in Argentine political culture, as noted by Oscar Landi: until Alfonsín's government the "impossible Argentina" was the nightmare created by the military and to which the country almost unanimously refused to return, despite the three military insurrections since 1984. After Carlos Menem's neoliberal-kitsch version of Peronism ascended to power and the deregulation of Argentine economy got under way, *impossible* was no longer the word used to describe the dystopian past that one refused; it was now reserved for the utopian project that one was led to abandon. The country was now being asked to forsake dreams of an "impossible future" and embrace the "realism" of the market.[47]

If the epochal transition from State to Market in Argentina is not carried through, it is at least made possible by the military regime. Let us not forget, 1983 marked the first time in forty years that Peronism was defeated in open elections; the victorious candidate was precisely the one who managed to frame the issue around the opposition between democracy and authoritarianism, the latter being repeatedly associated, in Alfonsín's speeches, not only with the dictatorship of the previous years but also with the authoritarianism of the armed Left in the early 1970s, as if those two kinds of violence were of the same order. The polarity between democracy and authoritarianism had become the doxa of our times.

The Naturalist Turn and the Imperative to Confess

The *romance-reportagem*, a particular brand of the journalistic novel, enjoyed a solid, though not uncontested, hegemony in Brazil during the 1970s. Taking the form of fictionalizations of bombastic, scandalous pieces of news reported by the media and displaying a naturalist aesthetic, the romance-reportagem paradoxically combined a cult of objectivity and neutrality with the myth of the valiant, undaunted reporter who overcomes all obstacles in his search for truth.[48] The romance-reportagem filled, if imaginarily, the information void in Brazilian society during a period of ferocious censorship over the mass media. The general feeling that "there's a whole lot going on that we don't know about" reinforced the fetishization of information as a precious commodity in itself, detached, as it were, from the social processes through which it was produced. This coincided with the arrival of a host of communication technologies in Brazil in the context of the dependent modernization propelled by the dictatorship. A completely depoliticized version of the communication sciences became the axis of both the modernizing rhetoric of the military—the new technology was presented as a proof that "Brazil had finally joined the first world"—and, ironically enough, much of the narrative written against it.

José Louzeiro's statement about his 1977 *Infância dos Mortos* synthesizes the romance-reportagem's naturalist rhetoric: "The facts that give substance to this narrative have been taken from our bitter everyday reality. The author did not worry about lining them up chronologically, nor did he abstain from describing brutal situations that show well the degree of dehumanization we have reached."[49] A remark that in another context might have sounded like a fictional trick of feigned verisimilitude now appeared as a nonironic claim to legitimacy for a "copy of the real" that believed in its own transparency. If the romance-reportagem ended up accounting for some of the greatest market successes in Brazil during the 1970s, the explanation may be found in this revamping of naturalist claims to neutrality and transparency within an aesthetic of abjection basically modeled after the mass media. It was the romance-reportagem's systematic masking of its own conditions of production that enabled the reader's cathartic identification with a warrior-reporter who seemed to float above all social tensions. Such heroicization of the journalist filled, again imaginarily, the void created by the defeat of the armed opposition to the dictatorship. Between 1968 and 1973 the guerrilla's putschist voluntarism nurtured the hope of bringing down the military regime through the isolated action of a self-entitled vanguard, in a reductionist militarization of politics. The "bravery" and "courage" of the reporter who "brings to light the censored truth" was tributary of an analogous operation: Brazilian politics was still narrated with military metaphors, even in the oppositional field. Here is an echo of the language that dominated Brazilian narrative during this time period: "Some risk their skins in war. Others do it in revolutions. John Reed was of them. Hemingway was one of them. Murilo de Carvalho is one of them. A man searching for stories to tell. A reality hunter. A reporter."[50] What was at stake here, of course, was not the truth value of such statements, but the process through which their very syntax mimed the mass media, while their semantics, although attempting to grasp politics, remained within military science.

Flora Süssekind was on the right track when she suggested that the function of the romance-reportagem was to offer a *symbolic compensation*.[51] Its compensatory function not only provided information blocked by censorship but also had an *affective* dimension. In a civil society faced with a demoralizing defeat, literature stepped forth to assure us that truth and reason were on "our" side. By playing into the Manichaean rhetorical

game of the dictatorship, naturalism not only failed to become a critical space for rethinking the mistakes of the resistance or the mythical
conceptions of the national-popular prevalent in the oppositional camp.
It also presented a compensatory substitution whereby the middle class
would expiate the guilt of having supported the coup and joined in the
anticommunist hysteria, all in the hope of a social ascension that would
ultimately be frustrated; hence the fact that the crisis of the romance-
reportagem can be argued to be coextensive and contemporaneous with
the collapse of a certain epic narrative of Brazilian politics. The romance-
reportagem knew no social types other than villains (dictators, torturers,
and traitors) or heroes (brave journalists in search of truth or news) because it purported to narrate the story of a fall, the trajectory of an irre-
deemable world, with the language of the classical genres—the tragedy
or the epic. That is, the illusion specific to the "journalist turn" was to
pretend to account for a fallen world (therefore a novelistic one, where
all heroism also triggers its parodic double) with prenovelistic, epic language. When it attempted to endow the plight of mundane, day-to-day
street characters with a tragic dimension, it produced a paradox. All
the sympathy and solidarity that their fate could inspire stemmed from
the fact that they were "one of us," common citizens—student activists,
workers, and so on—but the language that narrated it insisted on turning their fall into an event of tragic proportions, or their partial victories
against the regime into epic adventures, thereby removing those events
from the realm in which they had any meaning, that is, that of *experience.* In other words, the dead-end street in which that sector of Brazilian
literature found itself had to do with the thrust to construct a filled; classical subject in a world governed by the Lukácsian transcendental homelessness. The romance-reportagem's fundamental incompetence lay in its
inability to deal with *loss.*[52]

In addition to the privilege of journalism as a model for fiction writing in Brazil, the Southern Cone witnessed a proliferation of *confessional*
narratives by political actors in the oppositional camp, most often prisoners and victims of torture. Through texts such as Jacobo Timerman's
Preso sin nombre, celda sin número, Alicia Partnoy's *The Little School,* Fernando
Gabeira's *O Que É Isso, Companheiro?,* Hernán Valdés's *Tejas verdes,* and
numerous others, readers were forced to acknowledge the widespread
practice of torture in the continent. These texts placed the reader in the

face of absolute destitution. No roundabout wording was possible; no middle ground could be reached; no conciliation made sense when the regimes in question had developed such an arsenal of techniques: electric prods to the genitals, drownings, mock executions, rapes, beatings, humiliations of various kinds, and torture of children, all of which were applied to prisoners blindfolded or hooded, were assisted by doctors, and were converted into a science. It may not be useless to say this again, as a reminder of the character of the historical ground upon which the current free market stands. This is a necessary gesture, but as we know, insufficient. The accumulation of facts provided by testimonial literature represented a crucial step not only to convince those who insisted in denying the obvious but also for the juridical battles that have taken place and will yet ensue over the coming years.[53]

Compilation of data, however, is not yet the memory of the dictatorship. Memory far exceeds any factual recounting, however important the latter may turn out to be as an initial juridical or political step. The *memory* of the dictatorship, in the strong sense of the word, requires another language; and after reviewing the immense testimonial bibliography produced in the Southern Cone, one cannot avoid a discomforting conclusion: if these texts are treated with less condescension than has been the case, thus avoiding the trap of overlooking their rhetoric simply because they testify to the cruelty of a common enemy, it becomes clear that testimonial literature has left a very meager legacy for the reinvention of memory after the dictatorships. In other words, the worst disservice criticism can do to these texts, to the truth they bear—a factual one— is to treat them as much testimonio criticism has: as epochal ushers of some revolution that has finally allowed the subaltern to speak freely.

To be definitive, a study demonstrating the clear limits of the testimonial genre such as it evolved in the Southern Cone would need to be longer. It would entail, for example, showing how Jacobo Timerman's *Prisoner without a Name, Cell without a Number*, a report of his imprisonment and torture at the hands of the Argentine military, is permeated with the language of the dictatorship itself, drawing parasitically, in fact, upon that language, with its references to leftist militants as "terrorists";[54] the actions of the military as "excesses" (29); the mirage of a division between "radical" and "moderate" generals that could be exploited by prisoners, even during torture sessions—"one might say that my present freedom is a result of the patience exercised by the moderates" (29); the firm belief that "President Rafael Videla and General Roberto Viola tried to convert . . . [his] disappearance into an arrest in order to save . . . [his] life" (29); his overall indignation that a respectable liberal should share the misery of arbitrary imprisonment with leftist "terrorists"; his dismay that no Jewish leaders, under the nightmarish circumstances of the late 1970s, raised their voices in his defense (78); his certainty that, again, "moderate generals" had prevented a greater "outbreak of anti-Semitism" (70); his contentions that the liberal language of his newspaper, *La Opinión*, was "comprehensible and direct," while "leaders, politicians, and intellectuals" resorted to "euphemisms and circumlocutions" (23); a statement that by the way, could easily have been subscribed by the "moderate" Gal. Videla. Again, the need to defend this text, to defend the *truth* of the brutality that it makes known against all denegations coming from the military cannot possibly serve as an excuse for any condescension that would reinforce, as does Timerman, some of the mythology that made the coup possible in the first place.

Most of the testimonies, however, originated on the Left. Here, the analysis would take a slightly different route, although those familiar with the texts might not be surprised to find a stunning number of rhetorical coincidences with Timerman's *Prisoner without a Name*. Fernando Gabeira's *O Que É Isso, Companheiro?*, the most successful dictatorship memoir published in Brazil, reads like an adventure novel.[55] Everything in the text, from the lighthearted tone or the emphasis on miraculous escapes to the heroic portrayal of superhero militants, invites specular, unreflective identification and precludes the possibility of asking questions about the nature of that experience. The central episode revolves around the 1969 kidnapping of U.S. ambassador Charles Elbrick in exchange for the liberation of imprisoned guerrillas. Gabeira recounts the plans, the demands made by the organization, and the conversations with Elbrick about issues such as the Vietnam War, up to the not-so-happy denouement, when Elbrick and several political prisoners were released, most of the latter, however, only to be subsequently recaptured, with two of them dying under torture. The narrative alternates between two basic mechanisms of identification: the "adventurous" passages are narrated as an adult would narrate his naughty behavior as a child—no self-critique, but no restatement of principles either, just sheer enjoyment at the peripeteia, with experience erased along with politics. The second principle of identification is cathartic. The descriptions of torture scenes, replete with sentimental and emotional outpours, fully confident in language's potential of translating experience, make abundant use of abjection, only to return again to the superhero story, whose main protagonist emerges unscathed in the end. When *O Que É Isso, Companheiro?* was published, in 1979, the Brazilian middle class was noticeably anxious to purge away its guilty complicity with the military regime. Gabeira's text, among many others, helped the completion of that purification without major traumas, reworking of the past, or reelaboration of experience. It is indeed amazing, considering the rather literal descriptions of torture scenes, how little the book bothered the structure of feeling hegemonic in Brazil at the time. The book topped best-seller lists with successive editions. Politics had been narrated as a Batmanesque adventure and guilty consciences had been successfully swept under the carpet.

Several of the tropes typical of Latin American testimonialism recur in Miguel Bonasso's *Recuerdo de la muerte,* the memoirs of a *montonero* (guerrilla) activist captured in Montevideo and tortured by the Uruguayan police before being sent back to Argentina. Upon his capture, the first thought that crosses his mind sets the tone for the entire book: "The hood . . . obliges one to look inside. To ask oneself if he is going to resist. If he is going to come out of the test being the same or will become a traitor." [56] Again, it would take me a long and detailed reading of *Recuerdo de la muerte* to show that nothing in the subsequent development of the action, including the failures that piled up on the montoneros throughout the 1970s, changes the terms of the choice with which characters are confronted: you remain the same or you become a traitor. A genuine mythology of the macho who withstands torture and never betrays the cause substitutes for the examination of defeat that would be expected from such a testimony. The examples mount along the narrative: "The individual can always betray. What counts is the Party. Nothing, nothing. Betrayal looks like seduction. Like the image of the seduced woman" (135). As *betrayal*—an omnipresent word, as if politics had been reduced to the Christian polarity between betrayal and faithfulness— is progressively feminized, *the experience of defeat* is silenced, imaginarily compensated for by the image of the resolute macho-warrior. "Pelado wanted to know the history of Serafín, the melancholy toothless guy who had given him the first cigarette. He found out, with pity, that 'he had spoken during torture' and was surprised to realize that his mood was inclining toward forgiveness" (269). For the "feeble" ones who give out information under torture, what is left is either the label of traitor or at best pitiful forgiveness. Betrayal, pity, forgiveness: we know, all too well, where such a lexicon comes from. As the comforting language of Christianity fitfully complemented the heroic and militaristic rhetoric of the "armed vanguard," the dictatorship achieved a fundamental victory, for the language in which its atrocities were narrated was, in its essence, the very same language that it cultivated and promoted: macho militarism seasoned with pious Catholicism.

To be sure, it is not a matter of condemning the whole of testimonio as a genre. The denunciatory and even juridical weight of testimonial texts produced under conditions of oppression should not be underestimated. The key role played by testimonio in the resistance to the military, especially in the Chilean case, is undeniable. It is imperative, however, to interrogate the triumphant rhetoric with which the phenomenon was surrounded during the 1980s, especially in the United States and largely, I believe, as an imaginary compensation for the succession of defeats undergone by the Left in recent decades. In circumstances of political isolation it is all too comforting to imagine that redemption is just around the corner, being announced by a subaltern voice transparently coincident with its experience and supplying the critical-oppositional intellectual with the golden opportunity to satisfy a good conscience. No assertion that testimonio leads us into "postliterature" or that now "the subaltern other *really* speaks" will elide the rhetorical questions left unanswered by Southern Cone testimonialism, namely, the fact that a whole realm of experience was obliterated once the same victimized or heroic strategies—the two are not incompatible at all, as we have seen they actually complement each other quite well—were summoned to narrate facts that the current doxa is eager to forget. Oblivion was all the more facilitated once those atrocities were piled up in a language that very rarely asked questions about its own status—another instance of this being the insistent anunciatory tone of most testimonial texts in the subcontinent, more often than not fully confident that tomorrow the forces of justice would triumph.

The reinvention of memory after the military demands a critique of the legacy of testimonialism, however important it may be, I insist, to defend the truth of those texts. Their truth, that is, the truth of what happened to all of those who fell into the hands of the military regimes, is a factual one. Such truth is irreducible, and testimonialism has provided rich material to point to whenever we encounter, as we already have, denegations and denials of various kinds. The factual truth, however, is not yet the truth of defeat. The truth of defeat cannot emerge in a language that still has not incorporated the experience of defeat and thought it through. The truth of defeat, which is the truth of the Latin American experience in the past decades—not to say the past centuries—demands a narrative that does not limit itself to inviting solidarity. "Solidarity, which remains the essential summons of the testimonial text and that which radically distinguishes it from the literary text, is in perpetual risk of being turned into a rhetorical tropology."[57] The defeat, let us define it provisionally here, is *that moment of experience when all solidarity becomes a trope necessarily blind to the rhetorical structure that makes it possible.* Such blindness will only be exarcerbated if literary criticism insists on substituting the eulogy of testimonio for reflection on its conditions of possibility in times of defeat.

Allegory as the End of the Magical

Besides the return to naturalism, the literature written under dictatorship saw a proliferation of allegorical narratives that attempted to come to terms with what seemed like an unrepresentable catastrophe. Depicting fictitious countries terrorized by bloody tyrants, small towns occupied by iniquitous invaders or mysterious animals, and black masses replete with satanic allusions and sacrificial bodies, this literature confronts us with several imaginary dystopian towns: Hualacato in Daniel Moyano's *El vuelo del tigre*, Marulanda in José Donoso's *Casa de campo*, and Manarairema in José J. Veiga's *A Hora dos Ruminantes*, to name but the three I will briefly analyze here. As microcosms of a totality that now could be evoked only in allegorical fashion, these novels portray a certain interlude, a circumscribed period when history is suspended, and secular, onward-flowing time gives way to an eternalized time devoid of growth or progression, as if the ruling order were nothing less than that of Nature: a "strange combination of nature and history" whereby the latter is represented as "a petrified primordial landscape,"[58] that is, as *natural history*. As Benjamin notes in his analysis of allegory in the baroque, however, "nature" here does not stand for the transcendent exuberance that romanticism made known, but for an immanent process of putrefaction: "Nature was not seen by them in bud and bloom, but in the over-ripeness and decay of her creations. In nature they saw eternal transience, and here alone did the saturnine vision of this generation recognize history."[59]

"Eternal transience" is the Benjaminian oxymoron that alludes to that interval when history is suspended and contemplated in the starkness of its ruins. Nature becomes an emblem of death and decadence, a way of depicting a history that can no longer be grasped as a positive totality. "The word 'history' stands written on the countenance of nature in the characters of transience. The allegorical physiognomy of nature-history, which is put on stage in the *Trauerspiel*, is present in reality in the form of the ruin."[60] It is through the notion of ruins that the flourishing of allegory during times of political reaction can be best understood. As witness and expression of a political defeat, allegory emerges not because in order to escape censorship writers have to craft "allegorical" ways of saying things that they would otherwise be able to express "directly." Allegory is the aesthetic face of political defeat—for example, the baroque during the Counter Reformation, Baudelaire's allegorical poetry in the Second Empire, the revival of allegory in postmodernism—not due to some extrinsic controlling agency but because the petrified images of ruins, in their immanence, bear the only possibility of narrating the defeat. Ruins are the raw material that allegory possesses at its disposal.

I take the allegorical machines produced under dictatorship to represent a break with those strands of modern Latin American literature predicated primarily on certain "marvelous," "magical," or "fantastic" effects. Unlike magical realism, where the eruption of the uncanny element takes place within a mimetically credible universe (thereby staging the confrontation between opposing logics, which is the genre's defining trace), these allegorical fables let the reader know, from the beginning, that s/he is elsewhere. There is, therefore, no possible shock, no eruption of the unexpected or the magical in allegorical novels. In this respect they are akin to parables, in which the rules of verisimilitude are not violated within the tale, but rather suspended a priori, as a requirement for the story's very unfolding. Only by suspending verisimilitude can they set the stage to recount the monstrosity that is their proper object. Verisimilitude has to be previously suspended because the text will not bear the conflict between opposing logics—opposing conceptions of verisimilitude—which is the mark of modern "marvelous," "magical," or "fantastic" realism. As the novels I will discuss make clear, "allegory" takes place when the uncanny, the *unheimlich* element, hitherto identified as "marvelous" or "magical," has itself become *heimlich*: familiar, predictable, indeed inevitable.

Daniel Moyano's *El vuelo del tigre*, begun in Argentina and finished in the author's Spanish exile, relates the story of the occupation of Hualacato by "the Percussionists," of whom the reader knows nothing other than the regulations they impose upon a family, the Aballays. In one of the parallels between Hualacato and Argentina, the narrator states that "it is not the first time that they come. In forty years the old man has seen them come on horseback, in trucks, always at night."[61] The Percussionists take over the streets, impose a martial law, and designate a "savior" for each household. The text then sets out to tell the predicament of the Aballays under Nabu, their "savior": all the fear, interrogations, confiscation of letters and photographs, forbidden words, and so on. The family is forced to conceal their relationship with Cachimba, a man who has been married to one of their aunts and is now being searched by the occupying Percussionists. Moyano thus introduces the themes of disavowal and denegation: "It is not our fault that she [Avelina] is Cachimba's wife. That's her business. We can be friends or relatives of Avelina's but not of Cachimba's. She introduced him to me and I never saw him again" (51). The family's good behavior earns them a reclassification in the invaders' ranking: "This is not, apparently, a dangerous family, as it was thought at the beginning. It is now catalogued as simply suspicious, which implies some substantial changes." (95). The passage recalls the notorious classifications done by Latin American dictatorships, where citizens were pigeonholed into three or four official categories according to the degree of peril they could represent to the regime. The Aballays are allowed to take their first walk outside, after months during which they had already forgotten the sunlight.

The family is also, despite appearances of compliance, plotting a secret resistance. Animals are summoned to work as go-betweens for the resistance, and the crucial turning point comes from the family's observation of the birds' itinerary. Their flight seems to revolve around one single point that begins to appear to be endowed with a magical quality. The quasi-mystical communication that ensues between humans and birds provides the material needed for the "house of life," a fortress where "death could not enter." After the pseudorevolution, the people of Huala-cato begin to emerge from prisons and underground hideaways, count-ing their dead and contemplating the postcatastrophe scenario.

A similar motif runs through José Donoso's *Casa de campo,* arguably the most ambitious Latin American allegorical novel of the past few decades. Donoso's 500-plus-page tour de force marked a break with his earlier *cos-tumbrista,* or psychologizing, production; the change can undoubtedly be linked with that of Chilean society's. As Donoso indicates at the end of the novel, the period of its composition can be read allegorically. Begun "on September 18, 1973" (a week after the coup) and "finished on June 19, 1978," *Casa de campo* represents a major attempt, by a novelist not usually thought of as very political, to come to terms with the turmoil undergone by Chilean society. The text suggests a true table of equivalencies with Chile's trajectory from Allende to Pinochet. *Casa de campo* is the story of a country house belonging to the Venturas, who profited from the expro-priation of nearby gold mines from "native" hands for purposes of trade with all-powerful "foreigners," easily identifiable, through several hints, with multinational capital. The Venturas impose a tyrannical rule on the house, granting their servants "the right to organize spying networks and systems of punishment to impose the law."[62] The victims of such violence are mostly the children, deprived of any decision power, as well as the natives, the producers of the material foundation for the Venturas' richness. The family's political ambiguities are mirrored by the labyrin-thine structure of the house: the ground floor, living rooms, and parks host the public and hypocritical democratic rituals, while secret nego-tiations and deliberations take place in basements and adults' bedrooms.

The action is divided in two parts. "La partida," which narrates the adults' trip to the city, during which the children, allied with the natives, rebel against the order and make of Adriano Gomara, their only adult ally (and phantasmatic figure of Salvador Allende throughout the novel), the new leader. Protective bars are torn down, the natives are invited in, and egalitarian measures are taken, only to see, however, the adults return in the second part, "El regreso," and impose punishment and a

ferocious dictatorship upon children and natives, while displaying slav-
ish subservience toward the "foreigners" who had come to purchase and
take possession of the house. The adults' absence lasts, according to the
children and the natives, one year, but, according to the adults, only one
day, in a polemic that has an interesting historical counterpart in the
struggle over the meaning and legacy of the Allende government. *Casa
de campo,* unlike *El vuelo del tigre,* does not end with a revolutionary takeover but with the house being invaded by grass and seeds, making the
air unbreathable, throwing adults and children alike to the ground and
leaving a final image of chaos and destruction.

A bit like Moyano's *El vuelo del tigre,* the inhabitants of Manarairema in
José J. Veiga's *A Hora dos Ruminantes* wake up one day and notice a large
encampment by the river. Because the strangers never come to town,
do not seem interested in making friends, and do not respect any of
the hinterland courtesy rules, the townspeople grow increasingly uneasy
with their presence. In rare contacts with the foreigners, the townspeople are struck by their rudeness and contempt. Local conversations
begin to revolve around the foreigners' defiant standoffishness: they do
not appear to need the town for anything yet will not go away. Some
of the town's bravest men gradually turn into sheepish servants in the
outsiders' presence. During their stay, the town suffers two major cata-
strophic and surreal invasions, by dogs and later by oxen. The population
is first terrorized when the town is swarmed by starving dogs coming
from the strangers' encampment. They turn the city upside down, killing
chickens, scaring people away from their houses, relieving themselves
anywhere, and so forth. Here Veiga once again places emphasis on complicity generated by fear:

> Billy clubs, straps, and shotguns were slowly put away and in their
> place came fondlings, gentle words, and offers of food. . . . Respect
> for the dogs' rights was the order of the day. . . . If a dog approached
> a fountain in the streets, someone always rushed to cup his hands and
> spare the animal the inconvenience of drinking from the spout. (36–
> 7/55–6)[63]

When the dogs leave, it is time to swallow the humiliation and wel-
come oblivion: "nobody wanted even to think of the dogs, but the memory of them was everywhere" (38/58, translation modified). With the

second invasion, the town is virtually destroyed. Thousands of oxen appear as if coming from nowhere, jamming the streets and preventing anybody from leaving home: "once a window was opened, it was impossible to close it, nothing was strong enough to push back that mass of horns, heads, and necks that now took up every inch of space" (84/128). The occupation seems to last forever, as many of the townspeople starve to death, while others die attempting to make their way to a relative's house by walking on the oxen's backs. After a lengthy stay the oxen disappear the same way they came, and the villagers get together, euphoric but unable to reconstruct the mud-filled town. They light a bonfire at the top of the hill and gaze in disbelief at the desolate landscape. Someone informs them that the strangers too are now gone.

The first observation to be made about these allegorical representations of dictatorship—and about the many others produced in recent years—is that they take distance from the confrontation, characteristic of magical realism, between "marvelous," premodern cosmogonies and the modern, secular standpoint from which that precapitalist subalternity was represented. That is, the magical effect in Miguel Angel Asturias, García Márquez, or the Carpentier of *El reino de este mundo*, or yet the fantastic element in Cortázar, stemmed from some instance irreducible to the rationalization of modern capitalism, be it seductive indigenous/precapitalist cosmogonies in the former or the singular aesthetic epiphany that deautomatizes the repetition of atrophied experience in the latter. Magical (or fantastic, in the River Plate tradition) realism thus depended, for its effect, on the conflict between two irreconcilable logics. In the case of those more rural societies where magical realism of the Asturian variety flourished, this conflict could be recognized as that of two opposing modes of production, as the fully modern narrative apparatus wrestled with a folkloric or cosmogonic material that could not be incorporated without a previous taming, a constitutive subjugation by no means deprived of violence. Magical realism was always, from Miguel Angel Asturias's *Leyendas de Guatemala* to *Cien años de soledad* and Isabel Allende's *La casa de los espíritus*, inseparable from the demonization of a subaltern culture (subalternity occupied in Allende's novel by the signifier *woman*) carried out from the standpoint of modern capitalist forms ready to subsume them, the prototypical example being the submission of the circular, mythic time of the anecdote to the linear, onward-flowing time of writing in García Márquez's novel.[65] This dynamic should be kept in mind as one works through a critical bibliography that still reads magical realism as magical realism read itself, celebrating the genre's "subversion" of "Western" "rationalism" and its "openness to diversity," when not outright proposing it as the sum of Latin American identity.[66]

In the case of the more urban River Plate societies, magical realism symptomatically never established a tradition. That rather different, but historically analogous regional genre, the fantastic, emblematized another conflict, as is apparent in Felisberto Hernández or Julio Cortázar: the more typically modernist theme of alienation in face of a commodified reality, countered by the singular role of aesthetic experience as provider of *ostranenia*, that all-too-ephemeral epiphanic shock that provides a glimpse of what a redeemed world might look like. In Brazil, where the fantastic or the magical were not dominant strands, a similar conflict between opposing logics can be noted throughout the modernist mainstream, from Mário de Andrade's *Macunaíma* (where the antihero's *ai, que preguiça!* negated the world of rationalized labor much like a tropical flâneur) to the tormented consciousnesses of Clarice Lispector's characters, still able to find in the contemplation of daily objects (such as the cockroach in *A Paixão Segundo G.H.*) an epiphanic illumination that could reorder a reified experience.

These conflicts all but vanish in dictatorial allegories. The confrontation of opposing orders gives way to a total engulfing of the alternative logic by the rationality of the tyrannies portrayed. The enunciative locus from which the story is told has itself fallen into the immanence of the narrated material, in such a way that the terrifying totality is no more explainable to narrator or reader than to the bewildered characters. Because the fundamental principle has become invisible, the reader is confronted with a world deprived of all outside: not by coincidence these fables take place within a circumscribed space: a house, town, or imaginary republic—images of the petrification of history characteristic of all allegory. Beyond the allegorical walls a competing order or logic might exist, but that space has become unnarratable. The language of defeat can only narrate the radical immanence of defeat.

Furthermore, the notion of agency becomes problematic as the defeat appears to characters and reader alike as a product of nobody's will in particular, as if history had been submitted to a pervasive detranscendentalization that precluded the assignation of events to any consciousness or subject. The oppressive order displays such arbitrariness that it comes to be associated with Nature itself. Oxen invade and evacuate the town for no apparent reason in Veiga's *A Hora dos Ruminantes;* the adults defend an order upon which they have no control in Donoso's *Casa de campo.* It is as though the oppressors were as accidental to the framework of domination as the oppressed, both of them superfluous to the unfolding of a nightmare that seems to operate according to its own immanent rules, much like gravity laws or magnetic attraction. Inescapable and unascribable to any transcendental principle, the defeat emerges, in these allegorical texts, as an irreducible experience. Whereas in a symbolic poetic the immanence of the event can always be recuperable for an ontological principle, be it national identity or redemption through the aesthetic, allegory defies all transcendentalization, which is to say all interpretation: "allegorical interpretation is then first and foremost an interpretive operation which begins by acknowledging the impossibility of interpretation in the older sense, and by including that impossibility in its own provisional or even aleatory movements."[67]

Allegory thus lingers on immanence. If the arrival of the dictatorships and the ensuing transition from State to Market are coextensive with the end of the boom (the end of the compensatory, redemptive substitution of aesthetics for politics proper to the boom), then the emergence of these allegorical machines is also coextensive with the decadence of magical-realist or fantastic poetics in Latin America. If the latter had made of the *symbol* the principle of unification whereby the dispersion of events could be recollected and raised to a higher master code (hence all the metaphors of continental or national identity in the magical-realist boom), the end of the possibility of a nationally sustained capitalism and the passage to the planetary horizon of the Market coincide with the primacy of the allegorical. If the fundamental principle has become invisible, if one can no longer historicize a map that has covered the entire territory (as in Borges's short story, itself an allegorical anticipation of the present nightmare), then the unfractured totality of the symbol will give way to the fragmented hesitation of allegory. Whereas the boom narrated literature's unique power to put forth a national or continental synthesis, allegories of dictatorship narrate nothing but their powerlessness to read their object. Yet this impotence is not deprived of meaning, and it demands to be itself allegorized, that is, read as ruins of a lost, impossible totality. Although magical-realist novels were still being written as late as 1982, when Isabel Allende published *La casa de los espíritus* (or even later with the likes of Laura Esquivel), Allende's and Esquivel's texts bore witness to the fact that they could now only be read as kitsch, highly ideologized remnants of a mode of representation that, in order to subsist, must necessarily resort to sentimental, reactive, and often reactionary clichés.[68]

In sum, it is in the respective relationships of these two styles with *the other* or with *the outside* that the contrast between the allegorical and the magical becomes clearest. Magical realism, despite its history of appeals to Latin American originality and difference, has firm roots in the ethnographic thrust of the European avant-garde, specifically surrealism. Both of the key names in early formulations of the marvelous/magical, Miguel Angel Asturias and Alejo Carpentier, produced their first works in dialogue with the French avant-garde during and after lengthy stays in Paris. Of import for my argument here is not to what extent magical realism was not a "genuinely" Latin American phenomenon, or how organic its borrowings from surrealism were, but rather how much it partook in the conditions of possibility for what James Clifford has named "ethnographic surrealism," namely, the fact that "the 'primitive' societies of the planet were increasingly available as aesthetic, cosmological, and scientific resources."[69] As an other to what the avant-gardists perceived as "Western reason," those societies became available to fiction precisely as signs of an outside. Magical realism would take it upon itself to narrate that outside and extract its "marvelous" effect from it. This project entailed a double movement: the precapitalist cosmogonies had to be other enough to produce the magical effect yet familiar enough to be narratable in the language of modern Western literature. Magical realism thus defined itself in relation to an outside—without an outside there is no magical realism—but such outside had of necessity to be incorporated and demonized, appropriated and conjured. This dialectic of incorporation and othering defined the historical specificity of magical realism.

For postdictatorial allegories the outside has become unnarratable. All otherness, all oppositional or alternative principles have become predictable to the point of being turned into a moment of the tyrannical order's very unfolding. In other words, that historical tyranny appears as natural history. With all magical effect suspended, the allegorical event must linger on the immanence of its own facticity: it can no longer be referred to an outside that would endow it with an organizing principle. What is there "beyond" Hualacato, Marulanda, and Manarairema in the three novels discussed earlier? A competing order? A source of resistance? That space has become unapproachable by the novels because their own principle of verisimilitude cannot transcend, cannot but be coextensive with the microcosmic space of the imaginary towns. A competing order of verisimilitude cannot be brought into the novel. Hence the sensation of failure proper to allegory and replicated by these novels: the reader finishes them with the sense that the true story has not been told, that the other to which allegory alludes—*allos-agoreuein,* Greek for "speaking otherwise"—remains unspeakable. The outside is therefore not incorporated, domesticated, and conjured, as in magical realism, but rather maintained as a radical, unnamable outside. Paradoxically, then, it is precisely by circumscribing a world seemingly devoid of all otherness that allegorical novels *preserve* an outside—they preserve it at the price of being unable to name it.[70]

The Dissolution of the University in the Universality of the Market

No cultural apparatus dramatizes such logic of immanentization better than the university. My assumption in this final section is that whereas the modern university, whose emergence was documented and shaped in texts by Kant, Friedrich Wilhelm Joseph Schelling, Johann Gottlieb Fichte, Friedrich Ernst Daniel Schleiermacher, and Wilhelm von Humboldt,[71] allocated a site for reflection on the conditions of possibility of all knowledge, the ultimate ground not grounded by anything other than itself (that site represented, in the Kantian project, by the Faculty of Philosophy), contemporary transformations in the production of knowledge suggest that such reflection is no longer possible, the fundamental principle being all but invisible in a world of glossy technosurfaces and shimmering media images. In this sense the end of philosophy as the thinking of the ultimate ground coincides with the end of the university in its modern sense. The impossibility of foundational thinking explains the passage from modern "enthusiasm"—defined by Kant as the "symptom that foresees, demonstrates, and recalls mankind's moral disposition toward progress"—to postmodern boredom. "Fallen in the immanence of routine tasks, distrusting any narrative that could endow them with meaning and future,"[72] today's university can no longer pose the Kantian question: What is the Enlightenment? What is the present? "Our attempt to theorize the actuality of the university, in the sense of making visible its invisible conditions, is characterized by categorial and linguistic impotence."[73] If the existence of the university has always implied a tension between the production of instrumental, compartmentalized knowledge and the reflection on the ultimate conditions of possibility of that knowledge, the university's present state—one of thorough instrumentalization by and for the market—indicates that this reflection is no longer feasible, or at any rate no longer accessible to it. The impossibility of posing the Kantian question bespeaks, then, not the end of certain categories, somehow replaceable by others but the demise of the categorial as such.

My assumption is that this transformation is coextensive with the transition to transnational capital in its telematic, inescapable moment. Having reached the stage of a planetary, outsideless system and eliminated all coexistence with other modes of production, transnational capitalism has brought about, along with the dissolution of what one used to call irrationality (a product of the juxtaposed presence of capitalist and precapitalist forms), the collapse of the footholds that allowed the very grounds of rationality to be thought. "Postmodernity" remains, as Jameson has shown, the necessary name for this epochal horizon. If modern rationality constituted itself through an appeal to universality—a universality that, needless to say, lies at the foundation of the university in its modern sense—the persistence of noncommodified, nonreified corners provided for centuries the leverage for a critique of that same rationality, the Adornian-Horkheimian unveiling of the dialectic of the Enlightenment representing perhaps its most illustrious moment. When commodification reaches a truly universal stage, it is universality's very foundation that becomes unthinkable, due to the sheer absence of an outside from which its design can be observed. Dispossessed of its constitutive principle, the university witnesses its thorough saturation by the market, its metamorphosis into a technical school, "its dissolution in the telematic facticity."[74]

In Latin America the transition represented by the dictatorships marks this epochal passage to a postcritical, post-Kantian horizon. What are the specificities of this transition in a continent where the university was always closely associated with the state, in a moment when the state has been reduced at best to a piece in the workings of transnational capital and the old populist or liberal states, historically responsible for the regulation, disciplining, and instrumentalization of the knowledge produced in the university, have now given way to the reality of a post-State market? The historical coincidence witnessed today in Latin America between postmodernity and postdictatorship is, then, by no means accidental or gratuitous. Latin American postmodernity is postdictatorial—that is, the continent's transition to a postmodern horizon is carried out by the dictatorships—because the old populist or liberal states could not usher in this new phase of capital, because they were global capital's prospective victims themselves. Only the military technocracy was qualified, in the eyes of the ruling classes, to purge the social body of all elements resistant to this reconfiguration. Eduardo Galeano has put it emphatically: "in Uruguay, people were being tortured so that prices could be free."[75] Needless to say, this occurred not only in Uruguay.

What does the new phase imply for the university? The passage from State to Market brings about a fundamental shift. If the liberal-populist university could represent to the middle classes some realistic hope of social climbing and incorporation into the educated sector of the elites, today's university forms primarily a species that would have looked rather odd thirty years ago: the proletarian expert. Along with the technification of knowledge, the university observes a technification of the professionals that it produces, in such a way that the difference that separated them from manual workers becomes blurred. With the routinization and bureaucratization of what used to be called intellectual labor—a by-product of the aforementioned crisis in the possibility of posing the question about the foundation of knowledge—in today's capitalism there remains little of the self-reflexivity that used to differentiate intellectual from manual labor.[76] The blurring of this difference is perfectly expressed in the loss of status, social and economic, of the figure formerly known as intellectual. In the Latin American context the dictatorial transition implies, plain and simple, *the end of the university as a means of social ascension.* In the place of self-employed architects, doctors, lawyers, dentists, and so on one now has wage earners who are structurally prevented from any illusions that the laws of "free competition" may have something good in store for the dedicated worker. The irony is that Latin American middle classes offered their support for military coups in the expectation of university-based economic progress for their children, only to find out that the beneficiaries of the coups were oligopolies whose consolidation demanded the very elimination of that possibility.

Latin America has thus moved, to put it bluntly, from the old humanist to the technocratic, wage-earner-producing university. Under populist and liberal states the university was a privileged locus for manufacturing the lettered fraction of the elite in charge of the juridical and executive apparatuses, models of ideological reproduction, and administration of class conflicts. Insofar as it produced the thinking elite, that university was an Althusserian ideological state apparatus par excellence, Louis Althusser's framework representing itself the epitome of a modern reflection on the state.[77] Far from homogenous and certainly permeable to democratizing pressures, like all state apparatuses, the university in Latin America was nonetheless inseparable from the constitution of bodies of knowledge serving class hegemony. Already at the foundation of the University of Chile in the 1840s, Andrés Bello advances the "republic of letters" as a moral, disciplinary instance that "provided the necessary structure for rationalized sociability and formation of the citizen."[78] As an autonomous intellectual field began to emerge during the period of state consolidation in the late nineteenth century, the university became both the supplier of professional knowledge wedded to rationalization and the terrain in which a reactive assertion of "spiritual," "disinterested" values emanated from the humanities. The aestheticist understanding of *culture* (an omnipresent word in the literary essayists of 1900), proper to a tellurian Latin America, can be traced back to that historical juncture, one that provides the very genealogy of Latin Americanism as we know it today. Culture assumed the role of regulative and moderating force, a preservational barricade against the winds of industrial modernization, in a spiritualist rhetoric by no means alien to class contradictions: "the essayists refunctionalized normative, literary rhetoric, against social 'chaos' and massification, claiming for the humanities a rectorial place in the administration and control of a world where a new kind of 'barbarism' proliferated: the working 'mass.'"[79]

Whereas it is true that this elitist structure was shaken by the university reform of 1918, which did force the educational apparatus to a number of concessions, the gradual absorption of the reformist demands represented the definitive modernization needed in societies where the liberal bourgeoisie for the first time attained political power, as in the Argentine *radicalismo*, victorious with Yrigoyen in 1917, and as in the Brazilian *tenentistas* in 1930. For the humanities and specifically for literature the roles associated with discipline and citizenship (Bello), culturalist opposition to modernization (Enrique Rodó, Ricardo Rojas), and protection of the mother tongue against the immigrant lower classes (Rojas, Leopoldo Lugones) had become flagrantly anachronistic. From then on the role of the university would be in one way or another connected with the formation of elite politicians, legislators, moralists, managers, and functionaries, that is, with the production of *ideologues*. Systematically absorbed into the state apparatus (as in Brazil or Mexico) or not (as in Argentina), and with his productivity for the political system certainly varying—in Argentina Peronism, Radicalism, and obviously the military ruled without much recourse to university-generated legitimation—the ideologue was the main product of the modern Latin American university.

However, besides producing elite ideologues the modern university also produced *intellectuals*. These two categories frequently crisscross and contaminate one another, but they are far from being collapsible into each other. Educational modernization, in conformity with the bourgeois interests (but also conquered through the struggles of 1918, which forced concessions otherwise not obtainable) brought about a significant change in the university student's social profile. As middle and working classes gained some access to the university, the apparatus of ideological reproduction evolved into a terrain where counterhegemonic projects emerged. The same university that produced Roberto Campos also created Florestan Fernandes. The very professionalization of intellectual labor, a prerequisite for any capitalist society, intensified the contradictions between the university's ideological function and its actual productivity for capitalism. The period preceding the debacle of liberal and populist states witnessed the definitive unfolding of this contradiction. As the juridical, moral, and aesthetic roles associated with the humanists of yesteryear became outdated and the market no longer offered positions of economic stability and political leadership to university graduates, a

significant fraction of the educated sectors (no longer exclusively bourgeois in their class origins) moved toward *intellectual critique* in the strict
sense of the term.

This displacement was due to the structural contradiction between,
on the one hand, a university set up to form humanist ideologues and
moralists, that is, functionaries who had always enjoyed positions of
leadership, and on the other, the development of a mode of production
that increasingly dispensed with those figures, caused their proletarianization, and placed them under the impact of emergent lower sectors
gaining access to the educational apparatus. The struggle over knowledge in the liberal-populist moment was played out around this complex
dialectic between ideologues and intellectuals. Unlike ideologues, intellectuals forcibly think the *totality* of the social fabric, the fundamental
principles and ultimate conditions of possibility, and this is why the intellectual is a modern figure par excellence. As Beatriz Sarlo has argued,
the requirement for the existence of intellectuals is the lack of separation
between general normativity and the normativity of a specific field.[80]
The intellectual is not bound by any area of specialization, because the
mere assignment of particular fields to certain classes of individuals presupposes a previous mapping of knowledge, which is the very object of
intellectual critique. The existence of intellectuals is bound to the possibility of posing the Kantian, critical interrogation of the ultimate ground.
It is only fitting, then, that the historical period characterized by the definitive obliteration of the Kantian question also witnesses the decadence
of intellectuals, now forced to choose between a merely technical, instrumental academic specialization and a vegetative existence in public
spheres where their critical activity has been reduced to an opinion that
does not make a qualitative difference in the market's potentially infinite
menu of differences.

The present arrangement represents, then, the closing of the ephemeral cycle in which intellectual activity—in the Kantian, transcendental
sense outlined—seemed compatible with a professional commitment to
the university. In other words, there was a time in Latin America when it
seemed possible to be both an intellectual and an expert. In fact, the professionalization and modernization of the educational apparatus in the
decades following the university reform of 1918 opened a period when
the figure of the intellectual became inseparable from the university

apparatus as such. Whereas in the old agroexporting society it had been conceivable for, say, Mário de Andrade or Alfonso Reyes to intervene in the public sphere as intellectuals not immediately legitimated by the formalized knowledge of modern disciplines, developmentism eliminated any possible fringes separating intelligentsia and university. The times of erudite autodidacts were gone. By the time a landmark magazine such as *Contorno* emerged in Argentina (1953), all of its members—the cutting edge of Argentine thought at that moment: Ismael and David Viñas, Noé Jitrik, Juan José Sebreli, Adolfo Prieto, and so on—were already fully inscribed within a professionalized discursive structure. That obviously did not prevent them from operating powerfully outside university structures—as we know, *Contorno* was not merely an academic journal. But it did imply that the rules governing discursive production had changed. Intellectuals now spoke supported by a formalized knowledge produced within the modern disciplinary map. The *contornistas* were still intellectuals in the strict sense: thinkers of the totality, proponents of a political project, figures of the public sphere, and unveilers of dogmas and hidden presuppositions. But intellectual intervention now depended on competence and recognition within an institutionalized field of knowledge. The intellectual also had to be an *expert*.[81]

My assumption here is that the transition from State to Market—that is, the epochal transition represented by the dictatorships—witnesses the definitive victory of the expert over the intellectual: "For decades, experts coexisted with intellectuals of the old type: they were suspicious of each other, with good reason. Today the battle seems to have been won by the experts; they never present themselves as bearers of general values that transcend the sphere of their expertise and therefore they do not take charge of the political and social results based on them."[82] Until the collapse of the ideal of a nationally sustained capitalism, technological development had to be openly, clearly mixed with political decision-making in such a way that any appeal to the neutrality of technology had to be politically argued in public spheres, in contexts where it was immediately coded as a political argument. If the university's role then was to produce the governing elite, the formation of such castes was bound to be embedded in a political struggle. This is why the liberal and populist university gave birth both to ideologues (elite politicians, legislators, moralists, managers, and functionaries) and intellectuals. In contrast, the university left by the military regimes only residually produces one or the other: for ideologues have become all but superfluous in a moment when ideological reproduction is largely performed by the mass media, electronic and otherwise, and not in the public spheres where those ideologues used to operate, whereas the intelligentsia, forced into the corner of academic specialization, comes to the anguishing realization that it can no longer formulate a project for the totality. Ideologues (be they moralists, legislators, etc.), the indispensable enemies and competitors of intellectuals have undergone a similar demise, caused by the same historical transformation. Ideologues and intellectuals are thus revealed to have been a product of the same conditions, then mutually complicitous vis-à-vis the ground that made them possible and now equated by the erosion of that ground. Whereas one is no longer necessary, the other is no longer possible.

Defeated by the expert, made obsolete along with the ideologue, the modern intellectual has been transformed into a mere cultural commentator, academic or otherwise. In fact, it might not be far-fetched to postulate the emergence of Cultural Studies as a privileged symptom of the immanentization that precludes the formulation of a project of intellectual critique in the modern sense. If the thinking of the totality finds itself obstructed by an instrumentalization that limits all disciplines to their technical status, if all available epistemologies have been reduced to treating their objects technically, if therefore philosophy in the Kantian sense (the investigation of the ultimate ground) is no longer possible, is there anything accidental in the fact that the only recent politicization of knowledge in the humanities has taken place under the antitheoretical appeal to specificity—that battle cry most proper to the technical expert? The empiricism underlying Cultural Studies—its barely disguised resistance to theory—can be understood in this context. Having inherited the modern intellectual's political thrust, but being the product of the very immanentization, compartmentalization, and technification that eliminated the intellectual, Cultural Studies faces the task of reconciling its political vocation with its epistemologically technical status: in fact, "culture" has become today a technical way of talking about politics. In this sense Cultural Studies comes to replace not a moribund literary institution, as has often been affirmed—it could peacefully coexist with such an institution for decades without threatening it, as is already the case—but to symptomatize the impossibility of philosophy. Its privileged status as a symptom—Cultural Studies is after all the major arena where the links between polis and episteme can be negotiated today—stems from the very technification that has substituted the presumably neutral expert for yesteryear's politicized intellectual. It remains to be seen whether the political thrust that is nevertheless so vital a part of Cultural Studies will manage to offset the effects of this division of labor, this submission of the political to the technical and the instrumental that is the very condition of possibility of Cultural Studies as we know it today.

3. COUNTERTRADITIONS
The Allegorical Rewriting of the Past

Literature works with politics as conspiracy, as a war; politics as a grand para-noid and fictional machine. —RICARDO PIGLIA, *Crítica y ficción*[1]

Ricardo Piglia's postdictatorial novel *La ciudad ausente* (1992) rearranges a complex intertextual chain in which it is itself inserted as a mobile piece. To be sure, Piglia's narratives are always readings, *lecturas* in the strict sense, both of Argentine literature (Sarmiento, Borges, Macedonio Fernández, Roberto Arlt, Marechal, and Rodolfo Walsh, to mention the six major names in my view) and of selected moments in the Western canon—Joyce, Kafka, Brecht, and the American detective story. Before I tackle *La ciudad ausente* in the next chapter, I will consider Piglia's reframing of the Argentine literary tradition in his earlier work, especially in *Respiración artificial* and some of the stories collected in *Prisión perpetua* and *Nombre falso*, as well as critical pieces published in *Crítica y ficción* and *La Argentina en pedazos*. These texts elaborate on a series of questions: What does it mean to make of Macedonio Fernández and Roberto Arlt the two major pillars of the modern in Argentine fiction? What is the syntax of Piglia's appropriation of these signatures? What is the sense in which one could posit Borges as the culmination of nineteenth-century Argentine literature? How does Piglia deduce a theory of the Argentine state from the framework of the detective story?

In Piglia's two novels the remarkably ingenious plotlines do not gen-erate much interest unless those questions are posed. Narration is so tightly woven into metaliterary reflection that his novels have a way of preempting all commentary, entrapping it into confessing to be always already read by the very narrative it intends to analyze. Piglia's text offers itself as a lure into which the reader must be seduced, and from which s/he must, in a second moment, attempt to escape by means of criticism, in order not to become yet another grain engulfed and predicted by the text. Commentary is thus invited to be in that place where the text is not and from which its locus could potentially be described in its foundation. Most certainly, that putative place always turns out to be elsewhere, much like Alice's shelves, which invariably have a way of looking empty when all the others around them are full. Piglia's reader is often struck by the feeling that the spot from which s/he has decided to look at the novel proves to be a phantasmatic mirror reflection produced in advance by the novel itself, as though critical language were being led into a deceitful and bottomless abyss. In that sense Piglia, not Mujica Láinez as was often affirmed, wrote the novels that Borges never did.

Yet Borges occupies a very particular position within Piglia's reconstruction of the Argentine literary series, as the culmination of both of the major currents of nineteenth-century literature, that is, the modernizing, Europe-oriented tradition that runs from Sarmiento to Lucio Mansilla, Miguel Cané, and beyond, as well as, on the other hand, the lettered appropriation of the popular in the gauchesque, from Bartolomé Hidalgo to Estanislao del Campo, Hilario Ascasubi, and José Hernández. Borges represents the moment in which the devices proper to both forms face their ultimate demolition at the hands of parody:

> To take the case of Europeanism, cosmopolitanism, the foreign genealogy of our culture: a national tradition, it should be said, linked with basic problems clearly expressed by Borges's work. It would suffice to write the history of the system of citations, cultural references, allusions, plagiarism, translations, pastiches pervading Argentine literature from Sarmiento to Lugones to see to what extent Borges exacerbates this tradition, takes it to the limit of parody and the apocryphal. In fact, Borges's treatment of culture is a limit example of a literary system that has reached crisis and dissolution. (*CF* 107–8)

By the time the erudite tradition culminated in Borges, the possibility of an appeal to the literary as a sign of social distinction or as a marker of social class had withered considerably. Operating upon this historical limit, Borges's gesture voided citation of all authority and reliability, thereby closing the cycle of Europeanism and transforming its major rhetorical devices into so many chapters and books of the Babel library.

Erudition was thus deprived of all content to become pure device, empty syntax, or a mere structuring procedure. Literature was introduced, by means of parody, to its powerlessness to maintain the roles of civilizer and discipliner of barbarism (Sarmiento), self-reassuring autobiographical mirror for the elite (Cané, Mansilla), and purifier of national language against the neobarbarism of poor immigrants (Lugones). With Borges citation entered a rather different dialectic, in which it could no longer function as an instrument for the enforcement of propriety, the consolidation and reproduction of property, and the inviolability of the economico-ontological field of the proper. Borges disappropriated citation by placing in the agenda the relation between parody and ownership: this is one of the possibilities of reading him politically, over and above his rather unfortunate ideological choices. "Borges's truth has to be found elsewhere: in his fictional texts" (RA 157/125).

The other side of the coin lies in the gauchesque's appropriation of the popular, the counterpart of cosmopolitanism within nineteenth-century Argentina's literary system. Borges also closed that tradition, in interesting and often overlooked ways:

> On the one hand the gauchesque, from which he takes the traces of orality, popular speech and its artifices; in that he is frontally opposed to Lugones, who liked everything about the gauchesque except the popular language, thus seeing in *Don Segundo Sombra* the genre's culmination, the genre's theme but in lettered and *modernista* language. The gaucho war. To purify the national epic. Borges, in contrast, perceives the gauchesque more than anything as a style effect, a rhetoric, a narrative mode. That thing about how once you know the way a man speaks, his voice, his intonation, his syntax, you know his fate. (CF 124)

In order to rethink the national in Borges one does well to start with this central concern of his, one that persisted from the three collections of essays published in the 1920s, and which he subsequently renounced (*Inquisiciones*, *El tamaño de mi esperanza*, and *El idioma de los argentinos*), all the way to the stories depicting honor duels and displays of courage in his later fiction. There is, to be sure, a strong populist vein running through Borges's work, "the idea that libraries and books impoverish and the elemental lives of simple men are the truth" (CF 131). This opposition, however contrived and simplistic it may sound, remains essential to defining Borges's relationship with the gauchesque. Piglia recalls how, in the preface to *El idioma de los argentinos*, Borges referred to himself as "encyclopedic y *montonero*" (*AP* 103), two words that condensed the bodies of the two traditions. Populism versus avant-garde would persist as a major tension throughout Argentine literature. In the lettered appropriation of the gaucho's voice by the gauchesque, the genre itself signaled the gaucho's historical defeat, as if the cult of gaucho patriotism and heroism imaginarily compensated for their subjugation and proletarianization. In that sense the genre was itself a requiem for the gaucho, its high-sounding and epiclike tone resting upon the gaucho's historical defeat. Borges exacerbated that defeat, made visible its ineluctability. The gaucho universe, after Borges, could no longer be anything other than a lost object, as the gaucho was converted into *orillero*, dweller of those border zones that spatially allegorize the temporal transition from one social structure to another. One only has to think of all the stories in which Borges thematized the impossibility of heroism in a world that increasingly dispensed with it to realize that he wrote the genre's epitaph, its mournful anthem. "Borges works very explicitly with the idea of closing the gauchesque, of writing 'The End' for it" (*CF* 125).

From "Hombre de la esquina rosada" and "El fin" to "Historia de Rosendo Juárez,"[2] Borges developed a microscopy of the gauchesque's fading away by revealing the anachronism of the gaucho code of bravery. In "Hombre de la esquina rosada" the key is the shift of focus away from the public duel and defense of honor to the anonymous, unworthy murder committed by the narrator. No revenge is carried through, and the challenged man walks away without avenging his honor. Borges dissolved the genre's principle of intelligibility but maintained its tone, scenes, and especially the music of its voice; for Borges, the raw material for the genre was to be found in "the *truco* [a popular card game] and its conversations made of challenges, where language is all of a sudden another, in the milonga's rhythm of spoken war and feast, in the narratives of duels and revenges told among themselves by the poor."[3] Josefina Ludmer shows how Martín Fierro, the gauchesque popular hero, had ended José Hernández's *Vuelta* (1879)—the hero's return seven years after his debut in *La Ida* (1872)—where he speaks in legalistic and impersonal language and collapses justice and law, speaking, indeed, from the standpoint of law.

What Borges did to Hernández's Martín Fierro was to place him in the position where Hernández had left him in the *Vuelta*: a representative of emergent state legality who, in Borges's "El fin," finds defeat at the hands of popular justice now embodied by a black servant. The genre's closing moments had been Hernández's definitive abandonment of the ventriloquism of the gaucho "voice" in order to collapse the figure of the gaucho into the state. Borges restored oral popular justice, in its noncoincidence with the law, by making the servant take his revenge upon a Martín Fierro now completely turned into state functionary. In a way Borges did to Hernández what Hernández had done to Fierro: the memory of a popular hero had become, in Hernández's lettered appropriation of the gaucho, a transit zone already covered by the juridical state unification. Borges proceeded by rigorously taking the genre's most proper strategy to its limits. If Fierro had left the ranks of popular memory and turned into an example of domesticated patriotism, then he was to be sacrificed at the hands of the anonymous wretch, who beat the ex-outlaw Fierro in an open, just, utopian duel. Justice takes revenge upon the law, and the law of the genre finds its epochal closure.

Borges thus closed the two major lines of nineteenth-century Argentine literature. Hence Renzi's contention, in *Respiración artificial*, that Borges was the best nineteenth-century Argentine writer, "which is no small merit if you think that Sarmiento, Mansilla, del Campo, Hernández were writing back then" (*CF* 123). The deliberate anachronism of Piglia's claim, uttered in those epigrammatic, conclusive terms reserved for theoretical propositions embedded in fiction,[4] produced the healthy effect of placing Borges back into tradition and offering a counterpart to grandiose statements influenced by the boom, which often referred to Argentine literature as though it did not exist before Borges and Cortázar. Note Piglia's insistence that Borges operated within, never outside, the space delimited by Sarmiento: the delirious mixing of citations, equivocal references, the seduction of barbarism, the coexistence of fiction and nonfiction. Beginning with Sarmiento's *Facundo*, the latter polarity played a key role in Argentine culture. In order to narrate itself, its own genealogy and national project, the Argentine elite did not make use of fiction, but rather of (*auto*)*biography* (as can be seen in Sarmiento, Mansilla, Cané, and so on). Fiction emerged as a response to a different need, that of narrating the other (Indians, gauchos, blacks, and immigrants, in a word, barbarians). Barbarism demanded fictional language: "the class narrates itself in the form of autobiography and narrates the other with fiction" (*AP* 9). The specificity of Borges's intervention upon this tradition was to submit the autobiographical reference to the vertigo of fiction, causing his own systematic allusions to his grandmother, the English library, and so forth, to be read more as yet another Borgesian tale than as an ostentatious mechanism of self-legitimation. Borges took the primary literary mirror of the Argentine elite and, from within the logic of this very class, converted it into an empty device, making inescapable the contamination of civilization by barbarism (of nonfiction by fiction), which had been implicit in Argentina since Sarmiento.

If Borges was the last (and best) nineteenth-century Argentine writer, who opened up the twentieth century in Argentina? Who inaugurated the truly modern? Piglia's answer: Roberto Arlt. "Arlt starts from certain basic kernels, such as the relation between power and fiction, money and madness, truth and plotting, and converts them into form and narrative strategy" (*CF* 28). Arlt ushered in literary modernity because he was the first to understand the conspiratorial nucleus of modern Argentine politics. In opposition to naturalism, socialist realism and *costumbrismo*, which worked with merely conjunctural elements, Arlt wrote what is for Piglia the truly great political fiction, the one that captures the fundamental, secret core around which a given society structures itself. Falsification and deceit, the perennial conspiracy of Argentine politics, its clandestine plottings and visionary utopian/dystopian narratives: this is the stuff of which Arlt's novels are made. In Arlt's *Los siete locos* and *Los lanzallamas*, the Astrologer, a baroque discursive mixture of fascism, bolshevism, and technological mysticism, introduces a bleak and apocalyptic industrial technocracy in which "the majority will live scrupulously maintained in the most absolute ignorance, surrounded by apocryphal miracles."[5] Utopia here has degenerated into totalitarian paranoia, organized according to a rigorous, seductive, Machiavellian logic. The Astrologer stands for the prophet who lives technology as a visionary tale—"all science will be magic."[6] He dwells beyond all morality, in the genealogical realm, where he can see not the truth behind the veil but the constitutive dependence of truth upon the veil. Such characters invariably turn out to have prophetic visions: "Do you believe that future dictatorships will be military? No, sir. The military is worth nothing next to the industrialist. They can be his instrument, that's all. Future dictators will be the kings of oil, steel, wheat."[7] These words, uttered by Arlt's Astrologer in 1929, stand as an avant la lettre undoing of much sociological bibliography on the dictatorships of the 1970s. Instead of the focus on the derivative and superficial evolution of the juridicoparliamentary system, the Astrologer shoots for the ultimate ground; he is sheer will to power understood as will to class domination. The bleak dystopia of Arlt's Astrologer remains a matrix for the Argentine polis.

Arlt's language is essentially *impure*, a patchwork composed of residual materials of a peripheral modernity:

> A tango intermingled with military marches, Salvation Army anthems, revolutionary songs, a sort of anarchist tango singing social disgraces and mixing elements of lower culture: the occult sciences, spiritualism, Spanish translations of Dostoyevsky, a certain popular reading of the *Bible*, science and sexology manuals. Even Nietzsche's mark is very clear, the reading of Nietzsche that circulated within Argentine anarchist circles in the 1920s. What appeals to Arlt is this feuilleton element present in Nietzsche, acutely perceived by Gramsci when he noted the relation between the overman and serial novel heroes like Rocambole or the count of Monte Cristo. (*CF* 31)

Arlt stands in stark contrast to Lugones, the self-entitled protector of national language against immigrant workers, the national poet always horrified at anything mixed and impure. Arlt, against whom the elite ceaselessly flung the accusation that he wrote badly and violated Spanish syntax, brought into literature that delirious mix that is the mark of modernity. Handling contaminated fragments, filthy leftovers, Arlt "works with what really is the national language" (*RA* 169/134). In *Respiración artificial* Renzi makes the interesting point that Arlt was the first Argentine writer who bypassed bilingualism. Unlike all the major Argentine writers who preceded him, Arlt was a reader of translations, "he doesn't suffer from this doubling of the language of literature (read in another language) and the language in which one writes" (*RA* 170/135). Developing a style from the pitiful Spanish translations of Dostoyevsky and Nietzsche, Arlt imploded the standards of what had been considered "good" writing in Argentina. Whereas the ideal of "clean," "elegant" style, interspersed, when verisimilitude demanded, with picturesque reproductions of popular speech, is the norm for the group of writers surrounding Borges (such as Bioy Casares and Mujica Láinez, although not Borges himself, who knew better), in Arlt there is no raw transcription or copy of speech. Instead, his books offer a glimpse of a Babelian utopia constructed with the linguistic materials of Argentine modernity, from the impact of immigration upon River Plate Spanish to the languages of technology, usury, and popular science.

Money is not reducible to a theme in Roberto Arlt; it is rather a foundation and master metaphor for his fiction. Populated with humiliated, bullied middle-class wretches, Arlt's novels obsessively revolve around the elusive shine of money. His inventors, traitors, organizers of secret societies, charlatans, robbers, and pimps act motivated by visions of miraculous enrichment, all sharing the certainty that work only brings poverty and misery and that the truth of wage labor is the reproduction of exploitation. Arlt's typical character is the miserable petty bourgeois who knows too much to submit to the illusion of gradual amelioration through commitment to honesty and hard work. The paradigmatic economic operations in Arlt therefore take place *outside* the formal wage structure. "For Arlt there is no possible story in the world of labor" (*AP* 125). His plots are triggered by some illicit or ill-intentioned borrowing, ransacking, or sheer robbery, as if the very possibility of storytelling depended upon an alteration, however minimal and illusory, in the peaceful equilibrium between the wealthy and the destitute. Such alteration always comes from lawbreaking: petty robberies that stand as a pale miniature of the institutionalized robbery upon which the entire polis functions. In Arlt all enrichment is by definition illegal, criminal, and scandalous, and his characters find in temporary and compensatory enrichment the crime that grounds the possibility of writing.

The money thereby acquired is invariably spent on some mechanical invention, visionary utopia, or secret community. In any case, it is never reproduced. There is something in Arlt's characters that leads them to a logic of sheer expenditure, alien to all accumulation: "a countereconomy founded on loss and debt."[8] Thus arises the paradox behind their attitude toward money: facing money as the ultimate motor propelling everything, but at the same time as an object of contempt, Arlt's characters, like Dostoyevsky's, are often overtaken by the feeling that they could throw it all away or give it to the first bastard seen in the streets. The un-

reasonable act of generosity or self-dispossession signals the possibility
of overcoming the shame of petty calculations. Only by disdainfully
giving up money can one radically affirm one's freedom. This predicament is, no doubt, specific to the middle class. As Oscar Masotta has
affirmed in what is arguably the best book ever written on Arlt, the humiliation consists in belonging to the middle class.[9] In *El juguete rabioso*,
the poor adolescent explodes in disgust at his mother's humility and sacrifices: "I felt an urge to get up, grab her by the shoulders and shake her,
shout in her ears: don't talk about money, mom, please . . . ! Don't talk . . .
shut up!"[10]

Arlt's treatment of money is appropriated by Piglia as a privileged
metaphor for falsification, in ways that come to stand for fiction itself
(inviting, and I will get to that, interesting parallels with Baudelaire):

> For Arlt society rests upon fiction because its ultimate foundation
> is money. A magical object, this paper credited by the State is the
> empty sign of absolute power. To *make* money: Arlt takes this phrase
> as the essence of society and interprets it literally. To make money
> means to fabricate it: falsification is the central strategy of Arltian
> economy. The falsifier is an artist, the poet of capitalism. Falsification
> is an art of the age of mechanical reproduction. What is the false and
> what is the true? Arlt thinks about this question from the standpoint
> of money. How to pass off as legitimate that which is false? Therein
> he concentrates his poetic: falsification is the model for Arltian fic-
> tion. (*AP* 124)

If making money is to be understood literally as manufacturing it,
there is more to the connection between money and the world of inven-
tions and paratechnological discoveries of popular science. Money not
only constitutes the motive behind those practices; it also offers them
their ultimate matrix. The fabrication of little apparatuses encounters its
definitive model in the production of money, which becomes the very
allegory of technology: money as *techne*, a diabolical, modern and Faustian techne. This motif persists throughout Arlt's and Piglia's narratives.
In "En otro país," a collection of epigrammatic annotations from Piglia's
diary, we are told about an old man living somewhere by the Mississippi
River, obsessed with his shortwave transmitter, using it to send messages to Harry Truman, whom he still thought to be the president of

the United States. As an inventor worthy of a Roberto Arlt novel, "one of his [the old man's] favorite themes was usury, the satanic character of money" (*PP* 21). In "Luba," the story Piglia attributes to Arlt and includes in his *Nombre falso* (while presenting himself as a Max Brod–like editor), the bond between the runaway anarchist and Luba, the prostitute who hides him, proves irreversible when he offers her the stock of false money in his possession: "With this dough you'll start a new life, you too. It's false dough, but that doesn't matter: nobody will see the difference. It's perfect, made by South America's greatest forger" (*NF* 150). A bit like in Hal Hartley's films, where the characters say that all money is dirty money, in Arlt it is as though all money were false. The distinction between counterfeit and legal tender rests upon a prior falsification that grounds the very possibility of all manufacture. The opposition is made possible by one of its terms. If forgery is an art proper to the age of mechanical reproduction, the possibility of falsification lies in the decline of the aura; the postauratic announces the advent of falsifiability. It is well known that one of the definitions of the auratic object is that which cannot be falsified.[11] Arlt's characters only circumvent the auratic power of money by fabricating it, because the illusion of earning it on the market could only reinforce its auratic spell. Coming from the lower social strata, Arlt had nothing to gain by cultivating the aura, and he set to himself the task of destroying it in all its manifestations—the burning down of a library by Silvio Astier, the destitute and revolted adolescent in *El juguete rabioso*, being another instance of this relentless attack on the aura, this time the sacred aura of high culture.

But what is the relation among money, falsification and fiction? One needs to find mediations here, and Piglia finds an allegorical one in a recurrent element in Arlt's novels—the brothel, or prostitution:

> The Melancholy Pimp is the economist of Arlt's world. He knows about money, knows how to do business, knows the secret logic of capitalist exploitation. Prostitution is the perverse mirror where he sees the essence of society: to buy bodies with money, a perverse trick, a figured form of slavery, the representation of trade in its satanic purity. (Literature and prostitution are equivalent in Arlt: that's why the Pimp is the only one who talks about literature in his novels. The Pimp as a model for the literary critic.) (*AP* 125–26)

Prostitution serves as the matrix for business: inside the brothel, trade can surface in the most literal fashion. Prostitution is the degree zero of capitalist bad faith. All veils have been lifted over the commerce of bodies, and this is why the reflection on money often finds its privileged imagistic kernel in the brothel. Arlt's merit was thus to put forth a literary representation of prostitution in which all morality is revealed as parasitic upon an economic logic. In Piglia's "Luba" the anarchist refugee incites the prostitute's outrage by moving away from the language of trade to suggest that some deeper human complicity can develop between the two. When he attempts to turn her into a sort of pure, immaculate Dostoyevskian sufferer—for instance, *Crime and Punishment*'s Sonia, Raskolnikov's redeemer—she reacts infuriated: "What do you wanna do with me? You coward, son of a bitch. . . . You came here to mock me, to make me see how good you are" (*PP* 139). There is no room left for pity or solidarity in Arlt's characters; they are never measured by any transcendental value, moral or otherwise, but only by their sheer will to power.

In Piglia's reading the brothel also emerges as the great allegory for the literary institution; for Arlt being criticized implied, quite explicitly, losing money. Commentary was thus reduced to the nudity of its status as economic mediator and key to the selling of more books. In this perspective the literary critic is the one who handles, however precariously, the codes of access to market recognition. Here, as well, all bad faith has been abandoned, all morality suspended. Such suspension allows for the allegorization of the literary critic in the figure of the pimp. The literary canon takes the form of an immense market of bodies, where all use value has dissolved into exchange value. In *Los siete locos* and *Los lanzallamas*, Arlt depicts the Melancholy Pimp (would-be sponsor of the bolshevik-techno-mystical-fascist revolution planned by the Astrologer) as the artful and disingenuous reader of the world, the one who perceives that after all no qualitative difference separates a pimp from an industrialist. He quotes chronicler Bernal Díaz del Castillo, plans his retirement in Brazil or France "to read Victor Hugo and the follies of Clemenceau,"[12] and, as a sort of oxymoronic Nietzschean Socrates, introduces the character Erdosain into the amorality of all things. In effect, the Melancholy Pimp stands for that delving deeper into the essence, will to truth unveiled as will to power.

What interests me is primarily the way in which Piglia reads Arlt *alle-*

gorically, much like Benjamin read Baudelaire. Not only does Arlt emerge as the Argentine counterpart to Baudelaire, that is, as the first chronicler of a modernity marked by the shock experience in the crowd, the dizziness of the transitory, the death of God, and the becoming-dystopia of utopia. Not only do Arlt's concerns find several analogies in Baudelaire, as for example in the remarkable parallels that can be drawn between Arlt's treatment of money as falsification and the bewildering gesture of giving away counterfeit money as alms in Baudelaire's "La fausse monaie."[13] Besides all these convergences, Piglia's *procedure,* his protocol of reading, is itself allegorical: by isolating monads in Arlt's text and discerning in them the entire conflict between contradictory forces throughout Argentine literature, Piglia offers an alternative to the usual, symbolic method of presupposing a harmonious, unfractured totality only in a second moment to assign a position to each piece within an already domesticated whole. That is to say, instead of assuming the past history of Argentine literature to be an organic whole in which Arlt would be magnanimously assigned a corner in the pantheon—and thus made to coexist unproblematically with Sarmiento, Borges, and so on, all of them maybe testifying to the "richness" and "diversity" of the totality (instead of replicating the usual procedure of literary manuals and historicist critics who invariably empathize with the victor)[14]—Piglia reads in the texture of Arlt's work the furor of an interpellation of the present that puts such historical schemes in crisis. The allegorical interpreter of the past does not forget what s/he knows about the later course of history. The former procedure reads barbarism as a witness to the richness of culture. A study of postdictatorship, by definition, by the very gesture of reading the present as postdictatorial, cannot but embrace the latter protocol and attempt to read in every document of culture the barbarism that made it possible.

I would like to return to the allegories of the literary critic presented by Piglia, as the detective story also offers a model for the relation between commentary and text: "I often see criticism as a variant on the detective novel. The critic as a detective attempting to decipher a riddle even when there's no riddle. The great critic is an adventurer moving around texts searching for a secret that at times does not exist. It is a fascinating character: the decipherer of oracles, the tribe's reader. Benjamin reading Baudelaire's Paris. . . . In more than one sense the critic is the investigator and the writer is the criminal" (*CF* 20–21). Fictional encoding consists in erasing marks, heightening undecidability, disseminating false clues: the task of the criminal. The more carefully crafted a fictional work proves to be, the more it resembles a perfect crime. This perspective supports Piglia's contention regarding the special relationship that fiction holds with truth: fiction is not the realm where truth does not exist but the instance whereby truth can be suspended. The erasure of authorial signs in a fictional text, then, has nothing to do with "objectivity" understood in the realist-naturalist sense. Fiction eliminates authorial marks not in order that truth speak freely, in the luminosity of its self-presence, but all the contrary, as a way of submitting it to the vertigo of undecidability. The critic's role is to uncover this operation, reconstruct the evidence, discard false clues, and restore the coincidence between the crime's phenomenal manifestation and its truth: the image of literary criticism as a Cartesian-detectivesque canceling-out of the uncertainty that characterizes fiction.[15] The critic thus speaks in the name of truth, always and necessarily, even when proclaiming the multiplicity, instability, and slipperiness of truth. The model for the critic must be, therefore, the figure of the detective: the one who deciphers enigmas by means of "plotting, suspicion, double life, conspiracy, secret" (CF 21). For Piglia, the inaugural allegory of the literary critic in modern literature coalesces in Edgar Allan Poe's "The Murders in the Rue Morgue," where the mastery of reading and interpretation *methods*—a key word in Poe's story—displayed by detective Dupin (who, not gratuitously, first runs into the narrator in a bookstore) confirms the axiom that "the *truly* imaginative [are] never otherwise than analytic."[16]

To *decipher* has always been a central notion in Piglia. In *Respiración artificial* Professor Maggi sets out to reconstruct, in 1979, the trajectory of Enrique Ossorio, a mid-nineteenth-century Argentine exiled in New York during Rosas's dictatorship. Ossorio wrote his autobiography while planning a "romance in the future" in which the protagonist would receive letters from the Argentina of 1979 and attempt to imagine what that age would be like. Epistolary communication had, for him, the structure of a utopia—an address to an interlocutor who may or may not be there, a risky wager on what is yet to come. Ossorio countered his present defeat with a gesture toward the future. Symmetrically, Professor Maggi puts together the puzzle of the past in order to wake up from the nightmare of the present. Maggi's notes and letters are intercepted by Arocena, a censor and decipherer at the service of the state, a diabolical mind familiar with methods of minute textual interpretation who puts them to use in his search for secret, encoded clues to Maggi's "subversive" activities. Paranoid deciphering stands then not only for literary criticism but also for the conspiratorial matrix of Argentine politics. Ironically enough, most studies of *Respiración artificial* have replicated Arocena's procedure by reading the novel as an epiphenomenon of censorship, that is, by assuming that the text took the form it did because Piglia "could not" say what he wanted "explicitly" and had to "resort" to "veils," "metaphors," and "allegories" (now in the vulgar, romantic sense of the term), as if the story could somehow have been told in transparent fashion under different political circumstances. By so doing, these critics prove to be bad detectives in Poe's precise sense: for Dupin, bad detectives are those who search for a secret when there is none, look for the purloined letter in the most recondite hideaway when it is in fact staring them in the face. As Dupin makes clear in his methodological statement before solving the murder of Morgue Street: "Truth is not always in a well. In fact, as regards the more important knowledge, I do believe that she is invariably superficial."[17]

I will return later to the views of *Respiración artificial* (and of the literature written under dictatorships as a whole) as an epiphenomenon of censorship, but now I would like to continue disentangling the ways in which Piglia encodes the literary critic in his work. Perhaps the most felicitous and fruitful connection he has established in this regard is the one linking literary criticism and autobiography:

> As for criticism, I think it is one of the modern forms of autobiography. Someone writes his/her life while believing to be writing his/her reading. Isn't it the reverse of Don Quixote? The critic is the one who reconstructs her/his life within the texts s/he reads. Criticism is a post-Freudian form of autobiography. . . . The subject of criticism is often masked by the method (sometimes the subject is the method), but is always present, and reconstructing his/her history and locus is the best way of reading criticism. (*CF* 19)

The *bios* evoked by the *graphe* is not that of a unique, epiphanic experience conceived along romantic lines, but another *graphe*, that of the immense archive of the already read. *Bio-graphia* is thus *graphe* to the second degree. The critic's life is the history of a collection of books. Therefore, if it can be said that criticism is the culmination of the tradition inaugurated by Jean-Jacques Rousseau's *Confessions* — the culmination of modern autobiography — it is also true that it represents the undoing of this very tradition, for it unveils the illusion of supposedly unique personalities and unmistakable life stories. The extensiveness of the Babel library proves to be an antidote to all personalism and self-centered confessionalism. In this sense literature for Piglia has little to do with experience, if one takes experience as the anecdotal content of a personal trajectory, the mass of lived moments in all their banality. In a word, literature's material is not experience understood as *Erlebnis*,[18] *lo vivido*, the raw collection of empirie. In *Respiración artificial* Renzi acknowledges that "nothing really extraordinary can happen to us, nothing worth telling" (*RA* 34). In "En otro país" the protagonist faces absolute emptiness: he attempts to write his life, but "nothing happened, nothing ever really happens, but back then this worried me" (*PP* 15). The lack of meaningful stories to tell forces him to struggle with the diary format, first stealing stories from friends or yet inventing miraculous narratives about himself, which ends up leading him to fiction in the strict sense. Fiction thus emerges as a response to the banality of experience. In the end, the (fictional) diary becomes the locus for the *production* of experience: he comes to remember as his own only the apocryphal stories recorded in the diary, not the endless banality of "daily life."

Piglia reverses commonly held assumptions about fiction and criticism by thinking one from the point of view of what is supposedly most proper to the other, by contaminating them mutually. One of his preferred themes is the constitutive role of the fictional in criticism (e.g., literary criticism as a variation on the detective story) as well as the no-less-constitutive role of the analytical in fiction (scheming, plotting, and decoding as key operations in all fictionalization). Autobiography plays a singular role here, not exactly as the "middle of the road" between the two that it is often thought to be. Rather, it appears as the limit zone of fiction: stemming from the ultimate impossibility of autobiography (the absence of unique experiences to tell), fiction necessarily operates around the proper name, eluding it, opening up a space where one can narrate one's own history as if it belonged to another. Fiction is programmed as a machine to elude the weight of the proper name, escape the prison house of the proper name. In an interview conducted a few years after the appearance of *Respiración artificial*, Piglia recounted his desire that his next novel look "like it had been written by another writer" (*CF* 148). He was quick to add, though, that this was an impossible pretension. If this is impossible, it is because the proper name *returns*, and in places other than the cover and the title page. This return is what should be called "style" in Piglia: not the romantic uniqueness located in some interiority and later expressed in organicist fashion, but rather the anteriority of a written trace. I will have the opportunity to comment on Piglia's awareness of the iterative structure of signatures,[19] and his conscious effort to introduce fissures and ambiguities therein when I move on to *La ciudad ausente*. For now let me point out that these *graphei* are also marks of the past, tight binds that, to a great extent, define the subject's locus and condition of enunciation. They are less what is expressed than that which grounds expression and founds the possibility of a signature. Piglia's texts often deploy characters who, much like their creator, are perennially striving to disentangle themselves from their names and conquer anonymity. How can I learn to lose my proper name? is the question Piglia's characters are invariably led to ask. All anonymity has something utopian about it,[20] and literature unleashes that utopian potential by allowing the unduly appropriation of alien names. In that sense, Flaubert's gesture ("I am Madame Bovary"), as well as Nietzsche's ("I am Dionysus, I am the Crucified") are best grasped as novelistic and utopian par excellence, utopian because novelistic. Nietzsche, the only thinker who was able to philosophize with the proper name, was also the only one who succeeded in losing it. The powerful utopian energy released by Nietzsche's philosophy may be in many ways related to that labor on the proper name, that embrace and at the same time destruction of the proper name I am also observing in Piglia.

This theory of the signature is informed by a third Argentine writer who, along with Borges and Arlt, defines much of the space in which Piglia's fiction operates: Macedonio Fernández. No serious interpretation of Piglia's work can elude his indebtedness to this most paradoxical figure. Piglia makes him the central character of *La ciudad ausente*, and the novel's entire metaliterary dimension resides in his legacy. Macedonio, "this gray man who, in a mediocre Tribunales pension, discovered eternal problems as if he were Thales or Parmenides,"[21] was the great renewer of the Argentine novel in this century. A source of inspiration for the avant-garde, he differed considerably from our typical image of the avant-gardist writer: quiet, reserved, thoughtful, alien to oratorical disputes, Macedonio had a legendary disdain for publication. Always scribbling on every piece of paper available, accumulating stacks of manuscripts, leaving them behind every time he switched pensions, postponing what he called "the future novel," he was as puzzling a literary figure as you will ever find. Revered by several of the young poets congregated around the magazine *Martín Fierro* in the 1920s—Borges never tired of calling him "my master"—Macedonio only published his first book, *No toda es vigilia la de ojos abiertos* (1928), at fifty-four years of age, after emphatic insistence by Scalabrini Ortiz, Leopoldo Marechal, and Francisco Luis Bernárdez. From then on, and especially since the posthumous appearance of *Museo de la novela de la Eterna* (1967), Macedonio has become one of the major sources of alternatives to photographic naturalism and picturesque costumbrismo in the Argentine literary tradition.

The first feature of Macedonio's project that acquires special interest for Piglia is his conception of literature as challenge flung to the future:

> One of Macedonio's aspirations was to become *inédito* [unpublished]. To erase his traces, be read as if unknown, without previous notice. Several times he hinted he was writing a book of which no one would ever know a page. In his will he decided that it should be published secretly, around 1980. Nobody should know this book was his. At first he thought of publishing it anonymously. Then he thought it should be published in the name of a well-known writer. To attribute your own book to someone else: plagiarism in reverse. To be read as if you were *this* writer. In the end he decided to use a pseudonym that nobody could identify. . . . He liked the idea of working on a book designed to go unnoticed. A book lost in the sea of future books. The oeuvre voluntarily unknown, ciphered and concealed in the future, as a riddle cast to history.
>
> True legibility is always posthumous. (*PP* 92)

An authorless book, a false attribution, or a pseudonym: three strategies that operate differently upon the author function,[22] such as it has been understood at least since the invention of the printing press and the development of the intricate web linking intellectual property with a large field delimited by the uncertain notions of authorship, style, expression, and so on. Macedonio finally opted for the third alternative but in conceiving of the first two, far more unusual and transgressive, he announced a few paradoxes worth reflecting upon. The authorless book imagined by Macedonio is a most disconcerting object, for it blocks out all reference to any entity that transcends it (unlike apocryphal texts such as *Arabian Nights*, for which a certain contextual soil can be reconstructed) and demands to be read in its sheer immanence. It is an object deprived of any sustaining ground, existing as a pure monad beyond which all transcendence has been canceled out. In a sense, it is a replica of the world after the death of God. What interests Piglia is the idea of an anonymous book that proposes a riddle unsolvable by any recourse to a self, thus remaining illegible for the present, heralding the openness of what is yet to come, much like a utopian hieroglyph.

Macedonio's entire oeuvre is nothing but a harbinger for this most uncanny of all books. His major text, *Museo de la novela de la Eterna*, feeds on a double gesture. It looks back at the massive archive of the already written, humorously and guiltlessly asserting the impossibility of originality, the dead end of all novelty-driven art, the collapse of modern signature. "Everything has been written, said, heard, God was told, and he still had not created the world, nothing existed yet. I've been told that too, he rejoined from the old, submerged Nothingness. And he began."[23] On the other hand, the novel looks to the future, multiplying prefaces and introductions to a text that remains forever unwritten, "a book the very conception of which excluded the possibility of having an end" (PP 94). Everything in Macedonio had the character of an unfinished draft, or as he said, "a novel that will be futurist until it is written." In the "end" (the inconclusive end represented by the last corrected version of his manuscript),[24] Macedonio had amassed a total of fifty-six prefaces in which he expounded his poetics—an inventive and self-reflexive, antinaturalist, and anti-illusionist one—and turned the promise of a future novel into the very story to be narrated. The image of the novel that thinks its own ground or yet dreams to be thinking it entirely erases the border between the fictional and the theoretical. Throughout the prologues the novel exposes its characters as beings of belief, its writer as a hesitant producer, its entire existence hanging on its ability to imagine how and why it is being manufactured. This gesture would become part and parcel of Piglia's practice and indeed confuse more than a few critics. One of the accusations made against *Respiración artificial* was that "it did not tell a story," when in fact it told so many of them that the great challenge confronting the reader was to keep track of them all, to put them all together and compose the puzzle. In fact, the complaint belied the anxiety provoked by the mixture of genres and the contamination of fiction by theory. It was not the lack of a story, but the presence of theoretical thinking within fiction that bothered these critics, as though a novel that revolved around its own conceptual codes of reading represented the threat, the danger that after all literary critics were becoming obsolete.

For at least thirty years Macedonio would rewrite the unpublished *Museo*. By nurturing a legendary expectation around it, Macedonio insisted on leaving the future open as promise: "the desire animating me in the craft of my novel was to create a home for nonexistence" (22), the latter term meaning, for Macedonio, the interval between a promise and its realization; true nonexistence to him was the postponing of something on the verge of its coming into being. Therein resided the spell of fiction: in the apprenticeship of waiting. Macedonio's utopia promised a novel by making of that promise the novel's definitive necessity and impossibility. In the paradox of announcing, delaying, and prefacing failed hopes of a fulfilled teleology, it took the avant-garde thrust to its ultimate extreme. The assertion that "my novel is failed" (18), in Macedonio's prologues, thus refers not to a technical contingency but to the novel's essence as novel. *Only insofar as it was failed could it exist as a novel;* for Macedonio the novelistic did not make sense other than as an embrace of the failure to fulfill a promise: "novel whose existence was novelistic for so much announcement and giving up, and novelistic will be the reader who understands it" (15). The potentially endless wait preempted all compensatory recuperation. In opposition to the efficient object of the instrumental sciences, the novel intended to be an ur-object, the Borgesian "object educed by hope,"[25] a utopian object that only existed as a permanent claim to exist.

In the *Museo*'s diegetic sections as such—or "chapters," as opposed to the fifty-something "prologues," in that most uncertain of all distinctions when things Macedonian are concerned—many of the dialogues between characters and their creator, El Presidente, take the form of a perverse variation on the Socratic dialogue. The *Museo*—along with *Rayuela*,

Respiración artificial, and others—belongs in an Argentine tradition that interrogates and parodies the Socratic-dialogical method of inquiry into truth. Macedonio's utopia of dissolving all reality principle led the text to point to the impossibility, the chaotic and irreducible impossibility of the Socratic dialogue. As characters were turned into minuscule units deprived of all psychology and history, they invariably interpellated the author (phantasmatized as El Presidente) about their condition, where they were or would like to be, the grounds for their own existence, and the future of their pilgrimage. One of the typical responses by El Presidente was the invitation for them to derealize themselves through a fictional imagining, to dream that they were sheer objects of thinking. Being led to converse about their own precarious, derivative existence as objects brought about by hope, characters engaged in a fallen, parodic hermeneutic, through which the novel was forced to the abyss of never progressing as a demonstration of a principle of intelligibility. In a mostly un-Socratic manner, characters were led to contradict themselves in their inquiry, turn back, erase, or start all over, depending on the logical dead-end street where they had landed each particular time. Whereas the Socratic dialogue becomes readable by the rigorous necessity of each step upon the previous one, the carefully crafted architecture of the whole, the teleological progression toward the foundational question, the Macedonian strategy halts that teleology with a paradox, frustrates the detectivesque interrogation, reveals the fancied, imaginative nature of all links, and interrupts their verisimilitude. It introduces the sophist laughter in the high-tone seriousness of the hermeneutic march.

Whereas Piglia locates the antithesis of Roberto Arlt's Babelian utopianism in Leopoldo Lugones's quasi-fascist defense of linguistic purity, the antithesis of Macedonio Fernández's poetics of invention is to be found in the social realist fiction of Manuel Gálvez: "Implicit polemic between Macedonio and Manuel Gálvez. Here are the two traditions of the Argentine novel. Gálvez is his perfect antithesis: the hard-working, mediocre, successful, 'social' writer, who rests on literary common sense" (*PP* 93). This opposition has important resonance in the present Argentine and Latin American cultural debates. Postdictatorships witness a generalized return to "common sense" and "realism," understood as the accommodation to the limits of the possible. Radicals are supposed to have "learned a lesson" of "respect for democracy and life," and the pervasive absorption of progressive intellectuals, notably social scientists, into state apparatuses in recent years testifies to the strength of this doxa. The need for self-criticism on the part of the Left is all too easily collapsed into a well-behaved compliance with liberal democracy, a rather authoritarian and limited variety of liberal democracy at that. In the literary sphere, this antiutopian turn finds expression in a conservative version of postmodernism, which responds to the exhaustion of the modernist signature by resigning to a casual, "purely literary," experimentation-free model of storytelling. For Piglia, the heritage of Macedonio Fernández remains the most effective antidote against this ethos of acquiescence: "It is not a matter of seeing the presence of reality in fiction (realism), but rather the presence of fiction in reality (utopia). The realist man against the utopian man. In the end, these are two ways of conceiving efficacy and truth. Against the resignation of realist compromise, Macedonian anarchism and its irony" (CF 179). This anarchic project would later become the backbone of Ricardo Piglia's postdictatorial novel par excellence, *La ciudad ausente,* to which I now turn.

4. ENCRYPTING RESTITUTION

A Detective Story in the City of the Dead

The real was defined by the possible (and not by being). The truth/falsehood
opposition should be replaced by the opposition between possible and impossible. —RICARDO PIGLIA, *La ciudad ausente*

Ricardo Piglia's novel *La ciudad ausente* can be read as a treaty on postdictatorial affects and the tasks of mourning work. One of the key references
for my analysis will be Plato's *Republic,* Western philosophy's ultimate
taming of the unreasonableness of mourning. *La ciudad ausente* also engages in an explicit dialogue with James Joyce's *Finnegans Wake* in order
to establish the links between the Babelian and the Utopian. Macedonio
Fernández and his beloved Elena are the central characters, and Erdosain, Arlt's Raskolnikovian hero, makes a brief appearance. Finally, Edgar
Allan Poe's "William Wilson" provides the model for several of the novel's
embedded narratives, which proliferate out of the variation on the theme
of the double in Poe's story. As usual in Piglia, then, the reader has to
face the challenge of putting together the pieces of a narrative patchwork that points in several directions at the same time.

Piglia's alter ego in *La ciudad ausente* is Junior, a reporter in charge of
"special investigations" for *El Mundo.* A child of English parents, he lived a
nomadic life of peregrinations interspersed with short stays in hotels and
pensions. His father had been one of those failed English engineers stuck
in Argentina: a delirious, complex-ridden man, he spent his life listening
to BBC broadcasts, attempting to forget his personal history and reconnect with the lost homeland. Junior's father reminds one of Arlt's inventors, obsessed with mechanics and imagining that each little apparatus
may turn out to be the modern-day philosophers' stone, the "copper rose"
of Arlt's novels. He also resembles Renzi's father—Renzi being Piglia's

slightly aestheticist alter ego, a brilliant reader of literature and a character in almost everything else Piglia writes. Renzi's father too would spend
his life next to the radio, attempting to make sense of failure through the
distant sounds coming from broadcasts by the defeated Perón. These are
all untimely figures, in profound discord with their present, envisioning
its negation and making of their obsessions and idiosyncrasies a stark refusal of what is. Such refusal of the present has both an annunciatory
and mournful value: it cannot decide between recollection and utopia, as
it is challenged to extract the openness of what may be from the desolation of what was. Drawn between the imperative to mourn and the
imperative to promise, these characters emerge out of defeat to tell the
survivor's tale and imagine that the future will not repeat the past.

Junior shares with the modern detective the postulate of a principle
of justice independent of and irreducible to any law, any rights, and the
totality of any juridical system. His first mission is related to the preservation of Macedonio's museum of the novel, a bottomless source of
stories and permutations of narrative kernels. The museum starts as a
translation machine, then a processor of stories, en route to becoming
the only clandestine possibility of circulating narratives in an occupied
polis. Its basic paradigm comes from a story initially stuffed into it, Edgar
Allan Poe's "William Wilson," which narrates the discomfort produced
in the protagonist by the presence of his double.[1] After being fed with
"William Wilson," the museum redoes it as "Steve Stevensen," a first narrative model from which other variables are developed. Steve Stevensen
was himself a character of many lands, a stranger everywhere: "he had
been born in Oxford and all languages were his mother tongue" (103).
He eventually became a great natural scientist and adopted Argentina
as a second home, always attempting to carry out a lifelong project
of "constructing a miniature replica of the world" (104). As a utopian
figure, a producer of imaginary universes, he was much "like Fourier or
Macedonio Fernández" (103). Another of the living metaphors of alterity
was Hungarian Lazlo Malamüd, author of an acclaimed translation of
Martín Fierro. Forced to live in Argentina, being a pitiful *speaker* of Spanish, and having to survive as a teacher, he struggled to express himself
in a language of which he only knew its greatest poem. Only having
the memory of *Martín Fierro*'s unique lexicon, Malamüd spoke "an imaginary language, full of guttural R's and gauchesque interjections" (16). His

frustration and anxiety led him to a unique language that preserved the music of Hernández's poem: "No more—he said. Disgraceful life. Don't deserve so much humiliation. First a promise, then melancholy. The eyes cast tears, but pain heals not" (17).

As a narrator in a foreign language, Malamüd recalls *Respiración artificial*'s Polish exile and young philosopher Tardewski, publishing his research in an article for a Buenos Aires newspaper for which he had given up everything he had. His entire life and intellectual property, an insight into a possible encounter between Hitler and Kafka in Prague around 1909 to 1910, had been reduced to this *La Prensa* article, written by him in English and translated by someone else into Spanish. This was everything he was left with: an article he authored and could not read. In it Tardewski postulated the prophetic character of Kafka's work, which took literally the dystopia putatively narrated to him by Hitler in his Prague exile. Tardewski's insight allowed him to read Hitler's *Mein Kampf* both as the culmination of the philosophical tradition inaugurated by Descartes's *Discourse on Method* and as actualization of what Kafka foresaw in his fiction. The situation was Kafkian in more ways than one, as a young philosopher produced an interpretation of the present that now became unreadable to its author, existing in an unknown language, much like the texts that he could not decipher and was forced to copy in order to make a living in Argentina. Tardewski related to language as a Kafkian figure: facing his story in urgent and desperate fashion and extracting from it, as though from a dead object, a prophetic-allegorical dimension, he confronted the choice between complicity and failure. If the enterprise of Reason culminated in *Mein Kampf* and what Kafka narrated was the becoming-actual of such dystopia, then the only option left for a young philosopher was failure. Thought was thus reduced to acceptance and elaboration of failure. Coming up with Hitler's *Mein Kampf* had been the will of chance: searching for Hippias's fragments, accumulating material for his work on Martin Heidegger *in* the Pre-Socratics—that is, the retrospective impact of the author of *Being and Time* upon our perception of them—Tardewski ended up with Hitler's book due to a confusion in the "HI" catalog in the library. The striking irony was that a careful reading of the nightmare narrated by *Mein Kampf* made the earlier project on Heidegger and the Pre-Socratics useless. The issue was now Heidegger *in* Hitler; there was no sense in looking for Heidegger in Hippias or Parmenides. The twentieth century's greatest thinker was himself directing thought to Hitler, inviting the reader to see in the Führer the culmination of Western philosophy. In a world where Reason found two contemporaneous culminations in Heidegger and Hitler, the range of choices confronting Tardewski were reduced to two: complicity or failure. From a switch of bibliographical records in a public library, then, Tardewski came to see the end of philosophy: "So philosophy had begun to come to an end for me. The order of the HI catalog cards in the library. You see, a simple change of cards sufficed" (RA 248/194).

Junior's mission in La ciudad ausente entails the preservation of the Babelian diegetic machine illustrated by characters such as these, who deal with their personal stories as though they were apocryphal, impersonal, and irreducible to a signature. In his Holmesian task of following the hints to Macedonio's utopian machine, he comes up with one of the stories circulated by the machine, a testimony telling the life and death of the first Argentine anarchist. Images of violence against the working class abound: clandestine burial places, skulls, skeletons, and ruins of all kinds. "A map of grave sites as we see here in this mosaic, yes, that was the map, it looked like a map, after the soil was cold, black and white, huge, the map of hell" (39). As the embedded tales in the novel begin to take on allegorical signification as petrified maps of the polis, Junior comes to learn the collective dimension of his search. Once he realizes that the existence of any storytelling is in question, the tales come to appear to him as encrypted emblems of his interpretive struggle facing Macedonio's machine and his own present. The "absent city" in the title begins to allude to a city of the dead, in which some encrypted skulls have survived as hieroglyphs.

The unresolved work of mourning is the major propelling force behind Macedonio's machine:

> In those years he had lost his wife, Elena Obieta, and everything Macedonio had done since then (and above all the machine) was designed to make her present. She was the eternal one, el río del relato [the river of storytelling], the interminable voice that kept remembrance alive. He never accepted he had lost her. In that he was like Dante and like Dante he built a world to live with her. The machine was this world and it was his masterpiece. (49)

Macedonio's utopia is to construct an affective machine that could tell a story of grief and lost love, as an attempt to cancel out death in a virtual world. The remembrance of and mourning for Elena ground the unfolding of stories in the machine. Elena remains the phantasmatic origin, her image condensed in the struggle she puts up against death throughout her stay in hospitals, those hopeless institutions she and Macedonio hated so much. After Elena's death Macedonio took his civil life to the limit of renunciation, "abandoning everything, his children, his law degree, even his medicine and philosophy writings, and began to live on nothing, like a bum, with other anarchists" (156). Continuing to think of Elena as *la Eterna*, Macedonio nurtured the conviction that the storytelling machine—the museum of the novel—could bring together affective and political restitution. The remembrance of Elena was tied into the possibility of preserving some breathing room in a polis where the state exercised its control by inserting artificial memories, depriving subjects of their past, and forcing them to live in the third person, as if they were the mind of another. The elaboration of mourning work implies a confrontation with a postdictatorial doxa of oblivion, and this is Junior's first lesson as he attempts to grasp the trajectory of Macedonio's machine.

The machine is thus both affective and political, singular and collective, mournful and utopian. However, one must differentiate it from the idealizing-transcendentalizing thrust with which Platonizing Christianity has striven to achieve a fundamental end, that of "avoiding a certain terminal conflagration of flesh."[2] Harking back to Socrates' deep suspicion of mourning as a potential disseminator of uncontrollable grief, the business of philosophy has always had much to do with the wise administration of affects. The movement from empirical particulars to ideal universals never takes place independently of mourning, in the precise sense that the universal's great virtue lies in its transcending the mortality of the particular, thus revealing one's attachment to it to be unwise and unworthy of a philosopher: *the taming of mourning as the very origin of idealism*. This is a theme that runs through the entirety of Western literature, from the wailing and laments over the dead in Homer's *Iliad* to Dorian Gray's desperate attempt at immortalizing beauty in an artistic portrait. In *La ciudad ausente* Macedonio's answer to the loss of the loved object, to destitution, is the storytelling machine, but what is the nature of this machine? Is it a Platonic machine, a realm of ideal forms preserving a modern-day Beatrice? Is it a Christian machine, negating filthy flesh in favor of pure soul? Is this a compensatory machine? How do its stories relate to—evoke, *mime,* make present—the lost object? This is the knot to be disentangled in *La ciudad ausente,* a knot I propose to reduce to a single question: What is the nature of the bind linking mimesis to mourning?

Keeping in mind that Macedonio's attempt is to grasp "the primordial cell, the white knot, the origin of forms and words" (155), I will allow myself, before I return to *La ciudad ausente,* a short excursion into the text that delimits the field of those forms, that is, the Platonic text. In the well-known expatriation of poetic mimesis in Book 10 of the *Republic,* poetry is convicted for its complicity with "pains and pleasures of the soul" such as grief (605d), laughter (606c), and sex and anger (606d).[3] However, grief seems to enjoy a certain centrality as the most turbulent, the most dangerous of all affective threats to the Republic, as already in Book 3 the links between the mimetic and the mournful are shown to be of crucial concern for the philosopher-legislator. In the education of young souls, all privilege is to be accorded to "sayings that will make them least likely to fear death" (386a). Under this general precept, before the ban on the mimetic is ever considered the *Republic* announces the conviction of poetry for its links with certain clandestine affects, especially those that could influence youth to prefer the ultimate shames of slavery and defeat to death. What has to be taught is fearlessness of death: the goal of "boys and men who are destined to be free and more afraid of slavery than of death" (387b). Poetic imitation, however, by lending voice to lamentations and grieving by the gods, and abhorrent images of Hades, hallucinations, and ghosts, cannot but instill fear into young men, making them "more sensitive and soft than we would have them" (387b). In fact, "the entire vocabulary of terror and fear" is to be banned, because not only tragedy but also the epic fell prey to lamentation and sorrow. Anticipating the ban that will eventually ensue on poetic mimesis as such in Book 10—"we can admit no poetry into our city save only hymns to the gods and the praises of good men" (607a)—Plato hints at the possibility of purging mimesis of the pernicious influence of mourning:

> Again then we shall request Homer and the other poets not to portray Achilles, the son of a goddess, as "lying now on his side, and then again on his back, and again on his face" and then rising up and

"drifting distraught on the shore of the waste unharvested ocean," nor as clutching with both hands the sooty dust and strewing it over his head, nor as weeping and lamenting in the measure and manner attributed to him by the poet. (388a)

We thus face the knot that indissociably ties, on the one hand, the regulation of mimetic practices, that is, the disciplining and ultimate exile of the poem, and, on the other, the subduing of mourning as a social affect, the proliferation of which could, in the last analysis, undermine the foundations of order in the polis by provoking an uncontrollable explosion of grief. As it is made explicit also in *Laws*, caution is recommended against choirs that "plunge the city into sudden tears" with their "doleful strains" (800d).[4] Mourning is for the polis an unwelcome, perturbing enemy of wisdom, requiring from philosophy a regulative and subduing intervention. Philosophy is thus set up in opposition to poetry, which, according to Plato, tends to voice the imperative to mourn. The philosopher's wisdom bounds mourning, organizes the system of accepted reminiscences, blocks the public display of grief: "the city thus protects itself against funereal ceremonies, in which some cities even forbid their officials to participate, and against women, their emotionalism, and their excesses."[5] The control over mimetic practices is thus coextensive with the development of a number of official rites through which one attempts to curb the display of mournful grief, primarily identified, in Greek thought and art, with women.

As mourning rituals are, according to Plato, progressively gendered in the feminine, and women's acts of mourning increasingly identified with potential disorder, mimesis is convicted for its complicity with mourning and its refusal to maintain mourning work within proper, that is, domestic boundaries. This is complicity of a *submissive* kind, for poetry would presumably *bow* to mourning, accept its failure to heal, and embrace that failure as its most proper gesture: "poetic imitation . . . waters and fosters these feelings when what we ought to do is to dry them up, and it establishes them as our rulers when they ought to be ruled."[6] Poetry refuses to be the ruler of mourning and this is its definitive crime. The threat to the polis stems, then, not exactly from the mimetic but from the failure of the mimetic. In other words, it is the impossibility of mimesis, not its actuality, its frailty, not its effectiveness—in short, its failure as a controlling instance—that triggers the economy of mourning. In this sense, the victory of the Platonic reading is to have postulated a space where the failure of mimesis is identified with the troublesome lingering around of mourning. Poetry's very ineffectiveness turns it into an effective enemy of the social order. Poetry's failure was its triumph, and this is why it had to be silenced.

Yet no "overcoming" or "subverting" of Plato is at stake in *La ciudad ausente*: Macedonio's is a Platonic machine insofar as it assumes that most Platonic principle, that of poetic mimesis—in Piglia's novel, the reshuffling and recombination of stories—moved by a fundamental relationship with the grief provoked by the loss of a loved object. Much in tune with the tradition of mournful literature inaugurated by the *Iliad*, in *La ciudad ausente* "mourning . . . is represented as a structure of self-reflection in which the death of the other arouses automourning in the onlooker."[7] After Elena's death Macedonio confides to Russo: "that I think of her is natural, but that she thinks of me now, after she is dead, is something that causes me deep sorrow" (162). He cannot stand the thought of Elena, dead yet thinking of him and suffering with his loneliness; he mourns Elena's mourning, his inability to contain her mourning for him. Self-mourning is at work, then, but again of a specific sort, one that does not erect the self-protective shield of narcissism—a classic defensive mechanism against mourning—but rather hands the self over to the vertigo of affect. Macedonio, the poet who made of his oeuvre an endeavor to "unsettle the self, dislodge each one's comfort in their own self" refuses to incarcerate affect in the safe boundaries of a stable ego. Affects belong in the outside, and the storytelling machine is the bridge to this unknown, atopical outside. The machine is thus not a surrogate for Elena, a ventriloquial or masturbatory repetition; it brings her memory into presence as a future-oriented negation of oblivion.

As Junior tracks down the legacy of the machine he learns that Macedonio had a collaborator in his enterprise: Richter, a Swiss physics teacher who had passed for a German engineer in Argentina and ended up succeeding in selling to Perón the capability for an imaginary atomic bomb. With his heavy German accent he convinced Perón of his plans for producing nuclear fission through cold temperatures. Perón, who made a living out of fooling everyone around him, was flatly fooled by a fantastic story that promised an Argentine atomic bomb. This paranoid infiltration into the paranoid state was for Macedonio exemplary, and as soon as he met Richter he invited him to collaborate in the construction of the machine. This odd man ended up surviving Macedonio and had clues to the machine's clandestine whereabouts. One of the key tales received by Junior, "The white knots," serves as a coded ticket to the information possessed by Richter.

The story opens up with the image of Dr. Arana's clinic of reinsertion and recycling of memory, an exercise in reprogramming human recollection in the service of state counterintelligence. Dr. Arana harks back to the tradition of Arocena, the censor and interceptor of letters in *Respiración artificial*, who demonstrated a paranoid will to truth and social control in the form of minute deciphering of secret languages. Dr. Arana's clinic takes possession of the "white knots," condensed zones that define the "grammar of experience," an empty set of forms, fragments, and allegorical ruins that operate as a linguistic and genetic code. The clinic is a dystopian city where all those who look at themselves in a mirror see the face of another. The system of mirrors suggests a telematic panopticon, where one is "thrown into an alien memory, forced to live as another" (89–90), much like K. in *The Trial*, forced to deal with his past in the third person. The clinic is the miniature of a world where "they had unified the time all over the world to coordinate the eight o'clock news" (76). Dr. Arana's treatment consists in turning psychotics into addicts, regulating their delirium through extreme dependency. Medical, military, and communicational metaphors provide the clinic's basic vocabulary, invariably punctuated with an oft-repeated sentence in modern Argentine history: "I want names and addresses" (83).

Among the bodies and minds experimented upon by the clinic is Julia Gandini, a clandestine activist married to a Trotsko-Peronist now disappeared. Thrown into an alien story about her own past, forced to repeat the lesson of resignation and "realism," she is the postdictatorial figure par excellence. In the speech recited by Julia Gandini after she is submitted to this virtual lobotomy, Piglia parodies the self-mortifying, guilty rhetoric prevalent in postdictatorial confessions and self-critiques on the Argentine Left: "She recited the lesson. Mike had been wrong and had died because violence generates violence. . . . 'We had to go through this hecatomb to realize the value of life and respect for democracy.' She repeated the lesson like a parrot, with a tone so neutral that it sounded ironic. She was a penitent" (94–95). Julia Gandini's prosthetic memory implanted by the technoclinic state pictures the reemergence of *Realpolitik* in postdictatorship. The state moves from the surgical language of amputation (the subfield of medicine prevalent under the dictatorship, with special force in the military's conception of the country as a sick body with several incurable parts) to the psychologizing, comforting language of neobehaviorism. Regret and reconciliation are inserted into Gandini's brain as a way of controlling the symbolization of the past. Gandini is, in other words, the anti-Antigone, or a counterpart to Ismene, Antigone's sister who accepts Creon's injunction that Polynices, their brother and enemy of the state, will not be buried and honored. Gandini is thus submitted to a programmed lobotomy designed to preempt mourning work. The state now takes the form of a factory of recuperative narratives that imaginarily dissolve loss within an ethos of resignation. Such compensatory psychologizing targets bodies and memories alike, as the disciplining of remembrance goes hand in hand with geopolitical rearrangements in the city.

This "realism" contrasts with Elena's wager on the future in her investigative, detectivesque infiltration into the clinic. If Gandini represents the state's attempt cybernetically to produce Ismene, the circulation of storytelling depends upon Elena as Antigonal figure: like Antigone, Elena knows the importance of installing the symbolic articulation of the past at the heart of the polis's present reality.[8] Moving in an experimental, virtual world where "nobody seemed to have *recuerdos propios* [memories of their own]" (72), Elena faces the alliance between political surveillance and modern technology: TV sets, walkie-talkies, and cameras watch over the clinic, guarded by the paranoid postdictatorial state as a fortress holding national security information. The object of her intervention in Dr. Arana's clinic is the white knots, "marks on the bones, a map of a blind language common to all living beings. . . . From these primitive kernels, all of the world's languages had developed through the centuries" (84). Elena's only contact inside the clinic is a certain Reyes, a gangster, drug dealer, and professor of English literature. Along with him and a few foreign scientists, Macedonio and Elena constitute the novel's only alternative political network, which Junior now faces the task of reconstructing. Throughout his detectivesque mission the embedded narratives that populate the museum interrupt the flow of the major plotline, as Junior learns about the experiential memory accumulated in the machine. Besides the account of Elena's reconquest of the map to the white knots and the map of hell testified to by survivors of atrocities against the first Argentine anarchists, he is introduced to narrative kernels reprocessed by the storytelling machine after Poe's "William Wilson." Elaborating on the novel's central theses concerning language, mourning, and experience, these stories tell the fate of bullied characters, childhood failures, eccentric suicides, and linguistic disorders. The first of them is "Un gaucho invisible," which introduces a strange character who verges on the nameless.

The invisible gaucho is the anonymous and failed man. Ostracized daily among his fellows, ignored in conversation circles, he embodies the Arltian incommunicability across the borders that separate the different degrees of humiliation along the social ladder. More unfortunate than those around him, in the sense that social submission is for them imaginarily compensated through a macho self-assertion at the individual level, against women and men like himself, the invisible gaucho testifies to the wall that separates the humiliated from one another:

> They only spoke to him when giving him an order and never included him in conversations. They acted as if he weren't there. At night he would go to sleep before everybody and, stretched under the blankets, he would see them laugh and joke by the fire. He seemed to be living a bad dream. (46)

Much like Arlt's Erdosain or Astier, Burgos, the invisible gaucho, belongs in the lineage of wretches who cannot find community within the humiliated. "Arlt—who had read Dostoyevsky—knew very well that there is nothing tighter than the bind linking the executioner to the victim, the humiliated to the humiliator. But he also knew that this relation is, on the other hand, unlikely among the humiliated."[9] Only in entirely gratuitous acts does Burgos find a source of affective restitution, or an affirmative intervention in the world. For him, as not even murder, betrayal, or delation are available means, a momentary reversal of fortune depends on the possibility of stretching the pyramid of power to include yet another level, reproduce the hierarchical organization of bullies upon someone lower than himself.

Almost by chance he receives his shot at restitution while he struggles to lace up a calf drowning in the river several feet below him. As in the first attempts he manages to make the animal swallow a large amount of water and prolong its suffering, he provokes curiosity and amusement in the circle of gauchos, feeling for the first time that he is being assigned an active role. His is a discharge of ressentiment in compensatory fashion:

> Burgos laced it and raised it in the air; when the calf was way up he would let it go again. The other men celebrated the event with shouts and laughter. Burgos repeated the operation several times. Trying to elude the lace, the animal would submerge in the water. It'd swim, wishing to escape, and the men incited Burgos to fish it again. The game lasted for a while, among jokes and pranks, until he laced the calf when it was almost drowning and raised it up to the feet of his horse. The animal gasped in the mud, its eyes white with terror. Then one of the gauchos got off his horse and chopped its throat in one cut.
>
> —Done, kid. We'll eat fish barbecue tonight—. Everyone burst out laughing and for the first time Burgos felt the brotherhood of men. (48)

In the resentful achievement of temporary manhood, Burgos is at that moment more capable of bullying a weaker being than anyone else. Turned into a sheer reactive force, he is only offered the compensatory prize of envisioning a lower piece in the pecking order. Like Raskolnikov, Erdosain, and Astier, the invisible gaucho inhabits a world fled by the gods, where only the gratuitous affirmation of ressentiment can redeem, if momentarily, the debris accumulated under the pile of defeats. Because all transcendental principle of justice has dissolved for these characters, they are confronted with the will to power as the only structuring axis organizing what exists. Their response to the will to power, their own affirmation of it, can only be a reactive one: in the torture session upon the calf, in denouncing a poor friend (Astier) or strangling a cross-eyed woman (Erdosain), the hierarchical layering of bullies generates a resentful will for compensation. While these characters labor on the cathexis of daily losses, all affirmation of power has fallen prey to ressentiment. Being too well learned in the school of defeat to believe in any god, yet too weak to anticipate the overman, these are liminal, dusk-dwelling characters. In reducing will to power to a compensatory, temporarily healing act of restitution, they produce that oxymoronic mixture: a re-active affirmation, a negative and nihilist embrace of the yes.[10]

Yet in their very destitution these figures are given the opportunity to glance at the principles grounding their existence and the world around them. Having nothing to lose, they can incorporate the fundamental teaching conveyed by the tradition of the vanquished: "things can always get worse" (*PP* 12). In that sense they dwell beyond all bad faith, even if their ultimate attempt at affective restitution is a reactive and negative one. They are much like the selves that speak in so many tangos — subjects betrayed and abandoned, empowered by their defeats to see things as they really are, without any veils or distortions.[11] In any case, at such crossroads one is forced to learn about the discontinuity between justice and law, and the amorality immanent to all things. From the knowledge that no given system of laws and customs will ever coincide with justice, they derive their skepticism regarding all transcendental salvation. In a world where all action has been reduced to an affirmation of itself, these characters must embark on a final gratuitous act that can only be accom-plished in a realm beyond all morality.

Likewise in "Primer amor," the story of a childhood failed love, re-ciprocated but broken up by the law to which the protagonists must submit: "I knew we had fallen in love and we tried to hide it because we were kids and we knew we wanted something impossible" (52). Beaten up by the world, this Romeo is forced to communicate with his Juliet through the written word, "barely knowing how to write" (53), only to witness the little girl be dragged away from school never to be seen again. The question for the remembering narrator is then the elaboration on that loss, one that would populate fantasies and visions throughout his life. One discerns, underlying this metaphorization of primary loss, a reflection on mimesis and narcissism. The protagonist hears from his *mother* that any loved being can be brought to life with a mirror under the pillow; he is then led to take the *father's* shaving mirror at night to dream of the impossible Clara: "at night, when all were asleep, I would walk barefooted to the back patio and take down the mirror in which my father shaved every morning" (53). The protagonist begins to have dreams of multiple images of Clara in the mirror. The image has a funda-mentally cathectic function as a healing mechanism in the confrontation with loss. The Oedipal axis, however, becomes more complex: the protagonist sleeps with his father's mirror and through that mirror wishes to fulfill the mother's prophecy. In the attempt to offset the loss, the protagonist engages in mimetic exchanges with the mirror, the culmination of which lies years ahead, in a different stage in the elaboration of dream material. He dreams that he is dreaming of her in the mirror. In this potentiation of the image to the second degree, the mimetic proliferation brings about the sudden return of Oedipus. The protagonist sees Clara, the lost object of desire, as a little girl, coming to him "just like she was as a girl, with red hair and serious eyes. I was another, but she was the same and came to me, as if she were my daughter" (53–54). He thus fulfills the mother's prophecy by reactivating the mimetic powers of the father's mirror, only to see the Oedipal triangle return as the cathexis of defeat forces the identification with the father figure.

Mimesis has reinserted the father and led the protagonist to identify with him in his dreams. The father's borrowed mirror comes to speak through the protagonist's dreams. The mimetic serves the purpose of ultimately holding the explosion of grief at bay, suspending the complicity between mourning and mimesis—the status of the mimetic as a mouthpiece for mournful affects, so feared by Plato and since then installed at the heart of Western philosophy—by regulating mourning inside the Oedipal triangle. The mimetic here would no longer have to be a reason for concern to the philosopher-legislator. Far from being a dangerous instigator of mourning, mimesis prevents the overflow of mourning into an affective abyss by bringing it back into the Oedipal triangle, holding it in check under the law of the father. Much like the invisible gaucho, who can only find compensatory, reactive affirmation in torturing a calf, the protagonist of "Primer amor" holds mourning at bay through an Oedipalized metaphorical substitution of images.

In their elaboration of loss these characters leave behind the traces that will later become the object of Junior's search. In his visit to the museum Junior sees the father's mirror, another piece of debris left over from a lost experience that will eventually be transformed into another narrative kernel in the storytelling machine. In these first moments, the stories are relatively simple variations on the theme of the double. If "William Wilson" narrates the doomed trajectory of a man haunted by his double until he is led to kill himself and his replica, "Un gaucho invisible" relates Burgos's daily impossibility of replicating the will to power around him, until his ressentiment is temporarily redeemed by a further folding of the pecking order. In analogous fashion, "Primer amor" recounts the story of a protagonist projecting a mirror reflection of a lost love, thus fulfilling the mother's prophecy, while the image of that mother is replaced and restituted through the doubling of the girl that returns when the protagonist places himself in the locus of the father. After these initial, simpler combinations, the machine incorporates error and chance as a fundamental principle of operation:

> Junior began to understand. At first the machine errs. Error is the first principle. The machine "spontaneously" disassembles the elements in Poe's story and transforms them into fiction's potential nuclei. The initial plot came around like that. The myth of origins. All stories came therefrom. The future meaning of what was going on depended upon this story about the other and the yet-to-come. (103)

Along with the mirror, Junior finds a ring that has survived from another story, preserved and recycled by the machine.

The protagonist of "La nena" is a unique girl fascinated with little machines and bombs; she takes the movement of a fan as a model for the world. After her mother turns it off she begins to have trouble with language, burying in her memory the words she knows and losing the ability to use personal pronouns. As her language becomes more abstract and impersonal, she resorts to certain extremely creative and hallucinatory metaphors: "white sand" for sugar, "soft mud" for butter, and "humid air" for water. Since the medical establishment insists on electric "cures," her parents refuse to entrust her to a clinic, and decide, instead, to look for an empty form, a model of syntax that could replace the fan and give form to her language. The father, a frustrated musician who teaches high school math, eventually finds it in music:

> The father left Dr. Arana's clinic and began to treat the girl with a singing teacher. He needed her to incorporate a temporal sequence and he thought that music was an abstract model of the world's order. She sang Mozart's arias in German, with Madame Silenzky, a Polish pianist who directed the Lutheran church chorus in Carhué. The girl, sitting on a stool, howled following the rhythm and Madame Silenzky was terrified, for she thought the girl was a monster. (57–58)

She begins to hum along and articulate sound blocks modeled after the musical syntax, a sort of pure semiotic form from which all experience has been banned. As she suffers the loss of her mother, dead after two months in hospital, she begins to associate her death with a Schubert lied: "she sang as someone crying for a dead one and remembering the lost past" (58). Her entrance into language is mediated by mourning for her mother and for a lost tongue she attempts to recapture. As music endows her with an initial notion of syntax, her father sets out to work on her lexicon.

At first sitting on a couch and telling her a story as though singing an aria, the father searches in storytelling a model where each sentence is to become the "modulation of a possible experience" (59). This is why he opts for telling each time the same story in one of its infinite variations. One of the older versions is told in the twelfth century by William of Malmesbury in his *Chronicle of the Kings of England*: a noble young man from Rome plays a game with his friends in the garden during his wedding. He feels fearful of losing his ring and places it on one of the fingers of a statue. Upon his return he finds the stone fingers closed in a fist and realizes he will not be able to recover the ring. When he makes a second visit to the garden he finds out that the statue has disappeared. On his first night with his wife he hides the truth from her. However, when he lies down in bed, he notices that something has been interposed between their bodies. Shivering in terror, he hears a voice: "Hold me, today you've bound yourself to me in matrimony. I'm Venus and you've given me the ring of love" (59). This narrative kernel repeats itself in several variables: some twenty years after William of Malmesbury's book, a German compilation of fables entitled *Kaiserchronik* gives a different version, in which the statue was no longer of Venus but of the Virgin Mary. The young man develops a mystical passion for her and becomes a monk, after the mother of God chastely interposes between bride and groom on the nuptial night. The story survives in an anonymous painting of the time, where one can see Virgin Mary with a ring on one of her left fingers and an enigmatic smile on her lips. Another version, now with modern flashbacks and miraculous narrative turns, is told by Henry James in his "The Last of the Valerii," which relates the marriage between a rich American heiress and a noble Italian man in Risorgimento Rome. After a statue of Juno is found in excavations of his Villa, the count progressively falls prey to an intense fascination with it and eventually substitutes it for his wife altogether. Happiness only returns to the couple's life once the countess tears away the ring-bearing finger of the marble statue and buries it in the backyard.

This is the version that the little girl eventually learns in its entirety: "The girl left the story, as though walking through a door she got out of the tale's closed circle and asked her father to buy her a ring. She was there, humming, chirping, a sad, musical machine" (61). The ring stands as an emblematic figure for that primary kernel, a knot around which all possible narrative variables revolve. As a "white knot" in its own right, an originary mark on the bones and a starting point for all repetitions and restitutions, the ring emblematizes all the *relatos* (stories) that speak of the power of the relato: the little girl comes to learn of language and experience through storytelling, and the various rings pass on down as so many re-turns of the same tale. Her own ring survives as emblem of a lost language, thus finding an afterlife as an allegorically charged object. Concentrating in itself the restitutive power of the relato, the ring is a ruin that offers the past to be read as a monad, much like a baroque emblem. These are debris that bear within themselves the mark of a desolate time, traveling down history as encrypted images, allegories to be deciphered. The girl's ring replicates the wedding ring belonging to the protagonist of each tale, as the rings are always objects delimiting an impossibility, encircling and entrapping their owners in a desire they can neither fulfill nor comprehend. The ring, thus, not only functions allegorically in the proliferation of en abymes designed by Piglia (at least three levels: that of the various stories told to the little girl, her own story, and the novel's main plotline); it also stands as an allegorical representation of allegory itself, the emblem of allegory as a tropological confrontation with failure. In the little girl's silent brooding over the objects, or in her intoning a Schubert lied as a strange and unique mourning anthem, one recognizes that melancholy will for contemplation that affects all allegorical gazes: "this is the essence of melancholy immersion: that its ultimate objects . . . turn into allegories, that these allegories fill out and deny the void in which they are represented."[12] It should come as no surprise, then, that when Junior visits the museum he finds, along with the girl's ring, a copy of Burton's *Anatomy of Melancholy*, where, by the way, another variation on the same story is told.

Yet the ring also hints at that affirmation with which storytelling counters the melancholy of loss. The void referred to by Benjamin erupts, in Piglia's story, as the little girl loses her incipient speech when the fan stops; the void invites a catachrestic fulfillment, a trope that can name it, point to it, while maintaining it as an inscription to be deciphered, an open letter sent to the future: "this story was the tale of the power of storytelling . . . to narrate was to give life to a statue, make live someone who is afraid to live" (62). This use of storytelling reflects the ubiquity of the allegorical in Piglia: allegory is the enabling trope here because allegory takes up a ruin not to make it immediately codifiable but to preserve the untimeliness of its riddles. It both fills out the void and denies it. In these terms one could speak of a *restitutive* return of the allegorical in the form of storytelling in Piglia's work, for the relato is the only instance whereby the ring can redeem the memory of the lost object. As it encrypts itself as allegory, surviving as a ruin of the past, the ring points toward the void and demands restitution. But the objects to be restituted here, belonging, as they do, to the order of experience, can no longer be retrieved and are irrevocably lost. Storytelling knows this, and it sets to itself the unreasonable task of producing experience synthetically, a posteriori.[13] The task confronting storytelling is thus to offer restitution while knowing all too well that all restitution is impossible. It makes the acknowledgment of the impossibility of restitution its most restitutive gesture. As the telling of so many tales becomes the only life-affirming instance in an otherwise abyssal void of loss, their enigmas put forth a cryptic form of restitution, a hieroglyphic redemption ceaselessly announcing and deferring itself, like a visionary utopia of a future total, perfect book.

This is then the plan of *La ciudad ausente* as a whole: Macedonio's machine was to save that originary ring, preserve that primordial cell. While it replicates *Museo de la novela de la Eterna* in its attempt to approach that "possible form" located by Macedonio in the aesthetic-philosophical experience of self-derealization—the becoming-fictional of oneself, that most oxymoronic, unepiphanic kind of epiphany—*La ciudad ausente* encircles it within a plotline that mimes the detective story. Piglia thus continues *Respiración artificial*'s tribute to the *relato policial* but with a major discontinuity. Whereas *Respiración artificial* handles the relato policial model from the standpoint of the detective, *La ciudad ausente* tells perhaps the same story ("a crime or a journey, what else can one narrate?" Piglia has noted) but with a fundamental reversal: narration takes place from the locus of the criminal. The narrative machinery pays tribute to a conspiratorial desire. The entire politics of *La ciudad ausente* is at stake here, in the concept of the political as secret and paranoid fiction. *Respiración artificial* follows the clues of a succession of crimes and catastrophes later understood to be history itself. The attributes of the classical detective, the tracking down of clues and the restoration of meaning, guides the characters in their searches, be it the utopian redemption of the present (Ossorio and Maggi's problem) or the language that could narrate such utopian redemption (Renzi's question). Their tasks are delimited by a history that demands that they become detectives. *Respiración artificial* thus makes of the reader an accomplice in a deciphering operation. *La ciudad ausente* continues these deciphering operations but now as attributes of the criminal. Junior follows the tracks of Macedonio the outlaw and disseminates the underground utopia of a future story as the seed of a grand crime.

All detective narratives are, to be sure, prologues to a coming story: a detective novel only finds its fulfillment in the imperative of putting together the system of enigmas that, once resolved, opens up the possibility of narrating a tale. In this sense the detective genre is much like Macedonio's magnum opus where, however, such narratability only appears as a deferred promise. *La ciudad ausente* thus takes place in the contradictory juncture between the detective story's denouement-oriented poetics and Macedonio's open, unfinished, antidenouement novel. The virtual, yet-to-be-conquered *relato* organizes the architecture of the text, but the ending no longer obeys the classic dialectical model of the detective story, that of resolution of conflict and restoration of meaning. The denouement refuses to be a closure, and in that respect Piglia's tribute to the detective story remains a highly ambiguous one. *La ciudad ausente* is a Holmesian novel insofar as it turns the final tale, the *relato* to be conquered, into the object of desire and principle of organization of the whole. However, it affirms itself most of all as a Macedonian text; because that final tale is never final, it never takes the form of a dialectical synthesis of a trajectory, but rather that of a step to the outside. The *novela futura* is what every detective story promises, but it is also that instance in which every detective story finds its dissolution and deconstruction.

Junior's decisive step into the underground circuit is his visit to Ana Lidia (a near namesake of *Finnegans Wake*'s Ana Livia), a philosophy professor who leaves academia in order to turn her grandfather's bookstore into Buenos Aires's major center for research and reproduction of the museum-machine. Possessing the most lucid and radical mind in the novel, she operates in clandestine fashion, reprocessing and circulating apocryphal versions of the narratives preserved in the resistance. Dwelling in that position where views of the totality of the polis are far clearer, she is the opposite of Junior, who holds the confused belief in the undisturbed hegemony of forgetfulness in times postdictatorial: "I've seen several photocopies of stories from the 1950s, versions from wartime, science fiction stories. Pure realism" (110). The crucial information Ana passes down to him is, again, coded in a story, a tale of "an island, a sort of linguistic utopia on future life" (111).

Constructed as a series of propositions, "La Isla" occupies the climatic center of *La ciudad ausente*. It relates the story of "this place . . . populated with English, Irish, Russians, people coming from everywhere, persecuted by the authorities, political exiles being threatened with death" (123). "La Isla" is the phantasmatic image of a Joycean polis where languages last no longer than a few days or months and *Finnegans Wake* is the only book that survives in all languages, readable and transparent as a sacred scripture. Languages are not handled as a tool by a cogito. Rather, they succeed one another as a "white bird changing color in flight," giving the "illusion of unity in the passing of shades" (125), drowning their speakers in the immanence of their metamorphoses. The islanders "speak and comprehend instantaneously the new language, but forget the previous one" (126). They suffer from the absence of a transcendental consciousness that can take stock of the dizzying linguistic changes they undergo. All experience is dissolved along with the language in which it was concocted. Everything on the island is defined by the unstable character of language: letters reach their addressees, but their contents are no longer readable; men and women who loved each other in one language can hardly disguise their mutual hostility in the next. This is a world ruled by the emptiness of memory, as "one always forgets the language in which remembrances were fixed" (124). All masterpieces die as soon as the languages in which they were written disappear. No life on the island has remained untouched by forgetfulness: "only silence persists, clear as water, *igual* [identical] to itself" (128).

Linguistics is naturally the most advanced science on the island, and its epistemological foundation is provided by the mythical impossibility of coexistence between grandparents and their grandchildren, due to the belief that the former reincarnate in the latter. Historical linguistics is made possible by the belief in this most unique form of generational reincarnation, according to which "language accumulates the residues of the past in each generation and renovates the remembrance of all dead and lost languages" (127). One could say, then, that generational reincarnation is the form encountered by the islanders to reinvent the notion of tradition, lost as soon as they fell into the carousel of oblivion fomented by linguistic change. Grandchildren receive the inheritance as a way of "not forgetting the meaning words had in the days of their ancestors" (127). Although scientific linguistics disavows any links between language and natural phenomena, the island's tradition has it that languages suffer modifications during nights of full moon. The islanders follow the rituals and await "the coming of their mothers' language" (128). In the hopeful expectation of the return of a presemiotic babble, a substanceless language, made of sheer sound and materiality so as to resist daily wear and tear, they long for pre-lapsarian times when "words extended themselves with the serenity of the prairie" (124). On this utopian/dystopian island, all attempts at stabilizing language by artificial means have met with failure, because no one can devise a semiotic system that could maintain the same meanings through time. The consistency of a proposition lasts however long the terms in which it was formulated survive. On the island, therefore, "quickness is a category of truth" (132). The efforts to compose a bilingual dictionary that would allow some comparison between languages were unfulfilled: "translation is impossible, because only usage defines meaning and on the island they only know one language at a time" (131). The island eliminates translation because it dissolves the kinship among languages, which is the basis of translatability.[14] Those still working on the dictionary conceive of it as a book of mutations, "a sort of etymological dictionary that accounts for the history of the future of language" (131).

The islanders' entire notion of space is determined by language, in such a way that the highly unstable category of "the foreign" becomes a purely linguistic one. Because no image of the outside is available, each one's only homeland is "the language that all spoke at the moment of birth, but no one knows when they will be back there" (129). All *patrias* are thus at any given moment lost, not because one finds oneself "in exile," but rather because loss is the experience defining the subject's relation to them. They are linguistic patrias, and on the island language is the homeland of loss. The major spatial reference is the Liffey River— a crucial landmark in *Finnegans Wake's* Dublin—which runs through the island from North to South. "But Liffey is also the name for language and in the Liffey River are all the rivers in the world" (129). Space is thus fully temporalized: "the concept of border is a temporal one, and its limits are conjugated like those of a verb tense" (129). Mutations have taken over the whole of reality, and all that survives of past languages are a few ancient words "stamped on the walls of buildings in ruins" (130). The only tangible memory of the polis, however, is the written one, and a single book delimits the entire field of remembrance: "In fact the only book that lasts in this language is *Finnegans*, said Boas, because it is written in all languages. It reproduces the permutations of language in microscopic scale. It looks like a miniature model of the world" (139). In this insular realm ruled by the ephemeral, only *Finnegans Wake*, a system that tendentially embraces chaos, can ultimately last and survive through the linguistic changes. *Finnegans Wake* has been regarded as "a sacred book" (139) and is "read in churches" (139–40). Others believe it to be "a book of funereal ceremonies and study it as a text that founds religion on the island" (139).

Bob Mulligan is the only islander who has ever known two languages at the same time. He speaks "like a mystic, writing unknown sentences and saying that those were the words of the yet-to-come" (131). Mulligan's tales cannot be understood on the island, and judging by the few recordings preserved in the archives he seems to be speaking of a strange world only legible in the future:

> Oh New York city, yes, yes, New York city, the whole family went up there. . . . Women wore a veil over their heads, like Arab ladies, except that all of them had blonde hair. The grandfather's grandfather

was a policeman in Brooklyn and once he killed a limp man who was about to strangle a supermarket cashier." (131)

Mulligan's reference to uniformization and urban violence lends itself to be read as anticipation, and his schizophrenic speech appears as a prophesy that announces the wreckage of what is to come. Mulligan can speak of the future because he is above all moved by mourning: a widower one year after his marriage—as Belle Blue Boylan drowned in the Liffey River—he makes of his own life a hieroglyph unreadable to his present and becomes a vehicle for the echoes of what still not is. Piglia appropriates him as a figure for that class of prophets endowed with the knowledge conferred by failure, figures who can listen in the present to the murmurs of the future, much like Kafka knew how to discern the nightmare of what was to come in the words of Adolf Hitler, uttered in his Prague exile in 1910, according to the hypothesis of *Respiración artificial.* In *La ciudad ausente* Mulligan's little tale of New York is a microscopic version of a future dystopia that the reader can nonetheless recognize as his/her own present. In this small kernel of "La Isla," therefore, Piglia writes not a dystopia projected onto the future and modeled after an exacerbation of the present, à la Orwell, but rather a "realist," matter-of-fact account of the present projected by the past as a nightmare set in the future.

In fact, as the only bilingual person ever known, Mulligan is best grasped as the figure of the impossible *translator* on an island where all translation has been abolished. More than the researchers working on the futurist dictionary, Mulligan stands for the utopian translatability that could revolutionize life on the island. But he is mute, forever mute, because "nobody knew what he was saying, so Mulligan wrote this and other stories in this unknown language and one day he said he'd lost hearing" (132). The mute translator turns to writing. Living away from other people, silently brooding over a glass of beer, Mulligan is the translator who knows too much to continue attempting translation; let us say, a translator a priori in mourning for a failed task. As his speech and his very body encrypt themselves before their contemporaries like a diabolical, incomprehensible allegory, Mulligan embraces the translator's task as a true *Aufgabe*—a task that is always a giving-up, a renunciation leading to the embrace of defeat, that most proper lesson to all translators.

Also on the island, where the strangeness of each language vis-à-vis all the others has been taken to the limit, translation finds its metaphysical vocation of being "only a somewhat provisional way of coming to terms with the foreignness of languages."[15] The translator's predicament is here delimited by two symmetrical and opposing phenomena: on the one hand, the status of *Finnegans Wake* as the collapse of all translation — collapse understood as termination, but also as fulfillment — and on the other the succession of different languages like so many fragments of a broken vessel, dreaming of a pure language whereby the vessel would be recomposed. Such an Eden has been known on the island, at least mythically and retrospectively, as the time when "language was a plain where you could walk surpriselessly" (134). The mythical repertoire includes a rewriting of the Fall as entrance into language — "the tree of good and evil is the tree of language. As they eat the apple they begin to talk" (134) — the inauguration of the human word, in which "name no longer lives intact."[16] Adam and Eve begin to speak and thus lose the name — which was one with the essence of the thing — and resign themselves to the alienness of the sign. What has entirely been erased from the island, then, is the *name*, in everything that opposes it to the mere vehicular, instrumental, and bourgeois *sign*. The imperative to translate emerges as an attempt to recapture the echo of the name, of the pure language buried under signs worn out by use.

Such entrance into the human, fallen word necessarily implies the acceptance of translation as demand and impossibility, that is, acceptance of what is given out to translation, the gift of translation — the multiplicity and infinite foreignness of all languages — as well as the correlative acceptance of the renunciation entailed by all translation. What sets Mulligan apart from other islanders is his awareness of all that translation owes to failure — for his own tales are perceived as insane monstrosities, a bit like Hölderlin's versions of Sophocles, profuse in eccentric, visionary metaphors and incomprehensible to their present.[17] Such awareness constitutes precisely the knowledge that lies at the foundation of his melancholy. In contrast and correspondence with mute nature — "because she is mute, nature mourns"[18] — Mulligan is driven to silence by the profusion of languages and by his very bilingualism, as he finds himself telling tales that nobody understands. Benjamin's well-known linking of melancholia with speechlessness plays a crucial role both in his early essay on language and in his book on the German baroque drama. Piglia's island recasts the paradox: because s/he is endowed with more than one language, "La Isla" suggests, the translator mourns. S/he experiences more than anyone the fall from the name "into the abyss of the mediateness of all communication, of the word as means, of the empty word, the abyss of prattle."[19] The abyss of prattle is coextensive with the post-Babelian multiplicity of languages, the distressing consciousness of which the islanders are spared by living and recollecting only within the immanence of each language they happen to be speaking. Mulligan, the translator, cannot bypass such distress, and is led out of his cryptic and emblematic speech into silence. For him, then, the multiplicity of languages can take on allegorical dimension in the rigorous sense of the word, that is, as a tropological representation of a loss, the depiction of an object insofar as it offers itself as a lost object. It is from the standpoint of Mulligan's excessive knowledge that multilingualism comes to stand for the loss of the name: "something can take on allegorical form only for the man who has knowledge."[20]

Mulligan's untimely presence on the island of oblivion introduces the salvific motif of translation as revivification of memory. The fall into multilingualism on the Joycean island is also a fall into forgetfulness, and in this sense Piglia's tribute to Joyce is a highly ambiguous one as well. Because they have fallen prey to oblivion, the islanders are in dire need of translation. Translation here represents, in Benjaminian fashion, "one of the fundamental models of historical relation, similarly to criticism, collectionism and citation: the rescuing of Being at the instant of its abolition."[21] Piglia reads Joyce in cross-eyed fashion, looking at the wizard of *Finnegans* but keeping an eye and a thought on Kafka. Mulligan's monologue indeed recalls that of a Kafkian prophet dwelling in a Joycean universe. His speech is unreadable to his present yet allegorical for his future. Being an Irish speaker of English, he stands as a privileged analogue to a Prague Jew writing in German: both labor on that most literal, demetaphorized relation to the proper/alien tongue, voiding its symbols of the previously stable conventional meanings they had, taking language to a desert of literalness that evokes the echo of the name. As in *Respiración artificial*, the reading of Joyce cannot dispense with the Kafkian, salvific relation to language. In *Respiración artificial* the contrast is established between Joyce, who writes in order to wake from the nightmare of the present and Kafka, who makes of his writings an entrance into it.

The "fragmentary, incomparable work of Franz Kafka" is the only one that accomplished that "suicidal restitution of silence." Kafka "woke up, everyday, to *enter* that nightmare and try to write about it" (*RA* 272/213). Kafka appears as the one who cares too dearly about language, pays too high a price for it and thus knows that "to speak of the unspeakable is to put in danger the survival of language as a bearer of human truth" (*RA* 272/213). Kafka is the image of the prophet who has learned when to remain silent. Speaking of the unspeakable in 1980, Piglia had seen, through Kafka, that "the name of those who were dragged off to die *like dogs*, just like Joseph K., is legion" (*RA* 265/208); writing in the early nineties, he offers in "La Isla" an allegory of forgetfulness for postdictatorial times in which the only remaining attempt at translating memory is embodied by a Kafkian prophet who reads in the waters of history the desolation yet to come but cannot communicate it to his contemporaries, for his is an untimely language, incomprehensible on an island where the only transparent document is *Finnegans Wake*. The visionary prophet eventually despairs of language, "emphasizes his failure," as Benjamin would say of Kafka, and decides to burn his tales and fall into muteness. The postdictatorial attempt at translation of remembrance, then, allegorizes and points toward two convergent abysses, Babelism and Silence. Mulligan, as a translator, cannot reside outside the former but his condition on the (at any given point) monolingual island includes the acceptance of the latter. Babelism is the exhaustion of translation, unveiler of its impossibility, and cause of the translator's fall into the abyss of Silence. Drifting between Babelism and Silence, then, floats the island of oblivion, where people don't know that tomorrow they will be laughing at the same jokes in another language and where they still fail to understand a certain man who "dreams of incomprehensible words that had for him a transparent meaning" (131).[22]

Besides entering the plotline of *La ciudad ausente* as part of Junior's political and philosophical apprenticeship, "La isla" introduces Junior to the image of a mechanical one-eyed bird that used to fly over the island and survived in a museum, fascinating a man who collaborated with Macedonio in his processor of tales. This character turns out to be Russo, an immigrant whose awkward Spanish earned him his nickname among townspeople. Russo's closing testimony brings us back to the machine's origins, Macedonio's incomplete mourning for Elena, his unreasonable refusal to accept her death:

> He thought of memory persisting once the body is gone and the white knots that stay alive while the flesh falls apart. Stamped on the cranium bones, the invisible forms of the language of love remained alive and it might be possible to reconstruct them, to make memory live, like someone who fingers on a guitar the sounds of a song written in the air. That evening he conceived the idea of entering that remembrance and staying there, in the memory of her. Because the machine is the *remembrance* of Elena, it is the tale that returns, eternal like the river. (162–63)

The monologue by the virtual Elena that closes the novel exhibits traces of many other stories, internal and external to *La ciudad ausente*. The most salient is that of Molly Bloom, the Joycean heroine who knows a thing or two about mourning: "I am Amalia, if they hurry me I say I'm Molly, I'm her, locked up inside, desperate, I'm Irish, I say, then, I'm her and I'm all the others, I've been all the others, I'm Hypolite, the lame one, the little limp, I'm Temple Drake. . . . I've told this and other stories, it doesn't matter who is speaking" (173–74). Elena's Bloomesque (in Molly's, not Harold's or much less Allan's sense) monologue closes the novel by opening up the possibility of identification with all the names available in history. Much like Ossorio who, in *Respiración artificial*, hallucinates and identifies with Rosas and countless other figures, thus encountering the thread of Ariadne that can lead him out of the nightmare of the present, Elena makes of all recollection a wager on the future. Her virtual existence in the machine disseminates stories across a city controlled by a medicalized state and suffering from chronic oblivion. Her voice makes perceptible the echoes of voices of others, such as the girl in "La nena" who appears silently standing with the ring on her finger and gazing melancholically at the horizon, or Rajzarov, a friend of Macedonio's, a Russian student activist who had been totally disfigured by a bomb explosion in Odessa and later wandered around Argentina like a postrevolutionary Frankenstein, with his body full of metal prostheses. These untimely bodies bear the memory of the polis in postdictatorship: theirs is a radical wager on the openness of what is yet to come. The restitution they promise is encrypted in the tales they leave as a legacy—a gift—to the future.

"The death that exists in forgetfulness is the one that has led us to the error of believing in personal death,"[23] Macedonio affirmed in one of his many prologues to the *Museo*. Those familiar with his work know that what is at stake here is something radically other than the Christian notion of permanence and ascension of the soul after the putrefaction of the body. For Macedonio, negating death amounts to negating oblivion. Mimesis pays tribute to Mnemosyne. The mimetic machine elects Mnemosyne as inspiration and guide in its counterhegemonic war. Piglia takes up this motif and develops it into a program for postdictatorship: in a moment when the state abandons the surgical language of amputation and turns to a recuperative, psychologizing rhetoric, Piglia insists that what has been left out of this equation is the memory of an experience. As we have seen, however, such memory does not point toward an interiority but to an outside. Hence the paradox of the storytelling machine: it metaphorizes the possibility of creating new stories, but "new" and "create" need to be understood here in a most antiromantic sense. The machine handles combinations, plagiarism, apocryphal narratives, and disinteriorized affects. Piglia depersonalizes mourning and desubjectivizes affect. The crux of the matter coalesces in a fundamental literary and philosophical problem: How can one think an affect irreducible to the instance of the subject? How can one avoid the trap of narcissism as a protective shield against mourning? How can one think mourning as positivity, beyond all ressentiment? The machine starts from Macedonio's mourning, but instead of making its tales return to him, reinforcing his ego, and thus taking the facile, romantic way out, Piglia disseminates mourning as an apocryphal story. Stories roam around the city, circulate, and recompose the oblivious postdictatorial landscape. If the state invents false names, if it places its victims into alien, third-person memories, making them look at history through the eyes of another, the only alternative is to manufacture anonymity, to multiply eyes and names as so many impersonal war machines. As Russo explains to Junior: "I keep a possibility alive, understand me? A form still available, this is the logic of experience, always the possible, what is yet to come, a street in the future, an open door in a Tribunales pension, and the sound of a guitar" (CA 147).

To return to my original question, concerning the relation between the mimetic and the mournful in postdictatorship: for Piglia, mimesis can bring about restitution because storytelling is the one practice that allows for the dissemination and reshuffling of proper names. In this view, the accomplishment of mourning work demands above all a desubjectifying gesture, an escape from the prison house of the proper name, an act that ultimately displaces mourning away from egological boundaries into the realm of collective memory. *La ciudad ausente*'s crucial rhetorical operation is the identification of the apocryphal and the collective: that which is apocryphal belongs to all. However, the truly apocryphal, what truly bypasses the cage of the signature, is an event that is never affect free; on the contrary, it is itself a function of the singularity of an affect. From this observation emerges the paradox that Macedonio and Elena's most private language, their most singular remembrances—prior to and foundational of their own signatures—can establish a network of apocryphal storytelling in which the memory of the polis can be narrated. Taking the singularity of affect away from its association with an egological and romantic vocabulary in order to disseminate it through the polis: this is the spirallike path that restitution has to take, if it is to restitute anything at all. Restitution depends on the survival of storytelling because that which is to be restituted belongs in the order of memory. Only in this terrain, *La ciudad ausente* claims, can the tasks of mourning work be posed to thought.

5. PASTICHE, REPETITION, AND THE ANGEL OF HISTORY'S FORGED SIGNATURE

Christianity is a metaphysics of the hangman.

—FRIEDRICH NIETZSCHE, *Twilight of the Idols*

How was it that the devaluation of all higher values and the rejection of everything life affirming came to constitute the basis for all morality, the paradigm for all "good"? How was it that the negation of life, the negation of the only world there is, came to prevail over the guiltless embrace of life? Whence comes the power, the persuasive strength of what Nietzsche calls "that ghastly paradox of a 'God on the cross,' that mystery of an unimaginable ultimate cruelty and self-crucifixion of God *for the salvation of man*"?[1] Why was it that the thought of the slave, the thought of ressentiment, pity, and compassion in the end triumphed, if triumph is the very thing this thought denies in its ever deeper flow of self-debasement? How do we explain the paradox of a God who conquers and emerges victorious precisely by surrendering Himself to crucifixion *by His own followers*? Whence the attraction of the negative? These are, of course, questions familiar enough to any reader of Nietzsche. They are rehearsed here as a way of introducing the thread that will guide my reading of Silviano Santiago's *Em Liberdade*, the postdictatorial novel that goes furthest in interrogating the mythology of the negative within Latin American intelligentsia. Santiago's starting point can be read as a spin-off of Nietzsche's reevaluation of all values: what is the process through which the reactive ideology of suffering martyrs becomes the backbone of national imaginaries and identities?

In Nietzsche's genealogy the origin of a concept of moral superiority can always be referred back to a concept of *political* superiority, a difference in a relation of power. Only a posteriori does the positive or negative marking acquire moral connotations, invariably as a result of

one's position within a field of force. Morality is parasitic upon politics and economics, not the reverse. In a most fascinating passage of the
Genealogy (and one that is strikingly suggestive of early Marx), Nietzsche
traces the moral notion of *Schuld* (guilt) back to the material concept of
Schulden (debts), a first step in establishing the genesis of responsibility
and memory itself in the contractual relationship between debtor and
creditor.[2] The memorious are the ones in debt, Nietzsche seems to suggest. Guilt and conscience are memory functions that grow on the soil
of promises made to a creditor. It is thus memory, not forgetting, which
is the reactive, negative category in this dichotomy. In the Nietzschean
topology the superior, victorious force has no need to remember. It is
the slave who is condemned to memory. Remembrance and guilt (the
two seem inseparable in Nietzsche, as though recollection, by its very
nature, already implied the burden of a moral debt) are imposed whenever one faces defeat in a confrontation of forces. The legacy of defeat is
then a memory immersed in guilt, incapable of the active forgetting that
for Nietzsche characterizes all creative, life-affirming power.

In postdictatorial Brazil, where of late the most complicitous forms of
forgetting have thrived to the point of hegemonizing the polis and its
institutions—determining, even legislatively, how the past is to be dealt
with—to speak of any kind of forgetting, however active, can surely lead
to a good deal of misunderstanding. After all, can't literature contribute
to guard national memory, guarantee a mnemonic vigilance that alone
will prevent the past from ever repeating itself? Is the Nietzschean task of
active forgetting still valid when the defeat takes such proportions that it
seems to have destroyed one's very memory (that which, for Nietzsche,
characterizes the defeated as such), thus preventing even the consolidation of any guilt, of any recognition of a debt? How should the task of
active forgetting be posed when all is immersed, not in memory, but in
passive forgetting, the brand of oblivion that ignores itself as such, not
suspecting that it is the product of a powerful repressive operation? How
should one advance the accomplishment of mourning work, the restitution of the ego to its ever precarious, but nevertheless indispensable state
of negotiated equilibrium, when one is prey not to *depressive* mourning
(the refusal to heal and forget), but rather to *triumphant* mourning (the
illusion that one *has* healed and forgotten, maintained through a loud,
festive rhetoric that keeps loss from manifesting itself at the conscious

level)? Can one, in this context, posit the theme of mourning without making any concessions to a negative theology, a self-deprecating absorption in the abject? Can mourning be an affirmative practice? Can mourning be reinvented as positivity? Can one mourn in the manner in which Nietzsche advised us to write, that is, as if learning *how to dance?*

The decline of the Brazilian military regime in the early 1980s coincided with a reevaluation of literary modernism in which critic and novelist Silviano Santiago occupied a prominent position. Santiago insisted on the need to break with a long history of celebratory readings in order to open some fissures in the monolithic, suffocating edifice of modernism. "The question is: how does the aesthetic of the modernist novel generate today, for the young Brazilian writer, ideological and artistic traps from which s/he must free her/himself, so that s/he can cut off once and for all the umbilical cord that binds her/him to the masters of the past?"[3] It is difficult to overestimate the scope of this question. More than the Spanish American avant-gardes, Brazilian modernism for decades determined the horizon in which artistic practices and debates could take place. In order to answer his question, Santiago engaged in four tasks: an examination of modernism that included a reassessment of the canon, a rereading of the literary politics under Vargas's regime, an interrogation of the modern ideal of literacy, and a critique of parody.

1. An important part of this project was the recuperation of authors whose commitment to popular forms had led them to remain partially obscured within the modernist canon. Such was the case, for example, of Lima Barreto, whose aesthetic of *redundancy* was at odds with the modernist emphasis on *ellipsis.* Santiago insisted that Lima Barreto provided stylistic resources invaluable for today's novelist, who faces the thorny question of how to compete with the far more seductive aesthetic of the mass media.[4]

2. Basing himself on sociologist Sérgio Miceli's pioneering work, *Intelectuais e Classe Dirigente no Brasil,*[5] Santiago showed how the destructive, nihilist impulse of the first modernist days would later blur the complicitous alliance joining both left- and right-wing writers of the 1930s with the authoritarian project of Getúlio Vargas's corporative state. The study of this relative blurring of lines between progressive and conservative intellectuals in the 1930s and 1940s laid the groundwork for an investigation into the ways modernism stabilized itself as a canonical tradition.

3. Critically rereading the best modern Brazilian essayists, such as Antonio Candido, Santiago also demonstrated how, despite their emancipatory and popular perspective, they insisted on reducing citizenship to literacy, according to an Enlightenment-based model that ascribed a necessarily liberating content to lettered culture while excluding other forms such as mass-produced images.[6]

4. Finally, in a critical appropriation of what Octavio Paz has labeled "aesthetics of rupture," Santiago reflected on the progressive waning of parody, its congealment as an ultimately formulaic and sterile resource catalogued by the Brazilian modernist tradition as a title of literary maturity. Santiago's critical eye on the tradition of rupture established distance from a modernist legacy in which "everything done against its names and ideals was engulfed by its [modernism's] elastic throat."[7] His disengagement from the tradition of rupture maintained, at the same time, cautious distance from Paz's neoconservative "tradition of analogy" in which "at the very moment of secularization of knowledge the poet assumes the religious discourse of genesis."[8]

Already in 1971, in a key article entitled "The In-Betweenness [*entre-lugar*] of Latin American Discourse," Santiago defies the authority of the deeply seated criticism based on the notions of sources and influences. Taking as a point of departure both the Derridean *rature* (erasure) of the notion of origin, as well as Borges's dismantling of the linearity of literary history in his "Pierre Menard," Santiago argues for a criticism that takes difference, not faithfulness to a model, as its fundamental criterion. Critical fiction is to be conceived as "the use a writer makes of a text or literary technique which already belongs to the public domain . . . and our analysis will complete it with the description of this writer's technique in the moment of aggression against the original model, shaking the foundations that proposed it as the only object of an impossible reproduction."[9] The *"Entre-Lugar* of Latin American Discourse" is a text written with two hands at the same time, keeping at bay both the servile submission to the paradigms of sources and influences as well as a naive nativism that eludes confrontation with cultural dependency through facile affirmations of originality. Contemporary ethnography provided Santiago with invaluable arguments, insofar as it unveiled all the potentially unsettling effects of imitation, initially understood by a colonialist science as a proof of backwardness.[10] It was by negating the positivistic search for

coincidences and debts between model and copy, while making no concessions to the romantic notion of a spontaneous, free process of artistic
creation, that Santiago came to stake out the space of the in-between.
Such in-betweenness is not to be understood as moderation, or a middle
of the road, but rather as an interval, a rift that separates model and copy,
from which every Latin American cultural producer must start: "between
sacrifice and play, prison and transgression, submission to code and aggression, obedience and rebellion, assimilation and expression—there,
in this seemingly empty site, its temple and locus of clandestineness, the
anthropophagous ritual of Latin American literature takes place."[11]

Em Liberdade is undoubtedly the great actualization of this program.
Published in 1981, this novel-diary returns to the past but keeps a watch-
ful eye on the present. Santiago appropriates the voice of 1930s novelist Graciliano Ramos not in order to parody it (which would be a recourse already highly codified in Brazilian modernism, where the parodic
vein was hegemonic) but rather to present a *pastiche* in which no ironic
distance emerged between past and present. Graciliano represented, it
should be noted, the most rigorous, vigilant, and reflective voice in the
northeastern social novel that came to the fore in the 1930s following
the colorful and bombastic avant-garde of 1922. Whereas Jorge Amado
achieved international acclaim with his optimistic and Manichean socialist realism (which would later evolve into a kitsch, picturesque folklorism) and whereas José Lins do Rego presented his sagalike portrayal of
the sugar mills in such a way that all class differences and conflicts dissolved in a universalist ideology of cordiality and sweetness, Graciliano
made of literature an exercise in taking *critique* to its utmost limits. Thus,
in *São Bernardo* he is led beyond the boundaries of realism by making of
the very landowning protagonist the text's narrator, in order to dissect,
without recourse to an all-powerful, omniscient viewpoint, the ways in
which class domination (was) structured (by) syntax itself. By laying bare
the bad faith constitutive of the protagonist's autobiographical enterprise, Graciliano beats socialist realism on its own terrain, for his is a text
in which the very instance of enunciation is placed under the system
of reified social determinations (as opposed to socialist realist novels,
where the narrator's voice is always the voice of truth).[12] Likewise, *Vidas
Secas* relates the plight of northeastern migrant workers not by dema-

gogically endowing them with a class-conscious voice that would parrot the party line à la Jorge Amado but rather by making the text itself progressively fall into the guttural animalization and silence that occurs for the characters. Graciliano's style is unparalleled in Brazilian literature: cultivating a truly Flaubertian rigor and a surgical, minimalist precision, understanding literature as the product of labor and not of inspiration, leaving no political, psychological, or linguistic stone unturned, he was the fiercest enemy that romantic and neoromantic aesthetics ever faced in the country.

First and foremost, *Em Liberdade* engages in a dialogue with Graciliano's *Memórias do Cárcere*, a four-volume tour de force in which Graciliano relates his imprisonment by Getúlio Vargas's populist regime in 1936, with the subsequent ten months spent in a handful of jails across the country. His incarceration took place when Vargas prepared the way for the 1937 coup, which would consolidate until 1945 the fascist-leaning dictatorship known as Estado Novo. At least partially, Graciliano's reluctance in writing his prison memoirs (he only undertook the project a full ten years after being released) derived from his acute awareness of the trap of sentimentalism and victimization, the temptation of abandoning one's critical powers for the immediate narcissistic enjoyment in specular, cathartic identification. *Memórias do Cárcere*'s first chapter is an exemplary exercise in critical vigilance, a confrontation with all the perils that hover over the oppositional intellectual who has been subjected to political persecution. Aware of the risk of an egocentric overflow that could only further mythicize pain and suffering, Gracialiano resists the first person:

> I dislike the first person. All good and well if it is a fictional piece: a more or less imaginary subject speaks. This not being the case, it is bothersome to adopt the irritating little pronoun, albeit all the juggling to avoid it. I excuse myself arguing that it makes narration easier. Besides that I do not wish to go beyond my ordinary size. I will recoil to obscure corners, flee discussions, prudently hide behind those who deserve to patent themselves.[13]

The result of Graciliano's effort is astounding. Throughout *Memórias do Cárcere*, what emerges is a self unmatched in Brazilian memorialism, one that forecloses any specular identification by dissolving all personalism in the brute, coarse facticity of experience. The language is dry, concise, and untainted by any sentimentalist appeal. By not giving in to the ventriloquist temptation of speaking "on behalf" of his prison mates, Graciliano succeeds in portraying the abyss of silence and miscommunication among them, only occasionally bridged by the emergence of a tentative collective subject. *Memórias do Cárcere* thus continues the thrust of Graciliano's earlier work: the unveiling of the links between syntax and political power; the dismantling of the filled, whole, romantic confessional subject; the critique of pity and sentimentalism; the exploration of the representational limits of language, at times taking it to aporetic silence; the critical probing into the intellectual's predicament in a society dominated by contracts of favor and clientelism sponsored by a ubiquitous state.[14]

Silviano Santiago's *Em Liberdade* is, then, a counterpoint to *Memórias do Cárcere*; it pretends to be a diary written by Graciliano from 14 January to 26 March 1937, relating his first impressions as a free man after spending ten months in prison. "Editor" Silviano Santiago's introductory note presents the fictional trajectory of the unpublished manuscript, in a carefully planned strategy of verisimilitude: physical descriptions of the original with Graciliano's personal corrections, speculations on the exact moment when he might have written it, mention of his desire that twenty-five years pass after his death before the text should come to light, and even his last, Kafkian wish to have the diary burned. The fundamental rhetorical work in *Em Liberdade* is performed around the textual borders. Only on the cover of the book (which reads, "a fiction by Silviano Santiago") is the fabricated narrative about the text's origin disavowed. Once on the first page, the reader is confronted with a rigorously drawn, credible, verisimilar fictional space. Such rigor is that of a pastiche that assumes and endorses the past:

> I was not in any way critiquing Graciliano Ramos's style, which in my view is the best in modernism. . . . I wanted to activate G. Ramos's style, opting for other forms of transgression; I could have done a parody of him, but I did something that his family obviously only accepted with a good deal of difficulty, which was to assume his style and, even worse, his self. . . . This is one of the traces of the post-

modern, this capacity not of confronting Graciliano Ramos through parody, but of defining who is the author, what is the style you want to supplement. . . . Parody is more and more rupture, while pastiche is more and more imitation, which however generates forms of transgression that are not the canonical ones of parody.[15]

Silviano Santiago, editor of *Glossário de Derrida*,[16] does not use the word *supplement* innocently here. Santiago's diary-novel demands from the critic a reflection that links the problem of *signature* with that of *historical repetition*. His appropriation of Graciliano's voice is mirrored en abyme in the novel, when Graciliano conceives of a narrative in which he would speak through the self of eighteenth-century poet Cláudio Manuel da Costa. This piece, in its turn, displays several analogies between Cláudio Manuel's death in prison, after the republican rebellion in Minas Gerais in 1792, and the assassination of reporter Wladimir Herzog in his cell by the military dictatorship in 1975, in a pattern where the circulation of signatures uncovers a certain iterative element in Brazilian history. The uncovering of this iteration, then, must go hand in hand with the topological mapping of these various signatures, which will, in its turn, allow for a return to the Nietzschean question of active forgetting posed at the beginning of this chapter.

The paradox of all signatures lies in the tension between iterability and singularity. That is, in order to function like a signature at all, the written trace thus codified must be infinitely repeatable, liable to being brought to presence yet once again. Such a return to presence must always preserve a fundamental mark of identity with all its previous occurrences; it must indeed be the *memory* of them, or it will not be a signature at all. The first law to which a signature has to submit is, therefore, the law of iterability. However, a signature must of necessity be irreducibly singular as well, not only in relation to all other traces, but also in respect to all of its previous occurrences. A signature is an unrepeatable event that nevertheless brings within itself the imperative need for repetition. Seemingly complete in itself, a signature always demands a return (or at least the possibility of a return), for its very being coalesces in the paradox of a singular iteration, a unique event that nevertheless calls for a supplement. While marking a "having-been present in a past now,"[17] a signature interpellates its future by circumscribing the space where a new repetition can take place. This repetition will, in its turn, significantly alter that which it repeats.

Santiago's *Em Liberdade* implies that signatures demand restitution: a signature is also a *legacy*, all the more Graciliano's, which is itself a powerful reflection on what a legacy is. A legacy is not taken here to be a given, self-identical content that one could choose to receive or not. A legacy is a *task*, one that delimits the field in which it will be confronted.[18] Santiago's reply to this challenge in *Em Liberdade* is the repetition of the signature of he who most consistently explored what a signature is. But what is meant by "repetition" in a pastiche such as Santiago's? How is repetition a response to the task of accepting a legacy? One can begin to formulate an answer by recalling that a repetition, unlike a relationship of identity, can only involve something singular, without any possible equivalent. As opposed to identity or equality, which presuppose mutual interchangeability between terms (as in a mathematical equation, where the equal sign stands precisely for such possibility of substitution), a repetition is the re-turn of something that cannot be replaced.[19] Although seemingly oxymoronic, the phrase *differential repetition*, often used to define the structure of the pastiche, is in fact redundant. A repetition only takes place within difference: it necessarily differentiates itself from itself. To give an already classic example: Pierre Menard, by repeating Cervantes's text to the letter, forces Cervantes to differentiate himself from himself, interrupts the identity of Cervantes's signature with itself. "The most exact, the most strict repetition has as its correlate the maximum of difference."[20] The condition of possibility for the repetition of Graciliano Ramos's signature in *Em Liberdade* is, then, the self-differentation of this signature within the repetitive gesture. A pastiche is not a parody in the same way that a repetition is not an identity or that a difference is not a contradiction. The emblem of the rift between parody and pastiche is offered again by Pierre Menard: "he did not want to compose another *Quixote*—which is easy—but rather *the Quixote itself.*"[21] To insist on Borges's puzzling analogy, it might be argued that Santiago's project in *Em Liberdade* is not to construct "another" Graciliano, a parodic, caricaturesque, "updated" image of the modernist writer but rather to repeat Graciliano, letting the untimely eruption of his 1930s Portuguese interrupt and estrange the present. This example supports the deconstructive claim, endorsed in this study, that repetition modifies that which it repeats.

I will attempt to clarify these remarks by examining the mutual allegorizations between Santiago and Graciliano Ramos (and, within the diary, among Graciliano, Cláudio Manuel da Costa, and Wladimir Herzog). Santiago's Graciliano writes his diary in 1936, on the eve of a populist dictatorship with strong fascist overtones. Having already been jailed by the same regime in its "democratic" phase, thus living political closure from the standpoint of its consequences, he is, in the predictatorship, a postdictatorship intellectual. Santiago, on the other hand, writes in the early 1980s, during the dismantling of a twenty-year-long military rule, in a moment when the literary field was dominated by cathartic and confessional forms of testimonialism. The historical locations of Santiago and of his character Graciliano allegorize each other. Facing a modernist tradition long domesticated and canonized, where even the legacy of a text as radical as *Memórias do Cárcere* had been appended to a rather naive testimonialism, Santiago opts not for discarding this tradition but for searching within it the differential element that can activate repetition. The choice of Graciliano Ramos is due to his singularity within Brazilian modernism, that is, his suspicion of all nationalist fables, all social ventriloquism, and all triumphalism, and his uncompromising attitude vis-à-vis all sentimentalism, folklorism, or naturalism. *Em Liberdade* attempts to blast *Memórias do Cárcere* out of the conformism of this tradition. In this sense *Em Liberdade* is the *unconscious* of *Memórias do Cárcere*, the knowledge of the Brazilian literary tradition's failure to incorporate this unconscious without repressing it. *Em Liberdade*, being the postprison journal, is the diary that *Memórias do Cácere* could not be. The originality of *Em Liberdade* lies in the fact that this gesture, which structures the novel and makes it possible, is itself replicated, repeated within the text in several layers of meaning. As I show later, the reflection on repetition is the diary's motor, the force that moves Graciliano, the character, to write. His story on Cláudio Manuel da Costa replicates *Em Liberdade*'s relationship with *Memórias do Cárcere*, while at the same time interpellating the present (Santiago's present, the late 1970s) through a series of coincidences between Cláudio Manuel and Wladimir Herzog, the journalist murdered in his cell by the Brazilian military in 1975.

Em Liberdade deliberately comes across as a disappointing, anticlimactic text. The pious imaginary of martyrdom, so ingrained in the Latin American Left, anxiously awaits narratives of tortures and victimization, but who cares about the diary of a writer "in freedom"?

> Everybody demands—and this is unanimous—that I write my prison memoirs. Nobody asks me for the notes I am jotting down of my juggling with freedom.
>
> You son of a bitch. I won't fall into your trap. I am not giving you the book you demand from me.
>
> In exchange, I am giving you what you don't want. I am working with your disappointment. It is the precious raw material for this diary.[22]

The aporias confronted by Graciliano in the novel revolve around a thorny question posed to the oppositional intellectual: how and why to keep writing when there is an absence of any significant antihege-monic social practice, when one confronts isolation and political defeat, and above all, when one opts not to compromise with the widespread complacent desire to see one's life narrated in the language of suffering and resentment: "I wonder if [the reader] is only interested in the bleak side of a life" (*EL* 128). Graciliano directs his rage against the mystique of pain within the Left in a time when *integralismo*, the Brazilian version of fascism, gained political ground by maintaining precisely the same rhetoric.[23] One of *Em Liberdade*'s main axes is the dismantling of this aura. "The language of suffering is less original than one thinks; hence its all-inclusiveness. Each and all believe themselves identical in misery, sorrow and pain, i.e. all of them disgraced; but the one telling the story is always the most unfortunate of all mortals" (*EL* 29).

What links Graciliano Ramos and Silviano Santiago is the perception of a fundamental peril for the oppositional intellectual: to allow politics to be written with religious metaphors. "All political struggles relying on resentment and prison lead to nothing, at best to an ideology of cru-cified martyrs, ever-failed heroes of the cause" (*EL* 59). The redemptive conception of politics would lead, the novel seems to suggest, to a dis-astrous identification between *politicizing literature* and *substituting literature for politics* as such. *Em Liberdade* is also a critique of such confusion, under-stood as the critique of a tradition that manifested itself in an economist-determinist version in the 1930s, but with ramifications in other versions of naturalism, be they biologistic, as in the nineteenth century, or communicational-informational, as in the 1970s. Note the coincidence between the negative mystique attacked by Graciliano in the 1930s and the heroic-sacrificial rhetoric of the romance-reportagem I analyzed in chapter 2.[24]

The flip side of the imaginary of martyrdom is the ideology of cordiality, represented in the novel by writer José Lins do Rego, who hosts Graciliano and his wife, Heloísa, when the former is released from prison. For readers of the Brazilian northeastern novel of the 1930s it is well known how Lins do Rego's work, with its idyllic, romanticized, and nostalgic representation of the sugar mills (where class inequalities are dissolved within an assumed substratum of human goodness), stands in direct opposition to Graciliano's implacably critical fiction. Santiago explores this opposition to set up what will be one of the novel's guiding threads, the relation between past and present:

> See the case of Lins do Rego's four published novels. In taking stock of the sugarcane latifundium's past glory and present decadence, I notice in the novelist (and not only in the narrator) such emotional involvement with the portrayed material that pride and sadness are the dominant tones, respectively, for the pages of glory and the pages of decadence. The glorious days fill the novelist with pride; the decadent days make style somber. The social and economic disqualification of today's characters never reaches the point of "smearing" their ancestors. Present decadence does not come from the past; it is an exclusive offspring of today's men. How dare you touch the giants of the past. It would be a sacrilege. Past and present become stationary areas in fiction. (118)

In Lins do Rego's fiction the past is absolved from present decadence because the past is retrospectively thought of as the home of harmony, the dissolution of which alone explains present disgrace. Lins do Rego wants to write historical fiction that builds on the good old days, when in fact, Graciliano argues, the only radical accounts of the past are the ones that start from the *bad new days*. It is not enough for Graciliano, in order to deconstruct Lins do Rego's philosophy of history, to say that for the poor the past was not so great. This objection is valid, and it unveils Lins do Rego's class commitments, but it still remains insufficient if one wants to critique the foundations of his conception of history. There is a reason why it is the *past* that is described as good and happy, and Graciliano finds it in the link, retrospectively posited as broken, that allows Lins do Rego to think of the present as a *fall*. Graciliano is suspicious of this move because by postulating the past as free from all responsibility for present disgrace, it implicitly frees the present from all responsibility toward *past disgrace*. In other words, it prevents any possible embrace of the legacy left by one's enslaved ancestors. Graciliano's targets in the diary will then be twofold: on the one hand, an ideology of martyrdom that sees in past suffering an a priori transcendental redemption of the present, and on the other, an ideology of cordiality that brackets all past suffering in order to posit the bygone as the embodiment of human goodness, the fall from which would then alone explain present misery.

Santiago's portrayal of Lins do Rego frames the theme of *favor* in the diary. Graciliano, penniless and out of a job, with a large family to support and no short-term economic prospects, finds himself in the uncomfortable position of having to accept his friend's favors while at the same time dismantling the ideology of favor in his diary. To that it must be added Lins do Rego's adroit adaptation to Rio, where he was already well established in literary circles, in comparison with Graciliano's awkward, almost provincial insecurity in a milieu where sociability was a key requisite for success. From the point of view of Lins do Rego, a fan of soccer and carnival, a prototype of good intentions and conviviality, Graciliano is simply torturing himself unnecessarily. During their meals the tension mounts between Graciliano and Heloísa's uncompromising attitude vis-à-vis the myths of Brazilianness underlying Vargas's regime and Lins do Rego's wholesale belief in such myths, as well as his impatience with any peace-disrupting ideological dispute. It is Heloísa, more than Graciliano, who takes a clear stand against the ideology of cordiality. The climax occurs at a dinner, after Graciliano had reluctantly visited the Ministry of Education in search of information about a state-sponsored award for a children's literature book. Graciliano had walked by the minister and refused his effusive greeting, only to be later reproached by Lins do Rego:

> "How can you do this, to behave like a kid in front of a state minister! . . . I don't mean to say you should have behaved like an adult. Far from that. You should have acted like a *moleque* [naughty boy].

By gravely greeting the minister the former political prisoner would have become the embodiment of the Brazilian naughty boy. With irony and a smile. . . . Graça, you need to understand that this country is a total mess. Nobody here stays on their feet with a rigorous ethic. It's always a shameful, petty, and deceiving game of interests. In the national hodgepodge any logical and coherent attitude becomes inappropriate. Instead of benefiting from it, the correct person ends up being the only clown in the nation's general carnival. . . . The true clown is not the moleque or the *malandro* [rogue]. They are the smart, clever guys who can take advantage of the most adverse situations. The true clown is the correct man, who makes relationships rough, and makes it difficult to find easy solutions for every day's little problems.

Heloísa couldn't take it anymore and exploded:

—"It is by thinking like this that we go on accepting and justifying all dictatorships. Now it's man's natural selfishness, then it's Brazilian *malícia* [sagacity], then it's the so-called typical Brazilian democracy, where everyone is in charge because no one is in charge. And we keep rolling arguments in favor of the fascists, while they remain silent and thank us. . . . The country may be a mess, but that repression works in the right direction I have no doubt. . . . This Brazilian hodgepodge is terrible. It's terrible, not because a former political prisoner can speak cordially to a minister, but because a minister can send to jail someone with whom he talks for no reason other than the ones that may be going through his lunatic mind. Gráci acted correctly. Capanema didn't deserve his greeting. If people don't start staking out the differences, we'll all fall in the trap of the dictatorship, which is just around the corner, by the way. . . . No one is in charge in this country, right. But when an opposition group wants to take charge, you see arrest orders, prisoners are tortured and held incommunicable. You call that *molecagem* [naughtiness], Zé Lins. That's simplifying too much. If you had gone through half of what Gráci went through, you'd see that naughtiness is not the most appropriate word." (*EL* 131–33)

The passage shows the two irreducibly opposing views of Brazil that separate Lins do Rego from Graciliano and Heloísa. The argument, however, does not take place on a neutral field but in a context where the latter enjoy (and need) the former's favors and hospitality. In this sense the dinner dispute is a microcosm of the relationship that Graciliano is forced to entertain with the Brazilian state after he is released from prison. Personal relations replicate one's relationship with the state. The only difference is that after a few weeks Graciliano and Heloísa can dispense with Lins do Rego's generosity and (barely) stand on their feet by getting a room in a boardinghouse. As for the intellectual-state relationship, things turn out to be more complicated. Having to search for state-sponsored literary contests, clearly seeing what is at stake in the state's assuming responsibility for artistic patronage, Graciliano is led to grapple with the dialectic of favor throughout the diary:

> The only option for the intellectual in Brazil is to become a public employee, living reality in two halves, only grasping the truth by closing one eye. This condition is most castrating and tragic, because it leads one to be complicit with the powers that be. If the legislature and the judiciary are already servants of the Catete [presidential house at the time], what will happen to our thinkers, tied to the seductive machinery of the Ministry of Education and Health?
>
> They will write books in their free time. They will never be professionals of writing. They will spend the night reading and writing, intoxicating themselves with coffee and cigarettes, taking notes and correcting, typing up the originals. They'll write books that will be read by very reduced sections of the population, the few who have extra money to buy them. Or they won't be read at all: with signed dedications, they will serve as ornaments for five or six gigantic private libraries. (*EL* 36–37)

His reflections bear witness to a fundamental singularity of the modernization of the Brazilian literary field: professionalization is largely carried out through regulative and always interested state interventions, but instead of doing away with the premodern structure of favor, professionalization builds upon it. The mercantilization of intellectual labor does not eliminate a certain personalized patronage that operates in spite of, and in many instances in contradiction with, the impersonal logic of the market: "Professionalism splits man in half by performing a deep cut between the two sides. Professionalism gives him a home, food and well-being; it deprives him of sleep, tranquillity and good conscience. They're inimical halves, with no possibility of peace, since they're contradictory" (*EL* 181). As Roberto Schwarz makes clear with the notion of "misplaced ideas,"[25] capitalist market logic in Brazil does not set itself up in opposition to, but rather superimposes itself on, the rule of favor and friendship. Graciliano's critique of favor and cordiality must also entail a correlative critique of a professionalization that remains a tributary of patronage. In this sense each of the diary's two halves (the first from 01/14 to 02/14 and the second from 02/15 to 03/26) shows a predominance of one of the two themes. While living with Lins do Rego, Graciliano's entries in his diary obsessively revolve around the binds linking favor with the ideologies of cordiality and martyrdom;[26] after his move to a pension in the Catete neighborhood, Graciliano's diary is itself affected by the need to earn a living and thus tends to tackle more directly the shortcomings of the professionalization and autonomization of intellectual labor in Brazil. The two halves can, therefore, be taken as allegorical of the duplicity of Brazilian capitalism: a modern, secular, forward-looking enterprise that nevertheless can only establish itself by reinforcing a premodern clientelism.

It is within the framework of professionalization that *Em Liberdade* poses the question of the old modernist notion of *style*. Observing the widespread employment of writers in mass-circulation newspapers, Graciliano notes:

> They sit at the typewriter and in a few minutes have the requested report. . . . They know how to execute a specific task, but have reached the point of not feeling the need to do anything other than work imposed by someone else. . . .
>
> These are intellectuals who have lost the complex notion of personal style. They accept doing the job in the style of the communication medium that employs them. . . . I notice that there is something susceptible to definition independently of the subject who writes: the "journalistic style." It is not the style of journalist X or Y, but that of the newspaper, that is, the communication medium in itself. (*EL* 179)

The consequences of professionalism thus go beyond the writer's economic dependency upon corporate mass media; professionalism unleashes an assault upon signature itself. The vicarious identity of everything with everything else (all articles in a paper look alike; each paper seems identical to all the others) dissolves the singular iteration that characterizes signature. The technical is that realm where tendentially all signatures dissolve. For Graciliano this implies more than simply perceiving how limited his chances of economic survival are; it begins to narrow his options down to two: complicity or failure. The diary, and most of all the story on Cláudio Manuel that closes it, represent Graciliano's attempt to straddle these two poles. The irony here is that it is up to Graciliano Ramos, author of the most unmistakable style in modern Brazilian literature, to take stock of the definitive decadence of style. While Graciliano cannot make a reactionary, nostalgic critique of professionalism (the one founded on the values of the ineffable, the ethereal, the unique genius, inspiration, etc.), neither can he accept the terms in which professionalization has been carried through, completely controlled by monopolies, with virtually no space for dissent. The poles of complicity or failure begin to occupy the entire horizon of choices: "Rereading the paragraphs above, I realize that by writing I am digging my own future abyss. From this fall I will not be saved. . . . I feed myself in order to be the enemy's future dish" (EL 180–82). By the time Graciliano assesses his trajectory, shortly before beginning the story on Cláudio Manuel, his refusal to be an accomplice has decided matters for him:

> I am:
>> a journalist who doesn't work in a newsroom;
>> a novelist who doesn't go beyond the first edition;
>> a politician aborted in jail;
>> a single parent living in a pension;
>> a jobless worker.
> I won't continue with the list not to get even more depressed. (EL 199)

This acceptance of defeat in the arena of professionalism plays a major role in propelling Graciliano out of lethargy to write his exemplary story on Cláudio Manuel. It is by accepting defeat that Graciliano is led out of paralysis. It might still be worthwhile to underscore that the acceptance of defeat, the embrace of failure, has nothing to do with a self-indulgent masochistic celebration. Far from celebrating one's misery, the embrace of failure implies a recognition of the real conditions of intellectual production in the market, the only really radical response to the narcotic belief in progress. It is by accepting the *inheritance* of defeat that one opens oneself up to reading in each document of culture the barbarism that made it possible. Graciliano, having thought through the defeat of the forces that could have blocked Vargas's cryptofascist coup, the defeat of literature at the hands of corporate information industry, and the defeat of the utopia of modernist experimentation at the hands of musealization and canonization (in other words, the defeat of signature, of the poetical under the technical), decides to revisit the role of Cláudio Manuel da Costa in the Inconfidência Mineira. In the eighteenth-century republican revolt in Minas Gerais he sees a source of restitutive energy, a barely discernible remembrance dimly flashing underneath the pile of wreckage we call history. How is one to distinguish a singular interruption in the middle of catastrophes and defeats that pile up as if entirely within the identical? It is by facing this problem that he overcomes the anguish felt before the blank page and conceives his first literary project after prison.

Even before I propose an analysis of the tale, the reader may have noticed that Graciliano's relation to Cláudio Manuel replicates Silviano Santiago's relation to Graciliano Ramos. In that sense the story offers a key to the entire novel and brings us back to the theme of repetition. Graciliano Ramos rewrites Cláudio Manuel da Costa as an alter ego of Silviano Santiago rewriting Graciliano. Cláudio Manuel too was faced with the question of how to walk the fine line between servile compromise and individualistic voluntarism. For a critical intellectual, within a civil society barely organized independently of the state, there is only minimal room to maneuver between these two pseudoalternatives. *Em Liberdade* sets out to introduce pastiche within this politicostrategic problem. For the fiction writer pastiche opens the possibility of impersonal citation, the improper appropriation of proper names, and the narration of one's own story as if it belonged to another: "there has to be some identification with Cláudio, some sort of empathy that allows me to write his life as if it were mine, mine as if it were his. *It is a dangerous project, because people grant great value to the limits of the individual*" (EL 209). It is necessary to differentiate Graciliano's use of *empathy* here from the paralyzing *Einfühlung* of historicism, which attempts to create the illusion that one "really is" in the past, telling it as it "really happened" in order to excuse it, to find a justification for it. Graciliano's is, rather, a gesture that drags the past out of its continuum and makes it interpellate the present. While parodic irony condescendingly distances the past (with its implicit ideology that "now we've really got it," "we have now corrected the mistakes of the past"), pastiche allows the present to recognize itself in the past and recharge the past with the image of the now. Let us clarify this claim with an analysis of the story.

The official version of the late-eighteenth-century republican revolt in Minas Gerais is well known. Following an aborted insurrection against the Portuguese crown carried out both by the local elite and by the emerging middle-class intelligentsia, Cláudio Manuel supposedly committed suicide in jail, regretting his "betrayal" of his partners in the insurrection (his public call to arms, made from prison, directed at the elite members of the revolt). Meanwhile, Tiradentes, presented as a good-willed martyr, tropical embodiment of the crucified, supposedly took over the responsibility and offered his body to be hung and dismembered. Graciliano has a dream in which Cláudio Manuel is hung by a regional authority who was until then allied with the rebellion and now backed off in fear of being implicated by Cláudio's report. In Santiago's rereading of the Inconfidência Mineira, Cláudio's "betrayal" appears as a deliberate strategy to force the local ruling classes to stand by their republican commitment. In a somewhat proto-Brechtian move, "Cláudio tries and incriminates his own executioners ([state governor] Visconde de Barbacena in particular), so as not to grant them any special innocence and force them to assume the cause" (*EL* 204). Facing such risks, what was left for the tentative local elite was the elimination of Cláudio Manuel. In this alternative version, Tiradentes's gesture of assuming all responsibility gains a different meaning. More than a benevolent hero, Tiradentes turns out to be an accomplice of the Portuguese monarchy; by offering himself as the only subversive plotter, he provided them with the strength to pull out the repressive knockout punch. The rebellion could now be identified as the work of "a few" delinquents alien to the "people" of Minas Gerais. Tiradentes's heroism broke the political alliance that sustained the revolt: "didn't he act in conformity with the crown's design, more interested in sacrificing a scapegoat . . . ?" (*EL* 204). After his dream, Graciliano begins the research that would provide the basis for the story.

Graciliano conceives of a tale in which Cláudio's strategy appears as a deliberate critique of secrecy. Far from "betraying" elite members of the insurrection, at any rate already known by the Portuguese, Cláudio forces them to make their political decision *public* and thus be held accountable within civil society. Whereas members of the state elite were ready to negotiate with the Crown behind closed doors a solution that exemplarily punished a few middle-class intellectuals, Cláudio's decision answered the need for escaping both voluntarism and subservience. By publicly denouncing the earlier republican commitment of a bureaucracy now ready to back off, Cláudio attempted to bypass both the individual martyrdom of the sacrificial scapegoat—and therefore escape the heroicization of politics—and at the same time the equally undesirable strategy of negotiating a few crumbs in exchange for renouncing the revolutionary project. The former ends up being the image of the Inconfidência Mineira passed down by a narcotic historiography, crystallized in Tiradentes, invariably represented as Christlike figure—"the martyr swiftly climbed the twenty steps, without hesitating for a single moment: he only had eyes and heart for the Crucifix" (*EL* 203), reads a passage of a history manual quoted critically by Graciliano as he prepares the story. Tiradentes's Calvary is again a variant on the silencing of defeat, a way of eluding it *as defeat,* that is, of imaginarily transforming it into a victory in order to cushion it into a narrative according to which "something has been gained," "a lesson has been learned," and so forth. Martyrdom has been the most successful imaginary compensation for the incapacity or unwillingness to come to terms with defeat in Brazilian history: "Martyrdom is the noble category preferred by traditional historians, who see in it the objective measure of 'the great men of the past.' In possession of it they end up writing a religious history of man" (*EL* 203).

Brazil, unlike Spanish American nations, has no heroes of independence. Because Brazilian independence was not the product of a popular war, but rather a negotiation between a colonial elite and a Portuguese crown already barely distinguishable from one another (the latter had set roots in Brazil in 1808 fleeing from the Napoleonic Wars), it has been mostly up to Tiradentes to fill the heroic gap in the national imaginary. Undoing the myth of Tiradentes in Brazil is a bit like deconstructing San Martín in Argentina, or Bolívar in Venezuela, or yet Thomas Jefferson in the United States. The fundamental difference is that Tiradentes was the leader (or was retrospectively construed as such) of a *failed* rebellion. Whereas in Spanish America fables of national identity rest on victorious, macho military leaders whose only defeat is posthumous, located in their successors' implementation of their *legacy,* in Brazil the very legacy of independence is defeat itself, emblematized in the meaninglessness of 7 September for popular projects in the country. The defeat is then cushioned in the pacifying ideology of martyrdom; that is, imaginarily transformed into a victory, in a sense not unlike—in the Nietzschean analysis—Christianity, which paradoxically emerges victorious exactly by submitting unconditionally to defeat, by taking a morbid pleasure in it. The riddle of Tiradentes resembles the riddle of Christ in that both are figures who install a new value system by offering themselves as sacrificial scapegoats—this being, to be sure, their narcissistic trip.

What separates the sacrificial scapegoat from the victorious hero is, in a sense, the secret itself. Tiradentes holds the secret of the insurrection before his executioners by refusing to name names, and Christ holds the secret of his divinity by refusing the temptation of performing the public miracle that would prove it. The defeated thus reveal themselves victorious by holding a secret that contains the key to their defeat. This secret is what enables history to be reconstructed in such a manner that the defeat appears, retrospectively, as that which the defeated were in fact searching for all along. Could this not be taken to be the meaning of the Christian axiom that Jesus came down to earth *in order to* be crucified? Doesn't the official version of the Inconfidência Mineira tell us, surreptitiously, that the revolt's ultimate goal was not to achieve national independence but rather to offer the image of a martyr decapitated and dismembered, passing down to posterity this tremendous burden of guilt?

Graciliano's story on Cláudio Manuel unveils the roots of the politics of the secret, which is, after all, nothing but politics understood as conspiracy. Here one also needs to attend to the iterative element that runs through Brazilian history: In 1792, a local elite broke the republican alliance it had established with other social classes en route to solving its differences with the crown without touching on the structure of production. Graciliano writes in 1937, two years after an already Stalinized Communist Party (CP), which had been defending the quietist theory of "socialism in one country," attempted to regain some popular legitimacy with the aborted putschist, voluntarist, insurrection later known as Intentona Comunista (which, by the way, provided Vargas with the perfect excuse for repressive action). In the third turn of the spin, Santiago writes in the late 1970s, less than a decade after several left-wing groups, disillusioned with the CP's conciliatory politics, threw themselves into the tiger's mouth, in a guerrilla war completely deprived of popular support or political project. Here repetition takes the gregarious form of the eternal return of the same: "What a long and fastidious monologue our History is! The same facts repeated to exhaustion" (*EL* 34). And Graciliano reiterates, "historical truth imposes itself among us by fatigue" (*EL* 220).

The perception of an unbearable cycle of repetition—Portuguese monarchy, repressive populism, and military dictatorship—might corroborate a circular, cyclical vision of history, according to which what returns is nothing but the undifferentiated iteration of the same in its identity with itself. But Graciliano's story on Cláudio Manuel can be taken precisely as his way of breaching this understanding of historical repetition, of interrupting its almost self-evident, rounded coherence. What if, Graciliano seems to be asking, the identical that returns constituted itself exactly by obviating something untimely, something radically foreign and irretrievable by the present, which is however the present's very condition of possibility? What if each turn of the spin carried within itself its wholly other, buried underneath, repressed, yet preventing repetition from congealing into a simple cyclical iteration of the same, referring that repetition to a future moment in which it might be redeemed? The formulation I can offer for this foreign, untimely element is the following: *the untimely is that which has failed in history, but without which no history as such could have been constituted.*[27]

An emblem of this untimely element comes into being in Graciliano's allegorical dream, where he *is* Cláudio Manuel, spending in jail what would be his last night alive. The image of himself in the dream juxtaposes objects from the eighteenth century—now he holds a quill under candlelight—with modern ones—now he uses a pen and wears factory overalls. Sitting in front of him in the cell is Death itself, whom he attempts to entertain with some magic tricks. Clumsily handling a strip of cloth taken from his overalls, he desperately tries to induce laughter or applause in Death, to no avail. Death eventually gets up, walks toward him, picks up the torn pieces of a sheet of paper where the poet had scribbled "it is tiresome to wait," puts them together, forces him to sign it, produces a cloth belt, and makes a tight knot with it, showing the terrified poet that it could be tied to one of the window bars. He runs and hides behind the chair, which Death handily kicks away before grabbing his neck with both hands. As Death takes off the hood, Graciliano/Cláudio sees the rosy and smiling face of a Portuguese official.

Most obviously, the dream provides Graciliano with the hypothesis that the accepted version of Cláudio Manuel's death, given as a suicide, might be a hoax, and that he was in fact murdered in his cell by a government official threatened by Cláudio's strategy. The dream makes the past speak to the present when the eighteenth century appears to Graciliano as an allegory of his own predicament: his tiny pension room, where he attempts to elude death, is displaced and condensed in the cell where Cláudio Manuel spent his last days. The pension becomes a cell in the same way that his modern pen becomes Cláudio's quill. Like his eighteenth-century alter ego, Graciliano *waits*, immobilized by a turn of events that seems to close all political doors. The dream seems to extract its meaning from processes of condensation and displacement between the eighteenth century and the 1930s and from mutual allegorizations between Graciliano and Cláudio Manuel.

However, it only acquires its full force once we attend to several elements that set the text in the present in which *Santiago* is writing: the last days of the military dictatorship in Brazil. Cláudio's cloth belt, his garment, his tearing up a piece of paper, the chair, his coerced signature under a confession, Death's suggestion that the belt was long enough to hang him from a window bar (and thus dissimulate the strangling): all these pieces are taken directly from the farce set up by the military regime to justify the death of journalist Wladimir Herzog under torture in 1975. After his death the military released a note stating that Herzog, on the day of his imprisonment, "had been found" hanging from the "cloth belt he had been wearing" (which was something that prisoners, of course, were never given), tied to a window bar (which, in the photographs later released by the military, was shown to leave the other end of the belt standing at five feet, four inches, being thus at a lower level than Herzog's head, this meaning that in order to hang himself he would have awkwardly to bend his knees up toward his chest, when he had a chair and several higher bars at his disposal). In order to support their claims the military and complicitous doctors produced a fraudulent autopsy and the photographs, where Herzog appears in the most unconvincing suicide scene imaginable, with a chair and several torn pieces of paper on the floor (a sheet upon which, it was later discovered, Herzog had been forced to write a confession that he subsequently tore up, to the ire of his torturers).

Among the several Brazilians who died under torture, Herzog's case was unique because his wife and friends, human rights activists, and the journalists' union succeeded in proving in court, three years later, that Herzog had not hung himself but had been killed in his cell, subsequently strangled (to give the impression of death by asphyxia), and tied to one of the window bars. During the 1978 hearings several former prisoners testified not only to having heard Herzog's cries but also to having been tortured themselves; meanwhile army officials, torturers, and complicitous doctors contradicted not only each other but also their own earlier statements in the 1975 fake autopsy. The case was also exemplary because it generated a considerable amount of popular protest, including a massive ecumenical ceremony a week after Herzog's death, in which Father Evaristo Arns (one of the key leaders in the struggle for human rights in Brazil) and other religious figures led several thousand people to São Paulo's Praça da Sé, in a key episode in undermining the legitimacy of the military regime.[28]

The possibilities for mutual allegorizations between Graciliano's present (his oppositional stance against a repressive populist regime in 1937), his past (Cláudio Manuel's struggle against the Portuguese Crown in 1789), and his future (Herzog tortured and killed by the military in 1975) are manifold. By thinking his present and estranging himself from it, Graciliano dreams of the past. He dreams that he *is* the past. However, the past appears to him in the future's garment. History cannot be the place where he wakes up from the nightmare, because history is itself the nightmare. He dreams in order to wake up *to* the nightmare, his dreaming is itself the doorway to the nightmare, otherwise invisible through the foggy curtains of a reality that is, in fact, the only truly escapist dream. Parodying Joyce, one could say that Graciliano dreams not in order to wake from the nightmare of history but in order to enter it. But does Herzog appear to him, back from the future, as it were, to remind him to suspect the official version of Cláudio Manuel's death? Or does Cláudio Manuel rise from the dead to point out to him that he is discovering not only the past but also the future of his country? There is no deciding between these two alternatives, because the story deliberately prevents us from choosing whether the past is trying to awaken the present to the horrors of the future, or if the future, like the Benjaminian angel of history, is trying to come back and redeem the catastrophes of the past. Each present is here traversed by a fundamental discord with itself. Each anachronism, each temporal lack of coincidence in Graciliano's dream, is an index referring time to the need for redemption. Graciliano learns that the fate of the past will be played once again in the future. The meaning of "future" becomes for him just that: the arena where the dead will get another chance to be redeemed. And it is this redemption, conceived under the sign of the untimely, not the eternalized present of martyrs and heroes of the negative, that Graciliano pursues in writing the story.

In order to give another example of how the untimely operates in the triadic edifice composed by Cláudio Manuel, Graciliano, and Herzog, it may suffice to quote the history manual consulted by Graciliano while preparing the story. Alluding to Cláudio Manuel's "suicide," the manual affirms that "everything induces to believe that he was led to this crazed gesture by becoming conscious of his situation and regretting his *militância* [activism]" (*EL* 205). The word *militância*, anachronistic in eighteenth-century Portuguese, suggests that something else may be at stake. Indeed, the passage is a *literal* quote of the note released on 25 October 1975 in which the DOI-CODI (section of the Brazilian army in charge of political repression in the 1970s) unabashedly attempts to disclaim its responsibility for Herzog's death.[29] Again, the novel creates the uncanny feeling that the past is *citing* the future, in both senses of the verb: quoting it but at the same time summoning it to appear in court to be judged. The past's anachronistic quoting of the future becomes a way of interrogating it. This is another unsettling effect of the novel, for it does not produce the familiar feeling that the present (or the future) is quoting/judging the past, but the discomfiting sensation that the past—the dead—is endowed with the prerogative to judge the future. For if a fake explanation of a contemporary killing can serve as a fake explanation of an eighteenth-century death—and go relatively unnoticed in a contemporary novel—then it may be reasonable to conclude that the pattern of repetition in history has been naturalized to the extent that one does, indeed, perceive repetition as the inexorable, inevitable, eternal return of the same. The untimely, the anachronistic, is, then, in *Em Liberdade*, the crucial moment in which such naturalization is exposed, unveiled, and critiqued.

It would, therefore, be a mistake to take the iterative pattern in *Em Liberdade* as evidence that the novel endorses a cyclical, circular conception of historical repetition. If it submits history to the vertigo of the eternal return—in such a way that *history itself emerges as a product of iteration*—it does so by dissociating the notion of return from those of the cycle, the circle, the saga. What is at stake is thus not so much a refusal of the Nietzschean concept but of a certain understanding of it.[30] For it is not a matter of seeing the past reproduced in its identity and equality with a present that is nothing but the past's compulsive repetition. It is rather a question of receiving from an open future—from what Benjamin called an index to redemption, the narrow door through which the Messiah might enter (enacted in *Em Liberdade* by the irruption of 1975 into 1937 when 1937 dreamt of 1792)—the impact that makes the past repeat itself *as past* in the present, that is, that makes it interrupt the present's coincidence with itself, show the present's discord with itself and thus ground it in the untimely. It is not, of course, that Herzog's death retrospectively redeems anything for Graciliano (this would be the ideology of martyrdom) but that its emergence in his present opens the doors for the past to inscribe itself as past, in all its irreducibility. And that the past be inscribed as past, as irreducibly failed, becomes for him the very condition for the radically other to be imagined.

Thus *Em Liberdade* does not stage a confrontation between a conception of history that relies on repetition and one that does not. Rather, the novel assumes the insight that there is no history outside repetition—this being its anti-avant-gardist, antimodernist, or postmodern thrust—and proceeds to oppose one understanding of repetition as the identity of what returns in the cycle to another that takes it as the self-differentiating moment of the present as it is interrupted by the untimely. The former gives rise to a fatalist conception of history according to which past and present are bound by links of identity that invariably also imply a certain relationship of *necessity*; the latter, on the other hand, lays the foundation for a secular yet *messianic* notion of history, in the sense that the possibility of a link between past and present is never given but must be itself invented, redeemed, and rescued from the historical narrative in such a way that the future remains an open promise, rather than a necessary telos.[31] The fatalist, cyclical conception of history salvages in each barbaric moment of the past a glittering testimony to the progressive accumulation of culture. The messianic, radically opposed to such salvaging, probes into each cultural treasure of the past in order to burst out the failures, defeats, violence, and *barbarism* that lie at the foundation of culture. In this sense, the cyclical understanding of the eternal return alleviates all catastrophes, restoring an imaginary contentment that eludes the confrontation with mourning. On the contrary, the differential, messianic understanding of the eternal return embraces the ruins left over from catastrophes. It is thus from the beginning in danger of falling in the abyss of melancholia. Graciliano finds himself on the verge of such an abyss when he closes the diary: "I picked up Heloísa at the harbor today. She came back with our two younger daughters. I don't know how we're all going to fit in the tiny pension room" (*EL* 235).

Yet *Em Liberdade* is a text written with joy, *in* joy, I am tempted to say, and the entire critique of martyrdom would be misunderstood were we to ignore this crucial component. It is the paradox of a melancholic joy that must be grasped here. Few are the entries in which Graciliano does not make a reference to passion, to the exultation at the recovery of his corporeal energy, or to the conviction that only a truly gay science can oppose the steamroller of reactive ideology. Joy and melancholia are not simply juxtaposed; they do not simply coexist in Graciliano's diary. They are affirmed together, at the same time, such simultaneous affirmation of opposing poles being the very definition of paradox.[32] For it is the joy of melancholia, the joy derived from one's melancholia at political barbarism, that assures that one has not been numbed by the pile of catastrophes to the point of regarding them as natural; by the same token, it is the melancholia of joy, the acknowledgment of a limit, a fundamental powerlessness of one's joyous affirmation, that prevents joy from falling into the complacent happiness proper to those who are blind to the catastrophe. This paradox is thus *Em Liberdade*'s answer to the Nietzschean question of how to mourn affirmatively posed at this chapter's beginning. This answer has the unsettling and disturbing character proper to paradoxes, but paradox may well be the most adequate name for the project underwriting this novel: written in the first person, around and through proper names, yet anticonfessional; structured by repetition yet anticyclical; ruthless in its pillage of another signature yet conceived as a gesture of love; melancholic in its embrace of defeat yet making of this acceptance a joyous affirmation. *Em Liberdade* is saying yes, in a word, to the defeats suffered in the past so that a radical and uncompromising labor on the task of mourning can begin anew.

What is, then, if any, the notion of restitution one can derive from *Em Liberdade?* I observed in Ricardo Piglia's *La ciudad ausente* a process through which the rescuing of the past—most decisively embodied by the anarchic and utopian figure of Macedonio Fernández—recovered for the present the possibility of storytelling. In *La ciudad ausente* the past is rescued in the present. *Em Liberdade* underwrites a symmetrically opposed project: it is the present—each of the several presents of the novel— that is rescued by the past. Graciliano does not "appropriate" Cláudio Manuel; if anything he is appropriated by Cláudio, so Cláudio can speak not as present but as irreducibly past. The same relationship governs the link between Santiago and Graciliano, so what is restituted is not the possibility that the present narrate the past (that is, the thrust behind Piglia's novel) but rather that the past narrate itself *as past* in the present, this being the precondition for the present to be able to narrate itself and its future. In Piglia's restitution there is a debt with the future that can only be settled by an appropriation of the past. In Santiago's there is a debt with the *past,* the settling of which is the premise for the imagining of any future. As we will see later, *postdictatorship* is here simply the name given to the relationship of *necessary undecidability* established between these two thrusts.

6. OVERCODIFICATION OF THE MARGINS
The Figures of the Eternal Return and the Apocalypse

How does one desire not to keep? How does one desire mourning (assuming that to mourn, to work at mourning does not amount to keeping—and here we touch on what remains no doubt the unavoidable problem of mourning, of the relation between gift and grief, between what should be non-work, the non-work of gift, and the work of mourning)? How does one desire forgetting or the non-keeping of the gift if, implicitly, the gift is evaluated as good, indeed as the very origin of what is good, of the good, and of value.

—JACQUES DERRIDA, *Given Time: I. Counterfeit Money*

In Chile, the passage from Salvador Allende's Popular Unity government to Pinochet's bloody dictatorship was notably traumatic, and exile took a severe toll upon the country's cultural and artistic spheres. Activist, engagé pre-coup literature was forced to rethink its basic postulates, especially regarding its relationship with language. In this chapter I attempt a partial reading of two novels by the author of the most consistent narrative project to develop in the past decades in Chile: Diamela Eltit. In the renovated fiction that emerged toward the late 1970s, when the arts began the slow process of coming to terms with the violent 1973 interruption, no figure looms larger than that of Eltit. Having written the most innovative, risk-taking fiction of recent years in Chile, Eltit has helped inaugurate a new period in her country's literature. She can be connected with the problematic of this book because her work submits to a vertiginous fragmentation shatters of experience no longer representable as coherent wholes or as symbolic totalities. One cannot paraphrase Eltit's text; there is no such thing as a "plot" to be retold. Hers is a text that confronts the reader with snapshots, imagistic kernels that, whatever the various uneven relations they maintain with the novel in which they appear, also function as poetic monads. Of all the postdictatorial literature analyzed in this book, Eltit's is doubtless the one that goes furthest in breaking down the boundaries of genre, especially those that separate poetry, prose, and drama. The fundamental work performed by Diamela Eltit has to do with recapturing, through a violent encounter with writing, experiences, and memories irreducible to informational records. Few readers of Chilean literature would disagree that no recent Chilean fictionist reestablishes the charged question concerning the narrative status of experience in a more innovative and risk-taking fashion than Eltit has done in *Lumpérica, Por la patria, El cuarto mundo, El padre mío, Vaca sagrada, Los vigilantes,* and *El infarto del alma,* the latter coauthored with the singular photography of Paz Errázuriz.[1] Here I will analyze two of Eltit's novels, *Lumpérica* (1983) and *Los vigilantes* (1994), with a view to inquiring into the ways in which these two exemplary texts have dealt with the tasks, constraints, and challenges faced by post-dictatorship literary writing.

Eltit's first novel, *Lumpérica,* formed part of a larger artistic scenario. After the violent interruption caused by the 1973 coup, the crisis in activist art, and the phenomenon of exile, a series of written, visual, and performative works began, as early as 1975 and flourishing to the full around the end of the decade, to question the norms of representation and the relation among art, life, and politics in Chile. Named escena de avanzada by its most important theoretician, Nelly Richard, this variety of productions made Chile's symbolic memory their privileged focus of intervention. An inaugural moment in this process was the publication of *Manuscritos,* a one-issue magazine edited by Ronald Kay and designed by Catalina Parra, where the intertwining of image and text gave testimony to the decisive entrance of the urban space as a major interlocutor for the poetic text. Ronald Kay's collection of fragments entitled "Rewriting," which carries the subtitle "Street: The Physics of Poetic Mathematics," affirms that "the crowd's passing through the letter, the trace left by it, is the *impression* that one effectively has to read."[2] Words such as *trace, impression,* and *inscription* are indicative of a vocabulary that would gain prominence in Chilean art, especially in the theorization of memory. Kay's juxtaposition of text and grayish photos of Santiago offers an image of the break-punctuated urban experience under dictatorship, an experience the poetic voice could only perceive as unspeakable. One of the *avanzada*'s consistent concerns was the limits of the sayable, not as a result of external determinations such as censorship but instead as consequence of language's very limits. As Pablo Oyarzún would later point out, "the essential spin of the *avanzada*, in this regard, is to suffer the primary predicament of the unspeakable as something clandestine to its very speaker, which disarticulates the framework of individual and collective identities."[3]

In locating Diamela Eltit's work at least two discursive spectra must be kept in mind: that of the experimental visual arts, for example, the work of Carlos Leppe, Eugenio Dittborn, and Carlos Altamirano, and the Department of Humanistic Studies, where Ronald Kay, Raúl Zurita, Eugenia Brito, Rodrigo Cánovas, Eltit herself, and others collaborated in the production of new literary theories and practices.[4] Around 1979 the Colectivo de Acciones de Arte was formed. Composed of two writers (Diamela Eltit and Raúl Zurita), two visual artists (Lotty Rosenfeld and Juan Castillo), and a sociologist (Fernando Barcells), it was responsible for two major performances in the city. The first, "Para no morir de hambre en el arte" (1979), staged a distribution of powdered milk in a Santiago shantytown, accompanied by a poem—published in the magazine *Hoy*—exhorting the reader to "imagine that the shortage of milk in Chile today resembles this page" and by the public reading in five languages of a piece portraying the Chilean situation in front of the United Nations building in Santiago. A box containing milk, the *Hoy* issue, and a copy of the text read at the United Nations were left in the art gallery Centro Imagen, followed by a parade of milk trucks through the city and the hanging of a white sheet over the Museum, as a metaphor for "closure and continuing hunger."[5] In the second performance, "¡Ay Sudamérica!" (1981), the group threw 400,000 pamphlets over Santiago from a plane; the text read,

> the work of improving the accepted standard of living is the only
> valid art form
> the only exhibit(ion)
> the only worthwhile work of art. Everyone who works, even in the
> mind, to extend their living space is an artist.

Nelly Richard has noted the intricate rhetoric of such interventions: "preachy, exhortative, activist, utopian, consciousness-raising, prophetic, etc."[6] In forging a link with the city, these performances "operated in a space that provided an alternative to the art institution"[7] and would become key references for much postcoup Chilean literature.

At that moment the question of photography became central to the artistic debate in Chile,[8] from its role as "guardian of memory,"[9] to experimental disruptions conveyed by posing, simulation, and masquerade. Foregrounding the photographic space as a privileged trace of memory, Eugenio Dittborn worked on anonymous collective reminiscences in his 1977 "Fosa común," a collection of photographs focused on the task of mourning, and in *Caput mortuum red*, a photoserigraph that exhibited a discolored, worn-out image of a young man next to a serial number. This concern was also manifest in Lotty Rosenfeld's performance entitled "A Mile of Crosses on the Pavement," in which she glued a piece of white cloth across the dividing lines on the streets, to form a chain of crosses in Washington, D.C., the northern Chilean desert, and the border between Chile and Argentina. Rosenfeld thus mobilized the semantic field of "cross," thereby alluding to serial deaths and generalized mourning. Two other visual artists submitted the body to segmentation, denaturalization, and resignification. In *El perchero*, Carlos Leppe foregrounded as artifact a transgendered body rendered in pieces;[10] Juan Domingo Dávila "combines in his pictorial system the comic's narrativity, the nude tradition, psychoanalytic questioning and obscene provocation."[11] All these developments presupposed a convergence of various theoretical experiences in Chile: "semiology and poststructuralism, the concern for art's sociality at the uneven levels of media, modes and material support of artistic production, the critique of meaning-fixing, of the transparency of the real and of the politicomilitant consolidation of the creative will, the claiming of the signifier, margin, and interrogation of institutions have all functioned not only as descriptive, analytical or organizing ideas but also as imperatives for these productions."[12]

Much of the best literature that emerged at that moment—such as Diego Maqueira's *La tirana*, Raúl Zurita's *Purgatorio* and *Anteparaíso*, Diamela Eltit's *Lumpérica*, and Gonzalo Muñoz's *Exit* and *Este*—interacted with the visual arts and incorporated into itself dramatic referents as a principle of construction. Black masses, sacrifices, and a theatrical and travestied sexuality, invariably with much makeup and mise en scène, strove to unsettle the boundaries between life and art. Several of these texts proposed rituals and riddles, not infrequently overcodifying themselves into allegorical machines. Figuration became a major enabling device, as literature responded to "the appearance of the unsaid as language's ordering axis."[13] In the visual arts interruptive strategies (collage, cutup, montage, and quotation) became a privileged structuring principle. On the theoretical front, Patricio Marchant's writing—in dialogue with Nietzsche, Heidegger, Derrida, and the psychoanalytic tradition—elaborated extensively on the notion of *scene* in its psychoanalytic, performative, and poetic dimensions.[14] The new Chilean literature was decisively informed by critical theory and the visual arts. In this sense an inevitable cryptification ensued, as concern over art's conditions of production led into an investigation of its own existence: "the aspect of opacity that typifies many of these works [is] not due to arbitrary hermeticism, but rather to an overcodification of its elements and denotations: a certain version, then, of a ciphered language."[15]

Some texts rose to the status of emblems by condensing imagistic kernels that elaborated experience under dictatorship. Raúl Zurita, most notably, achieved quite an impact with the collection of poems entitled *Purgatorio* (1979) and *Anteparaíso* (1982). A telling phenomenon in the history of his reception was a blessing by Pe. Ignacio Valente, Chile's official literary critic and reviewer for the country's widest-circulating newspaper, the ultraconservative *El Mercurio*. Pe. Valente appropriated Zurita's grandiose resemantization of the Chilean landscape and his design of a Christian pattern of fall and salvation, lauding him as the true successor of Pablo Neruda and Nicanor Parra. His analysis enveloped Zurita's poetry in a conservative Catholic rhetoric that neutralized the unsettling assemblages of Zurita's poetic language. The text's destructive thrust to break down genres, images, historical messages, national ontologies, and so on, lost its battle with the Christian message also embedded in Zurita's text. In a struggle over the interpretation of one of Chile's most celebrated poets, the conservative establishment confronted an avant-gardism fascinated with "the voluntarism of his utterances,"[16] principles of both groups being represented in the very figure of Zurita. Meanwhile, Zurita's poetic production itself was absorbed by postdictatorial clichés, becoming increasingly patriotic and kitsch in its songs to and praises of the Chilean transition.[17]

Be that as it may, it is important to note the image of the polis as *wounded body* permeating Zurita's and Eltit's early work, as well as these works' offer of an aesthetic ritual that might effect a redemptive, quasi-religious form of restitution. To a series of practices that reposited the questions of art/life and art/politics, Zurita's work had the attractive attribute of "canceling and undermining the poetic self," proposing a "pathology of the individual that was also a pathology of society."[18] Nelly Richard has shed light on the symbolics of self-sacrificial practice, concluding that "at a time when the real is forbidden, there is a *demand for the symbolic,* a demand which their [Zurita's and Eltit's] Christian message is able to satisfy."[19] In a time when art no longer sang epic praises of political hope but could not avoid coming to terms with its social mode of existence either, self-sacrifice often became the privileged gesture of immersion into the collective. With Zurita, "art was Religion again, and from its platform it demanded belief as a mode of reading."[20] What was most seductive about Zurita's early poetry was its prosopopoeic potential, its staging of the wounded poet as "emissary goat that expiated the guilt and grief of the social body in a moment when the country found its symbolic expression in such penance."[21]

In order to contextualize Diamela Eltit's work, then, it is imperative to keep in mind these practices, in their trans–genre/gender operations upon the body and the urban space; their decidedly provocative, exhortative rhetoric; their radical fragmentation; and their redemptive-religious kernel. Like Diego Maqueira's *La tirana,* Eltit's *Lumpérica* displays the blasphemous, profane element proper to all black masses. Whereas *La tirana* takes as interlocutor the infinite mise en abyme of Diego Velázquez's *Las meninas*—the convergence of a geopolitical scene (America, Chile, and the mestizo) with an Oedipal one (mother/son and artist/artwork)—*Lumpérica's* filmic component highlights an acute awareness of the paradoxes of the gaze. The various layers of the signifier *Lumpérica* thus have to be attended to: the name evokes *America, lumpen,* and *woman,* but also (and crucially to the structure and politics of the novel) it brings to mind *lumen,* that is, light and the whole semantic web of vision.

In what follows I propose analyses of *Lumpérica* and *Los vigilantes,* while referring the reader, whenever possible, to the growing bibliography on Eltit.[22] As Marina Arrate has shown in the case of Eltit's *Por la patria*—"there is no story, just scenes"[23]—also in *Lumpérica* one finds not a paraphrasable plot but a scenic pattern, reemerging in different forms: a public square, alternately well and badly lit, inevitably cold as in the peak of the Santiago winter, occupied by a few beggars and the protagonist L. Iluminada. This scene dizzily becomes a black mass, a cinematic representation, a political takeover, an erotic communion, a poetic protest, and a nihilistic embrace of destitution. More often than not it becomes more than one thing at the same time, while frequently suspending that becoming in order to present an interrogation, a minimalist poem, or a metaliterary reflection, only to return again to the public square scene in the bitter cold of Santiago. L. Iluminada has undergone "loss of proper name" (10) and "the cold in this plaza is the time being marked to suppose oneself a proper name, given by the *letrero* [signboard], which will light up and fade away, rhythmic and ritual" (9). The text begins to establish a link between public sphere, proper name, and the lights. This oneiric space announces a possible restitution within what is otherwise a heap of destitutional remains. Djelal Kadir has noted that

> The lumpen of America in Eltit's *Lumpérica* has its personification, its ironically and paradoxically *unmasked* prosopopoeia, in the female figure of the novel's protagonist, L. Iluminada. A glaring figure that in turn glares, she is illumined starkness that sheds her *institutional* vestments so that by her light the *destitutional* remnants might come to life, take on discursive weight and political visibility, breach their ghostliness, reclaim their banished reality, and do so at the spatial and symbolic center of society's habitat—the town square, now become the permanent home of the homeless at strictly sanctioned hours of the day and spotlighted hours of the night.[24]

The body and voice of L. Iluminada collect these destitute remnants and offer them the fiction of a restitutive utopia: "the square lit up by the electric web guarantees a fiction in the city" (9). The spotlight's name-giving power lends form to this utopian scene. At the moments when the square empties and the spotlight is turned off, the mass of bodies tends to disappear in the background of a text that reads like a movie script. This is the moment of dissolution and loss of proper names. The reign of terror hovering over the city in *Lumpérica* thus has nothing to do with the "terror of the crowd" depicted in the flâneur tradition; it is rather the terror provoked by the *absence* of the beggars. In L. Iluminada's relation to the crowd there is immersion in the collective, not dandyesque voyeurism. The only exterior gaze left is the camera, the lights that operate from above and remind of all of the threats of the outside.

The first chapter, composed of a series of filmic takes of the public square, associates three semantic knots of great importance for the novel. As Eugenia Brito has pointed out, "writing in *Lumpérica* submerges (drowns) in three crossroads: woman, lumpen and america."[25] Eltit associates a minoritarian and indigent "america," suffocated by the cold city air, with a female body where makeup and wound converge. The first chapter's scenic dimensions include stage directions and later critiques of each take, producing a Brechtian effect whereby identification with the bodies of lumpen (*Lumpe-*) and woman (*-éric-a*) is precluded by carefully placed metafilmic interruptions. The reader is *shown* a scene and shown also that s/he is watching.

The camera is a source of true terror in *Lumpérica*. It presides over the feminization of the beggars' destitute bodies at the public square, as well as the transformation of L. Iluminada herself into a figure of prosopopoiec communion with them. The signboard "keeps handing out proper names" (21), constituting the instance whereby subjectification takes place, in the precise sense of being-before-interpellation, or being-before-the-law.[26] "The luminous board covers them with distinct tones, shades them, conditions them" (10); "So the spotlight, in full autonomy, calls them literary names" (11); "They're waiting for their turn, for the spotlight to confirm them as existence, to name them differently" (21). Under the scrutiny of such a gaze, an individual female body and the collective body of the destitute come into being. They emerge as a function of the gaze, that is, their proper names are endowed by it: "had the spotlight not fallen on the center of the square these would not have acceded to the privilege of the baptized one" (39). The "baptized one" is L. Iluminada herself, baptism appearing (as one among several Christian images in the novel) to announce the spotlight's name-giving powers, in a ritual that is either highly sexualized—"A primogenitor, she presents herself absent on guard, of her own will she is ready for the spotlight's control that, in darkness, acquires its deep penetration" (21)—or painfully eroticized—"she smashes her head against the tree time and again . . . shows herself in the *goce* [bliss] of her own wound, interrogates it with her nails, and if pain exists, it is obvious her state leads to ecstasies" (19).

The name-endowing instance is a phallic one, but L. Iluminada and the collective of indigent bodies in the plaza invent another sexuality, founded on *frotes* (rubbing), disseminated and decidedly anonymous. The cold in the plaza encourages rubbing and touching; the gesture of survival becomes indistinguishable from an erotic practice. Therein L. Iluminada undergoes her several becomings: her becoming-collective-voice, her own objectification by the violence of the lights (a subject formation scene in the most classical sense: constitution by interpellation of law), and also her becoming-subject-of-a-gaze, which, in its turn, objectifies the crowd of beggars. In a moment when they light the fire at the square, the narrative voice notes:

> They will remain protected from the cold, so she can continue contemplating them under the spotlight and examining them in the perfection of their poses. . . . That's why her gaze is attentive and her face desiring. The cold no longer matters, she would lose the pleasure of observation if she mixed with one of them. . . . Like a traveling camera, her gaze. (33)

Hence several gazes converge: the narrative voice, the lights—name givers and identity endowers in the scene—the camera that films, and L. Iluminada's eye following the anonymous mass of bodies at the square. The "seduced one"—L. Iluminada, *la seducida* (38)—is thus "conquered in conquering" (38). The text is then interrupted and the reader abruptly presented with the second chapter: a police interrogation under dictatorship. The plaza will eventually return, and the final movement of the novel—the tenth chapter of this "inverse *decameron*"[27]—concludes at dawn, with L. Iluminada shearing her hair in an empty and bitterly cold square where the dispossessed are no longer present. "Everything has been a rehearsal. Illumination is only for one night."[28]

In the second chapter, as the inquisitor's language spins logic around while questioning a man on his suspicious presence at the square with the beggars, Eltit proposes an anticathartic, analytical relation with the absurdity of the conversation. No outbursts of identification surface; all violence has been transferred to the bestiality of the inquisitor's language. Eltit points to the violence but does not victimize. Redundancies, logical contradictions, and repetitions all contribute to framing the scene for the reader, who is further forced to step back at the end of the interrogation, when the text fades into a movie script: "background, scene upon scene: interrogator and interrogated" (55). Five chapters later the questioning returns, now concerning this anonymous man's minute-long contact with L. Iluminada, as he once held her when she stumbled and fell at the square. There again the interrogation ends with the statements "The lights will be turned on at the square. The show will go on" (148), as the city assumes that inevitable appearance of normality most proper to the worst, truly terror-filled moments.

All who accused Diamela Eltit of obscurantism, hermeticism, and so on, were at least receiving the impact of a true question: Eltit's text is indeed illegible; certainly not in the sense they imagined but rather in the Barthesian sense of that which cannot be read, only written, the writerly text. Throughout the novel, with the possible exception of the police interrogations (chapters 2 and 7, written in a dry, demetaphorized Spanish, totally reduced to the nudity of its circular logic), Eltit submits language to a de-anecdotalization that defies paraphrase. One can always attempt to rewrite *Lumpérica* but never to "read" it with depth-hermeneutic apparatuses. Eltit is inserted into a tradition—to simplify an immense problem, let us call it the *baroque* tradition—for which there is no reserve of meaning that is not translated into the exteriority of language. Eltit takes her text to the limits of a calculated erasure of the anecdotal, the novelistic, in favor of the poetic as such, as in the following passages (each of which appears isolated on one page), where the orgiastic (*vac/a-nal* recalling *bacanal*), the eschatological, the animalesque (*mugir* means to bellow; *vaca* means cow), and the feminine (*muge/r*) come together to resignify the rubbing of bodies in the plaza:

> Woma/neighin' shaves and her hand finally feeds the green un-ties and maya she erects and orgi-astic her form.

> Anal'yzes the plot = weaving of the skin: the hand locks and phobia is a claw.

> Woma/neighing patrols bodily Brahma her wick ed hand that denounces her & bellows. (152–54)[29]

Besides invoking the baroque of Quevedo, Góngora, and Sor Juana and the neobaroque of Lezama Lima and Severo Sarduy, *Lumpérica* formally dialogues with a tradition of Chilean poetry reaching as far back as

Vicente Huidobro (in its filmic manner of cutting and interrupting discourse, the mimetic relation with film being one of the novel's major structural threads), through Gabriela Mistral on to Raúl Zurita. Like the work of Mistral, it investigates the attributes of certain scenes, dramatic condensations that take on the character of emblems. As in Zurita's work, that scene is often one of sacrifice, one in which language is used in a sacred register.

Lumpérica very consciously presents itself as a lure, a spectacle in a ten-round cyclical version. The third round is that of animalization, as the same scene in the square returns, now with protagonist and lumpen neighing and bellowing under the impassive lights and camera: "because neither her neighing nor the expert strength of her bellowing has succeeded in dissolving the powerful mark of this spotlight that has stolen her only presence before the pale ones, shielded behind its letters" (69). The protagonist takes over here in the persona of a mare, confounded with the lumpen, surviving by screaming and rubbing. She attempts "to erase the camera's expectation, to avoid the friction of scenes" (73). This is again a moment of disappearance of proper names, as the *animal lumpérico* "has no name other than that of its class" (75). The third chapter reinforces a recurrent motif in *Lumpérica*: the ideological function of the spotlight as namer, contrasted with the fleeting, ephemeral utopia of loss of name in the collective, which the protagonist experiences in the anonymous moments of darkness: "if the light, if the light were turned off, the plot would really start" (111).

The fourth chapter eroticizes the scene, as the camera closes in on the protagonist: "irreducible, her waist sets itself teasing by staking out erogenous zones in the rocking that makes room for her torso and the displacement of her muscles" (90). She is presented as a gazed-at body— "her eyes generate in my eyes the same twin gaze" (88)—until she "transposes her first scene" (91), bypasses the filming instance, as it were, in order to peek at a primal and violent sex encounter, a scene populated with specters of incest:

> Incest(ed) her caste recognizes in her face the face of the father,
> which the father's face sends to her when her hips, in the same
> form as the insatiable father. Animalesque hipped to her evil mother-

madonna, who raises her matrix in the soil peeled off by the pater's impulse

pulls back

the teat, this voluminous milky portion robs her and her starving muzzle sucks from the father his product loaned to continue her, the savage mater occluded and squeezing the teat with delight

the flow bursts forth
flooding her cervix
Milky-flooding the bare one with smoothing sticky liquid. (91–92)

For the protagonist, "*l'incesta el apellido* [the surname incests]" (92). The terror of incest reappears as inheritance of the name.[30] All naming brings with it a violence, a cut into the fabric of anonymity that assigns loci to each subject. All names are names of the father. Woman in *Lumpérica* comes into being by inheriting the father's name in a scene of incest: "the lewdness of the proper name moaned by the *pater* who consoles her" (92).

The abyss over which L. Iluminada hangs in her relation with the collective is the abyss of prosopopoeia, the possibility that she might lend a voice to an anonymous mass. Appearing as a phantasmic image joining the crowd of beggars, L. Iluminada is made subject of a prosopopoeia with the faded collective voice, in a utopian erasure of proper name. An excerpt entitled "Writing as Evasion," in the sequence of pieces on writing that make up the sixth chapter, concludes:

Intensely pale I adorn myself
daubed to mirror myself in these holes
multiplied by brain stimuli
that situate me on the verge of an abyss
which will irredeemably attract me. (128)

The poem is framed by a note written at the bottom of the page, giving another moment in the relation between the female protagonist and the lumpen:

She wrote:
I keep peeling myself off, a Madonna, right, I open myself. (128)

After this erotic expiation through writing, a piece on "Writing as Objective" ends with a "mode of concluding hope" (129), which announces the "reconstituted city" of "Writing as Illumination" on the following page. This section ends with a return to mournful destitution: "There were the defeated and the dead. Nothing else" (133). This acceptance of the task of mourning leads to the conclusion of the chapter:

> She wrote
> illumined, whole, lit up. (134)

At least twice the subject of writing collapses into the subject of the written, in a deliberate zooming of the protagonist into the persona of Diamela Eltit. The second, most decisive instance occurs when a dimly lit photograph of Diamela Eltit's wounded arms introduces the eighth chapter, the "General Rehearsal," which narrates one of the novel's self-sacrificial moments. In a true parody of the asepsis of medical discourse, the script relates with surgical precision how the protagonist performs a series of cuts upon her skin. The spatial-filmic reference is here completely taken over by hyperrealist minimalism. The scene recalls Eltit's performance entitled *Maipú* (1980), where she washed the sidewalk in front of a brothel, inflicted a series of wounds to herself, and read parts of *Lumpérica* to a group of prostitutes. Speaking of her interest in zones of exclusion (brothels, prisons, psychiatric hospitals, etc.), Eltit affirmed: "My concern is to expose these places, to become one with them with my physical presence. . . . It is a form of individual pain confronting the collective pain."[31] *Lumpérica* is, at the same time, a staging and a critique, a yearning for and skeptical disavowal of the possibility of such communion.

Lumpérica is a night-long reverie that closes down with the day dawning upon L. Iluminada in a deserted square. The ball of masks and prosopopoeias ends with the first morning pedestrian giving testimony to the city's return to the unbearable reality of "lights and proper names." *Lumpérica* announces the utopia of anonymity while foreshadowing its approaching defeat. Here resides one of the text's recurrent tensions: it purports to exist as an epic of marginality by turning the figure of the marginal into one of epic proportions. This desire exists, however, in tension with the novel's very structure, which is that of a ten-step walk along Calvary, concluded with the closing of the nocturnal cycle, that is, all in all the very structure of the *eternal return*. This framework suggests, then, that an epic of marginality can only be a fallacious one, for all epic is by definition an epic of the center. To marginals the possibility of speaking epically is not given. And when that possibility is granted them by prosopopoeia, they find themselves inevitably placed at the center, at best transformed into a rhetorical function of the center. Hence the dialogical duplicity of everything in *Lumpérica*: at the same time it presents a compensatory epic and a reflection on the impossibility of such epic. If the odyssey finds its coda in the circular conclusion of a cycle and, one may infer, prepares to resume the following night, prosopopoeic communion is deferred by means of the instance of control under which the scene displays itself, namely the spotlight. *Lumpérica* announces a religious communion rhetorically organized through prosopopoeia and dissolves this ceremony within the cynical atheism of the eternal return.

The restitutive gesture in Eltit hovers over an abyss represented by the accomplishment of restitution, that is, the perfect ventriloquism between the protagonist and the collective voice. This drives her work to face two border zones delimited by redemption and by silence. *Lumpérica* takes place in the interval between the two, deferring both the climactic moment of bodily communion with the destitute and the inevitable moment of silencing when lights are turned off in the morning. *Lumpérica* presents itself, indeed, as a *theater* of what ensues in such an interval, a drama relating the failure of prosopopoeic coincidence between L. Iluminada and the beggars. This failure is finally emblematized in the protagonist's chopping off her hair in the empty square, an act of "humiliation, contrition, mourning, excommunication and social exclusion"[32] that separates L. Iluminada's body and voice from a square in which "the totality [of cars] belongs to patrols who *vigilan* [watch over] the city" (198).

Eugenia Brito makes the crucial point that *Lumpérica* brought back to Chilean fiction the possibility of narrating the city.[33] Eltit answered the question of what language—beyond costumbrismo, local color, or symbolic fables or epics where "the individual" is neatly folded into the collective—could narrate the city. *Lumpérica* opened the path for a corporeal insertion into the fabric of the polis; it announced, in cryptic, hidden, clandestine form the image of the liberated city reconquered for storytelling and for experience. No traces of celebration, however, subsist in this rather melancholy novel. The reconquest should not be mistaken for

a celebration of some advent of freedom: the posteriority that characterizes *Lumpérica*'s imaginary vis-à-vis the dictatorship, that is, its postdictatorial nature as a novel (even though it was written during the height
of the Pinochet regime) stems not from some carnivalesque reversal but
from its acceptance of mourning. The reconquest of the city it stages is
thus the beginning of the confrontation with the imperative to narrate,
to rescue past experience, and to reactivate storytelling.

Lumpérica houses two rather different dimensions of the written: at one
end, *escritura* (writing) and *escribir* (to write) appear as *scenes*, moments of
illumination where the body is always actively involved: "this lumpen,
imaginary, write and erase, share the words, the fragments of letters,
erase their supposed mistakes, rehearse their handwriting, unload their
wrists, accede to print" (116). On the other hand, literature appears as
the sphere of institutions, names, records, and poses, that is, the realm of
representation in all senses. The opposition between the two is thus between a collective experience of inscription and its belated, inadequate
depiction. The utopian moment of *Lumpérica* is to glimpse into a residue of
experience—the fleeting moment when writing is collectively shared—
not captured by the representational apparatus named as literature in the
text: "no literature has depicted them in all their incommensurability, so
as everyday labor they hold on to their forms and each gesture when
they touch leads to climax" (107). The thrust of the novel is, then, to
highlight that residue of collective labor not containable by any literary
mechanism. This intent explains *Lumpérica*'s resistance to being literature,
most definitely expressed in its resistance to being a novel, and its insistence on a certain inscriptive, experiential dimension—let us call it
poetic—that the texts sees as *irreducible* to literature's representational machinery.

Eltit's *Los vigilantes* (1994) lends itself to be read in counterpoint with the
questions raised in the preceding interpretation, because *Los vigilantes* is,
quite consciously, a postdictatorial novel. It obsessively speaks of, and
in, mourning, linking this mourning with the "end of anguishing times."
But in this post-Pinochet novel the national allegory is not as transparent as it might seem. In the first instance, the collective realm appears
at the background of a domestic scene: love between mother and son in

the shadow of an absent father complicitous with the political order. The absent father is the addressee of a sequence of letters by the mother, her gesture of writing being the major obstacle in her relation with her starving, freezing son. This is, then, a national allegory unfolding within an Oedipal triangle, while at the same time re-posing the problem of writing. Opening and closing the text, the starving boy stutters along the page as he tries to elude his cold and hunger.

The shadow of an epidemic of uncontrollable grief lurks behind the scene of writing in *Los vigilantes*. It binds the gigantic task of mourning faced by the polis to writing and to a great physical effort: "you will know then that writing you represents to me a superhuman exercise" (35). "I must keep writing you, even though by doing it I jeopardize the fragile structure in which this mourning found my body" (103). Writing thus appears as the dimly envisioned possibility of an outside. By making the mother the only subject of writing—with the special exception of the two puzzling pieces that open and close the novel, uttered by the son—*Los vigilantes* truly installs the father as *absent*. That is, the mother writes when the father is absent.

This Oedipal triangle, however, does not remain confined within the boundaries of familialism,[34] opening itself up, rather, to a topography of the bodies that populate the city. The most nefarious image of the outside, hovering as a specter throughout her letters, are the "neighbors," those who watch over—one sense of *vigilantes*—the stability of the political transition. Neighbors are thus the guardians of the wretched pact in which she refuses to participate: "Voices are heard in the streets, noise, movements that confirm the climate is changing. The anguishing times are over. . . . The neighbors resolutely fight to impose new civic laws that will end up forming another tight circle" (63–64). The relationship to the outside has been reduced to hearing. Beyond the frontier separating the outside from the scene of writing, the neighbors watch and protect the reproduction of a self-satisfied postdictatorial consensus. The mother writes *to* this outside, attempting to write herself out of the confinement and hunger to which she has been condemned. In this scene, however, another centripetal force must be taken into account: the cold touches and piercing laughter of her young *infans*—etymologically, the mute one—who opens and closes the text *in pure speech*:

Mama writes. Mama is the only one who writes. (13)

I stick my fingers in my mouth to drag out the word that ponders among the few teeth I have. In some little hole I'll leave mama's leg when I get the word I still can't say. Mama's skin is salty. I don't like the sweet stuff, it makes you fat. Makes you fat. I throw up what's sweet, the salty stuff is rich. Now mama is bent over, mama begins to fuse with the page. (16)

In its initial section, before the mother's letters take over for the bulk of the book, *Los vigilantes* is a theater, *in speech,* of the infans's hopeless attempts to speak. Eltit, aware of the paradox, submits her Spanish to a tortuous, repetitive, broken syntax, an imaginary replica of the syntax expected from a speechless son existing in specular relationship with the mother. By endowing the son with the word, the novel dreams that it is taking place at the level of pure speech, that the infans's impossible talk is a pure *logos* not mediated by the inscription of the written trace.

The infans opens the text by speaking of his inability to speak—"Oh, if only I spoke. Just look how it would be if only I spoke" (14)—as he sees the mother "fusing with the page." Her writing introduces law by placing a barrier between her and his desire: "I take her fingers and twist them to make her forget the pages that separate and invent us. . . . But my silly head will begin to freeze if mama takes refuge among her pages" (19). In a scene where the father is absent, writing is the barrier reminding the son of the interdiction that separates him from the mother. Writing is here the *Nom-du-Père* that shields the mother's body from the speechless son—hence the precarious existence of the son's short opening piece (13-22), permanently hanging over the abyss of nonlanguage. The text sustains itself over this abyss by postulating a residue of affect—the son's desire for fusion with the mother—not exhausted by writing: "When he [*the Father, the Other*] writes to mama my heart steals his words. He writes trash to her. . . . I read the words he thinks and doesn't write" (14). The infans can thus unveil the father's writing; there is a reserve of affect not translated into the written trace. In *Lumpérica* the writing of L. Iluminada and the lumpen is coextensive with the novel's affectivity—it was the very form of this affect. This feature is reflected in the primacy of a baroque aesthetic in *Lumpérica*, for in a sense, the dissolution of all interiority into the exteriority of language is the baroque. *Los vigilantes*, in contrast, appears as a *romantic* text, insofar as it postulates a reserve of affect not exhausted by writing—a reserve the speechless son comes to embody.

Two major vectors operate to frame the mother's letters: the infans's desire and the father's absence. The father is the link with the outside, dominated by "neighbors" who find it "indispensable to guard the West's fate" (65). Concerning the scene of writing, then, one important observation has to be made on the difference between *Lumpérica* and *Los vigilantes*: whereas in the former the contact with the collective is one of communion, announcing a fleeting utopia at the square, in the latter the space of writing has been violently confined to a terror-stricken *inside*. The public space utopianly reconquered in *Lumpérica* has been, so the protagonist of *Los vigilantes* finds out, "only for one night." The square where L. Iluminada staged her camera-mediated prosopopoeia with the destitute has now been taken over by an "orgiastic arrogance of satisfaction" (111), a by-product of the "will to fuse with the West" (110), while the protagonist barely manages to "prepare to face the misery that encircles the borders of the West" (107). In 1983 it was still possible, accepted, in fact predicted, by the text, to read Eltit in the stereotypical Bakhtinian celebration of carnivalesque inversion. No traces of that possibility persist in the postdictatorial atmosphere of *Los vigilantes*.

Whereas *Lumpérica* is an orgiastic affirmation in the Chile of Pinochet's dictatorship, *Los vigilantes* faces the postdictatorial void, with nothing to affirm and no one to affirm it against (except the amorphous and generalized lethargy, which does not exactly qualify as a targetable enemy). *Lumpérica* is an affirmative allegory, a true allegory of affirmation—for this is one of the definitions of allegory: *a mimetic relation with the impossible*. Hence *Lumpérica*'s overcodification: because it opts to affirm only what is radically outside the codifiable by dictatorial and antidictatorial doxa, it can only dwell on the impossible. The condition of possibility of such impossible affirmation is its submission to the cycle of the eternal return of the same. Only by framing its affirmation within the logic of the eternal return—night, dawn, noon, sunset, and suggestion of a repeat the next night—can Eltit's first text affirm at all. It definitively installs its object as a *lost* object, the text's cryptic nature being a by-product of its simultaneous option for affirmation and acknowledgment of the object of such affirmation as a lost, impossible one.

Concerning allegory, then, the difference between *Lumpérica* and *Los vigilantes* is not that one is allegorical and the other is not but rather that the latter elevates allegory to a second degree where the possibility of affirmation has been dissolved. Despite the fact that it remains the bridge to the outside, writing in *Los vigilantes* is privatized, confined to the closed space of a room and the melancholy loneliness of a subject. The corporeal dimensions of writing are taken out of *Lumpérica*'s public square and brought to a suffocating regime of restrained space — "to become urban has constituted for me a painful apprenticeship" (83). The mother's confinement emblematizes her separation from the collective, in a time when the only organized collective is the guardians of order: this accounts for the novel's resistance to any affirmative statement. *Lumpérica*'s prosopopoeic moment of communion with the collective has been eliminated. Both the writer-protagonist of *Los vigilantes* and her son have been reduced to embracing a strategy of sheer survival: "My whole body howls, guessing the form that my condemnation will take. Your son, moving by my side, only plays defense now, terrified by the danger closing in on our heads" (99). There is no longer any room for the "pleasure of gazing" (33, 210) ubiquitous in *Lumpérica*, for the gaze has now been reduced to a looking down or away, most frequently by a being *watched over*. When the protagonist of *Los vigilantes* hides the destitute in her house, violating the city's rigid norms, she no longer affirms anything (such possibility is not given to her in the lethargic, forgetful postdictatorial order) but rather puts forth a desperate negation as her last gesture of resistance: "the house is now our only margin" (116). The difference between *Lumpérica* and *Los vigilantes*, a significant one in the context of the Latin American posttransitions, is thus between an affirmation of the impossible — an allegory — and a reflection on such affirmation *qua impossibility* — that is to say, an allegory to the second degree, an allegory of allegory, as it were, if we keep in mind that allegories are by definition representations of an impossibility.

Several recurrent phrases in the protagonist's letters lend themselves to be read in an allegorical key: the nightmarish crisis, the wretched pact (recalling all the odious transitional "democratic pacts"), the regulated normality, the guardians of consensus, and so forth, all of which evoke Chile's highly controlled, slow-paced, and oblivion-dominated return to liberal democracy. The major kernel here is the imperturbable forgetting that makes possible the reproduction of posttyrannical banality. The neighbors follow the complacent pact that promises a horizon where "the West can be within the reach of your hand" (110). These two irreducible, irreconcilable loci are represented by the two meanings of the word *vigilantes*: those who *vigilan* (watch over) and those who *guardan vigilia* (remain in vigil). On the one hand are represented all those who have chosen the sensible administration of the possible and have been led implacably to police the streets for any signs of unrest; on the other hand, the protagonist, victimized and bearing her mourning almost alone, "with my pernicious inclination for rituals that today all want to forget" (111). The protagonist's victimization brings the text back to self-sacrifice: "You will make of me the perfect victim because mine will be a judgment outside history" (100).[35]

Self-commiseration has also been privatized in *Los vigilantes*. *Lumpérica*'s frame as a novel reconnects L. Iluminada's (or Eltit's persona's) self-inflicted cuts with a whole complex of corporeal marks through which an experience of collective writing took place. For the protagonist of *Los vigilantes*, writing has become a *personal* ritual of expiation for a *collective* guilt from which she is exempt, while the infans remains outside language, unnamed, most often referred to indirectly, Oedipally, as "your child." In *Lumpérica*, L. Iluminada and the beggars at the square are co-authors, and their writing presupposed no addressee, because it simultaneously affirms and cancels itself. In *Los vigilantes*, the oedipal frame structures language around a phatic axis, making the protagonist's discourse revolve around the absent father, which justifies the epistolary format. Unlike *Lumpérica* (which bewilders the reader to such an extent that all transparency of addressing is suspended), *Los vigilantes* demands an empathizing position, both for the mother's mourning and for the child's hungry and cold rambling.

Although entrapped in a cycle of eternal return similar to *Lumpérica* (as the letters also follow a dawn-noon-dusk pattern), *Los vigilantes*, more than any other text in Eltit's production, embraces the apocalyptic as its fundamental mode of relationship with time. The text cannot bear another return, because Eltit makes her protagonist the *last* survivor, the last carrier of the word: "I no longer know who you are, I believe I never met you. Your mother is not a living figure either, the neighbors are only characters in the war. Only your son and myself are real" (112). Allusions to the multitude of dispossessed are now reduced to testifying to the narrator's philanthropy, as in her feeding, sheltering, and, in a climax of the Christian motif, washing their bodies in her house (96–97). If in *Lumpérica* the protagonist is constituted as subject only in her being one with the collective, in *Los vigilantes* the multitude, "shattered by panic, pain, and blood, barely bringing suffering as a memory of the blows" (102), has been made *extrinsic* to her, separated from her at the level of *experience*, and therefore only reachable through charity and compensatory expiation. This predicament explains the book's apocalyptic tone, its insistence on a war (involving North, South, West, and East), where "the great emblem auguring victory is the desperation of hunger that marks off borders" (112). Survival thus surpasses resistance or utopia as the protagonist's motivation to write.

It is certain that apocalypse is announced through a collective defeat shared by the protagonist, but now the constitution of the subject takes place not in the experience shared—for what is being shared is solidarity, not experience—but in the lonely gesture through which the protagonist addresses the Other, the absent one. The addressed "you" is the center of these letters, as can be noted in their profuse use of verbs in the second person, commands, or interrogatives. In this sense *Los vigilantes* is a love letter—that letter which makes of the addressee's absence its object and nucleus of desire—and thus demands to be read as symptom of this love. This predicament becomes visible in the tone of the mother's letters: repetitive, obsessive, self-torturing, and displaying a resistance to reading that is due no longer to morphosyntactic fragmentation and discontinuity (as in *Lumpérica*) but rather to the circular, dizzying display of symptoms. Like all love letters, they contemplate their own disappearance and silencing and are obsessed with end and death. *Los vigilantes* is an apocalyptico-eschatological chronicle of defeat. When the protagonist concludes her letters, before the word returns to the boy's delirious, broken speech, a mortuary scene appears as a postdictatorial image of mourning: "an age-old pile of bones deprived of memory, freed up from the burden produced by the desire that shakes and consumes life. Bones that keep their pulverization to make room for other bones coming into this unrealizable tomb, surrendering to so much darkness" (114). The circle of control around the postdictatorial city tightens, and writing is progressively equated with the sheer possibility of remaining alive. The protagonist commits to a "written, desperate, and aesthetic survival" (115) that pushes her to a corner of isolation and silence.

The infans, who opens the novel by experiencing his mother's writing as the pain of separation, closes it in the same atmosphere of hunger and cold that dominates the text. Now, however, the son sees the word return to him at the price of surrendering his desire to that of the mother, entering writing and accepting it as law: "Now I write. I write with mama grabbing my back" (126). This final surrender—more a conclusive defeat than a successful pedagogical experience—is expressed in the change in the boy's language, which syntactically and lexically becomes indistinguishable from his mother's: "we go toward the bonfire through the unyielding night to conclude this story that looks interminable" (126). The only desire left is the mother's written desire, while the boy has submitted to the oedipal order, closing what had been the only space untouched by the grid of language, which is always, as psychoanalysis has taught us, the grid of Law.

Los vigilantes is then exemplary as a postdictatorial text: what once was the dream of prosopopoeic communion with the destitute at the public plaza has now become an anguished, privatized attempt at survival. What once was the shared experience of affirmation has now been reduced to a unilateral gesture of philanthropic solidarity. From *Lumpérica* to *Los vigilantes* we move from the affirmation of the impossible—the affirmation of an orgiastic polis under dictatorship—to the impossibility of affirmation. As the relationship with the collective has been made *external* to experience, the restitutive gesture is engulfed by Christian redemption and fantasies of victimization or self-commiseration. The beggars that made up the utopian dimension of *Lumpérica* have now deserted the square, leaving it to the "neighbors" of *Los vigilantes* to see that the entrance into the realm of consumerism takes place unmolested by memory's troublesome negativity. In this context, Eltit's wager is that writing, no longer able to affirm any oppositional principle, can at least, by virtue of its mere existence, remain as bearer of an irreducible trace of memory and experience, such trace being, pure and simple, an insight into the wisdom conveyed by the tradition of the vanquished: that things keep going, that they keep reproducing themselves, that everything keeps *working; this* is the catastrophe.

7. BILDUNGSROMAN AT A STANDSTILL, OR THE WEAKENING OF STORYTELLING

Our time, then, this most essential part of lived experience, this greatest good of all goods, is no longer visible to us, no longer intelligible. It cannot be constructed. It is consumed, exhausted, and that is all. It leaves no traces. It is concealed in space, hidden under a pile of debris to be disposed of as soon as possible; after all, rubbish is a pollutant.

—HENRI LEFEBVRE, *The Production of Space*

In a dialogue with Juan José Saer published as *Por un relato futuro*, Ricardo Piglia identifies three major tendencies in the contemporary novel. The first springs from what he calls the "poetics of negativity," predicated on a refusal of all mass-cultural conventions and a position of radical negation, the ultimate result of which is silence. The examples noted by Piglia are Samuel Beckett and, in Argentina, Juan José Saer himself. They share a strategy that "refuses to partake in the manipulation presupposed by the culture industry"[1] and concentrate, instead, on destroying myths of direct communication and linguistic transparency. The poetics of negativity is thus a critique of all instrumental, pragmatic conceptions of language. To take an Argentine example, Saer's *Nadie nada nunca* repeatedly narrates the mystery surrounding a series of murders of horses.[2] By returning again and again to the events in circular and enigmatic fashion, the novel preempts all identification with the detectivesque search and calls attention, instead, to the problems of selection, exclusion, and organization involved in the act of narrating the past. Through a series of complex mediations, the impossibility of assigning agency to the crimes comes to allegorize the seemingly subjectless catastrophe that befell Argentina during the dictatorship. Never making any direct commentary on the country's political situation, *Nadie nada nunca* becomes an explosively political novel precisely by flirting with silence and the unsaid. Much like Piglia's own *Respiración artificial*, Saer's *Nadie nada nunca* believes that "concerning those things that cannot be said one had better silence." The poetics of negativity is thus an heir to the modernist, suicidal project of taking language to its most radical limit, a limit that may include the impossibility or undesirability of language altogether.

The second strand of the contemporary novel noted by Piglia is represented by what might be called the "postmodern strategy," that is, the attempt to erase the boundaries between erudite and mass cultures by combining procedures from both. Visible in authors such as Thomas Pynchon, Philip Dick, and, in Argentina, Manuel Puig, the postmodern strategy looks to recuperate the massive readership enjoyed by literature in the nineteenth century, now lost to the mass media. Instead of resolutely differentiating itself from all conventions of mass culture, as is the case with the poetics of negativity, the postmodern novel appropriates them and makes them part of its repertoire: cutting and montage, fluidity and quickness of style, suspense, dramatic identification, and so forth, are all stylistic traits borrowed from mass culture and now made central to the contemporary novel. As opposed to the poetics of negativity, which always tends toward silence, the postmodern text cultivates a proliferation of contradictory messages, saturating itself with a mosaic of citations. In its most critical forms, the postmodern novel lays a wager on the possibility that the stylistic procedures of mass culture may be appropriated for goals perhaps not achievable through mass culture and that the role of literature would be precisely to explore further that possibility.

The third strategy observed by Piglia attempts to renew literature by incorporating nonfictional material. The examples here are the various forms of *littérature-vérité*, narrative journalism, and testimonies. In Argentina, the pinnacle of this tradition is represented by the work of Rodolfo Walsh. During the recent Southern Cone dictatorships these genres experienced a substantial flourishing, accompanying the quest for alternative ways of circulating information in a time of severe censorship and control over the mass media. As Tânia Pelligrini has pointed out for Brazil, "this literature, whether allegorical, testimonial, memorialistic or journalistic in its form . . . seemed to be urgently driven to fill the vacuum created by censorship, which had forbidden all means of circulation of news and information."[3] The Brazilian romance-reportagem, critiqued earlier in this book, represented perhaps the most popular resurgence of this realist rhetoric in recent Latin American history. Moved by the need to narrate the real facts in a time when falsification is the rule in the media, journalistic and testimonial forms of narrative respond to the crisis of literature by abandoning fiction altogether. Their wager lies on the possibility of reconnecting experience and narrative by bringing to the latter the techniques of mass-circulation newspapers (immediatism, a certain sensationalism, an appeal to "reality," etc.), in a time when newspapers cannot fulfill the mission one usually expects of them. It is, then, through that substitutive role that testimonial or journalistic narrative legitimates itself in times of censorship.

It is clear that more sophisticated narrative projects such as Piglia's cannot be neatly classified under any of the three categories. Piglia shares with the poetics of negativity a deep suspicion of mass-cultural conventions and still maintains a firm confidence in literature's powers to deautomatize the numbed, inattentive perception proper to modern experience. In that sense Piglia is a true heir to the avant-garde. On the other hand, however experimental his work may be, it also incorporates that return to storytelling often associated with the postmodern strategy. Despite Piglia's rather negative view of postmodernism (*CF* 155), his debt to authors such as Manuel Puig is manifest. He does, for example, share with Puig the insight that "technical innovation and experimentalism are not contradictory with popular forms" (*AP* 115). Moreover, the third, nonfictional strategy also plays a role in Piglia's work, as he acknowledges his insertion into "a tradition of Argentine literature that says that in order to do politics with literature *no hay que hacer ficción* [one should not / does not have to do fiction], . . . that if one wants to intervene in politics one has to erase fiction" (*CF* 166). Therefore, Piglia's own position in his triad of responses to the crisis of literature is a highly complex one. Maintaining the negative impulse behind the avant-gardist poetics of negativity, but making use of popular, storytelling-driven forms such as science fiction and the detective story, all the while attempting to recover the potential for political intervention in Argentine history, Piglia knows that his synthesis of these three forms is likely to leave a remainder. If one attempts to synthesize avant-gardist negativity, postmodern storytelling, and testimonial truth-retrieving into a higher form, what is the dialectic that can account for this ascension? Would this synthesis not leave a few ashes, a remainder of traces that resist incorporation?[4] Could these ashes not represent the starting point for yet another narrative project, irreducible to the three strategies as well as to their synthesis in Piglia's work? What happens when literature is driven not by the will to synthesize—restore, recuperate, recover—but rather by the will to dissolve all syntheses? If all the projects described have a common goal of restoring a certain narratability to experience, could one imagine a literature that would be entirely alien to that effort? If literature surrenders to its divorce from experience, accepts that divorce as a fact, what can it still do? These are the questions I will pursue in order to frame the fiction of Brazilian writer João Gilberto Noll.

Noll debuted in 1980 with a collection of short stories entitled *O Cego e a Dançarina*. He followed it with *A Fúria do Corpo, Bandoleiros, Rastros do Verão, Hotel Atlântico, O Quieto Animal da Esquina,* and *Harmada,*[5] only the first two of which qualify as full-fledged novels, the others being more like novellas, with their eighty- to ninety-page accounts of characters remarkably shallower than those of the classic bourgeois novel. The length of Noll's texts is in itself an important element for analysis, because their concision functions as an index of their self-erasure and drive toward silence. Noll is moved by a profound disgust with what Brazilians call a *romanção*: the cosmogonic and totalizing narrative machinery that found its apogee in Honoré de Balzac's *La comédie humaine,* later to become a favorite model for the resurgence of various brands of regionalist and naturalist sagas in Brazil and all over Latin America. My focus here will be primarily on *Bandoleiros* and the four novellas that follow it, because they can be taken as a relatively homogenous group of texts where a sustained narrative project is developed.[6] As suggested by their titles, Noll's texts invariably allude to transitory places, pilgrimages, traces, and leftovers of experience. They systematically depict scenarios deprived of historicity, voided of becoming and time:

> Drying my hands with paper I felt the urge to look around for a clock. Then I sighed, as if saying: what for? (*RV* 9)

> This was old in me: to have the notion that I needed to do something without exactly knowing what: my habit was to stand halfway,

entertained by some detail that ended up changing my route. Now
I've lost all hopes of ever recovering the memory of what I had to do
back in the beginning. (RV 60)

Action is displaced to dark side streets that have lost their names,
abandoned houses, dumpsites, and public squares in state of decompo-
sition, all of them metropolitan images alien to the profusion of signs
and shocks that punctuated the drifting of the modern flâneur. Instead,
Noll's narrative camera offers scarce and rarefied shots at recondite, abandoned, "cold, pedestrian-only alleys, so narrow that the sun never bathes
the constant smell of piss" (QAE 7).[7] No historical marks remain in this
city; it lives in a perpetual "day after," bearing in itself the marks of
a destruction now blocked from memory. A few characters, much like
survivors, attempt to make sense of the deserted space. The frequent
travels—always luggageless: "before I gazed compulsively at the luggage
rack the thought occurred to me that I had brought nothing along" (RV
7–8)[8]—contrast with the strong feeling that all places look alike and that
alterity as such faces extinction, being thus a matter of utter indifference
to be in Rio de Janeiro or the South, Amazonas or the Northeast. Even
in a country supposedly so diverse as Brazil, the same postmodern banality covers the entire territory. Typically, Noll's narrator-protagonists
go through the most banal experiences, devoid of any temporal frame
other than the sheer schizo, noncausal succession of events following
one another: they get and lose jobs, find themselves arrested or dragged
into some psychiatric hospital, escape, get robbed or beaten up by the
police, run into people who do not seem to be going anywhere either
and invariably disappear without a trace. After a few pages the text halts,
in an arbitrary and anticlimatic coda, leaving the reader with a rather
uncomfortable sensation of incompleteness. The bulk of Noll's textual
labor is then to turn that banal sequence of events into a reflection on
the crisis of the narratability of experience.

   The paradox proper to Noll's texts is that nothing seems permanent
and everything is in flux, yet the notions of becoming and change have all
but disappeared. Noll is thus paradigmatic of a contemporary antinomy
mapped out by Fredric Jameson: "the equivalence between an unparalleled rate of change on all the levels of social life and an unparalleled
standardization of everything—feelings along with consumer goods, lan-

guage along with built space—that would seem incompatible with just such mutability."⁹ In order to analyze Noll's fiction it is necessary to trace the historical origins of the antinomy highlighted by Jameson, especially insofar as it bears on the question of experience. The discomfort produced by Noll's texts—that everything is in flux yet nothing changes, for experience never becomes narratable knowledge—has much to do with a displacement he imposes on the modern, Baudelairean tradition of the flâneur. For Walter Benjamin, the figure of the flâneur is an allegorical key to what he terms the crisis in the transmissibility of experience. Because I see Noll's characters as a radicalization of that crisis, I now briefly turn to Benjamin, who offers us the theoretical framework for understanding why Noll represents a form of narrative in which even the inattentive and superficial experience of the flâneur is no longer possible.

What Benjamin theorizes as the impossibility of turning the *Erlebnis* [lived moment] into narratable matter—which for him means "experience" in the strong sense of *Erfahrung*—is rooted in the endless repetition of the assembly line. In the assembly line, taken as an emblem of modern life, the subject is forced to relate to time as an entity external to his/her existence and personal history. Automated production stands as the paradigm for this voiding of time: "The unskilled worker is the one most deeply degraded by the drill of the machines. His work has been sealed off from experience."¹⁰ If "habits are the armature of experience,"¹¹ the modern assembly line transforms habit into an automatism where no movement ever depends on or learns from the preceding one. The subject's past is thus sealed off from the present. His/her work is therefore instrumental not in constructing memory but in liquidating it. Each operation is dissociated from the previous one for the very reason that it is its exact repetition. As a result, even moments of leisure become temporal voids, for the inability to experience—the impossibility of organizing what has been lived in a meaningful, coherent narrative—preempts the subject's relationship with time: "the man who loses his capacity to experience feels as though he is dropped from the calendar. The city-dweller knows this feeling on Sundays."¹² For Benjamin Sundays in the metropolis are the embodiment of atrophied experience, in a metaphor where "Sunday" evokes not leisure, much less entertainment, but rather experience that is lived, undergone, but not processed as narratable, meaningful material, that is, Erlebnis that does not ever fully achieve the status of Erfahrung. Benjamin refers to this decline of experience with a phrase borrowed from Nietzsche: the eternal return of the same.[13] Nietzsche's phrase describes, for Benjamin, the precise state of experience in the modern world: a sequence of returns in which no particular present accumulates or learns anything from the past. The theory of experience in modernity is thus a theory of the *impoverishment* of experience, a theory of the impossibility of narratively organizing it.

The epochally symptomatic character of the flâneur stems from this crisis in the transmissibility of experience: the flâneur testifies to a world where individual memories have been wrested away from collective tradition. What distinguishes the flâneur is the particular, paradoxical mixture of complicity and disdain that structures his relationship with the metropolitan masses. Being part of them, having in them a precondition for his own existence (*flânerie* is an urban phenomenon par excellence), yet disengaging himself from them with contemptuous distance, the flâneur represents that reserve of leisure still possible in a modern, incomplete stage in the evolution of capital: "the flâneur's leisure is a protest against the division of labor."[14] Comparing Edgar Allan Poe's "man of the crowd" with Baudelaire's flâneur, Benjamin notes that for the latter a certain composure was still available, as "Baudelaire's Paris preserved some features that dated back to the happy old days,"[15] for instance in the shielded comfort provided by glass-walled arcades from which the flâneur could see but not be seen. The flâneur is, therefore, a specimen proper to that moment of capital when some Archimedean foothold can still be maintained and a privileged view of the totality is still available. He depends for his survival on the persistence of tradition within the modern metropolis. After the implementation of Taylorism as the logic organizing production, the flâneur is all but swept away, for the flâneur's relation to time is one of sheer expenditure, clearly at odds with the Taylorist principle of maximum production in a minimum amount of time: "Taylor's obsession, and that of his collaborators and successors, is the 'war on *flânerie.*'"[16] The flâneur is thus a *modern* figure in the full sense, made possible by modernization and expelled by this very modernization once it reaches a more advanced stage.

It should not surprise us, then, that the art that witnesses the emergence of the flâneur, namely modernism, is also the art that makes of ostranenia—the novelty shock that deautomatizes perception—its major structuring principle. In the terms I have advanced here, this is the art to which Ricardo Piglia, for example, claims heritage. According to Benjamin, Baudelaire was well aware, when he published *Les fleurs du mal,* that "the climate for lyric poetry ha[d] become increasingly inhospitable,"[17] due to the (modern) fact that "only in rare instances is lyric poetry in rapport with the experience of its readers."[18] Therein lies the origin of the avant-gardist obsession with novelty: an art now obsolete in a commodified world would be forced to "make novelty its highest value."[19] What characterizes the Baudelairean gesture as such is the belief in the redeeming potential of the novelty shock, the hope that it could offer a glimpse into the eternal nucleus hidden behind the mercantile veil. "For Baudelaire it was a matter of blasting, through a heroic effort, the 'New' from the eternal return of the same."[20] The novelty shock has the function of recapturing the epiphanic moment that would redeem a reified experience. As Fredric Jameson has remarked in a recent essay, this was the moment in which "Being could again for a brief instant be deconcealed."[21] One of the ways in which that particular truth—what Jameson calls, following Heidegger, the deconcealment of Being—emerged in modern literature was precisely in the depiction of a radical otherness, an illuminating or epiphanic encounter with alterity. One of the fundamental tropes for that encounter was *the journey* in space or time. In fact, the flâneur can be seen as the traveler who makes of his explorations into his own city a voyage into the unknown. For Noll, then, the entire problem resides in the fact that the alterity that used to sustain and drive the journey in modern literature is no longer available.

Unlike the journeys that constituted one of modern literature's privileged genres, from Jonathan Swift to Alexander von Humboldt to Jack Kerouac, Noll's travels are not endowed with any liberating, pedagogical, or edifying function. The general architecture of Noll's text—the constant drifting, the focus on the first person, the individual attempt to make sense of the past, the temporary nature of everything—invites an approximation with the bildungsroman, except that there is never any *Bildung,* because characters have lost the ability to learn from experience or, which amounts to the same, experience can no longer be synthesized in a manner formative of an individual consciousness.[22] Growth, conflict, and resolution are inoperative categories here. Whereas the modern journey into a historical, geographical, or experiential otherness forced the hero to synthesize the past and take a qualitative leap in his/her formation, the drifting found in Noll's fiction leaves its protagonists even more impoverished and destitute. The eruption of past fragments does not awake protagonists from the temporal sameness to which they seem condemned. The process of subject formation stages a gaze back at the past that finds nothing to identify or recognize. Noll's nameless, single, jobless, and failed forty-year-olds are best grasped as a significant transformation in the modern tradition of the traveler/flâneur, more specifically as misfits, negators of the world around them, who, however, do not evolve into bearers of an alternative principle. As marginality has been deprived of all the redeeming potential it once possessed, these characters are no longer able to embody any affirmation. Noll's is thus a literature alien to all restitutive thrust. The negation of an unbearable reality does not take place in the name of anything that could transcend it but rather resigns itself to being radically immanent to what it negates. Whereas the flâneur "is always in full possession of his individuality,"[23] Noll's gray and anonymous characters have dissolved within the undifferentiated facticity of experience. Unlike the Proustian involuntary memory, recollections in Noll cannot set to themselves the task of "producing experience synthetically."[24] The reader ends up feeling that, despite the fragmentation and disorder in the protagonist's memory, there is ultimately no puzzle to be recomposed, because it does not matter much what happened before or after. In the undifferentiated progression of schizophrenia, time is not so much shuffled as it is suspended or erased. Some of the temporal confusion proper to the modernist patchwork remains, but now the redeeming potential once ascribed to its estranging and deautomatizing relationship with the linearity of time has definitively declined.

The short stories collected in *O Cego e a Dançarina* are set mostly in marginal areas of Brazil's metropolises. They depict the clash between signs of the frenetic modernization to which the country had been subjected and the state of hopelessness and symbolic destitution in which the impoverished middle classes found themselves at the end of the "economic miracle" of the 1970s.[25] *O Cego e a Dançarina* focuses primarily on certain eccentric types: adolescent children of political activists who had seen their parents defeated and now wonder what was to be (as in "Alguma Coisa Urgentemente"), little boys lost in a city enveloped by an atmosphere of fear and terror, where soldiers abound but where there does not seem to be any war going on (as in "Duelo antes da Noite"), and middle-aged men who take stock of their failures in a language deprived of all sentimentality (in "O Filho do Homem"). The book makes no direct allusion to the political process undergone by the country under the dictatorship, but its gallery of characters is barely comprehensible without an awareness of at least two parallel phenomena: the massive entrance of American mass culture in Brazil, most notably Hollywood, and the middle classes' disenchantment with the militant struggle against the regime and their subsequent fall into melancholia.

"Marilyn No Inferno," one of the best stories in the collection, relates the preparations for the "first Western shot in Brazil," where "the Baixada Fluminense imitates the prairies of Arizona" (CD 36). The movie is a copy to the Nth degree, where everything is fake or simulated, including the inevitable Mexicans, here played by Brazilian Indians. The story is told from the perspective of an extra, a teenager whose mother is dying of cancer in a filthy public hospital, while he dreams that after his minuscule part in this simulacrum of a Western he will be given an opportunity in the ultrapopular soap operas aired by the all-powerful Globo network. Noll's emphasis lies in the contrast between the epic dimensions of the Western as a genre, which nurture the teenager's grand dreams, and the pathetic poverty of his situation. As he fantasizes about Marilyn Monroe and Bette Davis, he hears humiliating insults coming from the director: "Hold this rifle strong, you idiot!" (CD 36). The story closes with the teenager grabbing one of the horses in the set and racing around the streets in a frenzied gallop. The race ends, most appropriately, in front of a theater that shows a Kung Fu movie, with the boy being thrown forward by the horse and ripping apart the front door poster, which metaphorically separates the miserable world of Caxias from the protagonist's glamorous fantasies of stardom. The final image is that of a fall into a bottomless abyss, represented by the torn Kung Fu poster that stands between an unbearable reality and an unattainable desire.

Most stories in *O Cego e a Dançarina* dramatize the disproportion between the allure of mass culture and the material and symbolic indigence in which it flourishes. However, unlike in works produced during the days of dependency-informed critiques of Americanization, in Noll's stories there is no trace of rejection of that imaginary. By leaving open the ending of "Marilyn No Inferno," and never passing judgment on the boy's dreams of stardom, Noll chooses simply to highlight the *formal* structure of his fantasy as nothing more than a poster, an image deprived of all depth, the destruction of which leads him to a free fall into an unknown beyond. The boy's fall from the horse onto the movie poster can be taken either as a dive into the simulacrum—an uncompromising embrace of his fantasy—or yet as a fall *through* fantasy *into* the real—the real understood precisely in the Lacanian sense of the unsymbolizable traumatic kernel that structures fantasy.[26] In any case, the crucial point is that the text provides no safe standpoint from which the reader can observe and judge the fall. Noll's texts are moved by a sort of complicity with the wretches and children of defeat who now make of TV and B-cinema waste their only possible homeland. Such complicity is hard to pin down, because it is never contaminated by any pity, resentment, or sentimentality. Hyperboles, exclamations, or sentimental overflows, so predominant in the testimonial and journalistic fiction written in the 1970s, are nowhere to be found. To take an analogy from a world dear to Noll, that of pop music, it might be argued that his narrators have much less to do with the early Beatles' smiling naïveté or the Rolling Stones' explosive histrionics and much more with the dark and cynic pessimism of the Velvet Underground.

Noll's second novel, *Bandoleiros*, takes place during the narrator's visit to the United States, after which he—himself a writer—is bothered by the feeling that he leaves having nothing to tell: "nobody would forgive this: I had been *na América-América* [in the real America] and had not extracted any fiction from it" (B 144). *Bandoleiros* stands as a melancholy counterpart to numerous travel narratives in which Europeans returned from America experientially enriched, invigorated by firsthand contact with an uncontaminated, alternative reality. All around him the narrator only sees parodic replicas of that most American of all myths: the uniquely individual life story. Throughout his stay he hears echoes of the rhetoric of a new moral crusade, suggestively recalling the puritanism and individualism of the Reagan years. Upon boarding the plane to Brazil he comes across a final specimen of the Panglossian character of American doxa, that unshaken belief that one lives in the best of all possible worlds:

The lady assisted me with the dull politeness of American service people. Not that I preferred a bad-tempered lady, but it was indisputably monotonous to confront yet again that flawless promptness, that discreet niceness of someone who is doing the most important thing in the world, that blind belief that each and everyone gives their share for the greatness of . . . a country. (*B* 152)

It would be instructive to compare the narrator's account of his stay in Boston with other contemporary travel narratives in America, most notably those of Peter Handke and Wim Wenders and Jean Baudrillard. César Guimarães has made the connection with Handke and Wenders, showing how, both in Handke's *Der kurze Brief zum langen Abschied* as well as in the several Wenders movies about America, "the myths constructed by Americans to explain their history (of which the grand fable remains the conquest of the West) represent not only a possibility of knowledge but also an opportunity to tell stories,"[27] whereas for Noll banality has saturated the horizon of the visible to such an extent that only at one point in the narrative can the narrator anticipate, in bad faith, that he "would go back to Brazil full of stories to tell in my books" (*B* 57). Whereas the protagonist of Handke's *Der kurze Brief* " 'learns' from American myths" and believes that "there is still something to see and tell, not only in the landscape, urban architecture, freeways and deserts, but also in the stories told by American cinema,"[28] Noll's narrators see not mass culture telling stories of lived experience but rather a reified and cliché-saturated experience being condemned to replay, ad infinitum, the rehearsed lines of some B movie or TV sitcom: "but all the words he said in that house, all that seemed to me like an old movie" (*HA* 38). As in Baudrillard's *Amérique*, the simulacrum has taken over. The distinction between Baudrillard and Noll, however, is that in the latter one finds no traces of the fascination that pervades Baudrillard's book, still all-too-modern in its weary European longing for America's "realized utopia." Baudrillard is then undoubtedly closer to Alexander von Humboldt and Alexis de Tocqueville than to Noll, in that precise anti-intellectual cult of lived experience (of whose aestheticized twentieth-century resurgence, by the way, Benjamin was so suspicious, seeing in it fascism itself): "drive ten thousand miles across America and you will know much more about this country than all the sociology and political science institutes put together."[29] Noll, to be sure, would take some distance from such traveler's optimism and certainly not out of any particular trust in sociology or political science.

Upon coming back to Rio the narrator of *Bandoleiros* reflects on the failure of his latest book, *Sol Macabro,* and on his aborted marriage with Ada, herself trying to recover from a disastrous stay in Boston. While assessing his past, he watches his best friend, João—his antithesis in everything, the image of the confident activist writer—slowly die of a mysterious disease, his pitiful demise being a commentary on his shiny optimism. Remembering "the special beings that we thought we were in our youth, all of us perfect failures" (*B* 10), the narrator anticipates a few images that become allegorical of Noll's textual universe. One of them is a blind tramp who lives in a shabby boardinghouse and spends his time playing the saxophone. As he has not paid the rent or heard any voices for months, "he began to suspect that the boardinghouse didn't exist anymore, that only he had remained there, a survivor" (*B* 27). The image of this blind man playing the sax alone in his room, not knowing whether the world has ended and whether he is the only survivor often reappears to the protagonist as an allegory of his own inability to perceive the passing of time other than as a homogeneous continuum: "It is very strange not to know it is Sunday morning. Any other day is fine. But if you don't know it's Sunday and you confess your ignorance, it sounds like you're drunk or nuts—a dangerous bum" (*B* 12).

After these first recollections, the narrator of *Bandoleiros* goes on one of his aimless bus rides and ends up in a district in the outskirts of Porto Alegre. Amidst dusty old shacks and a few dried-up trees he finds a man whom we later learn he had met in Boston, a certain Steve, an American who had spent part of his childhood in Porto Alegre, and "now came back, to see if he could restore the abandoned house and live there" (*B* 38). Steve is one of many obsessed, failed origin-searchers of Noll's novellas.[30] A former Harvard student, he was once almost drugged to death by doctors attempting to cure him of his depression. He ended up dropping out of school, totally amnesiac, unable even to recall the then recent assassination of John F. Kennedy. Meanwhile Ada, the narrator's wife, had gone to Boston to pursue a Ph.D. in "Minimal Societies," a new creed that was sweeping the entire world and to which she began to devote herself religiously: "She didn't see nationality as a measuring stick to evaluate any human content. Nations were doomed, with no exceptions. The only thing left was to join Minimal Societies" (*B* 45). Ada explained how Minimal Societies would solve the problem of mortality—"after you're dead you migrate to a more perfect Minimal Society" (*B* 46)—of information—"Information only makes sense under some danger. It is threat that makes us know. Minimals will self-manage, free as stars" (*B* 47)—and even of planning—"No need for people to know in which historical atmosphere they live. For that we have Planners" (*B* 63). Utopia here has degenerated into a totalitarian paranoia, a religious dogma defended by zealous militants. The narrator's visit to Ada in Boston coincides with her receiving two other Minimal militants, from whose delirious fanaticism he feels progressively alienated. It does not take him long to realize that his marriage with Ada has fallen apart. As the Minimals insist that "the task is to reconstruct the Universe within the space of your Minimal society" (*B* 45), the cynic and skeptical narrator gets kicked out of the house and finds himself forced to return early to Brazil. His lengthy wait at the Boston airport gives him the opportunity to meet Steve, whom he later reencounters in the abandoned shack outside Porto Alegre.

After being back in Brazil for some time the narrator receives an emergency call that closes the Minimal Society episode. Ada has been attacked while asleep by a Minimal fellow attempting to prove the sect's thesis that human beings are overtaken by a murderous desire whenever they contemplate someone sleeping. Ada is now confined to a wheelchair, having to be spoon-fed by the narrator, and, most important, apologizing the whole time, finding herself absolutely unable to contradict anybody. The experiment generates a best-seller on the dangers of sleep, written by Mary, a Kenyan Minimal militant. Mary's best-seller is one of four texts written within *Bandoleiros*, the other three being the narrator's *Sol Macabro*—an en abyme version of Noll's novel and a resounding bookstore failure—João's political, engagé manifestos—"He has just put out a hopeful novel. A love story in penury" (*B* 77)—and the "poetry of hunger" written by a young martyr who has decided to commit what was to him the only possible political act in a country like Brazil: the suicide-poem. If one takes these four texts as a caricature of the range of possibilities for postcatastrophe literature, the picture seems far from reassuring. The Minimals represent that eccentric, scandalous yet facile accommodation to a market eager for salable novelties; João's "visions of future grandeur" (B 77) remain impermeable to recent experiences of defeat and insist on hammering the same party line; the young fakir-poet, with his "naively sorrowful" (B 16) writings, offers himself as a sacrificial body, consumed in the act of affirming himself. Steve, the one who does not write, the utopian of pure lived experience, ends up drunk and destitute in the valley close to the ruins of his childhood house. In the context of these alternatives—market accommodation, naive activism, martyrdom, and *maudit*/beat-generation-style romanticism—the narrator's project of a reflexively mournful literature, corrosive and cynic but never self-sacrificial, appears to be the only alternative of some theoretical scope. But the narrator, much like Noll himself, faces an impasse and does not know how to proceed. Only in Noll's later texts does the semblance of an affirmative project emerge as an attempt to resolve this dilemma.

The voiding of memory and atrophy of experience are often allegorized by the characters' facelessness and anonymity. In *Rastros do Verão* the narrator-protagonist meets up with a boy at the bus station. When asked about his origins, the boy says that "anyone could show up and declare to be his father and he wouldn't have a way of knowing—the only image he had of him was of a faceless man" (RV 14). The narrative then unfolds as if the protagonist lacked meaningful events to tell: "I had been around all these years, yet what personal story could I tell? Through this tenuous geography, who had generated any lasting memory with me?" (RV 22) and "*Me faltavam as lembranças* [I . . . felt that I lacked the remembrances]. My past in Porto Alegre was yet another abstraction" (RV 30).

He is "uplifted by the fact that there still were stories to be made" (RV 46). These stories, however, do not seem to be available as personal experience: "I had lost the ability to get into a story with someone" (RV 28). Against this background, the protagonist goes through another set of banal events: beer with the boy at the station, a trip to the boy's house for a shower, snacks and top-40 radio, mutual masturbation, sex with the boy's mother while the boy packs up to join the marines the next day, and finally the protagonist remembering why he came to Porto Alegre when he finds a piece of paper with a message saying that his father is in the hospital, after which he heads to the hospital without ever finding his father. During the narrator's visit to the boy, the only measure of time is the succession of hit singles on the radio:

The host spoke of Elza Soares's fateful career. Then Elza sang the blues. . . . The boy said listen, what a great Legião Urbana song. . . . The host now announced Grace Jones coming up, to shake the floor. . . . The host said we'd heard Garotos da Rua. . . . Janis Joplin howled her *Summertime*. . . . The radio played Marina. . . . The radio played Fagner. . . . From the boy's room came B. B. King. (*RV* 44–60)

This is a syncopated, segmented time, an image of time that has been made *external to experience*. When experience drags along the endless repetition of the same, the only temporal punctuation comes from outside; in this case, most appropriate, the world of mass culture. The narrative structure replicates this segmentation: events unfold as if independently from each other, much like a series of filmic takes and cuts. From one scene to the next, nothing is accumulated or learned. The dialectic of experience here is one at a standstill, perennially facing the task of starting all over.

Hotel Atlântico narrates the drifting itinerary of a protagonist who wanders around the South of Brazil, staying temporarily in pensions and boardinghouses until he suffers an assault by the police in a small town and sees his right leg amputated. The town's doctor uses the "success" of the operation as an electoral triumph in his campaign for mayor, while the narrator progressively develops a strong complicity with Sebastião, the nurse who assists him and finally flees with him, the two nurturing the idea of visiting his childhood town. The narrator's trajectory becomes indistinguishable from the deterioration of his body: "In the mirror I looked at the deep black around my eyes, my scaly skin, my dried-up lips; I stuck my tongue in the infected cavity of a tooth, and thought that there was no point in staying here, counting signs that my body was falling apart" (*HA* 11). His memory's atrophy is physically allegorized by continuous losses of senses and body parts. He and Sebastião flee the hospital and embark on a genealogical search for the house of the latter's grandmother—guided by a Wenderian yellowish photo—and meet with the inevitable disappointment: "we saw that the blue wooden house was no longer there; he described it to me in the smallest details, in the hope that I would help him look for it" (*HA* 90–91). As they head toward the narrator's hometown in another failed search for origins, the narrator finds the end of his itinerary in the destitution of his own body.

On a beach from childhood times, he loses his hearing and his eyesight. Noll's sentences themselves become short, meager, lexically poor, as though tending toward silence:

> Sebastião sat me on the sand. He stayed by my side, with a hand firm on my neck.
>
> Then Sebastião looked at the sea. Me too, the South's dark sea.
>
> He then turned his head sideways and looked at me. By the movement of his lips I could only read the word sea.
>
> Then I was blind, I no longer saw the sea or Sebastião. (*HA* 98)

His encounter with origins ends in silence and blindness, with nothing accumulated or discovered in the pilgrimage. In contrast to much of the modernist tradition, no reserve of subversive potential remains in the romantic loner.

As opposed to the multiplication of names observed earlier in Ricardo Piglia and Silviano Santiago—a strategy that allows them to bypass the crisis in the narratability of experience by making available to fiction an infinity of apocryphal, impersonal experiences—Noll's failed search for origins highlights a fundamental impossibility of *constituting a proper name*. Being an iterative structure, a signature must be endlessly repeatable but absolutely unique in each one of its occurrences. In Noll, no true encounter with alterity, no epiphanic moment, provides the means to reorder past experience in order to allow for the emergence of a subject capable of a singular signature. The anonymity of all his narrator-protagonists is thus coherent with the content of the experience narrated. For subjects dissolved within sheer facticity, the proper name becomes a transcendental point of anchorage no longer available. Along with the possibility of a proper name, all interiority fades. "Even what would rigorously belong to the universe of subjectivity, of the private, is transformed by Noll's fiction into a sort of mixture or passageway between exhibition and intimacy."[31] The assault on names is extended to common substantives: "no, kid, not everything has a name in this disgraceful life" (*H* 53). The absence of a synthesizing instance makes world and characters drag along in the nameless. The windows and glass galleries that Flora Süssekind indicates as crucial in contemporary Brazilian literature—"the staging of a spectacular language, turning prose into a window where bottomless and privacy-less characters are exposed and observed, like video images on a mirrored text"[32]—also represent, then, a violent breach between subjects and some moment of their past, fundamentally precluding them from reordering their past experience. The opposition between Piglia/Santiago and Noll is thus a contrast between two different strategies of impersonality in the age of the decline of the proper name. The antinomy (or an ultimately dialectizable contradiction?) that must be grasped here is the one between Piglia or Santiago's impersonality-through-profusion and Noll's thin, rarefied impersonality. Whereas in Piglia and Santiago the multiplication of proper names guarantees some possibility of producing subjectivities, however apocryphal, in Noll the subject has been dissolved within the facticity of experience. The former strategy can be referred back to a constellation that includes both Italo Calvino and Thomas Pynchon—the profusion of stories, the infinity of the apocryphal, the multiplication of names—whereas the latter brings to mind a rather distinct lineage, more in tune with Peter Handke, Maurice Blanchot, and Pierre Klossowski—the slow fading away of the proper name.

Noll's Bildungsroman at a standstill thus chronicles the dissolution of that Archimedean foothold represented by the modern flâneur. Immersed in events whose significance is exhausted in their mere facticity, grasping time as voided and homogeneous, voyaging through lands that no longer offer a true otherness from which to assess identity, Noll's characters confront the impossibility of learning from experience and thus the impossibility of constituting a proper name. Walter Benjamin has taught us that experience in the strong sense presupposes an incorporation of individual memory into patterns of collective tradition. This may then be the time to ask the question concerning the status of the collective in these highly fragmented, privatized texts. Noll's later novellas, *O Quieto Animal da Esquina* and *Harmada*, provide an interesting frame in which to pose this problem, because they bring his typical, rarefied self-narratives into contact with the collective experience of the polis.

O Quieto Animal da Esquina is narrated by a young miserable poet mysteriously taken in by a rich family of German immigrant farmers, who become his benefactors for no apparent reason. Without asking for anything in return, except maybe to help them escape their boredom, they bring the poet—an ex-squatter and petty robber—to their opulent farm. The protagonist constantly oscillates between fleeing the farm in order to recover experience that carries some meaning for him or maintaining the comfort he has been given, at the cost of losing the possibility of living personal stories. Somewhere on the way he is struck by this doubt: "wouldn't it be better to get out of this room, try to forget Kurt's and Gerda's existences and go for a less blind situation" (QAE 46). Later on, the impulse is "to get used to the silence proper to all my reasons for staying here instead of being a squatter in an abandoned building; everything would be all right" (QAE 43). At times, the poor poet falls into sheer bad faith in his plans of future fortunes. He envisions "meeting a woman to be my company, Kurt had to bless this bind . . . , maybe he would give me half his treasure" (QAE 55). The protagonist is thus an individual who has been torn away from a collective existence, and experiences that separation, alternately, as a liberation and a reason for guilt and melancholia.

The barrier separating subjective and collective histories is shaken twice in the narrative, the first during a protest by landless peasants that creates some movement in the immense, uncultivated, and privately owned land. The landowners release the entire repressive apparatus of police and trained dogs, while the protagonist watches from inside the window, remembering his past in the slums:

> Further up the road the peasants lit matches, a meager flame disappeared and soon another one sparked; I leaned upon the window and the memory of a song that old buddies used to sing in the Glória neighborhood came to me, but I just couldn't get beyond the first verse, and even that line was kind of dissolving in my head, in a few minutes it was undone, actually it was like all of a sudden my fate had surpassed me and all the songs that used to come out of my mouth, so that there would be a time when I would look back and just not have anything to recognize. Pretty soon I won't have to lift a finger to avoid my past, I thought, relieved. (QAE 39)

The option for indifference is the only one possible here because there is no longer any organic tie between individual and collective memories. The protagonist sees "five ragged people, standing in expectant position and staring. What do they want from me? I asked myself, and rolled down the curtain" (QAE 50). The oblivion the childhood song has sunk into represents the forgetting of those lived moments that bore a concrete link with the collective. Subjective memory is transplanted to an outside lost to the subject and indicated by collective experience. At times, this loss is reason for "relief," as in the preceding quotation; it also frequently generates depression and melancholia: "wouldn't I be better off among convicts, who lack all appetite for rewards?" (*QAE* 70). *O Quieto Animal da Esquina* is a great study of ressentiment and bad faith; by endowing the young poet with the narrative voice and making his petty calculations and occasional doubts come to the textual surface, Noll again does not allow the emergence of any transcendental standpoint from which the ressentiment-driven poet could be judged. The ending, the protagonist's true embrace of conformism after a swim in the river—"now I would put on the dry clothes that Kurt was handing me, then I would go to bed, calm down, get some sleep, maybe dream" (*QAE* 80)—is an attempt at pacifying his memory, perturbed by the resonance of collective history outside his window, as well as by his own desire to abandon his Maecenas and relearn how to live personal stories.

Noll's story performs an interesting operation upon the opposition between the subjective and the collective. The text locates subjective lived moments in an outside space that is no longer contradictory but rather coextensive with collective experience as such, even if the latter is only phantasmatically evoked. There is no "opposition between the individual and the collective" here but rather a process of erasure of all subjectivity once it dissociates itself from the collective. In other words, the choice confronting Noll's poet is not between living personal stories or renouncing them for the collective. Instead, by closing the window on collective history he also chooses to remain barred from his proper name. The loss of personal stories to tell *is* the loss of collective history, that is, they are reconciled negatively—reconciled as loss, which is to say allegorically. Whereas for the hero of, say, Bertolt Brecht's *Trommeln in der Nacht*, the option is clearly between living a forgetful and ephemeral personal experience (the petty bourgeois life with his fiancée) or renouncing it for the revolution, in Noll not even an ephemeral individual story remains after the window is closed on collective history. For Noll the pale, anonymous outside of a lost collective experience bears the only possibility of recharging the also lost individual memory.

O Quieto Animal da Esquina thus depicts the political as pure negativity; that is, it depicts our inability to think the political. Coherent with his narrative project, Noll shows how the political is dissolved along with the dissolution of the proper name. In this sense, in Noll there is no "option for the individual over the collective," as has been affirmed and could be deduced from a superficial reading of his texts. Rather, what is at stake is a loss of the proper name that is *coextensive* with a loss of the political. The word *corner* in the title is then the corner the protagonist often feels he is about to turn without ever quite accomplishing it: "at any rate, if I tried to correct the delay, if I turned memory upside down to reconstruct this time, who would endorse my accuracy?" (*QAE* 52). After writing the poem entitled "O Quieto Animal da Esquina" he never writes a poem again, and this last piece becomes an emblem of his paralysis "on the corner." He is a "quiet animal," one tamed and now unable to choose the unknown over a mediocre, secure comfort. As always in Noll, however, the key is not to pass judgment on the character but to inquire into the conditions of possibility that make his choice inevitable. If the corner is never turned in *O Quieto Animal da Esquina*, the political theme returns in *Harmada*, Noll's latest novel, and this time a true encounter with the collective takes place.

The narrator-protagonist of *Harmada* is a jobless actor stuck in a homeless shelter. There he plays the role of "Storyteller of the Tribe," staging to his older fellow interns stories "that I said were episodes lived or witnessed by me" (*H* 46). In his weekly tale-telling sessions, he feels as though "this narrative were a fluid coming out of me, thinly, toward a still unknown world, where all stories would be protected from the mildew of forgetting, like an archive of time" (*H* 47). Noll's actor narrates as a collector preserving a rare object. His is a wager on the possibility of reaching that "brief collapse between the apparent and the intimate of things" (*H* 15). He wants to preserve experience in the more radical, Benjaminian sense of maintaining something alive as narratable material. In the same way that *Bandoleiros* depicts different writers, *Harmada* displays several performers and actors of identity fables: "I said that on that night I'd tell a story about my sources, that I'd spent the whole day reflecting on my strange origins" (*H* 48). Dramatic language takes over as the bearer of experience, and theater becomes the great metaphor for what will later in the book turn out to be an inquiry into the foundation of the city.

Throughout *Harmada* the propelling force behind the performance of such stories is the imperative to mourn. His storytelling sessions in the shelter begin after he suffers through seeing an older friend and guide die in his arms (*H* 51–52). Years later, after escaping the shelter, he sets up with his adopted daughter, Cris, the production of a mournful theatrical monologue:

> The play, a monologue by a Mexican author, spoke of a woman in mourning for believing in eternity with hatred and despair. Yes, she did not mourn, in her soul and body, for someone's death; no, her mourning, on the contrary, expressed sadness for the hard, immense heritage of eternity. (*H* 71)

This dramatic adaptation triggers a series of allusions to Juan Rulfo's *Pedro Páramo*, both in the tone of the home-returning motif as well as in the image of past specters' lingering around, reminding the present of the task of mourning. In *Pedro Páramo*, the return to the hometown is an imperative, a command passed down by the dying mother. For Rulfo such return spells failure insofar as the father proves to be also dead, as only echoes of his name still resonate in the "valley of tears."[33] Like *Pedro Páramo*, *Harmada* depicts an inheritance passed down as an imperative to mourn. The desolation of time, of history, is made present as a task for memory in the form of a scene that depicts a frustrated journey back home.

After being back home in the city of Harmada for some time, having accumulated some personal memories, reencountered old friends, and revisited ruined buildings, the protagonist's reconnection with his lost past leads to a climactic encounter with the legendary figure of Pedro Harmada, founder of the city named after him. In the last scene, the narrator recalls a mythical beginning in which a man "arrives on a beach by boat . . . gets off while holding his wounded arm and falls on his knees." The narrator continues, "Blood drops on the sand. He thinks: 'I'll found a city in these lands'" (*H* 124). The final meeting is a clash between mythical and historical times. The protagonist is led by a little boy to a man who identifies himself as Pedro Harmada. The past founder answers the present's call: "yes, I am Pedro Harmada—said the man while he opened the door" (*H* 126). The text refuses to tell what forms that encounter would take: Pedro Harmada's reply closes the narrative, and the question remains as to how the specter would speak to history.

The inquiry into the individual and collective past is further made ambiguous in *Harmada*: in addition to the fact that the protagonist is an actor—"everything I do is like I'm *representando* [acting] understand?" (*H* 27)—his adopted daughter learns from him the habit of inventing false stories about the past. As in *Bandoleiros*, the status of the narrative event (lived, dreamed, written, or performed?) is invariably in question. Pedro Harmada himself, arriving at the beach by boat and uttering a proto-typical foundational sentence, comes across as a rather theatrical, over-stylized image of the founder. The narrator is led to Pedro Harmada by a little boy whom he finds in the apartment just acquired with the money earned with his play. After trying to ask the boy where he came from, who his parents were, and so on, he realizes the boy does not answer him, because he is mute. They do not genuinely communicate until the narrator abandons verbal language and uses his theatrical skills to per-form a pantomime, in what is a crucial encounter in the novel:

> It was like a lightening, in one strike: I began to imitate a monkey to the boy, my hands opening my ears and blowing the wind, sud-denly I dissolved everything and made another face, then I rolled on the tiled floor, I overflowed myself in each gesture, blinking with no time to think about the next lunacy, everything was coming out of me instantaneously—as always, without thinking, I decided to pros-trate myself in front of the boy and kiss his feet; then he began to release the most fiery laughter, suddenly he was expelling the most obscure and indecipherable language followed by guffaw and gut-tural screams, coarse and possessed with extreme euphoria, and then I understood the boy was mute. (*H* 120)

This boy would later lead him by the hand to a deserted part of town, where among semidestroyed houses the protagonist would meet Pedro Harmada in the novel's final scene. It is then in bypassing the symbolic that he establishes a rapport with the boy, who, the text seems to sug-gest, bears within himself the riddle of the origins of the polis. In the inarticulate, babbling sounds produced by a mute boy the narrator finds the Ariadne thread that leads him to collective experience. Through-out *Harmada*, in fact, Noll places a good deal of emphasis on the utopia of a nonsymbolic language. One of the key moments in the narrator's search happens when he gets to know a blind man who "explored remote sounds" and "announced that finally we had arrived at an invertebrate language, one that lacks all master spine, does not wish to go anywhere and fades away in microexplosions" (*H* 80). This is the language that re-connects the narrator with the foundations of the polis: a language that opens itself up to the contingent, the aleatory, as in the purely affective babbling of a mute boy.

Harmada thus revisits the *romance de fundação*, the Brazilian novelistic tradition of inquiry into the foundations of the polis. It is well known among Brazilianists how this tradition, from José de Alencar to Jorge Amado and João Ubaldo Ribeiro, has offered some of the most ideologi-cal and totalitarian versions of Brazilian history. In theatrical and over-stylized fashion, *Harmada* revisits this tradition ironically: the portrait is no longer that of a heroic foundation but an act of memory that attempts to reconstruct ruins. Whereas Noll's earlier texts carefully deconstructed individual experience and the proper name, *Harmada* depicts the return of a phantasmatic, spectral image of the collective past. When the his-torical figure of the protagonist encounters the mythical founder of the city in the novel's closing scene, the reader is left hanging between the spectral return of past fragments and the image of a future that remains open. The return of the collective dimension, then, does not imply a confident, activist affirmation of a political program. The text's only af-firmative moment lies in the suggestion that it is in the babbling, pre-symbolic language of a mute boy that an alternative relationship with the polis can be established. The boy's incoherent murmurs seem to preserve specters and ghosts presumably exorcised in the authorized political dis-courses encountered elsewhere by the protagonist. Coming full circle, then, from the deconstruction of the proper name to a dim, fragile return of the collective, Noll seems to suggest that literature could still, at least, perform one task: to unveil the melancholia and unresolved mourning buried underneath the heroic myths of identities and foundations.

8. THE UNMOURNED DEAD AND THE PROMISE OF RESTITUTION

The real city crumbles down in memory, now it is only an imprint beat up and chiseled for the dream, rough, ancient, with this thick air previous to the storm aggravating monuments and stone facades. . . . It is the same little city. But why does it return? What accounts does it come settle, what recriminations does it fling, what bitter reproaches does it segregate? The dream is also this: a remembrance of what has not been lived, of that which unsuccessfully strove to leave a trace in us. —TUNUNA MERCADO, *Canon de alcoba*

In an article on what he terms the "crisis of witnessing" unleashed by the Holocaust, Dori Laub, a psychoanalyst and cofounder of the Fortunoff Video Archive for Holocaust Testimonies, recalls a survivor who made the following statement: "we wanted to survive so as to live one day after Hitler, in order to be able to tell our story."[1] The survivors' crisis of witnessing would then emerge from the abyss between the irreducible imperative to tell and the distressing perception that language cannot fully convey that experience, that no particular listener manages to capture its true dimension or even listen attentively and sympathetically enough. If in the most basic sense the work of mourning can only take place through the telling of a story, the survivor's dilemma lies in the irresolvable incommensurability between experience and narrative: the very diegetic organization of the past monstrosity is perceived either as an intensification or as a betrayal of one's suffering—or worse, of the suffering of another—and the survivor finds him or herself caught in a symbolic paralysis. Whereas the accomplishment of mourning work presupposes the elaboration of a story about the past, the survivor of genocide faces an extreme instance of the modern decline in the transmissibility of experience—that banalization of language and standardization of life that preempts the didactic power of storytelling and places storytelling in an acute, epochal crisis derived precisely from its divorce from experience.[2] In the case reported by Dori Laub, the survivor's new, recomposed family was continually perceived as "unempathetic strangers, because of the 'otherness' she sense[d] in them, because of their refusal to substitute for, and completely fit into, the world of parents, brothers, and children that was so abruptly destroyed."[3] The impossibility of replacing the lost object is reinforced by the presumed indifference of the surrogate object, which in its turn heightens the feeling that the experience of loss cannot be translated into language.

The survivor thus confronts a deadlock in the restitutive function of mourning. All mourning demands restitution, not exactly because it wishes to restore the state prior to the loss—the mourner generally knows this to be impossible and only refuses to accept it in extreme cases of fixation in the past conducive to radical melancholia[4]—but rather because mourning can only run its course successfully through a series of substitutive, metaphoric operations whereby the libido can reinvest new objects. The paralysis in mourning therefore indicates a breakdown in metaphor: the mourner perceives the uniqueness, the singularity of the lost object as staunchly resisting any substitution, that is, any metaphorical transaction. I go on to indicate why I conceive of this moment of resistance to metaphor not simply as a transitory, ultimately surmountable phase of mourning work but rather the very locus where mourning becomes an affirmative practice with clear political consequences. Latin American postdictatorial texts, and postcatastrophe literature in general, is challenged to subsume the stark, brute facticity of experience into a signifying chain in which such facticity perennially runs the risk of being turned into yet another trope. Mourning includes a necessary moment of confrontation with this risk and resistance to the metaphorical structure of mourning work. In this chapter I examine how this problem manifests itself in a testimonial novel by Tununa Mercado, an Argentine exile who returned to that country after the fall of the military regime, only to find out that the condition of possibility for so-called redemocratization was the erasure and forgetting of the experience of the victims.[5]

Tununa Mercado's *En estado de memoria*[6] narrates a series of events from the protagonist's exile in France (1967–70) during General Onganía's dictatorship in Argentina, and later in Mexico (1974–86), during the nightmarish period known as proceso, to the return to Argentina after the restoration of democracy. The background for Mercado's protagonist is the most violent period of modern Argentine history, at the end of which the number of deaths and disappearances mounted to 20,000. Beginning with the repression of the Peronist labor movement and the purges of progressive professors in the university after the coup of 1966, followed by the resurgence of popular resistance toward 1969, the ephemeral restoration of democracy in 1973, and the recrudescence of paramilitary violence preceding the coup of 1976, the question of exile was central for Argentine culture during almost twenty years. Contemplating the dictatorship's heritage after redemocratization, the country would be forced to confront the problem of mourning in a way rarely seen before. In addition to being a sophisticated reflection on mourning and trauma, *En estado de memoria* should also be understood as a political intervention in this context.

The novel begins with a most disturbing scene: a man named Cindal writhes in pain in a psychiatrist's waiting room, crying out that he has an ulcer. His is one of many somatizations of psychic disturbances to appear in a book where the line between physical and psychic pain is patiently called into question. The doctor's answer illustrates a certain relationship between experience and certain established bodies of knowledge. Cindal did not have an appointment, and even though other patients in the room, the narrator-protagonist included, were ready to give him their time slot, the doctor insisted on not receiving him, even after Cindal begged for the supreme humiliation: "please, intern me!" Michel Foucault reminds us that the modern clinic emerged when the symptom began to signify the disease without a remainder. The being of the disease could now be entirely stated in its truth, for the sovereignty of medical consciousness had transformed the symptom into a sign, in a process that is not, needless to say, deprived of violence: "But to look in order to know, to show in order to teach, is not this a tacit form of violence, all the more abusive for its silence, upon a sick body that demands to be comforted, not displayed? Can pain be a spectacle?"[7] As hope for alleviation leads to an offering of one's own body as a legible sign, Cindal announces a series of gestures later repeated by the protagonist, who receives her first lesson in the role of silence within structures of power/knowledge: "Time has been perfecting this tomblike analytic silence toward those who seek immediate answers to their desperation. Cindal hung himself that same night" (8).

En estado de memoria then sets out to relate the protagonist's "dependency on doctors of all sorts, including dentists, gynecologists, and above all witchdoctors, shamans, and 'masters'" (12). In this grouping psychoanalysis is not one practice among others, for the impossibility of establishing a lasting analytic scene is decisive:

> In strictly therapeutic terms, I have always been spared psychoanalysis. To tell the truth, I could never resort to an individual clinical treatment in which I offered, horizontally, my unconscious materials: for economic reasons, I always had to be in group therapies, where I effortlessly whisked my anguish and my vulnerability away from my mates' eyes and perhaps from the psychiatrist's sagacity. (11)

Besides the theoretical sophistication, the difference between psychoanalysis and all the other therapeutic practices undergone by the protagonist resides in this individual relationship, a precondition for the journey that distinguishes the talking cure: transference. The entire narrative hangs on the related problems of transference, translation, vicariousness, and substitution.[8] Early on the protagonist mentions the "immense capacity to transfer that characterizes me" (11–12). In a series of events she is forced to occupy the position of a surrogate, as in her job as a ghostwriter, composing texts later signed by others, reduced to being "a tutelary phantom over someone else's sentence" (25). She also has a long history of inheriting other people's clothes, the definitive metaphor of her vicariousness.[9] These clothes, "left as inheritance or memory of a friend who has just died," (52) bear in themselves those friends, as if clothes had turned into the privileged locus where the dead hang around. Because these objects still, in a way, belong to the dead, "one dares not throw or give them away" (53), which causes in the protagonist an interruption in transference, emblematized in the image of clothes hanging forever, useless in a closet from which one fears to remove them.

Reading *En estado de memoria*, one has the sense that psychoanalysis was the locus where all these impasses could be theorized at a higher level, but for economic reasons, for sheer incompetence of certain analysts, or for a crushing silence that overtakes the narrator on the only occasion where the opportunity does present itself, transference remains a symptom rather than a therapeutic strategy. In an episode that takes place upon her arrival in her French exile, she puts her hopes on a letter that an Argentine psychoanalyst had promised to send to a Swiss colleague, recommending her for sessions in Geneva, located only one hour away from her temporary home in Besançon. The letter elicits her remark "the assumption that I could have an existence as a *case* soothed me" (13). In Mercado's novel the process of endowing the other with that position of knowledge—a formal knowledge in which she could have an existence as a *case*—becomes central to the protagonist, the particular knowledge that fills it at any given moment being a matter of relative indifference. Drug treatments or self-help therapies, homeopathy, group endeavors, or even psychoanalysis are no more than different forms in which this fundamental lack is objectified in a subject-supposed-to-know. What differentiates psychoanalysis is, of course, its awareness that this process of transference is the fundamental enactment of the truth of the unconscious.[10] But the protagonist has to reach that insight through other means, and much of her transformation is embodied in her *transferring* that subject-supposed-to-know from these various external instances to her own practice of writing. By the time she completes the cycle narrated by the novel, she still does not know, *an other* knows in her place. Her trajectory does not lead to any harmonious reconciliation with the truth of her unconscious but instead concludes with the emergence of a practice, namely, writing, in which her ignorance can be articulated. The moment analogous to the psychoanalytic moment of rupture of transference—that moment when the subject recognizes that the other "does not have it" either—takes place in the emergence of writing as a privileged theater for the unconscious.

En estado de memoria is a text in which the only learning lies in coming to terms with that ignorance. A crucial moment takes place upon her return to Argentina, when she seeks aid from an old friend who is now running a "therapeutic altarpiece with Freudian psychoanalysis, Zen Buddhism and Taoism" (59). It soon becomes clear that the protagonist and the pseudoshaman speak entirely different languages:

> She began to list work "opportunities" like someone reading the classifieds page, not without first asking me, in a mysterious and com-

plicit tone, intending that I reveal some sort of concealed vice, *what I really wanted to do in Argentina, what interested me the most, what was it that disquieted me, incited me, but truly,* she said, *what is it you want to do,* marking the question in such a way that no doubt could remain as to its seriousness. . . .

With a lot of effort and after an immersion in my soul as in a confessional, I said that what interested me was to write, *fundamentally to write,* I said, feeling unfortunate and miserable, on the verge of tears and wishing I could flee as soon as possible. . . .

My desire was not any other: *to write,* I had said with the inflection of someone who makes herself pardoned for a fault; *to write,* I whispered, and this startled her; writing does not look like a labor decision, but she wanted to take me to a pragmatic terrain, telling me about people who prepared texts for marketing campaigns, or show-biz promoters who worked for dealers. I did not understand. How was it possible that my confession could only lead her to such hypotheses about my person? (60–61)

This is the first time the protagonist is confronted with that particular species of postdictatorial comforting and reassuring treatment, the typically postcatastrophic phenomenon represented by the rhetoric of self-help and adaptation. Individualizing all problems as matters of personal achievement, creating well-programmed subjects who intervene in the polis at best as consumers, the discourse of adaptation separates politics from experience and imposes a comforting compliance with the new market order: "to ask someone if they are well adapted is a commonplace of a whole social class eager to be tranquilized" (130). It is during the search for an alternative to this adaptive, conformist psychology that her writing opens up to the insistence of the unconscious, embodied in the insistence of unresolved mourning.

The confrontation with the recent Argentine political unconscious includes a critique of certain mythologies of identity that flourished during exile:

The attachment to the country we'd left conditioned all of our lives; there were those who could not overcome the sum of losses and spent the entire day thinking of their neighborhood, idealizing practices that one could not see why should be considered paradigmatic of a paradise lost; the Argentine substance being missed was embodied in mythologies of scarce interest. Seen from today . . . that "iconography" and the little cults to objects that then ruled fantasies, if judged beyond emotions, turn out to be a meaningless patrimony, with no intellectual or imaginary value. (33)

The text unveils the fundamental fallacy of all identitarian rhetoric by relating the predicament of a number of Argentine exiles who mystified an Argentine being and clung to national icons while away from home, only to complain after the return that those wonderful Mexican tortillas and chili could not be found in Buenos Aires. The most ideological facets of exile coalesced in these fetishes of an identity by definition alienated. These little objects, meaningless in themselves, appeared as substitutive, compensatory fictions for a political practice no longer available. "The reproduction of the void was the state proper to exile" (109). What distinguishes *En estado de memoria* is its insistence on mourning this void — by reflexively, symbolically incorporating it into its critical horizon — instead of merely providing a comforting surrogate to replenish the absence left by defeat.

The protagonist experiences exile as something that seems to occupy no particular place in time, as in a voided intermission that leaves no traces:

> Time takes place in a beyond, elsewhere, you hear it in the silences of the night, but you sever it, you don't want to perceive it because you suppose that homelessness will end, that it is a parenthesis that does not count in any becoming. . . . Provisional, time goes from week to week on a train of successive stops. (29)

This parenthesis surely proves to be illusory, because time *has* elapsed. Its weight, however, only makes itself felt retrospectively, after the return, emerging already as a belatedly perceived loss. The hitherto unnoticed destructive action of time is now retrospectively grasped, forcing many exiles into a spurious narrativization of something that cannot be narrativized. To use Benjamin's phrase, they resort to "the whore called 'Once upon a time'"[11] in order to cushion the distressing impact of the past. Speaking of the intolerable "Have you adapted yet?" question, Mercado's protagonist affirms:

The question is insignificant, but rarely does one have the strength to counter it with an *ex abrupto* or a refusal to answer, and all exiles . . . have had to begin by saying "well, at first my folks and I etc. etc. etc.," dividing in temporal fringes something that, being so dramatic, did not admit any slicing. And each one made up a story: there was a before, of flawed integration, then an improvement. (130)

Mercado here exposes the pacifying function of historicism, that narrative of progressive amelioration that implies that "there will be a future time of adaptation in which everything will be ordered in a satisfactory manner" (130). Remaining on guard against a narcotic belief in progress that can only generate a paralyzing optimism, the protagonist reaches a dead end: if the resolution of mourning depends on the elaboration of a narrative, what is to be done when all available narrative models rely on the premise of a gradual adaptation that cannot but repress and silence the work of mourning?

Her challenge is to offer her critical melancholia as an antidote to the optimistic progressivism underlying these exile narratives, while also preventing that melancholia from degenerating into a merely apocalyptic discourse. The refusal of all progressivism and historicism in dealing with the past and the refusal of the apocalyptic in the depiction of the future are in fact two sides of the same coin. Mercado distances herself from the "Once upon a time," one-thing-leads-to-another, gradualist narration of the past because she remains open to everything that, in the past, was silenced by that grand narrative: the fragmentary, the unaccomplished, the contingent, the uncanny, and the aleatory; in short, the remainders of what was defeated in the past. And it is the expectation triggered by these elements, the demand for restitution emanating from them, that prevents the future from congealing into an eschatological apocalypse—the other temptation for postdictatorial literature, parallel to the contented adaptation to the present. The unexpected, the wholly other with which the protagonist strives to have it out, cannot be mastered in any finalist narrative. While the relation to the past attempts to do justice to that which does not fit the progressivist model of historicism, the relation to the future takes the form of an expectation that cannot be domesticated into a telos, a gesture toward what is yet to come that refuses to confine it into a predetermined content, be it salvation or doom. In the protagonist's words, "to predict outcomes also constitutes a neurosis of destiny" (73). As she learns to bypass this neurosis, the future begins to take the form of a radical *outside* beyond all salvational or apocalyptic certainties.

In Mercado's text the past is often embodied in dead objects cut off from the utility they once had, stored in always provisional containers, accumulating in themselves a spectral charge:

> I opened [the trunks] upon my return to Argentina. Many weeks later I began to feel the effects: nightmares, sensation of emptiness, vertigo; the messages I received in opening them began to segregate doses of anxiety. I say it was the trunks, because the unconscious worked nonstop and gained, so to speak, the form of a cave of the human species, with bottoms and backgrounds that escaped consciousness by throwing heavy artillery at it; trapped in the most elementary feelings of terror before the unexpected and the lived, I fruitlessly resisted the dominant image: an open box letting out a pullulating reality. (133–34)

There is a sinister, uncanny character to the memories that spring out of the protagonist's boxes, or yet from her folders named *Recordatorio*, which catalogue experiences related to the friends murdered by the dictatorship.[12] These memories attest to how the past returns in the novel as the *Unheimlich* in the precise Freudian sense: something familiar, already lived, and processed by consciousness, which however can only be reminisced by triggering an unsettling, traumatic dimension that escapes consciousness as such. *En estado de memoria* portrays a mode of relating to the past that is perennially prey to this paradox: the past has become citable but at the price of eluding the consciousness that attempts to master it. The novel depicts an immense number of objects, images, written texts, and memories that catalog the past, but whereas this catalogue is supposed to enhance the subject's familiarity and control over the past, she constantly finds herself to be an *effect* of a mountain of souvenirs. In an episode upon her return, she visits the elementary school where she had studied in Córdoba, now melancholy-looking like all empty schools. The scenario activates the memory of her first day as a student, when she arrived after all children were already lined up to go to class. Standing alone in the courtyard as teachers unsuccessfully looked for her name on their class rolls, she went through the terror of not belonging and being alone in the intimidating emptiness of a school yard: "I am not on the lists, and this condition has been neither elating nor degrading; it has simply been constitutive" (137).

The most spectral instance of the past's return in the novel takes place in the protagonist's obsessive visits to Trotsky's house in Mexico. Trotsky's exile in Mexico pictures better than anything the fate of the Left in this century. As the fiercest enemy and victim of the disastrous bureaucratization of the worker's state in the Soviet Union, Trotsky remains the emblem of defeat. Along with his admirer, the also-Jewish Walter Benjamin, Trotsky understood as no one else the narrowing of historical options down to the choice between complicity and failure. Refusing to compromise with the quietist theory of "socialism in one country" — the religious dogma with which Stalinism helped bury several revolutionary insurrections in the first half of the century — Trotsky was led to confront a succession of failures, from his exclusion from the Communist Party in 1927, to exile in 1929, to a series of visa denials throughout the 1930s, and finally murder at the hands of a Stalinist agent. Mercado's protagonist, undergoing historical defeat in similar circumstances, comes to experience the spectral powers of the house, that ability to return from a failed past to interpellate the present. The spectral past repeats itself in the present, but each repetition produces a unique shock effect: "we'd leaf through the newspapers in several languages that announced the murder in large headlines; . . . we'd read it as one reads Shakespeare, knowing the outcome beforehand, but with an intense anguish, as though we had just found out about the news" (111). Their recurrent visits to the house, the repetitive rituals, the return of ghosts that could not be conjured other than by a political practice now lost, everything contributes to a somatization of historical failure as a compulsion to repeat. The drama here is that the protagonist is forced to resolve individually an impasse that can only be collectively addressed. Somatization becomes allegory in the form of dreams: the protagonist's nine-year-old daughter begins to

> *dream that we cannot leave Trotsky's house. . . . We were all in Trotsky's house with the dog and we could not leave,* that was the leitmotif and we then

> thought, before the vertigo engulfed us, that the sentence condensed
> the fate and history of the Left in the past forty years, our own his-
> tory and fate. (115)

Trapped inside Trotsky's house, trapped inside Trotsky's fate and history,
unable to escape the specter of Trotsky exiled, abandoned, and stabbed
to death from behind, the protagonist contemplates how her historical
defeats become the stuff of symptomatic dreams for her children, heirs
to the heap of disgraces handed down by the past. Like all heirs, they
are disturbed by ghosts, and like all heirs they are in mourning.[13] The
privileged instance of repetition in *En estado de memoria* is a ghost of the
past that, inconjurable because only collective practice could exorcise it,
is inherited in the present by her children as a historical burden, or as
the very burden of history.

And it is in the condition of an heir to another historical defeat,
that of the Spanish Civil War, that the protagonist undertakes her most
vicarious experience, a trip to Asturias, Spain, in place of Ovidio Gondi,
a socialist exile who had arrived in Mexico in 1939, at the age of twenty-
seven. He had been incapable of going back to Spain upon Franco's death
and now found that "I could not bear, physically or mentally, the return
to Asturias. In the world of memories Asturias remains a sort of mytho-
logical territory" (79). The protagonist believes she would be able to
"return in his place and tell him everything I'd seen, . . . give back to him
something of his history" (81). Hers is a restitutive mission that assumes
the secret agreement between the enslaved generations from the past
and the present. Restituting Ovidio Gondi's past is a way of approaching
her own confrontation with the Argentine catastrophe. Once in Asturias she is led by Gondi's only remaining friend in a fruitless search for
former acquaintances, until a seventy-something woman, dressed in strict
mourning, recognizes the name and unearths memories of activists, her
husband included, formerly executed by the fascist army. After recalling
Gondi's father—"they shot him three years after the end of the war, now
you imagine that" (83)—she finally produces an old, yellowish photo of
a piece of wasteland with a cross and the word *PAX* printed on it: "Right
here on this field they were shot. They got mine [her husband] with
another thirty-five on the boats, June 24. . . . Franco did the same to the
monument in the 1950s" (84). With the visit to Asturias the protagonist

begins to make the slow transition back to her own native soil. Again, the narrative progresses by substitutions; this time her position as a surrogate for a friend, as well as the trip's surrogate role for her return to Argentina, are based on a mutual destiny shared by Spanish and Argentine exiles, forty years apart, victims of different turns of the wheel of reaction.

The protagonist's restitutive will must thus straddle, on the one hand, the convergence, even the apparent equivalence between past and present desolation, and on the other the *Unheimlichkeit*, the unfamiliarity and strangeness of that which appears closest at hand. There is a remarkable play involving these two movements in the novel. The accumulation of popular defeats throughout history speaks to her almost as an allegorical household figure, while household items that bear her recent experience seem displaced, foreign, and unwilling to fulfill the restitutive mission with which she endows them, that is, to bear witness. Restitution, the major thrust behind her writing, is paralyzed, blocked, and inevitably enmeshed with the utmost destitution: the restitutive effort only realizes itself when it does not refrain from accepting and embracing destitution. After the return from exile, she experiences the disintegration of her sense of possession, caused by the perennially provisional state in which she has lived. She is overtaken by a sentence—"*Nothing of what surrounds me belongs to me.* And indeed, I'd look at the furniture, beds, books, and have a crystal clear, irrefutable understanding that nothing in the house was mine" (118)—even though everything there does belong to her. As in the opening of old trunks full of memories, the uncanny manifests itself when the familiar suddenly begins to be inhabited by the strange and the sinister. The protagonist and her desire are split by the Unheimlich, in such a way that her own possessions are symbolically torn away from her dwelling, estranged from it, as it were. "Dispossessed of this logic of appropriation common to humans" (117), she experiences the voiding of the concept of the proper, in the inseparable senses of propriety and property, ontological identity and economic ownership.

En estado de memoria thus narrates the epochal crisis of the proper. The protagonist's inability "to make mine the house I occupied" (117) signals a fundamental impossibility of dwelling that goes beyond the more literal phenomenon of exile. To be sure, exile is an instance of a crisis in dwelling not solvable by a mere "return home." If the very nature of dwelling is, as in Heidegger's reflection, "always a staying with things," a preservation that "safeguards each thing in its essence,"[14] the rupture of this being together with things dissolves the foundation that sustains dwelling. Homelessness appears in the novel not as a state in which the subject finds herself divorced from an abode still existent elsewhere; it is, rather, a break in the very principle of dwelling, operative not only upon the present but also retrospectively—estranging the protagonist from her own past, disseminating homelessness in the past—and, proleptically, preempting any utopian jointure in the future. She must, therefore, learn to come to terms with the breakup of dwelling as a *constitutive* condition, this being the reason why the question of exile, however crucial, does not encompass or bring about the crisis of the proper and the dissolution of dwelling but is instead encompassed by them.[15]

The question of the proper is thematized again in a chapter entitled "Fenomenología," where the protagonist relates the experience of a collective reading of Hegel in Mexico. She had bought Hyppolite's legendary translation and lengthy commentary in Paris, following the suggestion of a friend whom she had asked what to buy with only a few francs and the thought of possibly having to deprive herself of another book for the next thirty years. Thus begins the odyssey of what is at one moment conceived as a thirty-year journey through Hegel's *Phenomenology of Spirit*:

> We began to read and go through the thirty years with my Mexican friends. We'd read the French translation and almost simultaneously the Spanish Fondo de Cultura version. We'd read from both books and then go to the third, the Hyppolite. . . . None of us had any knowledge, we were as candid as unpredictably astute, because all of a sudden, with no competence to assimilate the text, each one believed s/he understood everything.
>
> The text would alternately escape us and hand itself to us; there were readings where we'd get into it and out of it like dolphins in the sea, rejoicing in these immersions and acrobatics, convinced that we'd seized the quintessence; but at times the elected fragment was like a rock of unapproachable cliffs on which we'd slip until falling on stupidity and emptiness. The reading was of *something else*, it was a sort of drug that elevated us and made us fly; sentence by sentence we would materially grab the words and I don't know through what odd power these words, over and above the concept, seized in their

pure saying, produced a deep agony in us. Those evenings we passed
from one canyon to another on the great rock and the substance we
touched was the pain of discovering. We did not go beyond page
fifty of the *Phenomenology,* not counting the trips to Hyppolite, but I
believe those sessions were ceremonies of an intense revelation of the
Spirit, a "philosophical" epiphany after which we were able to arrive,
in unrepeatable fashion, at knowledge, at *a* knowledge. (144)

It is fitting that Hegel's *Phenomenology* is the text occupying the protagonist in exile, a time when she weaves and knits more than she reads
or writes. Her reading experience summarizes all the attempts to grasp
truth at the heart of error. In her predicament, as in the labor of the
Hegelian negative, "the life of Spirit is not the life that shrinks from death
and keeps itself untouched by devastation, but rather the life that en-
dures it and maintains itself in it."[16] In a sense, *En estado de memoria* narrates
the protagonist's striving to overcome the separation between truth and
knowledge that founds the phenomenological scene. Such overcoming,
as in Hegel's phenomenology, only takes place once she comes to perceive what happens outside her as a moment of her very essence, that is,
in Hegel's terminology, when the substance proves to be also a subject.
To be sure, that incorporation of the outer into the inner, that digestion that is the very movement of the dialectic, finds itself interrupted
in the novel. The group's abandoning of the *Phenomenology* on page fifty
is thus another signal that the Spirit's journey, the great Bildungsroman
one could claim to be the literary equivalent of Hegel's masterpiece,
can no longer incorporate what resists it. This is due obviously not to
the readers' incompetence but rather to a fundamental change in one's
relation with the objects of knowledge. If Erfahrung in Hegel is the *"dialectical* movement exercised by consciousness on itself that affects both
its knowledge and its object,"[17] experience for Mercado's protagonist has
been reduced to a schizo group reading of the *Phenomenology* in which
that dialectics is paralyzed, frozen by the irreconcilable separation between consciousness and the objectal world, the latter subjected to an
order that defies the very possibility of any grasping by consciousness.
If the *Phenomenology* presupposes that "it is the nature of truth to prevail when its time has come,"[18] this statement for Hegel does not belie a
simple profession of faith in philosophy, marginal to the method elabo-

rated in the text; it is rather the heart of this method, the expression of its necessity. To Mercado's protagonist the possibility is not given of believing that it is the nature of truth to prevail once its time has come. As in Theodor Adorno's assessment of a world that has known Auschwitz, truth's vocation is no longer to prevail on time but rather to be delayed, to be perennially deferred, out of joint with its time. This breach, which dialectics has always mastered, has become unbridgeable in the novel and has come to be the only locus the subject can occupy. The constitution of the subject in *En estado de memoria* thus takes place in the failure of the phenomenological enterprise, a failure that, far from accidental, is the expression of the catastrophe, the manifestation of postdictatorial unresolved mourning.

The constitution of the subject in Mercado's novel thus occurs in a site marked by a not knowing. Led to compare the activities of reading and writing with that of weaving, she finds a resemblance in the solitude demanded by both. However,

> in the textile there is a sort of happiness *del no-ser y del no-estar* [in nonexisting and nonbeing], while in the textual . . . you only harvest misfortune, not as a personal feeling, but as an expression of a fundamental nakedness: not knowing, not being able to fill the void, not encompassing the universal. (146)

Again writing becomes the emblem for the frustration of the phenomenological journey. In a sense, the failure to read Hegel represents for the narrator the beginning of writing as the only practice coextensive with her destitution: one writes in order to experience the impossibility of filling the void and encompassing the universal. In a rather twisted form Hegel is confirmed: she takes hold of truth in the locus of error. In her state the failure to grasp truth is the only possible form in which truth manifests itself. The inability to "encompass the universal," to finish the phenomenological itinerary, is the prerequisite for the emergence of a truth that only writing can articulate. Her understanding of "the misfortune of writing," her coming to terms with it, already contains the entirety of Hegel's lesson, as if missing Hegel's point, failing to understand him, were today—after Auschwitz, after the dictatorial catastrophe—the only possible form of grasping him in his truth; in other words, as though the inability to make truth prevail in time were the very truth of our times.

The consequences of this painstaking (un)learning manifest themselves in the two allegorical chapters located in the middle and ending of the novel, entitled "Celdillas" and "El muro," both of them seeming somewhat isolated, with no obvious relation to the novel in its totality. "Honeycombs" offers an allegorical representation of the unconscious, where traditional images of depth (cave, river, and geological layers) give way to a perforated surface modeled after a honeycomb. The narrator is overtaken by "an irresistible biological desire to bite. Not biting with the teeth, but rather with some other general human device located not in the body but in the vague spaces of the so-called mind" (85). This desire stems from the fact that her whole visual universe is occupied by a line of identical cavities interconnected and absorbent, as in a sponge or a honeycomb, a hallucination that begins to provide the grid through which she grasps her reality. Her challenge is to comprehend this form, to which she refers as "the founding perforated surface" (91). The "cell effect," a symptom of a pathology that "refused to be described other than through a metaphor" (88), reduces her to "a minuscule and besieged being" (91). In her delirium she takes the image of the honeycomb divided in cells as the expression of a plight that affects everybody, and she feels disappointed at "not finding anyone to echo my restlessness or sympathize with my urgency to understand what was happening to me" (88). The delusional paranoia erases the line between the literal and the figurative; the protagonist takes the cells in "the honeycomb" as the structure of reality. Producing a deep anxiety, the "founding perforated surface all of a sudden becomes persecutory and uncontrollable" (91). The figure bespeaks a profound breakdown in the protagonist's production of images. Her only therapeutic reply to the pathology is a gradual attempt to sound out "some lost scene that may have configured the symptom" (92).

In this search "to situate the moment when the surface of the cell receives the sinister mark" (93), she comes across a particular word, *hacinamiento* (heaping), and an image, originated in the photographs of concentration camps filed by her parents more than forty years earlier: "dead bodies piled up; bodies lined up in ditches . . . ; the bowels of a gas chamber exposed in a transversal cut" (93). The painstaking analysis of the symptoms leads her to the understanding of her melancholia: at the root of her pathology was the burden of the unmourned dead whose anonymous, absurd, arbitrary deaths could not possibly be cathected and had thus been somatized through that belittling of the ego characteristic of melancholia.[19] In this context, the image of the Holocaust stands for death without burial, death without the possibility of mourning, death that sends the living to a world inhabited by ghosts and specters. The confrontation with the "founding perforated surface" offers the frame for a symptom that had appeared earlier in the novel, when the protagonist was haunted by the image of "the dead who entered through my eyes and left through my nape" (41). The entire restitutive mission of Mercado's text is to offer a symbolic burial for the dead, finding in writing a practice where the cathexis of this traumatic load can be worked out. The dead who have not been buried, who have been forced to or allowed to hang around the living as ghosts, cannot possibly be mourned. It is incumbent upon the living to restitute the dead to the realm of the dead and liberate them from the uncertain condition of being unnamed, unrecognizable, unmournable ghosts. To use an expression dear to Freud, her task is to transform a repetition into a memory.[20] Yet the restitution of the dead to the realm of the dead represents an ejection that, however crucial for the work of mourning, cannot but be perceived by the survivor as a betrayal, as though the completion of mourning were in fact a second killing of the dead. The transformation of the compulsive repetition into a *memory* can never be neatly differentiated from its submersion into the murky waters of forgetting. The protagonist learns that the reactivation of memory in postdictatorship, if successful, cannot but create the conditions for a reflexive, active forgetting, and this is again conducive to melancholia.[21]

Hence the novel conveys impossibility of associating the recognition of the origin of the symptom, the primary traumatic kernel, with *cure*, whatever status one may confer upon that word. Indeed, the chapter's final sentence preempts any euphoric conclusion regarding the identification of the sinister mark: "this order installed by terror repels and at the same time devours; if one eludes it, it triumphs anyway, and the cavity wins the game" (94). If this is the outcome, what is the use of coming to terms with the symptom? What is the point of being able to identify a pathological process that cannot be reversed? Why formulate the task of restitution when the order of terror will maintain the dead unnamed and unmourned? After all is said and done, where does *En estado de memoria* leave us? Is there a place for affirmation in Mercado's text? Can one mourn affirmatively? And what could that affirmation be?

The novel's final chapter, "The Wall," does not exactly answer these questions, but they refer the reader to a scene where they can be posed anew. Returning to the highly allegorical style of "Celdillos," "El muro" puts forth a certain spatial construction that superimposes a map of the city upon a map of the protagonist's melancholia. In a book full of interesting operations upon temporality, these two pieces are true treaties on the spatialization of affects, portraying an affective field embodied in allegorically charged images. Instead of the honeycomb cells, the final chapter presents a ubiquitous, immense gray wall, a "mantle spread over reality" (181). Knowing that she must eventually confront this wall, she begins to contemplate the space that separates her from it: "a wide and deep precipice . . . leaving a mysterious world out of my reach" (182). This "mysterious world" is nothing less than the outside, the civic life of the city, barred from the protagonist by the wall's restraining action. She gropingly finds her way around the city by visiting cafés, old buildings, and streets, but everywhere the wall makes itself felt in prohibitions, borders, and no-trespassing zones, even when these are "only" psychic.

The protagonist's confrontation with the wall is not to be taken as a conflict in military or militant terms. Defeating the postdictatorial wall, in the sense of eliminating it somehow to enjoy "freedom," is out of the question for Tununa Mercado. The chapter narrates the wall's gradual fading away into the background, but again there is no reason for euphoria. The narrator's "victory" over it, described in the last scene, where the wall surreptitiously slips down into a breach, triggers the process of mourning, understood as the beginning of the acceptance of loss, a process hitherto paralyzed. The wall thus also represents the repressive blockage that suspended mourning and forced it to remain unresolved. Not by chance, the moment of overcoming the wall coincides with a scene during which the protagonist enters into writing as though groping at an unknown reality that offers formidable obstacles:

> With small characters, awkward calligraphy and from the upper left corner I began to write. The pen tore up the surface and advanced with an uncertain design, producing small blocks of text. . . . [A]s

> though conditioned by terror at the unlimited surface, it created
> zones of reserve, baits of reference where it could return in case it
> got lost. (196)

As in a minuscule epic, a tale of war between a body and a disease, the
fate of the protagonist's affects, as well as of her public presence in the
city, are played out on the page. The repressive barrier stemming from
the traumatic experience has been lifted, although not destroyed:

> The wall . . . exposed to a hitherto unknown storm, constrained by
> the pit and dominated by a prolonged siege, literally began to fall
> upon the straight line of its base; it did not crumble throwing rub-
> bish like an earthquake building, but filtered itself upon its founding
> line, as a sheet of paper vertically slipping into a breach. (196–97)

En estado de memoria is thus a prolegomenon to postdictatorial writing
in that it narrates the conditions of possibility for writing after a catastrophe. The true story has not been told. Following the protagonist's
compelling refusal of all substitutive, compensatory mechanisms, and
her decision not to elude the abyss of depression and melancholia, the
final scene announces writing as the locus where the confrontation with
the pathology can truly take place beyond the mere identification of the
symptom, in a movement that is not simply a dive into the subject's interiority but a decisive reconnection with the outside. What might at first
appear to be a highly introspective text ends with a gesture toward an
unnamed, unknown outside that represents the only possibility of acti-
vating subjective memory along with a space of intervention in the polis.
One might refer to this outside as *the wholly other*, as the alterity that is
no longer a simple disguise for a repetition of the past traumatic kernel
(in Mercado's terms a new fold of the "founding perforated surface") but
rather an otherness unrepresentable by the present, an untimely other
that houses the possibility of memory and utopia. The wholly other announced by writing, the singular event as of yet unimaginable, becomes
the only desirable mode of relationship with the future, beyond all finalist, teleologic, apocalyptic, and historicist cushions. In yet another apparent paradox, therefore, *En estado de memoria*, a novel obsessed with the
impact of the past, reveals itself as a thoroughly future-oriented text.
More than asking what future can be imagined after the dictatorships,

however, it inquires into the mode, the modality, in which another relationship with the future can be established. This question remains, in Mercado, a formal question linked with the resolution of mourning.

En estado de memoria looks to the terrain whence postdictatorial symptomatology emerges, the unresolved dilemma of mourning, to imply that only the resolution of mourning will open up a space for the production of desires that would not be mere symptoms of loss. The only locus of a nonaberrant postdictatorial desire would thus be the soil from which all aberrations grow, in a final Hegelian irony in this most un-Hegelian text. This soil is the foundational, primary need that mourning run its course lest all desires become simply their own repressive, compensatory sublimation. In this sense postdictatorship stages both a desire for mourning—the embrace of mourning as the arena where the fate of the postdictatorial affective field will be played out—and mourning for desire—the acceptance of the defeat of all the desires swept away by the dictatorship. Tununa Mercado's *En estado de memoria* makes the most emphatic case for the role of writing in the accomplishment of this task: straddling the oppositions confronted by the protagonist and the postdictatorial affective field, writing is at the same time a solitary and collective, personal and anonymous, utopian and melancholic enterprise, much like the mourning it voices, and without the resolution of which postauthoritarian societies might face an unprecedented abyss of depression, barely masked underneath the triumphant neoliberal parade.

AFTERWORD Postdictatorship and Postmodernity

The main interest in life and work is to become someone else that you were not in the beginning. If you knew when you began a book what you would say at the end, do you think you would have the courage to write it? What is true for writing and a love relationship is true also for life. The game is worthwhile insofar as we don't know what will be the end.

—MICHEL FOUCAULT, "Truth Power and Self: An Interview with Michel Foucault"

While the Foucault epigraph that opens this afterword accurately describes my method of composition in this book, it also, and more importantly, captures my stance toward the underlying question guiding my engagement with postdictatorship: that of the status of literary writing in the age of the definitive decline of its links with experience. Whereas much of the literary-critical establishment has either migrated into other domains—supposedly or hopefully endowed with the experiential and social relevance one perceives to be waning in literature—or anguishedly frets over the future of its discipline, undertaking a preoccupied and at times paranoid drawing of disciplinary boundaries, I would like to return to the Nietzschean notion with which I opened this book, that of the untimely. An untimely approach to literature's recent defeats would stand in opposition both to the attempt to "adjust to the present conditions" (thereby embracing objects more palatable to a technified polis) as well as to the nostalgic, reactive defense of—or a refusal to mourn—what has been swept away by technification (in a word, the auratic quality of the literary). The untimely critic does not ever take the present as a given to adjust to it. S/he does not ever attempt to preserve a corner in a current configuration of things. Those who work under the sign of the untimely do not engage the future attempting to predict or circumscribe it. Insisting on a radical discord with the present precisely in order to foreground the absolute, *unimaginable*, unrepresentable openness of the future, the untimely only experiences the latter in the form of an open promise. Instead of "adjusting to the new times" and searching for a theoretical position, a vocabulary or a set of guidelines that might draw up for literature a self-satisfied corner in today's intellectual division of labor—thus bringing it "up to date" with the demands imposed by technification—I would rather insist on the reflection on the conditions of possibility of literature's very untimeliness in the current marketplace.

It is here, then, that for Latin America postmodernity meets postdictatorship: postmodernity, in its most rigorous, Jamesonian sense, alludes to that moment of thorough colonization of the planet by transnational capital, in such a way that even those once thought to be non-reified footholds—say, nature or the unconscious—have now been entirely engulfed into the machine of capital. This epochal horizon can be philosophically defined as a cognitive fall into sheer immanence, inasmuch as postmodernity designates the disappearance of all transcendental points of anchorage that used to allow the dispersion of events, the brute facticity of experience, to be conceptually raised to a higher level and thought as a positive totality. With the extensive colonization of the planet and the elimination of all coexistence of modes of production, the comprehension of the present as a historical, relative, and changeable reality has become problematic. It is nothing other than this that Fredric Jameson has in mind when he speaks of the "waning of the sense of history" in postmodernity. Nothing looks so much like nature as late capitalism, precisely the social system that has abolished it once and for all.

In Latin America the introduction of this new stage of capital was precisely the epochal role played by the dictatorships. Again, it is worthwhile to recall Eduardo Galeano's sentence: people were tortured so that prices could be free. If the function of the dictatorships was the epochal ushering of the postmodern stage of capital, the task facing literary writing in postmodern postdictatorships will necessarily differ from previous postdictatorships, in that now the imperative of mourning imposes itself in a context in which literature has been forced to abandon its privileged role in modernity—the imagination of an otherwise, the redemption of the poetic within the prosaism of daily alienated life, and the envisioning of a redemptive epiphany. As the once unique modernist signature is dissolved in anonymity or shuffled in a multiplicity of apocryphal names, it is the enterprise of modern literature—for its constitution centered on a fundamental relationship with the *proper name*—that seems to have met its epochal limit. In this sense literature's postdictatorial mourning already implies mourning for the literary.

By oscillating between the positions of subject and object of mourning, postdictatorial literature finds itself, then, perennially on the brink of melancholia. In its strict Freudian sense, the distinction between mourning and melancholia has to do with the locus of the loss, either situated outside the subject, having a profound impact upon him/her but being ultimately comprehensible as one's loss of something else (mourning), or yet ubiquitous to the point of engulfing the mourner him/herself in the loss, so the very separation between subject and object of loss disappears (melancholia). Several of the books analyzed here depict scenes in which it is perceived (by a character, a narrator-protagonist, or the implied author) that one can no longer write, that *writing is no longer possible*, and that writing's only remaining task is to account for that impossibility. The loss with which writing attempts to come to terms has, melancholically, swallowed writing itself, with the effect that the subject who mourns the other finds him/herself to be part of what has been dissolved. This discovery takes places in that murky gray area where mourning borders with melancholia. Melancholia thus emerges from a specific variety of mourning, one that has looped back around to engulf the mournful subject. In this sense, melancholia is nothing but a privileged symptom of a blockade in the resolution of mourning work.

From the aforementioned deadlock stems my insistence not only on the allegorical quality of the texts I analyze here but on the epochal primacy of allegory in postdictatorship tout court. Allegory is the trope of the impossible; by necessity it responds to a fundamental impossibility, an essential breakdown in representation. It builds that impossibility, in fact, into its emergence as a trope. If the historical defeat to the dictatorships also implied a defeat for literary writing, the task of allos-agoreuein, speaking otherwise, imposes itself. "Speaking otherwise" should not only be understood as a mere search for alternative forms of speech but also as speaking *of* the other (in the double sense of the genitive) and, first and foremost, as speaking *to* the other, of answering the call of the other. Postdictatorial literature speaks (the) other(wise). Allegorization takes place when that which is most familiar reveals itself as (an)other, when the most customary is interpreted as a ruin, and the pile of past catastrophes hitherto concealed under that storm called "progress" at last begins to be unearthed. The most familiar cultural documents become allegorical once they are referred back to the barbarism that lies at their origin.

As postdictatorial Latin American countries move on to monetarist stabilization programs, and the once totalizing figure of the intellectual gets replaced by the modest and efficient technician, with the more risk-taking aesthetic experiments being also pushed to the background by culturalism, the tendency is clearly for the issues outlined here to be repressed and forgotten. Very few voices still insist on them today. As the sociopolitical context evolves, the discourses I have highlighted should, themselves, progressively become allegorical ruins, much like the memories of past defeats they engage. This self-reflexive, potentially infinite chain of allegorization is not, as some versions of a self-satisfied postmodernism would have it, to be celebrated. On the contrary, the chain should always be brought to a halt, interrupted, and referred back to the desolation and misery that makes it possible. This, if it cannot properly be called a program for our times, should at least serve as the index of the infinity of a political and ethical task.

NOTES

Introduction

1　Benjamin, *The Origin of the German Tragic Drama*, trans. John Osborne (London and New York: Verso, 1977), 166.

2　Ibid., 217.

3　Paul de Man, "The Rhetoric of Temporality" (1969), in *Blindness and Insight: Essays in the Rhetoric of Contemporary Criticism* (1971), rev. 2d ed. (Minneapolis: U of Minnesota P, 1983), 207.

4　It should be pointed out that as far as Marx is concerned, what appears to be a symmetrical dichotomy between use and exchange is in fact a critical operation in which only the latter has a real epistemic status. As Jameson notes, "[use value] is 'always-already' if there ever was one: The minute commodities begin to speak . . . they have already become exchange-values. Use value is one of those lateral or marginal concepts which keeps moving to the edge of your field of vision as you displace its centre around the field, always a step ahead of you, never susceptible of being fixed or held." Frederic Jameson, "Marx's Purloined Letter," *New Left Review* 209 (1995): 92.

5　Jacques Derrida, *Cinders* (1987), trans. Ned Lukacher (Lincoln: U of Nebraska P, 1991), 55.

6　Quoted in Benjamin, *Origin*, 161.

7　Georg Wilhelm Friedrich Hegel, *Aesthetics* (1835), trans. T. M. Knox, vol. 1 (Oxford, England: Oxford UP, 1975), 399.

8　Ibid., 400.

9　Timothy Bahti, *Allegories of History: Literary Historiography after Hegel* (Baltimore and London: Johns Hopkins UP, 1992), 110.

10　"An allegory is but a translation of abstract notions into a picture-language, which is itself nothing but an abstraction from objects of the senses; the principal being more worthless even than its phantom proxy, both alike unsubstantial, and the former shapeless to boot. On the other hand a symbol . . . is characterized by a translucence of the special in the individual, or of the general in the special, or of the universal in the general; above all by the translucence of the eternal through and in the temporal." Quoted in Angus Fletcher, *Allegory: The Theory of a Symbolic Mode* (Ithaca, N.Y., and London: Cornell UP, 1964), 16.

11 Walter Benjamin, *Passagen-Werk,* ed. Rolf Tiedemann (Frankfurt a.M.: Suhrkamp Verlag, 1982), 362. All translations from the *Passagen,* as well as from all texts cited in languages other than English are mine, unless otherwise noted.

12 Benjamin, *Origin,* 162. This is naturally a coarse summary of a problem fraught with ambiguities. The counterargument must be considered as well: despite his condemnations, Hegel's *procedure* in the *Aesthetics* is itself allegorical. For a study of the foundational role of allegory in Hegel's writing of history, see Bahti, *Allegories of History,* 95–133.

13 Quoted in Jorge Luis Borges, "De las alegorías a las novelas," in *Otras inquisiciones* (1952), vol. 3 of *Prosa completa* (Buenos Aires: Emecé, 1979), 164.

14 Benjamin, *Origin,* 187.

15 Nicolas Abraham and Maria Torok, *The Wolf Man's Magic Word: A Cryptonymy,* foreword Jacques Derrida (1976), trans. Nicholas Rand (Minneapolis: U of Minnesota P, 1986).

16 For Freud's account of the Wolf Man case, see *The History of an Infantile Neurosis* (1918), vol. 17 of *The Standard Edition of the Complete Psychological Works of Sigmund Freud,* trans. James Strachey et al. (London: Hogarth, 1957).

17 Laurence A. Rickels, *Aberrations of Mourning: Writing on German Crypts* (Detroit: Wayne State UP, 1988), 5.

18 Abraham and Torok, *The Wolf Man's Magic Word,* 21.

19 Nicolas Abraham and Maria Torok, "Mourning *or* Melancholia: Introjection versus Incorporation" (1972), in *The Shell and the Kernel: Renewals of Psychoanalysis,* trans. and ed. Nicholas Rand (Chicago and London: U of Chicago P, 1994), 127.

20 Ricardo Piglia, *Crítica y ficción* (1986), 2d ed. (Buenos Aires: Siglo XXI and Universidad Nacional del Litoral, 1993), 158–59.

21 Benjamin, "A Berlin Chronicle," in *Reflections: Essays, Aphorisms, Autobiographical Writings,* trans. Edmund Jephcott (New York: Schocken, 1978), 25.

22 Fredric Jameson, "Third-World Literature in the Age of Multinational Capitalism," *Social Text* 15 (1986): 81.

23 João Gilberto Noll, *Hotel Atlântico,* 4th ed. (Rio de Janeiro: Rocco, 1989).

24 Friedrich Nietzsche, "On the Uses and Disadvantages of History for Life," in *Untimely Meditations,* trans. R. J. Hollingdale (Cambridge: Cambridge UP, 1983), 60.

25 In this sense the untimely represents the eruption of everything that does not conform to the affective field dominant in postdictatorship, such as analyzed by Alberto Moreiras under the rubrics of paranoid, hysterical,

and schizo desires. See his pioneering article "Postdictadura y reforma del pensamiento," *Revista de Crítica Cultural* 7 (1993): 26–35.

1 Oedipus in Post-auratic Times

1 *Affect* is etymologically related to the Latin *facere* (to do). *Affectus,* the preterite form of *afficere* (to influence, to attack) stems from the composite form *ad* (to, toward) plus *facere. Affectare,* in Latin, has not only the sense of "to have an effect upon" but also "to strive for." See the key role played by Spinoza's theory of affect in an immanentist and processual notion of desire such as Gilles Deleuze's: "Desire is . . . a process, rather than a genesis or structure; it is affect, rather than *sentiment* [feeling]." "Désire et plaisir," *Magazine Littéraire* 325 (1994), 63. Spinoza's elaborations on immanence of affect are to be found in the third part of his *Ethics* (1677), *A Spinoza Reader: The Ethics and Other Works,* trans. Edwin Curley (Princeton, N.J.: Princeton UP, 1994), 85–265.

2 John Beverley, *Against Literature* (Minneapolis and London: U of Minnesota P, 1993), 98. Beverley's narrative depends on several translations, which demand closer interrogation, notably, the one that equates *lo letrado* and *lo literario:* "Tomás in Cervantes's novel is a *letrado* or 'man of letters,' meaning in practice both a university graduate—a *licenciado*—and, as the name suggests, an almost always masculine subject formed *by* and to some extent *for* literature (in Renaissance Spanish, *letras*)" (29). Such an equation (between "literature" and *letras* in "Renaissance Spanish") is novel enough to lead the reader to expect a demonstration of what it is that authorizes it. For if Beverley's reading of Garcilaso de la Vega's twenty-third sonnet as one that "sublimates and eternalizes its subject" (36) is to prove that an ideology of the literary already operated in early sixteenth-century poetry, then one has to ask oneself what has been made of the category of literature in everything that opposes it to rhetoric, poetry, epic, and so on, namely, a certain connection with the individual signature, a constitutive relationship with property as such, a quite locatable role in the separation of social spheres toward the end of the eighteenth century, and so forth. If no attention is paid to that, collapsing *letras* (or *poetry,* in the sense that it can have in Garcilaso) into literature remains a dogmatic and opportunistic move, a retrospective fallacy designed to justify a supposedly liberating break to be ascribed to testimonio. A more careful historicization might note that not only for Garcilaso in the 1520s but even for Baltazar Gracián, more than a century later, the "eloquence and good writing" that Beverley associates with the "ideology of the literary" (38) were rigorously circumscribed as *rhetoric* and therefore only in a quite distorted form collapsible

into literature in the modern sense. The problem is surely immense, and I return to it in chapter two. Two important considerations of Beverley's thesis can be found in Alberto Moreiras, "The Aura of Testimonio," in *The "Real" Thing: Testimonial Discourse and Latin America*, ed. George M. Gugelberger (Durham, N.C.: Duke UP, 1996), and Neil Larsen, *Reading North by South: On Latin American Literature, Culture, and Politics* (Minneapolis and London: U of Minnesota P, 1995), where Larsen compellingly shows how the countercanonization of testimonio is the great reassertion of modernist, aestheticist, boom-defined values, because high modernism is assumed to have an exclusive claim on the literary as such. For an attentive treatment of the history of the category of *letrado* in Latin America, see Angel Rama, *La ciudad letrada* (Hanover: Ediciones del Norte, 1984); for the acutest genealogy of the notion of literature in Spanish America, see Julio Ramos, *Desencuentros de la modernidad en América Latina: Literatura y política en el siglo XIX* (Mexico City: Siglo XXI, 1989).

3   The first quote is from "Postmodernism in the Periphery," *South Atlantic Quarterly* 92 (1993): 554. The other two are from "Testimonio and Postmodernism," *Latin American Perspectives* 18 (1991): 20, 26. In his recent work Yúdice has elaborated on the status of the literary—a reflection already informed by a renewed understanding of cultural policy—in ways that productively displace the thematic of consciousness. In his critique of Fuentes and Paz, Yúdice shows how the political argument around identity can give way to what I would call a topology of forces in the public sphere, in which the category of liberated consciousness would presumably be in question. See his "Postmodernity and Transnational Capitalism," in *On Edge: The Crisis of Contemporary Latin American Culture*, ed. George Yúdice, Juan Flores, and Jean Franco (Minneapolis and London: Minnesota UP, 1992), 11–15. See also his critique of a certain will to embrace multicultural redemption in the way U.S. intellectuals relate to global culture, in "We Are *Not* the World," *Social Text* 31–32 (1992): 202–16.

4   Jean Franco, "Remapping Culture," *Latin American Literary Review* 20 (1992): 40.

5   Miguel Barnet, "La novela-testimonio: socio-literatura," in *Testimonio y literatura*, ed. René Jara and Hernán Vidal (Minneapolis: U of Minnesota P, 1986), 285.

6   Carlos Fuentes, *La nueva novela hispanoamericana* (Mexico City: Joaquín Mortiz, 1969), 13.

7   Ibid., 14. In the same logic, see the following statement: "*Los de abajo, La sombra del caudillo* and *Si me han de matar mañana* . . . , over and above their possible technical shortcomings and despite their documentary remnants,

introduced an original note in the Spanish-American novel: they introduced ambiguity" (15). Again, the conception is that history unfolds by gradual amelioration.

8   Ibid., 30, 36.

9   Emir Rodríguez Monegal, *Narradores de esta América*, 2 vols. (Montevideo: Alfa, 1969), 10.

10 Ibid., 11.

11 Ibid., 41.

12 Ibid., 11.

13 Fuentes, *La nueva novela hispanoamericana*, 35.

14 On the concept of discursive formation, see Michel Foucault, *The Archaeology of Knowledge* (1969), trans. Alan Sheridan Smith (New York: Pantheon Books, 1972), especially the notion of discursive regularities.

15 Alejo Carpentier, "La novela latinoamericana en vísperas de un nuevo siglo," in *Ensayos* (Havana: Letras Cubanas, 1984), 155.

16 Vargas Llosa, quoted in George R. Coulthard, "La pluralidad cultural," in *América Latina en su literatura*, ed. César Fernández Moreno (Mexico: UNESCO and Siglo XXI, 1972), 71.

17 Angel Rama, "El boom en perspectiva," in *La crítica de la cultura en América Latina* (Caracas: Biblioteca Ayacucho, 1985), 293–96.

18 Julio Cortázar, quoted in Rama, "El boom," 272–73.

19 Beatriz Sarlo, "El campo intelectual: un espacio doblemente fracturado," *Represión y reconstrucción de una cultura: el caso argentino*, ed. Saúl Sosnowski (Buenos Aires: EUDEBA, 1988), 96.

20 Rama, "El boom," 286. I cannot refrain from retelling an anecdote that illustrates my point. Borges relates how he stormed into his mother's house in 1930, jubilant over the sale of twenty-seven copies of one of his books. His mother, filled with emotion, replied: "Twenty-seven books is an incredible number! You're becoming a famous man, Georgie." Roberto Alifano, *Conversaciones con Borges* (Buenos Aires: Atlántida, 1984), 94.

21 Preliminary work for national situations has been done, especially regarding the turn of the century. For Argentina, see Carlos Altamirano and Beatriz Sarlo, "La Argentina del centenario: campo intelectual y temas ideológicos," *Hispamérica* 9 (1980): 35–59; for Chile, see the excellent essay by Gonzalo Catalán, "Antecedentes sobre la transformación del campo literario en Chile entre 1890 y 1920," in *Cinco estudios sobre cultura y sociedad*, by José Joaquín Brunner and Gonzalo Catalán (Santiago: FLACSO, 1985), 69–175.

22 Walter Benjamin, "The Work of Art in the Age of Mechanical Reproduction," in *Illuminations*, trans. Harry Zohn (New York: Schocken, 1968),

224. For Benjamin the aura stands for that "unique phenomenon of a distance" characteristic of a residual cult value of the artwork, ultimately extinguished only with the advent of modern means of reproduction.

23   The definitive study of this process remains Jürgen Habermas, *The Structural Transformation of the Public Sphere: An Inquiry into a Category of Bourgeois Society* (1962), trans. Thomas Burger and Frederick Lawrence (Cambridge, Mass.: MIT, 1989), 27–56.

24   Rama, *La ciudad,* 33. In the Brazilian tradition Antonio Candido was the first to devote systematic critical attention to literature's class-specific status in the country, by examining the dialectic between two factors: (1) the confinement of literature to a small reading public, which in turn reinforced (2) Brazilian literature's notorious complicity with colonial and postcolonial elites. Candido is careful, however, not to reduce the effects of the literary to such complicity, which would mean blinding oneself to all the inconsistencies, contradictions, aporias, paradoxes, and failures of the hegemonic projects one hopes to examine. See "Literatura e Subdesenvolvimento," in *A Educação pela Noite e Outros Ensaios* (São Paulo: Atica, 1984), 140–62; see also "Literatura de Dois Gumes," in *A Educação,* 163–80, the *dois gumes* (two edges) in the title suggesting precisely that duplicity.

25   Sigmund Freud, "Mourning and Melancholia" (1916), in vol. 14 of *The Standard Edition of the Complete Psychological Works of Sigmund Freud,* trans. James Strachey (London: Hogarth, 1957), 237–58. Freud associates the "phase of triumph" (255) with mania as such, that is, the regime in which the ego has surmounted and is triumphing over something that remains hidden from it. See also the *economic* logic that makes possible the phase of triumph, as in the reflection on debt and expenditure (253–58). In Nicholas Abraham and Maria Torok's rereading of Freud's conceptual pair, it is the notion of *incorporation*—the introduction of all or part of the love object into one's own body as an intrapsychic tomb where the other is buried alive—which emerges as coextensive with this triumphant moment of blocked mourning. See *The Wolf Man's Magic Word* and "Mourning *or* Melancholia."

26   Jean Franco, "Memoria, narración y repetición: la narrativa latinoamericana en la época de la cultura de masas," in *Más allá del boom: literatura y mercado,* ed. Angel Rama et al. (Mexico City: Marcha, 1981), 116. On the boom's denial of tradition, see Doris Sommer, "Irresistible Romance: The Foundational Fictions of Latin America," in *Nation and Narration,* ed. Homi Bhabha (New York and London: Routledge, 1990), 71.

27   Enrique Pupo-Walker, *La vocación literaria del pensamiento histórico en América: desarrollo de la prosa de ficción, siglos XVI, XVII, XVIII, XIX* (Madrid: Gredos, 1982).

28 Jorge Aguilar Mora, "Sobre el lado moridor de la 'nueva narrativa' hispano-americana," in *Más allá del boom*, ed. Angel Rama et al., 241.

29 Roberto González Echevarría, *Myth and Archive: A Theory of Latin American Narrative* (Cambridge: Cambridge UP, 1990), 21–22.

30 González Echevarría has signaled in the same direction in noting how Melquíades alludes to Jorge Luis Borges: "In fact, Melquíades is a figure of the Argentine writer. Old beyond age, enigmatic, blind, entirely devoted to writing, Melquíades stands for Borges, the librarian and keeper of the archive." Ibid., 23.

31 Alberto Morciras, "Pastiche Identity and Allegory of Allegory," in *Latin American Identity and Constructions of Difference*, ed. Amaryll Chanady (Minneapolis and London: U of Minnesota P, 1994), 205. The temporality of accomplished identity represents that nightmare of a "definitive exorcism of spectres and spectrality, the beginning of a market universe which is a perpetual present, as well as the instauration of truth." Jameson, "Marx's Purloined Letter," 108. For Derrida's elaborations on the apocalyptic, see *Specters of Marx: The State of the Debt, the Work of Mourning and the New International* (1993), trans. Peggy Kamuf (New York and London: Routledge, 1994), and "On a Newly Arisen Apocalyptic Tone in Philosophy" (1981), in *Raising the Tone in Philosophy*, ed. Peter Fenves (Baltimore: Johns Hopkins UP, 1993). For a discussion of Derrida's and Jameson's positions on the spectral, see my "Marx, en inminencia y urgencia," *Revista de Crítica Cultural* 11 (1994): 63–66, and "El espectro en la temporalidad de lo mesiánico: Derrida y Jameson a propósito de la firma Marx," in *Espectros y pensamiento utópico*, vol. 2 of *La invención y la herencia*, ed. Federico Galende (Santiago: ARCIS-LOM, 1995).

32 Roberto Schwarz, "Nacional por Subtração," in *Que Horas São?* (São Paulo: Companhia das Letras, 1987), 4.

33 For the culminating political moment of said convergence between the thinking of dependency and that of modernization, see, of course, the trajectory of ("former," he insists) sociologist and present implementer of neoliberalism Fernando Henrique Cardoso.

34 Derrida has named that paradox "the irreducibility of the 'effect of deferral,'" a delay that produces its own object and whose temporality comes to be linked by Derrida to that of writing. See "Freud and the Scene of Writing" (1966), in *Writing and Difference*, trans. Alan Bass (Chicago: U of Chicago P, 1978), 196–231.

35 Julio Cortázar, *Rayuela* (1963), Colección Archivos, ed. Julio Ortega and Saúl Yurkievich (Madrid: CSIC, 1991), 183.

36 Andreas Huyssen, *Twilight Memories: Marking Time in a Culture of Amnesia* (New York and London: Routledge, 1995), 33.

37   These axes define much of what the boom produced on Borges and Argue-
      das, from Monegal to Vargas Llosa. In the case of Arguedas a significant
      change would occur as a result of remarkable analyses by Antonio Cornejo
      Polar, *Los universos narrativos de José María Arguedas* (Lima: Instituto de Estu-
      dios Peruanos, 1973), and "Un ensayo sobre 'los zorros' de Arguedas," in *El
      zorro de arriba y el zorro de abajo,* by José María Arguedas, ed. Eve-Marie Fell
      (Madrid: Archivos, 1990), 296-306; William Rowe, "El nuevo lenguaje de
      Arguedas en *El zorro de arriba y el zorro de abajo,*" *Texto Crítico* 11 (1978): 198-
      212, and "Deseo, escritura y fuerzas productivas," in *El zorro de arriba,* 333-40;
      Martin Lienhard, *Cultura popular andina y forma novelesca: zorros y danzantes en la
      última novela de Arguedas* (Caracas: Universidad Central de Venezuela, 1981).
      All of these critics could only reach this critical assessment of Arguedas by
      deliberately distancing themselves from the rhetoric of the criticism asso-
      ciated with the boom.
38   Quoted in Elisabeth Garrels, "Resumen de la discusión," in *Más allá del boom,*
      ed. Angel Rama et al., 293.
39   Ricardo Piglia and Juan José Saer, *Por un relato futuro* (Santa Fé, Argentina:
      Universidad Nacional del Litoral, 1990), 23-24.

2 *The Genealogy of a Defeat: Latin American Culture under Dictatorship*

1   For the episodes immediately following 31 March, see Nélson Werneck
      Sodré, *História da História Nova* (Petrópolis, Brazil: Vozes, 1986).
2   Roberto Schwarz, "Cultura e Política, 1964-1969" (1970), in *O Pai de Família
      e Outros Estudos* (Rio de Janeiro: Paz e Terra, 1978), 62.
3   Ibid., 63. I have chosen to provide my own translations of "Cultura e Polí-
      tica," for John Gledson's version mistranslates *teórica* as "doctrinal," *produção
      artística* as "artistic expression," *público dos melhores filmes* as "those who en-
      joyed the best films," and so on. See Roberto Schwarz, *Misplaced Ideas: Essays
      on Brazilian Culture,* trans. and ed. John Gledson (London and New York:
      Verso, 1992), 126-59.
4   Flora Süssekind, *Literatura e Vida Literária* (São Paulo: Zahar, 1985), 18.
5   Ibid., 12.
6   Renato Ortiz, *Cultura Brasileira e Identidade Nacional* (São Paulo: Brasiliense,
      1985), 87.
7   Quoted in ibid., 119-20. See also Néston García Canclini's analysis of the
      privatization of initiative in the art institution and the still state-national
      domain of patrimony in *Hybrid Cultures: Strategies for Entering and Leaving Moder-
      nity* (1989), trans. Christopher Chiappari and Silvia López (Minneapolis:
      U of Minnesota P, 1995).

8   Ibid.

9   For an excellent study of state cultural policies in Brazil during the dictatorship, see Ortiz, *Cultura Brasileira*, 79–142. On the polemic over "theory" in literature departments, see Süssekind, *Literatura*, 28–34; on the naturalist hegemony during the 1970s, see Flora Süssekind, *Tal Brasil, Qual Romance?* (Rio de Janeiro: Achiamé, 1984), 172–94.

10 Bernardo Subercaseaux, *Historia, literatura y sociedad: ensayos de hermenéutica cultural* (Santiago: CESOC and CENECA, 1991), 123.

11 Bernardo Subercaseaux, *La industria cultural y el libro en Chile (1930–1984)* (Santiago: CENECA, 1984), 130–31.

12 Carlos Catalán, *Estado y campo cultural en Chile*, Serie Material de Discusión 115 (Santiago: FLACSO, 1988), 26.

13 Anny Rivera, *Transformaciones culturales y movimiento artístico en el orden autoritario: Chile, 1973–1982* (Santiago: CENECA, 1983), 24–25.

14 Pablo Oyarzún, "Arte en Chile de veinte, treinta años," *Georgia Series on Hispanic Thought* 22–25 (1987–88): 303.

15 Jaime Collyer, "De las hogueras a la imprenta: el arduo renacer de la narrativa chilena," *Cuadernos Hispanoamericanos* 482–83 (1990): 126.

16 Subercaseaux, *Industria*, 80.

17 Carlos Orellana, "La cultura chilena en el momento del cambio," *Cuadernos Hispanoamericanos* 482–83 (1990): 50.

18 José Joaquín Brunner, "Entre la cultura autoritaria y la cultura democrática," in *Un espejo trizado: ensayos sobre culturas y políticas culturales* (Santiago: FLACSO, 1988), 87.

19 Pablo Sapag, "Chile: experiencia sociopolítica y medios de comunicación," *Cuadernos Hispanoamericanos* 482–83 (1990): 63–70.

20 For the best analyses of Chilean art under dictatorship, see Pablo Oyarzún, "Arte en Chile," and Nelly Richard, *Margins and Institutions: Art in Chile since 1973*, bilingual edition (Melbourne: Art and Text, 1986). For a useful compilation of cultural transformations during this period, with a complete social-scientific bibliography, see José Joaquín Brunner, Alicia Barros, and Carlos Catalán, *Chile: Transformaciones culturales y modernidad* (Santiago: FLACSO, 1989).

21 Gabriel Salazar, "Historiografía y dictadura en Chile (1973–1990)," *Cuadernos Hispanoamericanos* 482–83 (1990): 87.

22 Oscar Terán, *Nuestros años sesentas: la formación de la nueva izquierda intelectual en Argentina, 1956–1966* (Buenos Aires: Puntosur, 1991), 52–53.

23 Silvia Sigal, *Intelectuales y poder en la década del sesenta* (Buenos Aires: Puntosur, 1991), 153.

24 Sarlo, "El campo intelectual," 98.

25 Piglia, *Crítica y ficción*, 118. For a detailed analysis of the intellectual field in Argentina during the sixties, see Terán, *Nuestros años sesentas*, and Sigal, *Intelectuales y poder*. For a study of the crossroads between the literary boom and Argentine literature, see Adolfo Prieto, "Los años sesenta," *Revista Iberoamericana* 125 (1983): 891–901.

26 Noé Jitrik, *Las armas y las razones: ensayos sobre el peronismo, el exilio y la literatura, 1975–1980* (Buenos Aires: Sudamericana, 1984), 210.

27 Evelyn Picón Garfield, "Cortázar por Cortázar," in Cortazar, *Rayuela*, 785.

28 Francine Masiello, "La Argentina durante el proceso: las múltiples resistencias de la cultura," in *Ficción y política: la narrativa argentina durante el proceso militar* (Buenos Aires and Minneapolis: Alianza Editorial and the Institute for the Study of Ideologies and Literatures, 1987).

29 Liliana Heker, "Los talleres literarios," *Cuadernos Hispanoamericanos* 217–19 (1993): 187–94.

30 Andrés Avellaneda, "Realismo, antirrealismo, territorios canónicos: Argentina literaría después de los militares" in Hernán Vidal, ed., *Fascismo y experiencia literaria: reflexiones para una canonización* (Minneapolis: Institute for the Study of Languages and Literatures, 1985), 582. For the most thorough compilation of censored works in Argentina, see Avellenada's *Censura, autoritarismo y cultura: Argentina, 1960–1983*, 2 vols. (Buenos Aires: Centro Editor de América Latina, 1986).

31 Fernando Reati, *Nombrar lo innombrable: violencia política y novela argentina, 1975–1985* (Buenos Aires: Legasa, 1992).

32 See Osvaldo Pellettieri, "Los 80: el teatro porteño entre la dictadura y la democracia," *Cuadernos Hispanoamericanos* 517–19 (1993): 313–22. The original twenty-one plays performed in 1981 have been reprinted in Miguel Angel Giella, ed., *Teatro Abierto 1981: teatro argentino bajo vigilancia* (Buenos Aires: Corregidor, 1992).

33 On recent Argentine cinema, see José Agustín Mahieu, "Cine argentino: las nuevas fronteras," *Cuadernos Hispanoamericanos* 517–19 (1993): 289–304.

34 For a more detailed view of the evolution of this fraction of the intellectual field in Argentina, consult *Punto de Vista* (1978–present); see also John King, "Las revistas culturales de la dictadura a la democracia: el caso de 'Punto de Vista,'" in *Literatura argentina hoy: de la dictadura a la democracia*, ed. Karl Kohut and Andrea Pagni (Frankfurt a.M.: Vervuert Verlag, 1989). The entire volume is, in fact, excellent. See, as well, Beatriz Sarlo and Hilda Sábato's testimonies in Roy Hora and Javier Trimboli, *Pensar la Argentina hoy: los historiadores hablan de historia y política* (Buenos Aires: El Cielo por Asalto, 1994). For an initial mapping of cultural magazines in recent Argentine history, see Jorge Warley, "Revistas culturales de dos décadas (1970-1990)," *Cuadernos Hispanoamericanos* 517-19 (1993): 195-207.

35 José Joaquín Brunner, "Cultura autoritaria y cultura escolar: 1973–1984," in *Cinco estudios sobre cultura y sociedad,* ed. J. J. Brunner and Gonzalo Catalán (Santiago: FLACSO, 1985), 418.

36 See Guillermo O'Donnell's formulations of the theory of the bureaucratic-authoritarian state in *Modernization and Bureaucratic-Authoritarianism* (Berkeley: U of California P, 1973), and "Tensions in the Bureaucratic-Authoritarian State and the Question of Democracy," in *The New Authoritarianism,* ed. David Collier (Princeton, N.J.: Princeton UP, 1979).

37 José Joaquín Brunner, *La cultura autoritaria en Chile* (Santiago: FLACSO, 1981), 29.

38 Ibid., 53.

39 Brunner, "Cultura autoritaria," 420.

40 Brunner, *La cultura autoritaria,* 61.

41 Brunner, "Entre la cultura autoritaria y la cultura democrática," in *Un espejo trizado: ensayos sobre culturas y políticas culturales* (Santiago: FLACSO, 1988), 98.

42 Ibid., 100.

43 Fernando Henrique Cardoso, *Autoritarismo e Democratização* (Rio de Janeiro: Paz e Terra, 1975), 98.

44 Ibid., 133. Emphasis added.

45 Ibid., 199.

46 Willy Thayer, "Crisis categorial de la universidad," typescript, 2.

47 For a more detailed analysis of this interesting discursive phenomenon, see Oscar Landi, *Reconstrucciones: las nuevas formas de la cultura política* (Buenos Aires: Puntosur, 1988).

48 Two of the typical texts of the journalistic turn are Aguinaldo Silva's *O Crime Antes da Festa* (Rio de Janeiro: Lidador, 1977), and José Louzeiro's *A Infância dos Mortos* (Rio de Janeiro: Record, 1977). For a full bibliography, see Flora Süssekind, *Tal Brasil* and *Literatura.* See also Davi Ariguccis Jr.'s analysis in "Jornal, Realismo, Alegoria: O Romance Brasileiro Recente," in *Achados e Perdidos* (São Paulo: Polis, 1979), 79–115.

49 Louzeiro, quoted in Süssekind, *Literatura,* 58.

50 Faerman, quoted in ibid., 178.

51 Süssekind, *Literatura,* 177.

52 For a similar critique of scandalous, seemingly radical naturalism in the Argentine context, see Francine Masiello, "Contemporary Argentine Fiction: Liberal (Pre-)Texts in a Reign of Terror," *Latin American Research Review* 16 (1981): 218–24.

53 Another of these juridical battles has recently been won, when the Brazilian Congress approved a motion to provide an indemnity to relatives of the almost 200 documented disappeared citizens during the dictatorship.

See "Câmara Aprova Indenizações," *Folha de São Paulo*, 14 September 1995, "Caderno Brasil," page 9.

54   Jacobo Timerman, *Prisoner without a Name, Cell without a Number*, trans. Toby Talbot (New York: Knopf, 1981), 48, 51–75, passim. Page references to this work are hereafter given parenthetically in the text.

55   Fernando Gabeira, *O Que É Isso, Companheiro?* (Rio de Janeiro: Codecri, 1979).

56   Miguel Bonasso, *Recuerdo de la muerte* (Mexico City: Era, 1984), 37. Page references to this work are hereafter given parenthetically in the text.

57   Moreiras, "The Aura," 9. If it is true that much of the earlier triumphalism around testimonio—as in the days when it was actually claimed that testimonio represented some form of "postliterature"—has subsided, the debates over its canonization into our undergraduate and graduate programs have just begun. For initial work in this second cycle of testimonio criticism, see the excellent volume edited by George M. Gugelberger, *The "Real" Thing: Testimonial Discourse and Latin America* (Durham, N.C.: Duke UP, 1996).

58   Benjamin, *Origin*, 166–67.

59   Ibid., 179.

60   Ibid., 177.

61   Daniel Moyano, *El vuelo del tigre* (Barcelona: Plaza y Janés, 1984), 15. Page references to this work are hereafter given parenthetically in the text. As for the reference to the many times Percussionists have arrived in the past "forty years," note that Moyano's novel is published around the time of Peronism's fortieth anniversary.

62   José Donoso, *Casa de campo* (Barcelona, Caracas, and Mexico City: Seix Barral, 1978), 40.

63   Page numbers, given parenthetically in the text, refer first to the Portuguese original, *A Hora dos Ruminantes*, 1966, 16th ed. (São Paulo: DIFEL, 1984), and then to the English translation, *The Three Trials of Manairema*, trans. Pamela G. Bird (New York: Alfred A. Knopf, 1970).

64   See, among others, Osvaldo Soriano, *Cuarteles de invierno* (Buenos Aires: Sudamericana, 1988), where sports come to allegorize the struggle among the various Argentine classes over the Peronist legacy, or Érico Veríssimo, *Incidente em Antares* (1971), 29th ed. (Rio de Janeiro: Globo, 1978), where the imaginary town of Antares is both a microcosmic representation of Brazilian oligarchic politics and an unsettling stage where the dead rise in order to assert their rights.

65   For an analysis of the conflict between mythic-circular and historic-linear times in *Cien años de soledad*, see Roberto González Echevarría, *Myth and Archive: A Theory of Latin American Narrative* (Cambridge: Cambridge UP, 1990).

66 This move dates back to Alejo Carpentier's preface to *El reino de este mundo*, in its proposition of Latin America as a rich marvelous antidote to an artistically decadent Europe. The self-congratulatory tone continues in two influential essays in the magical realist canon, Angel Flores's "Magical Realism in Spanish American Fiction" and Luis Leal's "Magical Realism in Spanish American Literature." They set the tone for future logo-etno-phonocentric proclamations of magical realism as the very voice of Latin America. For recent developments in the field, see Lois Parkinson Zamora and Wendy B. Faris, ed., *Magical Realism: Theory, History, Community* (Durham, N.C., and London: Duke UP, 1995). Fredric Jameson has introduced the notion that I am attempting to develop here, that of magical realism as a product of a clash between different modes of production. See "On Magic Realism in Film," *Critical Inquiry*, 12 (1986): 301–25.

67 Jameson, *Postmodernism, or, the Cultural Logic of Late Capitalism* (Durham, N.C.: Duke UP, 1991), 168. See also Paul de Man, "allegorical narratives tell the story of the failure to read," in *Allegories of Reading: Figural Language in Rousseau, Nietzsche, Rilke, and Proust* (New Haven and London: Yale UP, 1979), 205.

68 For a critique of Isabel Allende's kitsch monument, see my "*La casa de los espíritus*: la historia del mito y el mito de la historia," *Revista Chilena de Literatura* 43 (1993): 67–74.

69 James Clifford, *The Predicament of Culture: Twentieth-Century Ethnography, Literature, and Art* (Cambridge, Mass., and London: Harvard UP, 1988), 120.

70 In the best study available of Brazilian literature under the dictatorship, Flora Süssekind lumps together, however, allegory and the magical/fantastic, chastising allegorical novels as "literature whose axis is reference and not work with language." *Literatura*, 61. The direct table of equivalences she observes between allegories and the histories to which they allude leads her to dismiss these allegories because presumably "the text's signification is determined authoritarianly" (60). As I have argued here, however, this determination is itself what must be unveiled and analyzed as indicative of a historical break, instead of taken at face value and dismissed. For an initial theoretical treatment of allegory in postdictatorship, see my "Alegoría y postdictadura: Notas sobre la memoria del mercado," *Revista de Crítica Cultural* 14 (1997): 22–27.

71 For an overview of these debates, see Charles E. McClelland, *State, Society, and University in Germany, 1700–1914* (Cambridge: Cambridge UP, 1980).

72 Willy Thayer, *La Crisis no moderna de la universidad moderna (epílogo del conflicto de las facultades)* (Santiago: Cuarto Propio, 1996), 26. See also Adriana Valdés and Pablo Oyarzún, "Fragmentos de una conversación en torno a la universidad" *Lo* 1 (1992): 22–31.

73 Ibid., 31.

74 Ibid., 83.

75 Quoted in Lawrence Weschler, *A Miracle, a Universe: Settling Accounts with Torturers* (New York: Penguin, 1990), 147.

76 On this point, see Willy Thayer's remarkable essay "Fin del 'trabajo intelectual' y fin idealista/capitalista de la historia en la 'era de la subsunción real del capital,'" in *Espectros y pensamiento utópico*, vol. 2 of *La invención y la herencia* (Santiago: ARCIS-LOM, 1995), 172-93.

77 See Althusser's "Ideology and Ideological State Apparatuses," in *Lenin and Philosophy*, trans. Ben Brewster (New York and London: Monthly Review, 1971), 127-86.

78 Ramos, *Desencuentros*, 43.

79 Ibid., 217.

80 Beatriz Sarlo, "¿Arcaicos o marginales? Situación de los intelectuales en fin de siglo," *Revista de Crítica Cultural* 9 (1994): 12.

81 I am grateful to Julio Ramos for pointing out problems in a previous version of this argument. Any remaining inconsistencies are, of course, my own responsibility.

82 Beatriz Sarlo, *Escenas de la vida posmoderna: intelectuales, arte y videocultura en Argentina* (Buenos Aires: Ariel, 1994), 182.

3 *Countertraditions: The Allegorical Rewriting of the Past*

1 *Crítica y ficción*, 121; hereafter cited as *CF*. Other works by Piglia cited in this study are *La ciudad ausente* (Buenos Aires: Sudamericana, 1992); *Respiración artificial* (Buenos Aires: Sudamericana, 1980); *Prisión perpetua* (Buenos Aires: Sudamericana, 1988); *Nombre falso* (1975), definitive edition (Buenos Aires: Seix Barral, 1994); and *La Argentina en pedazos* (Buenos Aires: Ediciones de la Urraca, 1993). They are hereafter identified, respectively, as *CA, RA, PP, NF*, and *AP*, with page numbers given in parentheses. References to *RA* include page numbers for Daniel Balderston's English translation: *Artificial Respiration* (Durham, N.C., and London: Duke UP, 1994). Page references to *Ciudad ausente* in the next chapter are not preceded by *CA*.

2 Published, respectively, in *Historia universal de la infamia* (1935), vol. 1 of *Prosa completa* (Buenos Aires: Emecé, 1979), 291-98; *Ficciones* (1944), vol. 2 of *Prosa completa*, 221-24; and *El informe de Brodie* (1970), vol. 4 of *Prosa completa*, 25-30.

3 Josefina Ludmer, *El género gauchesco: un tratado sobre la patria* (Buenos Aires: Sudamericana, 1988), 225. Ludmer's working hypotheses to define the genre coalesce in the formula "La voz (del) 'gaucho,'" where both the quotation marks and the preposition in parentheses introducing the genitive

are highly significant. The genre separates legality and illegality, defines the space of possible statements on the gaucho, and maps and disciplines bodies over a regulated grid. As the system of laws according to which the representation of the gaucho comes to be conceivable, the genre is a "treaty on the differential uses of voices and words that defines the meaning of the uses to which bodies are put" (31). For the genre, the gaucho exists as a usable body, coextensive with the emergence of the social sign of the patriot gaucho. As such, gauchos become *citable* by the genre at the price of being ultimately incorporated into the unifying enterprise of the state. The *gauchesca* makes legible this epoch, "since it is written in the voice, in the writing of the other's voice" (43). The genre chronicles the exile of the "gaucho" voice. If the closing of the genre takes place with José Hernández's *Vuelta de Martín Fierro* (1879), where the "gaucho" voice becomes an institution in itself, absorbed and closed as a cycle in state legitimacy, Borges puts an end to that subsequent historical moment characterized by "the use of the genre to *pasar a* [transit to] another literary genre" (41).

4 On the epigrammatic in Piglia's fiction, see Marina Kaplan, "Between Arlt and Borges: Interview with Ricardo Piglia," *New Orleans Review* 16 (1989): 64–74.

5 Roberto Arlt, *Los siete locos* (1929) and *Los lanzallamas* (1931) (Buenos Aires: Biblioteca Ayacucho, 1986), 94. For an analysis of a similar degeneration of utopia into dystopia in José Saramago's masterful and often overlooked *O Ano de 1993*, see my "*O Ano de 1993*: Sobre as Ruínas da Anti-Utopia," *Letras e Letras* 99 (1993): 39–42.

6 Ibid., 180.

7 Ibid., 26–27.

8 Ricardo Piglia, "Roberto Arlt: una crítica de la economía literaria," *Los Libros* 29 (1973): 25.

9 Oscar Masotta, *Sexo y traición en Roberto Arlt* (Buenos Aires: Centro Editor de América Latina, 1982), 31.

10 Arlt, *El juguete rabioso*, 74. 1926. Barcelona: Bruguera, 1979.

11 In arguments Benjamin made in "The Work of Art" about the role of mechanical reproduction in the decline of the aura, there is a thread to be followed from what one might call the *retrospective production of authenticity* to the *advent of falsifiability*. Because "a medieval picture of the Madonna could not yet be said to be 'authentic'" (243), the effect of reproduction lies not only in its progressive fabrication of that authenticity—"mechanical processes of reproduction were instrumental in differentiating and grading authenticity" (243)—but also in opening up the possibility of counterfeiting that accompanies all authenticity as its ineluctable supplement. If "the presence

of the original is the prerequisite to the concept of authenticity" (220), and the original only comes into being as such by being copied, then the very possibility of authenticity as a concept becomes tied with that of falsification. One could read in the decay of the aura, therefore, the link between reproducibility and falsifiability explored by Arlt in his novels.

12   Arlt, *Los siete locos* 231.

13   For a commentary on Baudelaire's "La fausse monnaie" within a reflection on the gift and paradoxes of giving, see Jacques Derrida's *Given Time I: Counterfeit Money* (1991), trans. Peggy Kamuf (Chicago and London: U of Chicago P, 1992). Derrida's question revolves around what happens to a gift that "seems to give nothing" (115) and cancels itself as gift: the gift of false money.

14   *Einfühlung* (empathy) in the interpretation of the past is historicism's most proper move, unveiled by Benjamin as an embrace of the victorious version, the understanding of history as a parade of cultural treasures. For Benjamin the great anaesthetic effect of historicism stems from its belief in seeing the past the way the past saw itself, as though blocking out the ulterior course of history; hence the axiom that historicism imagines time as "empty and homogeneous." Walter Benjamin, "Theses on the Philosophy of History," in *Illuminations*, 261. This is the empathy that the historical materialist counters with a seizing of "an image that flashes up at the instant when it can be recognized and is never seen again" (255). Unlike a historicist, and contradicting Keller's reassuring axiom, a historical materialist knows that truth can indeed run away.

15   The hypothesis advanced by Tardewski in *Respiración artificial* is that Descartes's *Discours sur le méthode* was the first modern novel, a monologue that narrates not the (hi)story of a passion but of an idea: "one could say that Descartes wrote a detective novel: How can the investigator, without moving from his armchair before the fire, without leaving his room, using only his reason, eliminate all the false leads, destroy his doubts one by one, until he finally succeeds in discovering the criminal, that is, the cogito. Because the cogito is the murderer, of that I have not the slightest doubt, said Tardewski" (*RA* 244–45/192). Or yet, maintaining the analogy but departing from Tardewski's conclusion, it might be argued that what eventually comes into being as cogito stands not so much for the criminal but for the detective himself, for the death sentence over the criminal, that is, for the emergence of the detective as the instrument of Reason. If one reads *Discours sur le méthode* as a murder mystery, in my view, one has to acknowledge that the criminal is the *doubt*, not the cogito. Doubt is the plot's starting point and also that which must be eliminated (the very role of the criminal in a murder mystery). As a detective story, Descartes's text narrates the triumph of the cogito-detective over the criminal-doubt.

16   Edgar Allan Poe, "The Murders in the Rue Morgue" (1841) in *Works of Edgar Allan Poe* (New York: Chatham River, 1985), 248.

17   Ibid., 256. This is also a theme that pervades Nietzsche's thought. Here is a taste of it: "To find everything profound—that is an inconvenient trait. It makes one strain one's eyes all the time, and in the end one finds more than one might have wished." Friedrich Nietzsche, *The Gay Science* (1882), trans. Walter Kaufman and R. J. Hollingdale (New York: Random House, 1974), 198.

18   Benjamin opposes *Erlebnis* and *Erfahrung* several times, seeing in the first a suspicious "cult of experience" and the history of its connections with "agricultural orientation, the racial ideology and Buber's 'blood and experience' [*Erlebnis*] arguments." Walter Benjamin, quoted in Gershom Scholem, *Walter Benjamin: The Story of a Friendship* (1975), trans. Harry Zohn (New York, Schocken, 1981), 29. Benjamin's letter to Buber, a radical critique of Buber's notion of Erlebnis, was published in Benjamin, *Briefe*, ed. Gershom Scholem and Theodor Adorno (Frankfurt a.M.: Suhrkamp Verlag, 1966), 125-28. For a thorough commentary on Benjamin's critique of Max Brod's "Buberization" of Kafka, see Hans Mayer, "Walter Benjamin and Franz Kafka" (1979), trans. Gary Smith and Thomas S. Hansen, in *On Walter Benjamin: Critical Essays and Recollections*, ed. Gary Smith (Cambridge, Mass.: MIT, 1988), 185-209. Benjamin reserves Erfahrung as a concept most especially for the philosophical question of the crisis in the transmissibility of experience; this entails that the concept is decisively affected by the notions of narrative and narratability. See, on Erlebnis and Erfahrung, "On Some Motifs in Baudelaire" (1939), in *Illuminations*, 155-200; on the decline of Erfahrung, "The Storyteller" (1936), in *Illuminations*, 83-109.

19   For Derrida's elaborations on the law of iterability, see "Signature Event Context" (1972), in *Margins of Philosophy*, trans. Alan Bass (Chicago: U of Chicago P, 1982), 307-30; on the iterative and the autobiographical, see his reading of Nietzsche in "Otobiographies: The Teachings of Nietzsche and the Politics of the Proper Name" (1982), in *The Ear of the Other: Otobiography, Transference, Translation*, trans. Peggy Kamuf (Lincoln and London: U of Nebraska P, 1985), 3-38.

20   For an argument on the utopian nature of anonymity, see Jameson, "On Literary and Cultural Import-Substitution in the Third World: The Case of Testimonio," *Margins* 1 (1991): 11-34.

21   Jorge Luis Borges, "Macedonio Fernández," *Sur* 209-10 (1952), 146.

22   The reference to author as a function, over and above any psychological or biographical content, was proposed by Michel Foucault in "What Is an Author?" (1969), in *Language, Counter-Memory, Practice*, trans. Donald Bouchard and Sherry Simon (Ithaca, N.Y.: Cornell UP, 1977), 133-38.

23   Macedonio Fernández, *Museo de la novela de la Eterna* (1967), ed. Ana María
     Camblong and Adolfo de Obieta (Paris: Archivos, 1993), 8. Page numbers
     refer to this edition and are hereafter given parenthetically in the text.

24   After first-caliber minute textual research, Ana María Camblong establishes
     the basic text for her critical Archivos edition of *Museo de la novela de la
     Eterna* (1993) from the last typescript corrected by Macedonio, around 1947
     to 1948, and eventually given to Scalabrini Ortiz. Besides a critical dossier
     with some of the best that has been written on Macedonio, the Archivos
     edition includes variations found in several other copies and prefaces that
     Macedonio did not incorporate to the last drafts. It expands considerably
     upon the three other editions, all of which had been impeccably orga-
     nized, prefaced, and annotated by Macedonio's son Adolfo de Obieta: the
     first in Centro Editor de América Latina (1967), the second as volume VI
     of Corregidor's *Obras Completas* (1975), and the third in Ayacucho (1982),
     with a prologue by César Fernández Moreno, which included a selection
     of Macedonio's other writings.

25   Jorge Luis Borges, "Tlön Uqbar, Orbis Tertius," in *Ficciones* (1944), vol. 2
     of *Prosa completa*, 120. Along the lines proposed by Borges, see Alberto
     Moreiras's distinction between efficient and tenuous objects, not as two
     different objects, but as two modes of approaching writing. Whereas the
     efficient mode operates in the object to organize an ontology, the tenuous
     disorganizes and deconstructs it. The tenuous object unveils blind spots
     and moments of decomposition or inversion of the efficient object. If all
     hermeneutics must necessarily constitute an efficient object for its decod-
     ing operations, the tenuous object points to that which does not offer itself
     to symbolic totalization and interpretation. The efficient object strives to
     present the unpresentable (shed light upon the ultimate ground, decode
     the foundational axiom), whereas the tenuous object insists upon the un-
     representability of the presented (that instance where representation col-
     lapses). See Moreiras's usage of this distinction to reflect on the status of
     Latin America as an object for Latin Americanism. "Epistemología tenue
     (sobre el latinoamericanismo)," *Revista de Crítica Cultural* 10 (1995): 48–54.

4 Encrypting Restitution

1   The emphasis in Poe's "William Wilson" resides in the ineluctability of the
     bind that joins the protagonist to his double. His final act of murder, of the
     double and thus of himself, is part of a logic he cannot circumscribe and
     to which he only gains insight from the double's last words: "Thou have
     conquered, and I yield. Yet, henceforward art thou also dead — dead to the
     World, to Heaven and to Hope! In me didst thou exist — and in my death,

see by this image, which is thine own, how utterly hast thou murdered thyself." Edgar Allan Poe, "William Wilson" (1839), in *Works of Edgar Allan Poe*, 225.

2 Henry Staten, *Eros in Mourning: From Homer to Lacan* (Baltimore: Johns Hopkins UP, 1994), 1.

3 Plato, *Republic*, trans. Paul Shorey, in *The Collected Dialogues*, ed. Edith Hamilton and Huntington Cairns (Princeton, N.J.: Princeton UP, 1961), 575–844.

4 Plato, *Laws*, trans. A. E. Taylor, in *The Collected Dialogues*, 1225–513.

5 Nicoles Loraux, *Women in Mourning*, trans. Corinne Pache (Ithaca, N.Y., and London: Cornell UP, 1998), 26. See Loraux for an insightful analysis of the Greek management of mourning and the strategies for its containment within the sphere of close family ties. Of relevance for the study of the strategies for subduing mourning in ancient Greece is Page DuBois's reminder that "the rule that tragedy should not address contemporary events was established in part because of the overwhelming impact on the Athenian audience of Phrynikhos's tragedy on the taking of Miletus by the Persians in 494." Page DuBois, *Torture and Truth* (New York and London: Routledge, 1991), 64. Herodotus recalls how the author suffered punishment for bringing a recent loss into the civic memory: "When Phrynichus produced his play, *The Capture of Miletus*, the audience in the theater burst into tears. The author was fined a thousand drachmae for reminding them of a disaster which touched them so closely, and they forbade everybody ever to put the play on the stage again" (Herodotus, quoted in DuBois, *Torture and Truth*, 64).

6 Plato, *Republic*, 606d.

7 Staten, *Eros in Mourning*, 40.

8 If in Sophocles' play Antigone's definite resolution to bury and honor her dead brother is bound to her perception that "I shall have to spend more time pleasing those below than those here" (75), the major conflict between her will and Creon's prohibition does not stem exactly from a split between divine and human law, as many since Hegel have argued. Neither is Creon uncontested as representative of human law, nor Antigone unambiguously moved only by a religious injunction. There is irreconcilability, rather, between Antigone's attempt to sanction the work of mourning in the polis (which shakes the gendered separation between public and private, the affective and the political), and on the other hand the interest of a political status quo that constitutively excludes that possibility. For a reading of the play from the standpoint of Antigone's acknowledgement of the bond constitutive of the subject—the bond of the name, of the signifier that links her to Polynices—see Jacques Lacan, *The Seminar of Jacques Lacan, Book VII: The Ethics of Psychoanalysis, 1959–60*, ed. Jacques-Alain Miller, trans. Dennis Porter (New York and London: Norton, 1992). See also Peggy Phe-

lan's elegant critique in *Mourning Sex: Performing Public Memories* (New York and London: Routledge, 1997), 13–18.

9   Masotta, *Sexo y traición*, 23.

10   For an interpretation of Nietzsche from the standpoint of the opposition between active and reactive forces, see Gilles Deleuze's *Nietzsche and Philosophy* (1962), trans. Hugh Tomlinson (New York: Columbia UP, 1983), especially "Active and Reactive," 39–72. Tracing the anti-Hegelian, antidialectical thrust that pervades Nietzsche's work, Deleuze shows how the "inversion of the value-positing eye" takes place in the move from dialectical negation—which for Nietzsche always represents the thought of the slave—to genealogical affirmation. For an excellent account of how Deleuze delineates an *ethical horizon* in Nietzsche's work, and ultimately displaces the debate away from the dialectical terrain, see Michael Hardt, *Gilles Deleuze: An Apprenticeship in Philosophy* (Minneapolis: U of Minnesota P, 1993), 26–55.

11   The melancholy epiphany characteristic of the self that speaks in the tango has not escaped Piglia's attention: "The tango reiterates two or three basic formulas. The central framework is clear: the man who has lost his woman looks at the world cynically and disenchantedly. This woman's betrayal is the *condition* for the tango's hero to acquire this turbid lucidity that allows him to philosophize about the past, the neighborhood, lost purity, the meaning of life. Disgrace, it must be said, is the foundation of popular philosophy" (*AP* 79).

12   Benjamin, *Origin*, 232–33.

13   Benjamin regards the synthetic, artificial production of experience as one of the tasks of modern literature: "*Matière et mémoire* defines the nature of experience in the *durée* in such a way that the reader is bound to conclude that only a poet can be the adequate subject of such an experience. And it was indeed a poet who put Bergson's theory of experience to the test. Proust's work *À la Recherche du temps perdu* may be regarded as an attempt to produce experience synthetically, as Bergson imagines it, under today's conditions, for there is less and less hope that it will come into being naturally." Benjamin, "On Some Motifs in Baudelaire," 157.

14   "All suprahistorical kinship of languages rests in the intention underlying each language as a whole—an intention, however, which no single language can attain by itself but which is realized only by the totality of their intentions supplementing each other: pure language." Walter Benjamin, "The Task of the Translator" (1923), in *Illuminations*, 74. What the island does to translation, then, is to erase the echoes of the pure language to which all translation bears witness. It makes translation impossible—at any rate it makes visible, ineluctable its impossibility—while immersing its inhabitants

in the immanence of an ever-different little fragment of the broken vessel of pure language.

15   Ibid., 75.

16   Walter Benjamin, "On Language as Such and on the Language of Man" (1955), in *Reflections*, 327.

17   On Hölderlin's versions of Sophocles as untimely confrontations with his present, see Haroldo de Campos, "A Palavra Vermelha de Hölderlin" (1969), in *A Arte no Horizonte do Provável*, 4th ed. (São Paulo: Perspectiva, 1977), 93–107.

18   Benjamin, "On Language," 329.

19   Ibid., 328.

20   Benjamin, *Origin*, 229.

21   Pablo Oyarzún, "Sobre el concepto benjaminiano de traducción," *Seminarios de Filosofía* 6 (1993): 91–92.

22   Speaking of drifts, I'd like to reserve this note for mourning the impossibility of extending, for the moment, the reference to the philosophical problematic of translation. As for the Benjaminian reflection on the translator, it will be necessary to keep in mind all the paradoxes of the Aufgabe, as Pablo Oyarzún has developed in a remarkable essay: "*Aufgabe* is on the one hand task, task understood as an imposing, destinating gift (*Gabe*). Something must be given, from which translation is begun and its process inchoated; something must be given as the origin of translation: something, as an original, must be given. It *must* be, so that it may be possible to give it again (*wiedergeben*), to render it: to translate. And if it is generally impossible for an original to give itself to the one who wishes to give it again—since it is most proper to it to evade itself—the origin effect is irrevocably guaranteed as the given constitutes itself as demand. The impossible gift is, then, also an imperative, a command: the given is legacy and delegation. The translator is found then under the command—that is, the dictate—of what is given (to) translation, and the commitment of a care: the care of the (de)legated." Ibid., 94. As the task imposes itself as gift, the legacy of the gift, it is interrupted by an Aufgabe that also names an impossibility: "But *Aufgabe* is also giving up, abandoning. The command of the given—the dictate of the gift, the dictate in which the gift consists—that constitutes and institutes translation as such, that defines the translator's mission (shipment, charge, message), is determined in the translator, but at the same time before the translator, by an equally constitutive renunciation" (94).

For the genealogy of the constitutive embrace of translation as failure, see Oyarzún's trail from the disobliviation of the name from under the instrumental bourgeois sign in Benjamin's "On Language as Such and on the

Language of Man," through the links between allegorical representation and mournfulness in *The Origin of German Tragic Drama,* to the vertigos of the Benjaminian theory of translation. See also, for a reflection that roughly points to the same horizon, Paul de Man, "Conclusions: Walter Benjamin's 'The Task of the Translator'" (1985), in *The Resistance to Theory* (Minneapolis: U of Minnesota P, 1986), 73–105, notable in its analysis of translation as a prosaicization of the original and revelation that the original was already dead. Another imperative reference here is Derrida's piece on translation, "Des tours de Babel" (1977), in *Difference in Translation,* ed. Joseph F. Graham (Ithaca, N.Y.: Cornell UP, 1985), 165–207, especially for what refers translation to post-Babelian multilingualism and inaugurates it as task and gift.

23   Fernández, *Museo,* 40.

5 Pastiche, Repetition, and the Angel of History's Forged Signature

1   Nietzsche, *On the Genealogy of Morals* (1887), trans. Walter Kaufman and R. J. Hollingdale (New York: Random House, 1967), 35.

2   Ibid., 58–65.

3   Silviano Santiago, "Fechado para Balanço (Sessenta Anos de Modernismo)," in *Nas Malhas da Letra* (São Paulo: Companhia das Letras, 1989), 76.

4   Ibid., 88–93.

5   Sérgio Miceli, *Intelectuais e Classe Dirigente no Brasil, 1920–1945* (São Paulo: DIFEL, 1979).

6   Silviano Santiago, "Reading and Discursive Intensities," in *The Postmodernism Debate in Latin America: A Special Issue of boundary 2,* ed. John Beverley and José Oviedo (1993): 194–202.

7   Santiago, "Fechado para Balanço," 77.

8   Silviano Santiago, "A Permanência do Discurso da Tradição no Modernismo," in *Nas Malhas da Letra,* 114.

9   Silviano Santiago, "O Entre-Lugar do Discurso Latino-Americano," in *Uma Literatura nos Trópicos* (São Paulo: Perspectiva, 1978), 22–23.

10   An exploration of the unsettling powers of mimesis that shares much with Santiago's can be found in Michael Taussig, *Mimesis and Alterity: A Particular History of the Senses* (New York and London: Routledge, 1993). See especially Taussig's perceptive reading of Benjamin's thesis on the rebirth of the mimetic in modern mechanical reproduction (19–43).

11   Santiago, "O Entre-Lugar," 28.

12   Graciliano Ramos, *São Bernardo* (1934), 51st ed. (Rio de Janeiro: Record, 1989). For two elegant treatments of G. Ramos's singularity in Brazilian literature, see João Luiz Lafetá, "O Mundo à Revelia," afterword to Ramos,

São Bernardo, 189–213, and the classic analysis by Antonio Candido, *Ficção e Confissão* (Rio de Janeiro: José Olympio, 1956).

13 Graciliano Ramos, *Memórias do Cárcere* (1953), 21st ed., 2 vols. (Rio de Janeiro and São Paulo: Record, 1986), 1:37.

14 Pressed by economic needs, Graciliano would get a bitter taste of such clientelism in 1941, when he took a job at the Department of Press and Propaganda of Getúlio Vargas's dictatorial regime, the same regime that had incarcerated him five years earlier. Graciliano wrote several stories and chronicles for magazines such as *Atlântico* and *Cultura Política*, in which, however, one cannot disentangle political complicity with the Estado Novo in any facile fashion, in spite of certain rather mechanical connections recently made, following Pierre Bourdieu, between professional positionality and political content. For an initial analysis of the episode that takes full account of what some would call "merely textual problems," see Raúl Antelo, *Literatura em Revista* (São Paulo: Atica, 1984), 27–56. For an application of the Lejeunian theory of the "autobiographical pact" to Santiago, see Wander Melo Miranda, *Corpos Escritos: Graciliano Ramos e Silviano Santiago* (São Paulo and Belo Horizonte: EDUSP and UFMG, 1992).

15 Santiago, "A Permanência," 116–17.

16 Silviano Santiago, ed. *Glossário de Derrida* (Rio de Janeiro: Francisco Alves, 1976).

17 Derrida, "Signature Event Context," 328. For a thorough explanation of the paradoxes of signature—along with the entire set of problems they mobilize: those of iterability, repeatability, speech acts, performativity, citation, and so on—see Derrida's response to J. Searle, "Limited Inc a b c . . ." (1977), in *Limited Inc*, trans. Samuel Weber (Evanston: Northwestern UP, 1988), 29–110.

18 "If the readability of a legacy were given, natural, transparent, univocal, if it did not call for and at the same time defy interpretation, we would never have anything to inherit from it." Derrida, *Specters of Marx*, 16.

19 Gilles Deleuze, *Difference and Repetition* (1968), trans. Paul Patton (New York: Columbia UP, 1994), 1–2.

20 Ibid., xxii.

21 Jorge Luis Borges, "Pierre Menard, autor del *Quijote*," in *Ficciones* (1944), vol. 2 of *Prosa completa*, 128.

22 Silviano Santiago, *Em Liberdade* (Rio de Janeiro: Paz e Terra, 1981), 128. This work is hereafter cited in the text as *EL*.

23 See the exemplary exchange included by Santiago in the novel: Getúlio Vargas, in a conversation with *integralista* leader Plínio Salgado, warned him of the danger represented by the candidacy of José Américo, an enemy of

the tropical fascists. Salgado's reply is to the point: "the day we begin to be persecuted nationally our growth will be extraordinary, because it is the very nature of our movement to grow through the mystique of martyrdom" (*EL* 182).

24   The thesis of a threefold cycle of Brazilian naturalism (biologistic in the 1880s, economist in the 1930s, communicational in the 1970s) was synthesized in Flora Süssekind's *Tal Brasil, Qual Romance?* but it is the maturing of a critical process that includes Nélson Werneck Sodré's Marxist interpretation in *O Naturalismo no Brasil* (Rio de Janeiro: Civilização Brasileira, 1965), and João Alexandre Barbosa's *A Tradição do Impasse* (São Paulo: Atica, 1974). See also Antonio Candido's analysis of naturalism as a utopia of immediate experience in "De Cortiço a Cortiço," in *O Discurso e a Cidade* (São Paulo: Duas Cidades, 1993), 123–52.

25   Schwarz's concept of *idéias fora do lugar* describes the necessary contradiction of a society structured by slavery-based latifundia but submitted to an already capitalist international market. As a consequence, the same landowning class forced toward liberalism in order to integrate itself in the world market was also forced to violate the most obvious liberal principles. In Schwarz's words, "liberal ideas could not be put into practice, yet they could not be discarded." "Misplaced Ideas: Literature and Society in Late-Nineteenth-Century Brazil" (1973), trans. Edmund Leites and Roberto Schwarz, in *Misplaced Ideas*, 28. If the rationale behind Taylorist capitalism has it that work should be accomplished in the minimum amount of time, what the slave owner needed in a society such as that of nineteenth-century Brazil was exactly the opposite, that is, to stretch the slave's work to a maximum length of time so that s/he would be kept busy and disciplined for the whole day. Modernizing and rationalizing production were absolutely pointless, but narratives of modernization were part and parcel of the ideological edifice through which the rural oligarchy governed. Liberalism did not make sense, but structurally it could not disappear. It was useless and useful, or rather its usefulness stemmed from the fact that it was useless. Liberalism was, then, according to Schwarz, *mistranslated* in Brazil. Not that it was ever true in its self-identity in Europe or anywhere, but its predicament in the periphery of capitalism lay in the fact that the possibility of taking liberalism to all its consequences was not given. Unlike in Europe, where the transition to capitalism destroyed residues of previous modes of production, in Brazil liberalism could only exist by feeding on precapitalist structures, that is, by coexisting with and deriving its legitimacy from everything that undermined the very possibility of being a liberal.

   The answer historically articulated in Brazil to that paradox took a specific form in the practice of *favor*. In addition to justifying the "freedom" to sell one's labor force on the market, liberalism masked the relationship between beneficiary and benefactor as a transaction deprived of any constraints. After all, everybody is free to ask, concede, and deny favors. Beneficiaries and benefactors were attached to each other by a perverse bind: the latter wanted and needed the former to accept their favor so that their power to concede it could be reinforced. Beneficiaries, in turn, would acknowledge the favor in order to establish credit for future requests. The structure of favor has affected social life in Brazil to the present day, from politics to the legal system, public services, health, education, trade, and so on. Therefore, the notion of misplaced ideas has nothing to do with a "discrepancy between representation and reality" as William Rowe and Vivian Schelling suggest in their *Memory and Modernity: Popular Culture in Latin America* (London and New York: Verso, 1991), 37. It is a disjunction *installed at the very heart of the Real*, a condition of possibility of representation itself, rather than a naively asserted noncoincidence between representation and "reality" following a classical notion of truth as *adequatio*. Once the matter is posed in this fashion, to suggest that "far from being a negative fact this discrepancy allows for critical distance from other forms of thought claiming dubious universality" (37), as Rowe and Schelling do, can only function as a consolation in bad faith, which, by the way, never appears in Schwarz's theorization of the concept. For a sustained engagement with the notion of misplaced ideas, see Neil Larsen, *Reading North by South*, where Larsen makes the best English-language presentation of Schwarz's work. See, especially, "Hegemony or Ideology?" (93–99) and "Brazilian Critical Theory and the Question of Cultural Studies" (205–16).

26 In fact, the novel suggests a constitutive bind between the ideology of cordiality and reactionary thought; for example, "A political prisoner, hearing me say that a certain fascist guy was, in spite of everything, a *simpático* [agreeable] person, alerted me: 'have you ever seen a fascist who is not an agreeable person?' " (*EL* 121).

27 This can be read in light of Gilles Deleuze's reversal of a traditional understanding of the eternal return as cyclical movement. For Deleuze, it is no longer being that returns in its sameness, but return itself is what constitutes being. What returns then is the very being of becoming, not a fixed being supposedly going through several becomings. In other words, there is no repetition independent of the singularity—nonnegative difference, what I am here referring to as the untimely—that structures becoming. See *Nietzsche and Philosophy*, 22–29, 46–49, 68–72, passim.

28 For a complete account of the killing of Herzog and the long process of

proving the truth in court, as well as the pertinent iconographic material, see Fernando Jordão, *Dossiê Herzog: Prisão, Tortura e Morte no Brasil* (São Paulo: Global, 1979).

29   See ibid., 20.

30   After all, wasn't it Zarathustra himself who reproached the dwarf for collapsing the eternal return into the time of the cycle?

"All that is straight lies," the dwarf murmured contemptuously. "All truth is crooked; time is itself a circle."

"You spirit of gravity," I said angrily, "do not make things too easy for yourself! Or I shall let you crouch where you are crouching, lamefoot; and it was I that carried you this *height*." Friedrich Nietzsche, *Thus Spoke Zarathustra* (1883–85), in *The Portable Nietzsche*, ed. and trans. Walter Kaufman (New York: Viking Penguin, 1968), 270. On the critique of the cyclical hypothesis, see also Deleuze, *Nietzsche and Philosophy* and *Difference and Repetition.*

31   Since its inception, deconstruction has insisted that the metaphysical conception of time assigns to the future, be it in its eschatological, teleological, apocalyptic, or any other actualization, a conceptual locus inseparable from presence as such. That is to say, the future imaginable by metaphysics— never, to be sure, to be opposed to another, "truer" "more adequate" representation of it—is entirely circumscribed as *future present*, that is, as that which will be *Anwesenheit* (presence) in a *Gegenwart* (present) that still is not. See Jacques Derrida, "*Ousia* and *Gramme*: Note on a Note from *Being and Time*" (1968), in *Margins of Philosophy*, 29–67, for a confrontation with the most vigilant manifestation of this reduction, that is, the Heideggerian analytic of *Dasein*. It is in Walter Benjamin that the spark of a concept of future not reducible to presence can be envisioned, and it is for such spark that Derrida has reserved the names of justice, promise, and the gift. For what links the future as open promise to the undeconstructability of justice— justice that is always to be radically distinguished from law and the totality of any juridical system—see *Specters of Marx*, 16–48, passim. For what links the thought of utopia with the task of tarrying with the impossible, see the remarkable essay by Jameson, "Marx's Purloined Letter." I have attempted to treat the problem in "Marx, en inminencia y urgencia" and "El espectro en la temporalidad de lo mesiánico."

32   "Good sense affirms that in all things there is a determinable sense or direction [*sens*]; but paradox is the affirmation of both senses or directions at the same time." Gilles Deleuze, *The Logic of Sense* (1969), trans. Mark Lester with Charles Stivale (New York: Columbia UP, 1990), 1.

6 *Overcodification of the Margins*

1 Diamela Eltit, *Lumpérica* (Santiago: Ediciones del Ornitorrinco, 1983), *Por la patria* (Santiago: Ediciones del Ornitorrinco, 1986), *El cuarto mundo* (Santiago: Planeta, 1988), *El padre mío* (Santiago: Francisco Zegers, 1989), *Vaca sagrada* (Santiago and Buenos Aires: Planeta, 1991), *Los vigilantes* (Santiago: Sudamericana, 1994). Diamela Eltit and Paz Errázuriz, *El infarto del alma* (Santiago: Francisco Zegers, 1994). I hereafter refer to these works parenthetically in the text.

2 Ronald Kay, ed., *Manuscritos* (Santiago: DEH, 1975), 26.

3 Oyarzún, "Arte en Chile," 311.

4 Eugenia Brito, *Campos minados: Literatura post-golpe en Chile* (Santiago: Cuarto Propio, 1990), 75.

5 Richard, *Margins and Institutions*, 56.

6 Richard, *La insubordinación de los signos: cambio político, transformaciones culturales y poéticas de la crisis*, 40.

7 Richard, *Margins and Institutions*, 57.

8 Pablo Oyarzún, "Parpadeo y piedad," *Cirugía Plástica* (1989): 32.

9 Richard, *Margins and Institutions*, 41.

10 On Carlos Leppe's multifaceted and provocative work, see, in addition to Richard's *Margins and Institutions*, her highly poetic *Cuerpo correccional* (Santiago: Visual, 1980), where the artist is referred to in the second person, and criticism incorporates the object being addressed in its tone and layout on the page. See also Fátima Bercht, ed., *Contemporary Art from Chile*, bilingual catalog (New York: Americas Society, 1991), a catalogue of an art exhibit put forth in New York in 1991. On the evolution of recent art in Chile, see Oyarzún, "Arte en Chile" and "Parpadeo y piedad." Ineluctable reflections on photography by one of Chile's best are to be found in Ronald Kay's *Del espacio de acá* (Santiago: Visual, 1990).

11 Oyarzún, "Arte en Chile," 323. On Dávila's painting, see three remarkable texts by Gustavo Buntinx, Carlos Pérez, and Nelly Richard, in *El fulgor de lo obsceno* (Santiago: Francisco Zegers, n.d.). In Dávila's recent work see the parodic and transgendered representation of one of Latin America's macho icons: Simón Bolívar. With makeup and conspicuous traces, making an obscene gesture, Dávila's portrayal of Bolívar set up a space where masculine imagery was politically queered. The painting provoked a hysterical response from the governments of Venezuela, Colombia, and Ecuador, as well as an embarrassed, out-of-place apology by the Chilean executive. See the excellent dossier, "El caso 'Simón Bolívar,' o el arte como zona de disturbios," in *Revista de Crítica Cultural* 9 (1994): 25–36, most decisively the

letter signed by several scholars, writers, art producers, philosophers, and composers, in which they manifest concern over the precedent of censorship (34).

12 Oyarzún, "Arte en Chile," 322.

13 Raúl Zurita, *Literatura, lenguaje y sociedad* (Santiago: CENECA, 1983), 6.

14 See, in Patricio Marchant's *Sobre árboles y madres* (Santiago: Gato Murr, 1984), the rhetorical mapping of the fate of two desires: (1) the possibility, total feasibility, that a twenty-year-old Chilean utter "I am a poet"—the fact that this desire may or not fulfill itself, or to what degree, is another question; (2) total impossibility, unfeasibility, on the other hand, that the same Chilean could possibly say: "I am a philosopher." An immediate correction —a translation of one's desire—is requested by the latter sentence, argues Marchant: "You mean a professor of philosophy." See the entire architecture and the thinking of the scene in *Sobre árboles y madres* for the impact of the thought of the impossibility of philosophy in Spanish, in Chile, and in Latin America, and the acceptance of the task to "think what is primarily real for us: Spanish, our language, and Latin America; and as Chileans, to think Chilean poetry, conceptual like few, a gift for thinking" (86). For an analysis of the ethical questions raised by the impossibility of philosophy in Latin America, see my "Deconstruction, Liberal Universalism, and the Ethics of Interpretation," forthcoming in *SubStance* (1999).

15 Oyarzún, "Arte en Chile," 311.

16 Richard, *Margins and Institutions*, 79.

17 For a rigorous analysis of Zurita's trajectory from the standpoint of its culmination in the kitsch monument *La vida nueva* (Santiago: Universitaria, 1994), see Carlos Pérez, "El manifiesto místico-político-teológico de Zurita," *Revista de Crítica Cultural* 10 (1995): 55–59. Pérez retrospectively reads the coherence of the eschatological matrix present in the early collections of poems *Purgatorio* and *Anteparaíso* as it evolves into the later grandiosity of his epiphanic "sermon of new life" and the pretension of being a "*Canto General*, the general chant of new times" (57). See also the perceptive readings of *Purgatorio* and *Anteparaíso* by Brito in *Campos minados* (75–142), where she maps out Zurita's semiotization of a feminine body within the texture of biblical metaphors, as well as Rodrigo Cánovas's analysis of how Zurita composed emblematic images of the national and the continental, at times in syllogistic form, as in a replica of the analytical text. Rodrigo Cánovas, *Lihn, Zurita, Ictus, Radrigán: literatura chilena y experiencia autoritaria* (Santiago: FLACSO, 1986), 57–92.

18 Adriana Valdés, quoted in Cánovas, *Lihn, Zurita, Ictus, Radrigán*, 81.

19 Richard, *Margins and Institutions*, 68.

20 Brito, *Campos minados*, 87.

21 Pérez, "El manifiesto," 55.

22 My reading of Eltit is indebted to various essays in which Nelly Richard insightfully tackles Eltit's literature and the larger artistic context of CADA and the escena de avanzada. On the artistic scene in Chile under Pinochet, see her *Margins and Institutions*, which analyzes Eltit's and Zurita's performatic work in "The Rhetoric of the Body" (65-73); on Eltit's *El padre mío*—a text based on a recording made by Eltit of the convulsive linguistic delirium of a Chilean beggar—as an ironic and deconstructive unsettling of metropolitan desires for testimonio, see her "Bordes, diseminación, postmodernismo: una metáfora latinoamericana de fin de siglo" in *Las culturas de fin de siglo en América Latina*, ed. Josefina Ludmer (Buenos Aires: Beatriz Viterbo, 1994), 240-48. For the most intricate and dense exploration of the signifiers of memory, mourning, trace, residue, metaphoricity, and so on, in Chilean postdictatorship, see Richard's *Residuos y metáforas: ensayos de crítica cultural sobre el Chile de la transición* (Santiago: Cuarto Propio, 1998), a book in fact too recent to be fully engaged here as it would deserve. On *El padre mío*, see also Ivette Malverde Disselkoen, "Esquizofrenia y literatura: el discurso de padre e hija en *El padre mío* de Diamela Eltit," *Acta Literaria* 16 (1991): 69-76. On *Por la patria*, a novel that I will not touch here, consult Marina Arrate's elegant and rigorous analysis in "Una novela como radiografia: *Por la patria*," Master's thesis, Universidad de Concepción, Santiago, 1992, as well as Rodrigo Cánovas, "Apuntes sobre la novela *Por la patria*, de Diamela Eltit," *Acta Literaria* 15 (1990): 147-60, and Raquel Olea, "*Por la patria*: una épica de la marginalidad," *Lar* 11 (1987): 2-6. On the whole of Eltit's fiction, see Richard, "Tres funciones de escritura: deconstrucción, simulación, hibridación," in *Una poética de literatura menor: la narrativa de Diamela Eltit*, ed. Juan Carlos Lértora (Santiago: Cuarto Propio, 1993), 37-51, as well as the other articles included therein. On *Lumpérica* and *Por la patria*, see Djelal Kadir's excellent *The Other Writing: Essays in Latin America's Writing Culture* (West Lafayette, Ind.: Purdue UP, 1993), 177-201, and Julio Ortega, *El discurso de la abundancia* (Caracas: Monte Avila, 1990), 255-77. For the most informed and thorough analysis of landmarks of postcoup literature in Chile (Eltit, Zurita, Muñoz, Maqueira, Fariña, Juan Luiz Martínez, Berenguer, etc.), see Brito's *Campos minados*. On contemporary Latin American and especially Chilean women's literature see Carmen Berenguer et al., *Escribir en los bordes: congreso internacional de literatura femenina latinoamericana* (Santiago: Cuarto Propio, 1990). Of variable interest are the articles mapping Chilean culture under dictatorship, compiled in the special issue of *Cuadernos Hispanoamericanos* 482-83 (1990).

23 Arrate, "Una novela como radiografía," 81.

24 Kadir, *The Other Writing*, 183.

25   Brito, *Campos minados*, 196.

26   On the constitution of the subject as product of an interpellation by the law —the external, controlling instance represented in *Lumpérica* by the lights coming from the signboard—see Althusser's theory of ideology, elaborated in "Ideology."

27   Kadir, *The Other Writing*, 185.

28   Brito, *Campos minados*, 198.

29   Naturally, my translation is only a coarse approximation that loses not only the alliterations and assonances but also several anagrammatic effects (such as the connection between weaving and hardness in *trama=dura*, the orgiastic and the anal in *vac/a-nal*, etc.). The original reads: "Muge/r/apa y su mano se nutre final-mente el verde des-ata y maya se erige y vac/a-nal su forma. / Anal'iza la trama=dura de la piel: la mano prende y la fobia es/garra. / Muge/r'onda corporal Brahma su ma la mano que la denuncia & brama."

30   For Jacques Derrida, the inheritance of the name is not an inheritance among others. It provides the matrix, as it were, for investigation of what it means to inherit and to posit oneself before the task of inheriting the other's legacy. See the collection of essays published in English as *On the Name*, especially "Passions: 'An Oblique Offering,'" ed. Thomas Dutoit (Stanford: Stanford UP, 1995).

31   Eltit, quoted in Richard, *Margins and Institutions*, 73.

32   Kadir, *The Other Writing*, 191.

33   "She would provide the lights, the gaze, the screen, extensively to see the city in all its disarticulation as a center of a country's social and cultural life." Brito, *Campos minados*, 12.

34   For a devastating dismantling of familialism that does not exhaust itself in the negativity of critique but chooses to reconnect with the collective in affirmative fashion—laying the groundwork for a new ethics—see Gilles Deleuze and Félix Guattari, *Anti-Oedipus: Capitalism and Schizophrenia I* (1972), trans. Robert Hurley, Mark Seem, and Elen Lane (Minneapolis: U of Minnesota P, 1977).

35   See also the protagonist's self-mutilation dreams (29) and the omnipresent associations between writing and suffering (35, passim) or the apocalyptic anticipation: "Did you walk thinking of the final instant of my fall? Did you laugh? Did you enjoy guessing the shape of my bones? Is this coming end fulfilling the exactitude of your desires?" (100).

7 Bildungsroman at a Standstill

1   Piglia and Saer, *Por un relato futuro*, 14.

2   See Juan José Saer, *Nadie nada nunca*, 1980 (Buenos Aires: Seix Barral, 1995).

3 Tânia Pellegrini, "Brazil in the 1970s: Literature and Politics," *Latin American Perspectives* 21 (1994): 65.

4 The theme of dialectics, and of the ashes it inevitably leaves behind in its work, is the center of Jacques Derrida, *Glas*, which makes a case for mourning as a privileged figure for that residue never fully incorporated, never entirely synthesizable by dialectics. See *Glas* (1974), trans. John P. Leavey Jr. and Richard Rand (Lincoln: U of Nebraska P, 1986).

5 João Gilberto Noll, *O Cego e a Dançarina* (1980), 2d ed. (Porto Alegre: L&PM, 1986); *A Fúria do Corpo* (Rio de Janeiro: Rocco, 1981); *Bandoleiros* (Rio de Janeiro: Nova Fronteira, 1985); *Rastros do Verão* (Rio de Janeiro: Rocco, 1986); *Hotel Atlântico*, 4th ed. (Rio de Janeiro: Rocco, 1989); *O Quieto Animal da Esquina* (Rio de Janeiro: Rocco, 1991); *Harmada* (São Paulo: Companhia das Letras, 1993), hereafter designated parenthetically in the text by their initials, *CD, B, RV, HA,* and *QAE,* respectively, with the exception of *A Fúria do Corpo.*

6 *A Fúria do Corpo* is a remarkable novel, indeed one of the finest published of late in Brazil, but it differs considerably from the others and would thus deserve separate treatment. For an analysis of *A Fúria do Corpo,* see Silviano Santiago, "O Evangelho Segundo São João," in *Nas Malhas da Letra,* 62–67.

7 Note also the scenario in *Rastros do Verão:* "Deep silence. I didn't see pedestrians or cars. I took the first lateral street to piss. At one end of it you could see the harbor, at the other small stores, all closed. . . . A few steps later I saw the old Market on the borders of Quinze Square. Through the square I trod upon remains of fruit and felt various consistencies under my feet, as I crushed day-old grapes. No one went by. A few buses rested at the terminal" (10–11). "Store windows turned the lights off, a man leaned on a lamp post and looked at his fingers, at every block the streets were more deserted" (92).

8 Or in *Hotel Atlântico,* where the protagonist checks into a hotel under a false name, lies about his marital status, and tries to elude the clerks' suspicions when they see that he carries no luggage (8–10).

9 Fredric Jameson, "The Antinomies of Postmodernism," *The Seeds of Time* (New York: Columbia UP, 1994), 15.

10 Benjamin, "On Some Motifs in Baudelaire," 176.

11 Benjamin, *Passagen,* 355.

12 Benjamin, "On Some Motifs in Baudelaire," 184–85.

13 Several passages of Benjamin's *Passagen-Werk* depict Nietzsche's doctrine as the complicit counterpart of historicist progressivism: "the belief in progress and in infinite perfectibility—an endless task for morality—and the representation of the eternal return are complementary" (144); "the eternal return is the *fundamental* form of the mythical, prehistorical consciousness"

(143); "In one fragment, Nietzsche leaves the exposition of his doctrine to the care of Caesar, instead of Zarathustra. This is of great importance, for it underscores that Nietzsche perceived the complicity that exists between his doctrine and imperialism" (142). As argued in chapter 6, however, there are surprising ways in which the Benjaminian messianic could be reconciled with a differential, noncyclical understanding of the eternal return.

14   Benjamin, *Passagen,* 445.

15   Benjamin, "On Some Motifs in Baudelaire," 172.

16   Friedmann, quoted in Benjamin, *Passagen,* 453.

17   Benjamin, "On Some Motifs in Baudelaire," 155.

18   Ibid., 156.

19   Benjamin, "Paris: Capital of the Nineteenth Century," in *Reflections,* 158.

20   Benjamin, *Passagen,* 351.

21   Fredric Jameson, "Utopia, Modernism, and Death," in *The Seeds of Time,* 85.

22   As César Guimarães has noted, Noll has replaced the journey that provided the model for the Bildungsroman with another kind of displacement, namely, *deriva* [drifting]. If, as Wim Wenders affirms, "the journey as a time of apprenticeship to understand the world is a dream no longer thinkable for us" (quoted in Guimarães, "As Imagens da Memória: Fonemas, Grafemas e Cinemas nas Narrativas da Contemporaneidade." Ph.D. diss., Universidade Federal de Minas Gerais, 1995, 164), the traveling self has been "deprived of all becoming, with his/her movement of changing into a different person finding itself paralyzed" (164); hence Guimarães's contention that Noll's characters "experiment without constituting experience" (160), in contrast to Peter Handke's fiction, which can still provide the utopia of a unique relationship with objects and thus recapture some narratability in experience. See Guimarães's fine analysis in "As Imagens."

23   Fournel, quoted in Benjamin, *Passagen,* 447.

24   Benjamin, "On Some Motifs in Baudelaire," 157.

25   "The entire book, from the first to the last story, juxtaposes the most extravagant realities of the Brazilian imaginary at the end of the 1970s." Francisco Caetano Lopes Jr., "A Questão Pós-moderna Vista da Periferia: O Caso João Gilberto Noll," *Hispania* 74 (1991): 600.

26   For a compelling articulation of the late Lacanian notion of fantasy as the very structuring axis through which an anchor can be set in the Real, see Slavoj Žižek, *The Sublime Object of Ideology* (London and New York: Verso, 1989), 43–49, passim.

27   Guimarães, "As Imagens," 161.

28   Ibid., 161–62.

29   Jean Baudrillard, *Amérique* (Paris: Bernard Grasset, 1986), 109.

30   Also in *Hotel Atlântico,* the narrator-protagonist hears of a defeated origin-

searcher: "one afternoon I heard someone playing the organ in the chapel. I later found out it was a kid who had studied conductorship in Germany, and knowing he had terminal cancer came back to die in Arraiol, his *terra de origem* [hometown] (*HA* 84).

31   Flora Süssekind, "Ficção 80: Dobradiças e Vitrines," in *Papéis Colados* (Rio de Janeiro: UFRJ, 1993), 243.

32   Ibid., 240.

33   Juan Rulfo, *Pedro Páramo* (1955) (Barcelona: Planeta, 1990), 29.

8   *The Unmourned Dead and the Promise of Restitution*

1   Dori Laub, "Truth and Testimony: The Process and the Struggle," in *Trauma: Explorations in Memory*, ed. Carol Caruth (Baltimore and London: Johns Hopkins UP, 1995), 63.

2   For the standard account of the decline in the transmissibility of experience in its links with the crisis of storytelling, see Walter Benjamin, "The Storyteller" (1936), in *Illuminations*, trans. Harry Zohn (New York: Schocken, 1968), 83–110.

3   Dori Laub, "Truth and Testimony," 63. On the vicissitudes of witnessing after historical catastrophes, see also Shoshana Felman and Dori Laub, *Testimony: Crisis of Witnessing in Literature, Psychoanalysis, and History* (New York and London: Routledge, 1992).

4   Freud, "Mourning and Melancholia," 237–58.

5   Speaking of Uruguay, Hugo Achugar has noted the *ethical* dilemma of postdictatorship: "A feeling of guilt arises from the fact that Uruguayan society knows . . . that it has come out of the dictatorial catastrophe without being able to clarify doubts and misgivings, or punish those responsible. . . . The bad conscience of an important part of the country has preferred to live with guilt rather than risk achieving justice." *La balsa de la medusa: ensayos sobre identidad, cultura y fin de siglo en Uruguay* (Montevideo: Trilce, 1992), 45. *En estado de memoria* is a novel written against, and as an autopsy of, precisely such bad faith.

6   Tununa Mercado, *En estado de memoria* (Buenos Aires: Ada Korn, 1990). Page references to this work are hereafter given parenthetically in the text. Tununa Mercado's first book, *Celebrar a la mujer como una pascua*, was published in 1967 and received an honorary mention at Cuba's Casa de las Américas Award. Her second book was *Canon de alcoba* (Buenos Aires: Ada Korn, 1988), a series of richly allegorical stories that give testimony on some of Mercado's major concerns: the question of writing in times of defeat, the impact of exile upon memory, and the status of the dead among the living. Next was *La letra de lo mínimo* (Buenos Aires: Beatriz Viterbo, 1994), a col-

lection of minimalist texts and travel notes about the United States. Most recently, she has published *La madriguera* (Buenos Aires: TusQuets, 1996), childhood memoirs where the past appears as a mobile and multilayered labyrinth revolving around a lost object.

7   Michel Foucault, *The Birth of the Clinic: An Archaeology of Medical Perception* (1963), trans. A. M. Sheridan Smith (New York: Vintage, 1973), 84.

8   For an exploration of the links between transference and translation, especially as regards autobiography and the singularity of a signature in the work of Friedrich Nietzsche, see Derrida, *The Ear of the Other.*

9   The protagonist's vicarious nature has been noted by Jean Franco in her analysis of the novel. See Jean Franco, "Going Public: Reinhabiting the Private," in Yúdice, Flores, and Franco, ed., *On Edge,* 78–80.

10 Jacques Lacan, in his *The Four Fundamental Concepts of Psychoanalysis* (1973), trans. Alan Sheridan (New York and London: Norton, 1981), critiques a common misunderstanding about the nature of transference (associated by him with the puritanism of American ego psychology), namely, the notion that links transference with illusion and error, leading up to the fallacy of a supposedly desirable intervention of the analyst to "correct" it through "an alliance with the healthy part of the subject's ego" (130–31). To that Lacan opposes a concept of transference as the repetition of a missed encounter, an *event* that *takes place,* "the enactment of the reality of the unconscious" (146), rather than a manipulatable means for correcting delusions.

11 Benjamin, "Theses on the Philosophy of History," in *Illuminations,* 262.

12 In similar fashion, see Mercado's *Canon de alcoba:* "Tired people, true computers of repression: years gathering clippings, assembling files, writing testimonies" (82). Again, the past emerges as a storage of uncanny memories that do not cease to return.

13 On the themes of inheritance, spectrality, mourning, and restitution, see Jacques Derrida, *Specters of Marx.* See also Jameson's extensive discussion of it in "Marx's Purloined Letter." I have addressed the crucial role of Benjamin in the renewed dialogue between Jameson and Derrida in "El espectro en la temporalidad de lo mesiánico.

14 Martin Heidegger, "Building Dwelling Thinking" (1951), trans. Albert Hofstadter, in *Basic Writings,* ed. David Farrell Krell (San Francisco: Harper-Collins, 1977), 353, 351.

15 The metaphor of the house returns in "La casa está en orden," an unpublished essay in which Mercado reflects upon the "day after" in Argentina, from her shock at the widespread proliferation of euphemisms in the references to the military regime (the disappearance of the words *genocide* and *annihilation,* the replacement of *military dictatorship* with *proceso,* the term chosen by the dictators), to the gradual victory of forgetting over memory

in the laws known as "Due Obedience" and "Final Stop," to the rearrangement of the literary sphere in postdictatorship along the values imposed by the market.

16 Georg Wilhelm Friedrich Hegel, *Phenomenology of Spirit* (1807), trans. A. V. Miller (Oxford, England: Oxford UP, 1977), 19.

17 Ibid., 55.

18 Ibid., 44.

19 In her *The Gendering of Melancholia: Feminism, Psychoanalysis, and the Symbolics of Loss in Renaissance Literature* (Ithaca, N.Y., and London: Cornell UP, 1992), Juliana Schiesari unveils the rhetorical mechanisms through which the distinction between melancholia and mourning has been gendered, with the former being historically assigned to men precisely as a sign of their exceptionality (hence the mythical image of the melancholic genius, always a man), as opposed to the "*devaluing* of the historical reality of women's disempowerment and of the ritual function that has traditionally been theirs in the West, that of mourning" (12). It would be instructive to confront Mercado's novel with Schiesari's study, for Mercado's protagonist speaks as a woman for whom mourning does not exclude that heightened self-awareness and creative impulse traditionally assigned to melancholia and historically gendered in the masculine. In other words, her mourning does not replace melancholia but rather establishes the conditions for a critical, self-reflexive, melancholic work of mourning, while all along speaking distinctively as a woman. The key for this possibility is, as I have been arguing, the relationship with the collective, perhaps absent or only dimly envisioned in the first world texts analyzed by Schiesari. It is in the relation with the collective that Mercado advances Schiesari's call for "new symbolic orders" in which "a radical affirmation of mourning" could take place and mourning would be understood "to be not just the undermining of the ego but a positive form of social and psychical reasoning" (267).

20 "We overcome the transference by pointing out to the patient that his feelings do not arise from the present situation and do not apply to the doctor, but that they are repeating something that happened to him earlier. In this way we oblige him to transform a repetition into a memory." Sigmund Freud, *Introductory Lectures on Psycho-Analysis* (1917), vol. 16 of *Standard Edition*, 444.

21 As Cathy Caruth points out in a fine study of trauma: "to cure oneself— whether by drugs or the telling of one's story or both—seems to many survivors to imply the giving-up of an important reality, or the dilution of a special truth into the reassuring terms of therapy. Indeed, in Freud's own early writings on trauma, the possibility of integrating the lost event into a series of associative memories, as part of the cure, was seen precisely as

a way to permit the event to be forgotten." "Preface," *Trauma*, vii. The protagonist of *In State of Memory* is keenly aware of this paradox—the therapeutic remembrance of the trauma has the purpose of producing oblivion of
it—and this awareness lies at the root of her melancholia. Freud's distinction between mourning and melancholia thus receives another spin here: it
is the postdictatorial *possibility* of successful mourning work, not its impossibility, that generates melancholia.

WORKS CITED

Abraham, Nicolas, and Maria Torok. "Mourning *or* Melancholia: Introjection versus Incorporation" (1972). *The Shell and the Kernel: Renewals of Psychoanalysis.* Trans. and ed. Nicholas Rand. Chicago and London: U of Chicago P, 1994, 125–38.

———. *The Wolf Man's Magic Word: A Cryptonymy.* Foreword by Jacques Derrida (1976). Trans. Nicholas Rand. Minneapolis: U of Minnesota P, 1986.

Achugar, Hugo. *La balsa de la medusa: ensayos sobre identidad, cultura y fin de siglo en Uruguay.* Montevideo: Trilce, 1992.

Aguilar Mora, Jorge. "Sobre el lado moridor de la 'nueva narrativa' hispanoamericana." In Rama, *Más allá,* 237–254.

Alifano, Roberto. *Conversaciones con Borges.* Buenos Aires: Atlántida, 1984.

Allende, Isabel. *La casa de los espíritus.* Barcelona: Plaza y Janés, 1982.

Altamirano, Carlos, and Beatriz Sarlo. "La Argentina del centenario: campo intelectual y temas ideológicos." *Hispamérica* 9 (1980): 35–59.

Althusser, Louis. "Ideology and Ideological State Apparatuses" (1970). In *Lenin and Philosophy.* Trans. Ben Brewster. New York and London: Monthly Review, 1971, 127–86.

Andrade, Mário de. *Macunaíma.* 1928. Belo Horizonte: Itatiaia, 1984.

Antelo, Raúl. *Literatura em Revista.* São Paulo: Ática, 1984.

Arigucci Jr., Davi. "Jornal, Realismo, Alegoria: O Romance Brasileiro Recente." In *Achados e Perdidos.* São Paulo: Polis, 1979, 79–115.

Arlt, Roberto. *El juguete rabioso.* 1926. Barcelona: Bruguera, 1979.

Arlt. *Los siete locos* (1929). *Los lanzallamas* (1931). Caracas: Biblioteca Ayacucho, 1986.

Arrate, Marina. "Una novela como radiografía: *Por la patria.*" Master's thesis, Universidad de Concepción, Santiago, 1992.

Asturias, Miguel Angel. *Leyendas de Guatemala.* 1930. Buenos Aires: Losada, 1970.

Avelar, Idelber. "O Ano de 1993: Sobre as Ruínas da Anti-Utopia." *Letras e Letras* 99 (1993): 39–42.

———. "Bares desiertos y calles sin nombre: literatura y experiencia en tiempos sombríos." *Revista de Crítica Cultural* 9 (1994): 37–43.

———. "*La casa de los espíritus:* la historia del mito y el mito de la historia." *Revista Chilena de Literatura* 43 (1993): 67–74.

———. "Deconstruction, Liberal Universalism, and the Ethics of Interpretation." *SubStance* (1999). Forthcoming.

———. "El espectro en la temporalidad de lo mesiánico: Derrida y Jameson a propósito de la firma Marx." In *Espectros y pensamiento utópico,* vol. 2 of *La invención y la herencia.* Ed. Federico Galende. Santiago: ARCIS-LOM, 1995, 22–32.

———. "Marx, en inminencia y urgencia." *Revista de Crítica Cultural* 11 (1995): 63–66.

Avellaneda, Andrés. *Censura, autoritarismo y cultura: Argentina, 1960–1983.* 2 vols. Buenos Aires: Centro Editor de América Latina, 1986.

———. "Realismo, antirrealismo, territorios canónicos: Argentina literaria después de los militares." In Vidal, *Fascismo,* 578–88.

Bahti, Timothy. *Allegories of History: Literary Historiography after Hegel.* Baltimore and London: Johns Hopkins UP, 1992.

Barbosa, João Alexandre. *A Tradição do Impasse.* São Paulo: Ática, 1974.

Barnet, Miguel. "La novela-testimonio: socio-literatura." In *Testimonio y literatura.* Ed. René Jara and Hernán Vidal. Minneapolis: U of Minnesota P, 1986, 280–302.

Baudelaire, Charles. "La fausse monnaie." In Derrida, *Given Time.* Appendix.

Baudrillard, Jean. *Amérique.* Paris: Grasset, 1986.

Benjamin, Walter. "A Berlin Chronicle." In *Reflections,* 3–60.

———. *Briefe.* Ed. Gershom Scholem and Theodor Adorno. Frankfurt a.M.: Suhrkamp Verlag, 1966.

———: *Illuminations.* Trans. Harry Zohn. New York: Schocken, 1968.

———. "On Language as Such and on the Language of Man" (1955). In *Reflections,* 314–32.

———. "On Some Motifs in Baudelaire" (1939). In *Illuminations,* 155–200.

———. *The Origin of German Tragic Drama.* 1928. Trans. John Osborne. London and New York: Verso, 1977.

———. "Paris: Capital of the Nineteenth Century." In *Reflections,* 146–62.

———. *Passagen-Werk.* Ed. Rolf Tiedemann. Frankfurt a.M.: Suhrkamp Verlag, 1982.

———. *Reflections: Essays, Aphorisms, Autobiographical Writings.* Trans. Edmund Jephcott. New York: Schocken, 1978.

———. "The Storyteller" (1936). In *Illuminations,* 83–109.

———. "The Task of the Translator" (1923). In *Illuminations,* 69–82.

———. "Theses on the Philosophy of History." In *Illuminations,* 253–64.

———. "The Work of Art in the Age of Mechanical Reproduction" (1936). In *Illuminations,* 217–51.

Bercht, Fátima, ed. *Contemporary Art from Chile.* Bilingual catalog. New York: Americas Society, 1991.

Berenguer, Carmen, *Escribir en los bordes: congreso internacional de literatura femenina latinoamericana.* Santiago: Cuarto Propio, 1990.

Beverley, John. *Against Literature.* Minneapolis and London: U of Minnesota P, 1993.

Bonasso, Miguel. *Recuerdo de la muerte.* Mexico City: Era, 1984.

Borges, Jorge Luis. "De las alegorías a las novelas." In *Otras inquisiciones* (1952), vol. 3 of *Prosa completa,* 163–66.

———. "El fin." In *Ficciones* (1944), vol. 2 of *Prosa completa,* 221–24.

———. "Historia de Rosendo Juárez." In *El informe de Brodie* (1970), vol. 4 of *Prosa completa,* 25–30.

———. "Hombre de la esquina rosada." In *Historia universal de la infamia* (1935), vol. 1 of *Prosa completa,* 291–28.

———. *El idioma de los argentinos.* 1928. Buenos Aires: Seix Barral, 1994.

———. *El informe de Brodie.* 1970. Vol. 4 of *Prosa completa.*

———. *Inquiciones.* Buenos Aires: Proa, 1925.

———. "Macedonio Fernández." *Sur* 209–10 (1952): 145–47.

———. *Prosa completa.* 4 vols. Buenos Aires: Emecé, 1979.

———. "Pierre Menard, autor del *Quijote.*" In *Ficciones* (1944), vol. 2 of *Prosa completa,* 125–40.

———. *El tamaño de mi esperanza.* 1926. Buenos Aires: Seix Barral, 1993.

———. "Tlön Uqbar, Orbis Tertius." In *Ficciones* (1944), vol. 2 of *Prosa completa,* 109–24.

Brecht, Bertolt. *Trommeln in der Nacht.* In *Stücke 1,* vol. 1 of *Berliner und Frankfurter Ausgabe.* Berlin, Weimar, and Frankfurt: Aufbau and Suhrkamp, 1989, 175–239.

Brito, Eugenia. *Campos minados: literatura post-golpe en Chile.* Santiago: Cuarto Propio, 1990.

Brunner, José Joaquín. *La cultura autoritaria en Chile.* Santiago: FLACSO, 1981.

———. "Cultura autoritaria y cultura escolar: 1973–1984." In *Cinco estudios sobre cultura y sociedad.* By José Joaquín Brunner and Gonzalo Catalán. Santiago: FLACSO, 1985, 415–53.

———. *Un espejo trizado: ensayos sobre culturas y políticas culturales.* Santiago: FLACSO, 1988.

———. "Entre la cultura autoritaria y la cultura democrática." In Brunner, *Espejo,* 79–101.

———. "Intelectuales y democracia." In Brunner, *Espejo,* 439–66.

Brunner, José Joaquín, Alicia Barros, and Carlos Catalán. *Chile: Transformaciones culturales y modernidad.* Santiago: FLACSO, 1989.

Buntinx, Gustavo, Carlos Pérez, and Nelly Richard. *El fulgor de lo obsceno.* Santiago: Francisco Zegers, n.d.

Burton, Robert. *The Anatomy of Melancholy.* 1621. Oxford: Clarendon, 1989.

"Câmara Aprova Indenizações." *Folha de São Paulo,* 14 September 1995, "Caderno Brasil," p. 9.

Campos, Haroldo de. "A Palavra Vermelha de Hölderlin" (1969). In *A Arte no Horizonte do Provável.* 4th ed. São Paulo: Perspectiva, 1977, 93-107.

Candido, Antonio. "De Cortiço a Cortiço." In *O Discurso e a Cidade.* São Paulo: Duas Cidades, 1993, 123-52.

————. *A Educação pela Noite e Outros Ensaios.* São Paulo: Ática, 1987.

————. *Ficção e Confissão.* Rio de Janeiro: José Olympio, 1956.

————. "Literatura de Dois Gumes." In Candido, *Educação,* 163-80.

————. "Literatura e Subdesenvolvimento." In Candido, *Educação,* 140-62.

Cánovas, Rodrigo. "Apuntes sobre la novela *Por la patria* (1986), de Diamela Eltit." *Acta Literaria* 15 (1990): 147-60.

————. *Lihn, Zurita, Ictus, Radrigán: literatura chilena y experiencia autoritaria.* Santiago: FLACSO, 1986.

Cardoso, Fernando Henrique. *Autoritarismo e Democratização.* Rio de Janeiro: Paz e Terra, 1975.

Carpentier, Alejo. *La novela latinoamericana en vísperas de un nuevo siglo y otros ensayas.* Mexico: Siglo veintiuno, 1981.

————. *El reino de este mundo.* 1949. Montevideo: Arca, 1966.

————. *Los pasos perdidos.* 1953. Ed. Roberto González Echevarría. Madrid: Cátedra, 1985.

Caruth, Carol, ed. *Trauma: Explorations in Memory* (Baltimore and London: Johns Hopkins UP, 1995).

"El caso 'Simón Bolívar,' o el arte como zona de disturbios." Dossier de prensa. *Revista de Crítica Cultural* 9 (1994): 25-36.

Castañeda, Jorge. *Utopia Unarmed: The Latin American Left after the Cold War.* New York: Random House, 1993.

Catalán, Carlos. *Estado y campo cultural en Chile.* Serie Material de Discusión 115. Santiago: FLACSO, 1988.

Catalán, Gonzalo. "Antecedentes sobre la transformación del campo literario en Chile entre 1890 y 1920." In *Cinco estudios sobre cultura y sociedad.* By José Joaquín Brunner and Gonzalo Catalán. Santiago: FLACSO, 1985, 69-175.

Caws, Mary Ann, ed. *City Images.* New York: Gordon and Breach, 1991.

Clifford, James. *The Predicament of Culture: Twentieth-Century Ethnography, Literature, and Art.* Cambridge: Harvard UP, 1988.

Collyer, Jaime. "De las hogueras a la imprenta: el arduo renacer de la narrativa chilena." *Cuadernos Hispanoamericanos* 482-83 (1990): 123-35.

Cornejo Polar, Antonio. "Un ensayo sobre 'los zorros' de Arguedas." In *El zorro de arriba y el zorro de abajo.* By José María Arguedas. Ed. Eve-Marie Fell. Paris: Archivos, 1990, 296-306.

————. *Los universos narrativos de José María Arguedas.* Lima: Instituto de Estudios Peruanos, 1973.

Cortázar, Julio. *Rayuela* (1963). In Colección Archivos. Ed. Julio Ortega and Saúl Yurkievich. Madrid: CSIC, 1991.

Coulthard, George. "La pluralidad cultural." In *América Latina en su literatura.* Ed. César Fernández Moreno. Mexico: UNESCO and Siglo XIX, 1972, 53-72.

de Man, Paul. *Allegories of Reading: Figural Language in Rousseau, Nietzsche, Rilke, and Proust.* New Haven and London: Yale UP, 1979.

————. "Conclusions: Walter Benjamin's 'The Task of the Translator'" (1985). In *The Resistance to Theory.* Minneapolis: U of Minnesota P, 1986, 73-105.

————. "The Rhetoric of Temporality" (1969). In *Blindness and Insight: Essays in the Rhetoric of Contemporary Criticism* (1971). Rev. 2d ed. Minneapolis: U of Minnesota P, 1983, 187-228.

Deleuze, Gilles. "Désire et plaisir." *Magazine Littéraire* 325 (1994): 59-65.

————. *Difference and Repetition* (1968). Trans. Paul Patton. New York: Columbia UP, 1994.

————. *The Logic of Sense* (1969). Trans. Mark Lester with Charles Stivale. New York: Columbia UP, 1990.

————. *Nietzsche and Philosophy* (1962). Trans. Hugh Tomlinson. New York: Columbia UP, 1983.

Deleuze, Gilles, and Félix Guattari. *Anti-Oedipus: Capitalism and Schizophrenia I* (1972). Trans. Robert Hurley, Mark Seem, and Elen Lane. Minneapolis: U of Minnesota P, 1977.

Derrida, Jacques. *Cinders* (1987). Trans. Ned Lukacher. Lincoln: U of Nebraska P, 1991.

————. "Des tours de Babel" (1977). In *Difference in Translation.* Ed. Joseph F. Graham. Ithaca, N.Y.: Cornell UP, 1985, 165-207.

————. *The Ear of the Other: Otobiography, Transference, Translation.* Trans. Peggy Kamuf. Lincoln: U of Nebraska P, 1985.

————. *Given Time: I. Counterfeit Money* (1991). Trans. Peggy Kamuf. Chicago and London: U of Chicago P, 1992.

————. *Glas* (1974). Trans. John P. Leavey Jr. and Richard Rand. Lincoln: U of Nebraska P, 1986.

————. "Freud and the Scene of Writing" (1966). In *Writing and Difference.* Trans. Alan Bass. Chicago: U of Chicago P, 1978, 196-231.

————. "Limited Inc a b c. . . ." (1977). In *Limited Inc.* Trans. Samuel Weber. Evanston: Northwestern UP, 1988, 29-110.

————. *Margins of Philosophy* (1972). Trans. Alan Bass. Chicago: U of Chicago P, 1982.

————. "On a Newly Arisen Apocalyptic Tone in Philosophy" (1981). In *Raising* the Tone of Philosophy: Late Essays by Immanuel Kant, Transformative Critique by* Jacques Derrida. Ed. Peter Fenves. Baltimore: Johns Hopkins UP, 1993, 117–71.

———. "Ousia and *Gramme:* Note on a Note from *Being and Time*" (1968). In *Margins of Philosophy,* 29–67.

———. "Signature Event Context" (1972). In *Margins of Philosophy,* 307–30.

———. *Specters of Marx: The State of the Debt, the Work of Mourning and the New International* (1993). Trans. Peggy Kamuf. New York and London: Routledge, 1994.

Disselkoen, Ivette Malverde. "Esquizofrenia y literatura: el discurso de padre e hija en *El padre mío* de Diamela Eltit." *Acta Literaria* 16 (1991): 69–76.

Donoso, José. *Casa de campo.* Barcelona, Caracas, and Mexico City: Seix Barral, 1978.

DuBois, Page. *Torture and Truth.* New York and London: Routledge, 1991.

Eltit, Diamela. *El cuarto mundo.* Santiago: Planeta, 1988.

———. *Lumpérica.* Santiago: Ediciones del Ornitorrinco, 1983.

———. *El padre mío.* Santiago: Francisco Zegers, 1989.

———. *Por la patria.* Santiago: Ediciones del Ornitorrinco, 1986.

———. *Vaca sagrada.* Santiago and Buenos Aires: Planeta, 1991.

———. *Los vigilantes.* Santiago: Sudamericana, 1994.

Eltit, Diamela, and Paz Errázuriz. *El infarto del alma.* Santiago: Francisco Zegers, 1994.

Felman, Shoshana, and Dori Laub. *Testimony: Crisis of Witnessing in Literature, Psychoanalysis, and History.* New York and London: Routledge, 1992.

Fernández, Macedonio. *Museo de la novela de la Eterna* (1967). Colección Archivos. Ed. Ana María Camblong and Adolfo de Obieta. Paris: Archivos, 1993.

———. *No toda es vigilia la de ojos abiertos.* 1928. Buenos Aires: Centro Editor de América Latina. 1977.

Fletcher, Angus. *Allegory: The Theory of a Symbolic Mode.* Ithaca, N.Y., and London: Cornell UP, 1964.

Flores, Angel. "Magical Realism in Spanish American Fiction." In Zamora and Faris, *Magical Realism* 109–17.

Foucault, Michel. *The Archaeology of Knowledge* (1969). Trans. Alan Sheridan Smith. New York: Pantheon Books, 1972.

———. *The Birth of the Clinic: An Archaeology of Medical Perception* (1963). Trans. A. M. Sheridan Smith. New York: Vintage, 1973.

———. "What Is an Author?" (1969). In *Language, Counter-Memory, Practice.* Trans. Donald Bouchard and Sherry Simon. Ithaca, N.Y.: Cornell UP, 1977, 133–38.

Franco, Jean. "Going Public: Reinhabiting the Private." In Yúdice, Franco, and Flores, *On Edge,* 65–83.

———. "Memoria, narración y repetición: la narrativa hispanoamericana en la época de la cultura de masas." In *Más allá del boom: literatura y mercado.* Ed. Angel Rama et al. Mexico: Marcha, 1981, 111–29.

———. "Remapping culture." *Latin American Literary Review* 20 (1992): 38–40.

Freud, Sigmund. *The History of an Infantile Neurosis* (1918), vol. 17 of *Standard Edition* (1960).

———. *Introductory Lectures on Psycho-Analysis* (1917), vol. 14 of *Standard Edition* (1957).

———. "Mourning and Melancholia" (1916), in vol. 14 of *Standard Edition* (1957), 237–58.

———. *The Standard Edition of the Complete Psychological Works of Sigmund Freud.* Trans. James Strachey et al. London: Hogarth, 1953–66.

Fuentes, Carlos. *La nueva novela hispanoamericana.* Mexico City: Joaquín Mortiz, 1969.

Gabeira, Fernando. *O Que é Isso, Companheiro?* Rio de Janeiro: Codecri, 1979.

García Canclini, Néstor. *Hybrid Cultures: Strategies for Entering and Leaving Modernity.* Trans. Christopher Chiappari and Silvia López. Minneapolis: U of Minnesota P, 1995. Original in Spanish: *Culturas híbridas: Estrategias para entrar y salir de la modernidad.* Mexico City: Grijalbo, 1989.

García Márquez, Gabriel. *Cien años de soledad.* 1967. 59th ed. Buenos Aires: Sudamericana, 1990.

Garfield, Evelyn Picon. "Cortázar por Cortázar." In *Rayuela.* By Julio Cortázar. Ed. Julio Ortega and Saúl Yurkievich. Paris: Archivos, 1991, 778–89.

Garrels, Elisabeth. "Resumen de la discusión." In Rama, *Más allá,* 287–326.

Giella, Miguel Angel, ed. *Teatro Abierto 1981: Teatro argentino bajo vigilancia.* Buenos Aires: Corregidor, 1992.

Gomes, Renato Cordeiro. *Todas as Cidades, a Cidade: Literatura e Experiência Urbana.* Rio de Janeiro: Rocco, 1994.

González Echevarría, Roberto. *Myth and Archive: A Theory of Latin American Narrative.* Cambridge: Cambridge UP, 1990.

Gugelberger, George M., ed. *The "Real" Thing: Testimonial Discourse and Latin America.* Durham, N.C.: Duke UP, 1996.

Guimarães, César. "As Imagens da Memória: Fonemas, Grafemas e Cinemas nas Narrativas da Contemporaneidade." Ph.D. diss. Universidade Federal de Minas Gerais, 1995.

Habermas, Jürgen. *The Structural Transformation of the Public Sphere: An Inquiry into a Category of Bourgeois Society* (1962). Trans. Thomas Burger and Frederick Lawrence. Cambridge, Mass.: MIT, 1989.

Hardt, Michael. *Gilles Deleuze: An Apprenticeship in Philosophy.* Minneapolis: U of Minnesota P, 1993.

Hegel, Georg Wilhelm Friederich. *Aesthetics* (1835). Trans. T. M. Knox. Vol. 1. Oxford, England: Oxford UP, 1975.

————. *Phenomenology of Spirit.* 1807. Trans. A. V. Miller. Oxford, England: Oxford UP, 1977.

Heidegger, Martin. "Building Dwelling Thinking" (1951). Trans. Albert Hofstadter. In *Basic Writings.* Ed. David Farrell Krell. San Francisco: HarperCollins, 1977.

Heker, Liliana. "Los talleres literarios." *Cuadernos Hispanoamericanos* 217–19 (1993): 187–94.

Hölderlin, Friedrich. "Becoming in Dissolution." In *Essays and Letters on Theory.* Trans. and ed. Thomas Pfau. Albany: State U of New York P, 1988, 96–100.

Hora, Roy, and Javier Trimboli. *Pensar la Argentina: los historiadores hablan de historia y política.* Buenos Aires: El Cielo por Asalto, 1994.

Huyssen, Andreas. *Twilight memories: Marking Time in a Culture of Amnesia.* New York and London: Routledge, 1995.

James, Henry. "The Last of the Valerii." *The Tales of Henry James. Volume 2: 1870–74.* Ed. Maqbool Aziz. Oxford: Clarendon, 1978, 259–83.

Jameson, Fredric. "Actually Existing Marxism." *Polygraph* 6/7 (1993): 170–95.

————. "The Antinomies of Postmodernity." In Jameson, *Seeds,* 1–71.

————. "Marx's Purloined Letter." *New Left Review* 209 (1995): 75–109.

————. "On Literary and Cultural Import-Substitution in the Third World: The Case of the Testimonio." *Margins* 1 (1991): 11–34.

————. "On Magic Realism in Film." *Critical Inquiry* 12 (1986): 301–25.

————. *Postmodernism, or, the Cultural Logic of Late Capitalism.* Durham, N.C.: Duke UP, 1991.

————. *The Seeds of Time.* New York: Columbia UP, 1994.

————. "Third-World Literature in the Age of Multinational Capital." *Social Text* 15 (1986): 65–88.

————. "Utopia, Modernism, and Death." In Jameson, *Seeds,* 73–128.

Jitrik, Noé. *Las armas y las razones: ensayos sobre el peronismo, el exilio y la literatura, 1975–1980.* Buenos Aires: Sudamericana, 1984.

————. "Miradas desde el borde: el exilio y la literatura argentina." In Sosnowski, *Represión,* 133–47.

Jordão, Fernando. *Dossiê Herzog: Prisão, Tortura e Morte no Brasil.* São Paulo: Global, 1979.

Joyce, James. *Finnegans Wake.* 1939. New York: Viking, 1976.

Kadir, Djelal. *The Other Writing: Essays in Latin America's Writing Culture.* West Lafayette, Ind.: Purdue UP, 1993.

Kaplan, Marina. "Between Arlt and Borges: Interview with Ricardo Piglia." *New Orleans Review* 16 (1989): 64–74.

Kay, Ronald. *Del espacio de acá.* Santiago: Visual, 1990.

————, ed. *Manuscritos.* Santiago: DEH, 1975.

King, John. "Las revistas culturales de la dictadura a la democracia: el caso de

'Punto de Vista.'" In *Literatura argentina hoy: de la dictadura a la democracia*. Ed. Karl Kohut and Andrea Pagni. Frankfurt a.M.: Vervuert Verlag, 1989, 180–221.

Lacan, Jacques. *The Four Fundamental Concepts of Psychoanalysis* (1973). Trans. Alan Sheridan. New York and London: Norton, 1981.

———. *The Seminar of Jacques Lacan, Book VII: The Ethics of Psychoanalysis, 1959–60*. Ed. Jacques-Alain Miller. Trans. Dennis Porter. New York and London: Norton, 1992.

Lafetá, João Luiz. "O Mundo à Revelia." Afterword. In Ramos, *São Bernardo*, 189–213.

Landi, Oscar. *Reconstrucciones: las nuevas formas de la cultura política*. Buenos Aires: Puntosur, 1988.

Larsen, Neil. *Reading North by South: On Latin American Literature, Culture, and Politics*. Minneapolis and London: U of Minnesota P, 1995.

Laub, Dori. "Truth and Testimony: The Process and the Struggle." In *Trauma: Explorations in Memory*, ed. Caruth, 117–48.

Leal, Luis. "Magical Realism in Spanish American Literature." In Zamora and Faris, *Magical Realism*, 119–24.

Lefebvre, Henri. *The Production of Space* (1974). Trans. Donald Nicholson-Smith. Oxford and Cambridge: Blackwell, 1991.

Lértora, Juan Carlos, ed. *Una poética de literatura menor: la narrativa de Diamela Eltit*. Santiago: Cuarto Propio, 1993.

Lienhard, Martin. *Cultura popular andina y forma novelesca: zorros y danzantes en la última novela de Arguedas*. Caracas: Universidad Central de Venezuela, 1981.

Lispector, Clarice. *A Paixão Segundo G.H.* 1964. Critical Edition by Benedito Nunes. Florianópolis: UFSC, 1988.

Lopes Francisco Caetano, Jr. "A Questão Pós-moderna Vista da Periferia: O Caso João Gilberto Noll." *Hispania* 74 (1991): 598–603.

Loraux, Nicoles. *Women in Mourning*. Trans. Corinne Pache. Ithaca, N.Y., and London: Cornell UP, 1998.

Louzeiro, José. *A Infância dos Mortos*. Rio de Janeiro: Record, 1977.

Ludmer, Josefina. *El género gauchesco: un tratado sobre la patria*. Buenos Aires: Sudamericana, 1988.

Mahieu, José Agustín. "Cine argentino: las nuevas fronteras." *Cuadernos Hispanoamericanos* 517–19 (1993): 289–304.

Maqueira, Diego. *La tirana*. Santiago: Tempus Tacendi, 1983.

Marchant, Patricio. *Sobre árboles y madres*. Santiago: Gato Murr, 1984.

Martin, Luthers, Huck Gutman, and Patrick Hutton, eds. *Technologies of the Self: A Seminar with Michel Foucault*. London: Tavistock, 1988.

Masiello, Francine. "La Argentina durante el proceso: las múltiples resistencias de la cultura." In *Ficción y política: la narrativa argentina durante el proceso militar*.

Buenos Aires and Minneapolis: Alianza Editorial and the Institute for the Study of Ideologies and Literatures, 1987, 11–29.

———. "Contemporary Argentine Fiction: Liberal Pre-texts in a Reign of Horror." *Latin American Research Review* 16 (1981): 218–24.

Masotta, Oscar. *Sexo y traición en Roberto Arlt.* Buenos Aires: Centro Editor de América Latina, 1982.

Mayer, Hans. "Walter Benjamin and Franz Kafka" (1979). Trans. Gary Smith and Thomas S. Hansen. In *On Walter Benjamin: Critical Essays and Recollections.* Ed. Gary Smith. Cambridge, Mass.: MIT P, 1988, 185–209.

McClelland, Charles E. *State, Society, and University in Germany, 1700–1914.* Cambridge: Cambridge UP, 1980.

Mercado, Tununa. *Canon de alcoba.* Buenos Aires: Ada Korn, 1988.

———. "La casa está en orden." Typescript.

———. "Las escritoras y el tema del sexo." *Nuevo Texto Crítico* 2 (1989): 11–13.

———. *En estado de memoria.* Buenos Aires: Ada Korn, 1990.

———. "Fuegos fatuos: escribir en Buenos Aires." *Casa de las Américas* 34 (1994): 98–101.

———. *La letra de lo mínimo.* Buenos Aires: Beatriz Viterbo, 1994.

———. *La madriguera.* Buenos Aires: TusQuets, 1996.

Miceli, Sérgio. *Intelectuais e Classe Dirigente no Brasil, 1920–1945.* São Paulo: DIFEL, 1979.

Miranda, Wander Melo. *Corpos Escritos: Graciliano Ramos e Silviano Santiago.* São Paulo and Belo Horizonte: EDUSP and UFMG, 1992.

Moreiras, Alberto. "The Aura of Testimonio." In *The "Real" Thing: Testimonial Discourse and Latin America.* Ed. George M. Gugelberger. Durham, N.C.: Duke UP, 1996.

———. "Epistemología tenue (sobre el latinoamericanismo)." *Revista de Crítica Cultural* 10 (1995): 48–54.

———. "Pastiche Identity and Allegory of Allegory." In *Latin American Identity and Constructions of Difference.* Ed. Amaryll Chanady. Minneapolis and London: Minnesota UP, 1994, 204–37.

———. "Postdictadura y reforma del pensamiento." *Revista de Crítica Cultural* 7 (1993): 26–35.

Moyano, Daniel. *El vuelo del tigre.* Barcelona: Plaza y Janés, 1984.

Muñoz, Gonzalo. *Exit.* Santiago: Archivo, 1981.

Nietzsche, Friedrich. *The Gay Science* (1882). Trans. Walter Kaufman. New York: Random House, 1974.

———. *On the Genealogy of Morals* (1887). Trans. Walter Kaufman and R. J. Hollingdale. New York: Random House, 1967.

———. "On the Uses and Disadvantages of History for Life" (1873). In *Untimely*

Meditations. Trans. R. J. Hollingdale. Cambridge: Cambridge UP, 1983, 57–123.

———. *The Portable Nietzsche.* Ed. and trans. Walter Kaufman. New York: Viking Penguin, 1968.

———. *Thus Spoke Zarathustra* (1883–85). *The Portable,* 103–439.

———. *Twilight of the Idols* (1889). *The Portable,* 463–563.

Noll, João Gilberto. *Bandoleiros.* Rio de Janeiro: Nova Fronteira, 1985.

———. *O Cego e a Dançarina* (1980). 2d ed. Porto Alegre: L&PM, 1986.

———. *A Fúria do Corpo.* Rio de Janeiro: Rocco, 1981.

———. *Harmada.* São Paulo: Companhia das Letras, 1993.

———. *Hotel Atlântico.* 4th ed. Rio de Janeiro: Rocco, 1989.

———. *O Quieto Animal da Esquina.* Rio de Janeiro: Rocco, 1991.

———. *Rastros do Verão.* Rio de Janeiro: Rocco, 1986.

O'Donnell, Guillermo. *Modernization and Bureaucratic-Authoritarianism.* Berkeley: University of California, 1973.

———. "Tensions in the Bureaucratic-Authoritarian State and the Question of Democracy." In *The New Authoritarianism in Latin America.* Ed. David Collier. Princeton, N.J.: Princeton UP, 1979, 285–318.

Olea, Raquel. "*Por la patria:* una épica de la marginalidad." *Lar* 11 (1987): 2–6.

Orellana, Carlos. "La cultura chilena en el momento del cambio." *Cuadernos Hispanoamericanos* 482–83 (1990): 49–54.

Ortiz, Renato. *Cultura Brasileira e Identidade Nacional.* São Paulo: Brasiliense, 1985.

Oyarzún, Pablo. "Arte en Chile de veinte, treinta años." *Georgia Series on Hispanic Thought* 22–25 (1987–88): 291–324.

———. "Parpadeo y piedad." *Cirugía Plástica* (1989).

———. "Sobre el concepto benjaminiano de traducción." *Seminarios de Filosofía* 6 (1993): 67–101.

Pellegrini, Tânia. "Brazil in the 1970s: Literature and Politics." *Latin American Perspectives* 21 (1994): 56–71.

Pellettieri, Osvaldo. "Los 80: el teatro porteño entre la dictadura y la democracia." *Cuadernos Hispanoamericanos* 517–19 (1993): 313–22.

Pérez, Carlos. "El manifiesto místico-político-teológico de Zurita." *Revista de Crítica Cultural* 10 (1995): 55–59.

Phelan, Peggy. *Mourning Sex: Performing Public Memories.* New York and London: Routledge, 1997.

Piglia, Ricardo. *La Argentina en pedazos.* Buenos Aires: Ediciones de la Urraca, 1993.

———. *La ciudad ausente.* Buenos Aires: Sudamericana, 1992.

———. *Crítica y ficción* (1986). 2d ed. Buenos Aires: Siglo XX and Universidad Nacional del Litoral, 1993.

———. *Nombre falso* (1975). Definitive edition. Buenos Aires: Seix Barral, 1994.

————. *Prisión perpetua*. Buenos Aires: Sudamericana, 1988.

————. *Respiración artificial*. Buenos Aires: Sudamericana, 1980. English translation: *Artificial Respiration*. Trans. Daniel Balderston. Durham, N.C., and London: Duke UP, 1994.

————. "Roberto Arlt: una crítica de la economía literaria." *Los Libros* 29 (1973): 22–27.

Piglia, Ricardo, and Juan José Saer. *Por un relato futuro*. Santa Fé, Argentina: Universidad Nacional del Litoral, 1990.

Plato. *The Collected Dialogues*. Ed. Edith Hamilton and Huntington Cairns. Princeton, N.J.: Princeton UP, 1961.

————. *Laws*. Trans. A. E. Taylor. *The Collected Dialogues*, 1225–513.

————. *Republic*. Trans. Paul Shorey. *The Collected Dialogues*, 575–844.

Plotnik, Viviana. "Alegoría y proceso de reorganización nacional: propuesta de una categoría de mediación socio-histórica para el análisis discursivo." In Vidal, *Fascismo*, 532–77.

Poe, Edgar Allan. "The Murders in the Rue Morgue" (1841). In *Works*, 246–68.

————. "William Wilson" (1839). In *Works*, 212–25.

————. *Works of Edgar Allan Poe*. New York: Chatham River, 1985.

Prieto, Adolfo. "Los años sesenta." *Revista Iberoamericana* 125 (1983): 891–901.

Pupo-Walker, Enrique. *La vocación literaria del pensamiento histórico en América: desarrollo de la prosa de ficción, siglos XVI, XVII, XVIII, XIX*. Madrid: Gredos, 1982.

Rama, Angel. "El boom en perspectiva" (1982). In *La crítica de la cultura en América Latina*. Caracas: Biblioteca Ayacucho, 1985, 266–306.

————. *La ciudad letrada*. Hannover: Ediciones del Norte, 1984.

Rama, Angel et al. *Más allá del boom: literatura y mercado*. Mexico City: Marcha, 1981.

Ramos, Graciliano. *Memórias do Cárcere* (1953). 21st ed. 2 vols. Rio de Janeiro and São Paulo: Record, 1986.

————. *São Bernardo* (1934). 51st ed. Rio de Janeiro: Record, 1989.

Ramos, Julio. *Desencuentros de la modernidad en América Latina: literatura y política en el siglo XIX*. Mexico City: Siglo XXI, 1989.

Reati, Fernando. *Nombrar lo innombrable: violencia política y novela argentina, 1975–1985*. Buenos Aires: Legasa, 1992.

Richard, Nelly. "Bordes, diseminación, postmodernismo: una metáfora latinoamericana de fin de siglo." In *Las culturas de fin de siglo en América Latina*. Ed. Josefina Ludmer. Buenos Aires: Beatriz Viterbo, 1994, 240–48.

————. *Cuerpo correccional*. Santiago: Visual, 1980.

————. *La insubordinación de los signos: cambio político, transformaciones culturales y poéticas de la crisis*. Santiago: Cuarto Propio, 1994.

————. *Margins and Institutions: Art in Chile since 1973*. Bilingual ed. Melbourne: Art and Text, 1986.

————. *Residuos y metáforas: ensayos de crítica cultural sobre el Chile de la Transición.* Santiago: Cuarto Propio, 1998.

————. "Tres funciones de escritura: deconstrucción, simulación, hibridación." In Lértora, *Una poética,* 37–51.

Richard, Nelly et al. *Arte en Chile desde 1973: escena de avanzada y sociedad.* Santiago: FLACSO, 1987.

Rickels, Laurence A. *Aberrations of Mourning: Writing on German Crypts.* Detroit: Wayne State UP, 1988.

Rivera, Anny. *Transformaciones culturales y movimiento artístico en el orden autoritario: Chile, 1973–1982.* Santiago: CENECA, 1983.

Rodríguez Monegal, Emir. *Narradores de esta América.* 2 vols. Montevideo: Alfa, 1969.

Rosa, Guimarães. *Grande Sertão: Veredas.* 1956. Rio de Janeiro: José Olympio, 1972.

Rowe, William. "Deseo, escritura y fuerzas productivas." In *El zorro de arriba y el zorro de abajo.* By José María Arguedas. Ed. Eve-Marie Fell. Colección Archivos. Madrid: CSIC, 1990, 333–40.

————. "El nuevo lenguaje de Arguedas en *El zorro de arriba y el zorro de abajo.*" *Texto Crítico* 11 (1978): 198–212.

Rowe, William, and Vivian Schelling. *Memory and Modernity: Popular Culture in Latin America.* London and New York: Verso, 1991.

Rulfo, Juan. *Pedro Páramo* (1955). Barcelona: Planeta, 1990.

Sader, Emir. "Da Teoria do Autoritarismo ao Deus Mercado." *Folha de São Paulo,* 11 June 1995, "Caderno Mais," p. 3.

Saer, Juan José. *Nadie nada nunca* (1980). Buenos Aires: Seix Barral, 1995.

Salazar, Gabriel. "Historiografía y dictadura en Chile (1973-1990)." *Cuadernos Hispanoamericanos* 482–83 (1990): 81–94.

Santiago, Silviano. *Em Liberdade.* Rio de Janeiro: Paz e Terra, 1981.

————. "O Entre-Lugar do Discurso Latino-Americano." In *Uma Literatura nos Trópicos.* São Paulo: Perspectiva, 1978, 11–28.

————. "O Evangelho Segundo São João." In *Nas Malhas da Letra,* 62–67.

————. "Fechado para Balanço (Sessenta Anos de Modernismo)." In *Nas Malhas da Letra,* 75–93.

————. *Nas Malhas da Letra.* São Paulo: Companhia das Letras, 1989.

————. "A Permanência do Discurso da Tradição no Modernismo." In *Nas Malhas da Letra,* 94–123.

————. "Reading and Discursive Intensities." In *The Postmodernism Debate in Latin America: A Special Issue of boundary 2.* Ed. John Beverley and José Oviedo (1993): 194–202.

————. "Repressão e Censura no Campo das Artes na Década de 70." In *Vale Quanto Pesa: Ensaios sobre Questões Político-Culturais.* Rio: Paz e Terra, 1982, 47–55.

————, ed. *Glossário de Derrida*. Rio de Janeiro: Francisco Alves, 1976.

Sapag, Pablo. "Chile: experiencia sociopolítica y medios de comunicación." *Cuadernos Hispanoamericanos* 482–83 (1990): 63–70.

Saramago, José. *O Ano de 1993* (1973). Lisbon: Caminho, 1987.

Sarlo, Beatriz. "¿Arcaicos o marginales? Situación de los intelectuales en fin de siglo." *Revista de Crítica Cultural* 9 (1994): 8–13.

————. "El campo intelectual: un espacio doblemente fracturado." In Sosnowski, *Represión*, 95–107.

————. *Escenas de la vida posmoderna: intelectuales, arte y videocultura en Argentina*. Buenos Aires: Ariel, 1994.

————. "El relativismo absoluto o cómo el mercado y la sociología reflexionan sobre estética." *Punto de vista* 48 (1994): 27–31.

Sarmiento, Domingo. *Facundo, o Civilización y barbarie*. 1845. Prologue by Noé Jitrik. Caracas: Ayacucho, 1977.

Schiesari, Juliana. *The Gendering of Melancholia: Feminism, Psychoanalysis, and the Symbolics of Loss in Renaissance Literature*. Ithaca, N.Y., and London: Cornell UP, 1992.

Scholem, Gershom. *Walter Benjamin: The Story of a Friendship* (1975). Trans. Harry Zohn. New York: Schocken, 1981.

Schwarz, Roberto. "Cultura e Política: 1964–1969" (1970). In *O Pai de Família e Outros Estudos*. Rio de Janeiro: Paz e Terra, 1978, 61–92.

————. *Misplaced Ideas: Essays on Brazilian Culture*. Trans. and Ed. John Gledson. London and New York: Verso, 1992.

————. "Misplaced Ideas: Literature and Society in Late-Nineteenth-Century Brazil" (1973). Trans. Edmund Leites and Roberto Schwarz. In *Misplaced Ideas*, 126–59.

————. "Nacional por Subtração." In *Que Horas São?* São Paulo: Companhia das Letras, 1987, 29–48.

Sigal, Silvia. *Intelectuales y poder en la década del sesenta*. Buenos Aires: Puntosur, 1991.

Silva, Aguinaldo. *O Crime Antes da Festa*. Rio de Janeiro: Lidador, 1977.

Sodré, Nélson Werneck. *História da História Nova*. Petrópolis, Brazil: Vozes, 1986.

————. *O Naturalismo no Brasil*. Rio de Janeiro: Civilização Brasileira, 1965.

Sommer, Doris. "Irresistible Romance: The Foundational Fictions of Latin America." In *Nation and Narration*. Ed. Homi Bhabha. London and New York: Routledge, 1990, 71–98.

Sophocles. *Antigone*. Bilingual ed. Trans. and ed. Andrew Brown. Wiltshire: Aris and Philips, 1987.

Soriano, Osvaldo. *Cuarteles de invierno*. Buenos Aires: Sudamericana, 1988.

Sosnowski, Saúl, ed. *Represión y reconstrucción de una cultura: el caso argentino*. Buenos Aires: EUDEBA, 1988.

Spinoza, Baruch. *The Ethics* (1677). *A Spinoza Reader: The Ethics and Other Works.* Trans. Edwin Curley. Princeton, N.J.: Princeton UP, 1994, 85-265.

Staten, Henry. *Eros in Mourning: From Homer to Lacan.* Baltimore: Johns Hopkins UP, 1994.

Subercaseaux, Bernardo. *Historia, literatura y sociedad: ensayos de hermenéutica cultural.* Santiago: CESOC and CENECA, 1991.

————. *La industria editorial y el libro en Chile (1930–1984).* Santiago: CENECA, 1984.

Süssekind, Flora. "Ficção 80: Dobradiças e Vitrines." In *Papéis Colados.* Rio de Janeiro: UFRJ, 1993, 239-52.

————. *Literatura e Vida Literária.* São Paulo: Zahar, 1985.

————. *Tal Brasil, Qual Romance?* Rio de Janeiro: Achiamé, 1984.

Taussig, Michael. *Mimesis and Alterity: A Particular History of the Senses.* New York and London: Routledge, 1993.

Terán, Oscar. *Nuestros años sesentas: la formación de la nueva izquierda intelectual en la Argentina, 1956–1966.* Buenos Aires: Puntosur, 1991.

Timerman, Jacobo. *Prisoner without a Name, Cell without a Number.* Trans. Toby Talbot. New York: Knopf, 1981.

Thayer, Willy. "Crisis categorial de la universidad." Typescript.

————. *La crisis no moderna de la universidad moderna (epílogo del conflicto de las facultades).* Santiago: Cuarto Propio, 1996.

————. "Fin del. 'trabajo intelectual' y fin idealista/capitalista de la historia en la era de la subsunción real del capital. In *Espectros y pensamiento utópico.* Vol. 2 of *La invención y la herencia.* Santiago: ARCIS-LOM, 1995, 172-93.

Valdés, Adriana, and Pablo Oyarzún. "Fragmentos de una conversación en torno a la universidad " *Lo* 1 (1992): 22-31.

Vargas Llosa, Mario. *La casa verde.* 1966. Barcelona: Seix Barral, 1983.

Vidal, Hernán, ed. *Fascismo y experiencia literaria: reflexiones para una canonización.* Minneapolis: Institute for the Study of Languages and Literatures, 1985.

Veiga, José J. *A Hora dos Ruminantes* (1966). 16th ed. São Paulo: DIFEL, 1984. English translation: *The Three Trials of Manirema.* Trans. Pamela G. Bird. New York: Alfred A. Knopf, 1970.

Veríssimo, Érico. *Incidente em Antares* (1971). 29th ed. Rio de Janeiro: Globo, 1978.

Warley, Jorge. "Revistas culturales de dos décadas (1970-1990)." *Cuadernos Hispanoamericanos* 517-19 (1993): 195-207.

Weschler, Lawrence. *A Miracle, a Universe: Settling Accounts with Torturers.* New York: Penguin, 1990.

William of Malmesbury. *Chronicle of the Kings of England.* London: Bell, 1895.

Yúdice, George. "Postmodernism in the Periphery." *South Atlantic Quarterly* 92 (1993): 543-56.

————. "Postmodernity and Transnational Capitalism." In Yúdice, Flores, and Franco, *On Edge,* 1-28.

————. "Testimonio and Postmodernism." *Latin American Perspectives* 18 (1991): 15–31.

————. "We Are *Not* the World." *Social Text* 31–32 (1992): 202–16.

Yúdice, George, Juan Flores, and Jean Franco, ed. *On Edge: The Crisis of Contemporary Latin American Culture.* Minneapolis and London: U of Minnesota P, 1992.

Zamora, Lois Parkinson, and Wendy B. Faris, ed. *Magical Realism: Theory, History, Community.* Durham, N.C., and London: Duke UP, 1995.

Žižek, Slavoj. *The Sublime Object of Ideology.* London and New York: Verso, 1989.

Zurita, Raúl. *Anteparaíso.* Santiago: Editores Asociados, 1982.

————. *Literatura, lenguaje y sociedad.* Santiago: CENECA, 1983.

————. *Purgatorio.* Santiago: Universitaria, 1979.

————. *La Vida nueva.* Santiago: Universitaria, 1994.

INDEX

Abraham, Nicolas, 7–8, 240 n.25

Achugar, Hugo, 267 n.5

Adorno, Theodor, 78, 224

Alencar, José de, 209

Alfonsín, Raúl, 53, 60–61

allegory, 3–11, 14–15, 232–33, 235–36 n.10; etymology of, 11, 77; and impossibility, 75, 181–83, 247 n.67; and literary history, 96–97; vs. magical realism and the fantastic, 68–77, 246–47 n.66, 247 n.70; and mourning 3–5, 123–24; and time 4–5, 68–69

Allende, Isabel, 73, 76, 247 n.68

Allende, Salvador, 13, 35–37, 39, 40, 71–72, 164

Altamirano, Carlos (Argentina), 53, 239 n.21

Altamirano, Carlos (Chile), 166

Althusser, Louis, 80, 264 n.26

Amado, Jorge, 140–41, 209

Andrade, Mário de, 74, 83

Antelo, Raúl, 257 n.14

apocalypse, 18, 21, 178–85, 217–18, 264 n.35

Argentine culture under dictatorship, 9–10, 48–54, 59–61

Arguedas, José María, 34, 242 n.37

Aricó, Pancho, 54

Arigucci, Davi, 245 n.48

Aristaráin, Adolfo, 52

Arlt, Roberto, 50, 86, 91–97, 101, 105, 107, 117

Arraes, Miguel, 40

Arrate, Marina, 169, 263 n.22

Ascasubi, Hilario, 87

Asturias, Miguel Angel, 73, 76

authoritarianism, the sociology of, 13–14; 54–61

Avellaneda, Andrés, 52, 244 n.30

Bahti, Timothy, 236 n.12

Bakhtin, Mikhail, 181

Balzac, Honoré de, 26, 189

Barbosa, João Alexandre, 258 n.24

Barcells, Fernando, 166

Barnet, Miguel, 24

Barreto, Lima, 138

Barros, Alicia, 243 n.20

Barthes, Roland, 173

Bassani, Giorgio, 27

Baudelaire, Charles, 6, 19, 97, 191–94

Baudrillard, Jean, 19

Beatles, The, 196

Belli, Carlos Germán, 27

Bello, Andrés, 29, 80–81

Benjamin, Walter, 1–4, 6, 10, 21, 69, 97, 124, 130–32, 160–61, 191–94, 197, 216, 219, 236 n.11, 239–40 n.22, 249–50 n.11, 250 n.14, 251 n.18, 254 n.13, 254–55 n.14, 255 n.22, 256 n.10, 260 n.31, 265–66 n.13, 267 n.3

Bernárdez, Francisco Luis, 102
Beverley, John, 13, 23–24, 35, 237–38
 n.2
Bioy Casares, Adolfo, 50, 93
Blake, Peter, 13
Blanchot, Maurice, 203
Boccaccio, Giovanni, 45
Bolívar, Simón, 155, 261 n.11
Bonasso, Miguel, 66–67
boom of Latin American literature,
 11–13, 24–37; and literary history,
 24–27; as mourning for the auratic,
 30–35; and nationhood, 35–37;
 as a substitution of aesthetics for
 politics, 27–32
Borges, Jorge Luis, 29, 34, 50, 75, 86–
 91, 97, 101–2, 139, 144, 239 n.20,
 249 n.3, 252 n.25
Bourdieu, Pierre, 53
Brazilian culture under dictatorship,
 39–44, 158–61, 243 n.9
Brecht, Bertolt, 10, 40, 86, 171, 205
Brito, Eugenia, 166, 171, 177, 262 n.17,
 263 n.22, 264 n.33
Brizola, Leonel, 40
Brod, Max, 95
Brunner, José Joaquín, 14, 46, 54–56,
 243 n.20
Buarque de Hollanda, Chico, 40
Buntinx, Gustavo, 261 n.11
Burton, Robert, 123

Calvino, Italo, 203
Campos, Haroldo de, 255 n.17
Campos, Roberto, 45, 81
Candido, Antonio, 139, 240 n.24, 257
 n.12, 258 n.24
Cané, Miguel, 87–88
Cánovas, Rodrigo, 166, 262 n.17, 263
 n.22

Cardoso, Fernando Henrique, 14, 22,
 54, 56–58, 241 n.33
Carpentier, Alejo, 11–12, 24, 26–28,
 31, 34, 73, 76, 246–47 n.66
Caruth, Cathy, 269–70 n.21
Carvalho, Murilo de, 62
Castelo Branco, 40
Castillo, Bernal Díaz del, 96
Castillo, Juan, 166
Catalán, Carlos, 243 n.20
Catalán, Gonzalo, 239 n.21
Cervantes, Miguel de, 145, 237 n.2
Chilean culture under dictatorship,
 44–48, 164–69, 243 n.20
Chocano, Santos, 27
Clifford, James, 76
Coleridge, Samuel, 6, 255–36 n.10
Collyer, Jaime, 45
Cornejo Polar, Antonio, 242 n.37
Cortázar, Julio, 11–12, 25–29, 31, 34,
 36, 51, 73–74, 90
Costa, Cláudio Manuel da, 17, 143,
 152–63
Croce, Benedetto, 7

Dante, 110
Dávila, Juan Domingo, 167, 261 n.11
Del Campo, Estanislao, 87, 90
Deleuze, Gilles, 237 n.1, 254 n.10, 259
 n.27, 260 n.30, 260 n.32, 264 n.34
De Man, Paul, 4, 247 n.67, 256 n.22
Demo, Pedro, 42
Derrida, Jacques, 139, 143, 164, 168,
 241 n.31, 241 n.34, 250 n.13, 251
 n.19, 256 n.22, 257 n.17, 257 n.18,
 260 n.31, 264 n.30, 265 n.4, 268
 n.8, 268 n.13
Descartes, René, 109, 250 n.15
Dick, Philip, 187
Disselkoen, Ivette, 263 n.22

Dittborn, Eugenio, 166–67
Donoso, José, 15, 68, 71–72, 75
Dos Passos, John, 26
Dostoyevsky, Fyodor, 45, 92–93, 96, 107, 117–18
DuBois, Page, 253 n.5

Eltit, Diamela, 15–16, 18, 20, 37, 48, 164–85, 263 n.22
Errázuriz, Paz, 165
Esquivel, Laura, 76
eternal return, the, 18, 157–62, 172–77, 181–85, 259 n.27, 265–66 n.13
experience, 18–19, 189–94, 196–97, 200–201, 222–25, 251 n.18, 254 n.13

Faulkner, William, 50
Felman, Shoshana, 267 n.3
Fernandes, Florestan, 81
Fernández, Macedonio, 16, 17, 50, 86, 101–35 passim, 252 n.24
Fichte, Johann, 77
Fischerman, Alberto, 53
Fitzgerald, Scott, 50
Flaubert, Gustave, 101, 141
Flores, Angel, 247 n.66
Foucault, Michel, 212, 230, 239 n.14, 251 n.22
Fourier, Charles, 108
Franco, Jean, 31, 240 n.26, 268 n.9
Frei, Eduardo, 39
Freud, Sigmund, 7–8, 30, 33, 99, 218, 232, 236 n.16, 240 n.25, 269 n.20, 269–70 n.21
Freyre, Gilberto, 42, 45–46
Frondizi, Arturo, 49
Fuentes, Carlos, 11–12, 24, 26–28, 30, 238 n.3, 238–39 n.7
Furtado, Celso, 40

Gabeira, Fernando, 63, 65–66
Galdós, Benito, 26
Galeano, Eduardo, 79, 231
Gallegos, Rómulo, 24
Gálvez, Manuel, 104
García Canclini, Néstor, 242 n.7
García Márquez, Gabriel, 12, 26, 29, 31–34, 73–74, 246 n.65
Giehlow, Karl, 7
Gil, Gilberto, 40
Goethe, Johann Wolfgang von, 5
Gogol, Nikolay, 45
Góngora, Luis de, 173
González Echevarría, Roberto, 32, 241 n.30, 246 n.65
Goulart, João, 39–40
Gracián, Baltazar, 237 n.2
Gramsci, Antonio, 49, 92
Gramuglio, María Teresa, 53
Greene, Graham, 50
Guarnieri, Gianfrancesco, 40
Guattari, Félix, 264 n.34
Guimarães, César, 197, 266 n.22

Habermas, Jürgen, 240 n.23
Handke, Peter, 197, 203, 266 n.22
Hardt, Michael, 254 n.10
Hartley, Hal, 95
Hegel, Georg, 5–6, 10, 19, 221–24, 236 n.12, 253 n.8
Heidegger, Martin, 109–10, 168, 193, 221–22, 260 n.31
Heker, Liliana, 52
Hemingway, Ernest, 62
Hernández, Felisberto, 74
Hernández, José, 89–90, 108–9, 249 n.3
Herodotus, 253 n.5
Herzog, Wladimir, 17, 143, 145, 158–61, 259–60 n.28

Hidalgo, Bartolomé, 87
Hippias, 109
Hitler, Adolf, 109–10, 129, 210
Hölderlin, Friedrich, 1, 21, 130, 255
    n.17
Homer, 111–13
Horkheimer, Max, 78
Hugo, Victor, 96
Huidobro, Vicente, 174
Humboldt, Wilhelm von, 77, 193, 197
Huxley, Aldous, 50
Huyssen, Andreas, 34

incorporation, vs. introjection 7–9
Inés de la Cruz, Sor Juana, 173
intellectual, the, 77–85; vs. the ex-
    pert, 82–85; vs. the ideologue,
    79–82

James, Henry, 122
Jameson, Fredric, 10, 190, 193, 235 n.4,
    241 n.31, 247 n.66, 251 n.20, 260
    n.31, 268 n.13
Jefferson, Thomas, 155
Jitrik, Noé, 83
Jordão, Fernando, 259–60 n.28
Joyce, James, 16, 26–27, 50, 86, 107,
    126, 128–33

Kadir, Djelal, 170, 263 n.22
Kafka, Franz, 86, 109, 115, 129, 131–32,
    142
Kant, Immanuel, 14, 29, 77–79, 82, 84
Kay, Ronald, 165–66, 261 n.10
Kennedy, John F., 198
Kerouac, Jack, 193
Kéti, Zé, 40
Klossowski, Pierre, 203

Lacan, Jacques, 196, 253 n.8, 266 n.26,
    268 n.10

Lafetá, João Luiz, 256–57 n.12
Landi, Oscar, 60, 245 n.47
Larsen, Neil, 238 n.2, 259 n.25
Laub, Dori, 210–11, 267 n.3
Leal, Luis, 247 n.66
Leão, Nara, 40
Leppe, Carlos, 166–67, 261 n.10
Lienhard, Martin, 242 n.37
Lima, Lezama, 173
Lispector, Clarice, 74
Lobo, Edu, 40
Loraux, Nicoles, 253 n.5
Louzeiro, José, 62, 245 n.48
Loyola, Hernán, 44
Ludmer, Josefina, 89, 248–49 n.3
Lugones, Leopoldo, 81, 87–88, 92, 105
Lukács, György, 10, 63

Mansilla, Lucio, 87–88, 90
Maqueira, Diego, 167, 169
Marchant, Patricio, 168, 262 n.14
Marechal, Leopoldo, 50, 86, 102
Martí, José, 29
Martín, San, 155
Martini, Juan, 54
Marx, Karl, 235 n.4, 241 n.31
Masiello, Francine, 52, 245 n.52
Masotta, Oscar, 94
McClelland, Charles, 247 n.71
melancholia, 7–10, 130–31, 210–12,
    269 n.19, 269–70 n.21
Menem, Carlos, 22, 60
Mercado, Tununa, 9, 16, 19–20, 37,
    210–29, 267–68 n.6, 269 n.19
messianic, the, 161–63, 265–66 n.13
Miceli, Sérgio, 138
mimesis, 110–14, 119–23, 135
Mistral, Gabriela, 45, 174
Moravia, Alberto, 26
Moreiras, Alberto, 236–37 n.25, 238

n.2, 241 n.31, 252 n.25, 268 n.12, 268–69 n.15

mourning, 7–9, 30–31, 137–38, 210–12, 225–29; and allegory, 3–5, 123–24; and gender, 112–17, 253 n. 5, 253–54 n.8, 269 n.19; and idealism, 111–12; and mimesis, 110–14, 119–23, 135; and storytelling, 20–21, 121–24, 132–35; and translation, 126–32, 240 n.25; and value, 4–5, 164

Moyano, Daniel, 15, 54, 68, 70–72, 246 n.61

Mozart, Wolfgang, 121

Mujica Láinez, Manuel, 50, 89, 93

Muñoz, Gonzalo, 167

Neruda, Pablo, 45, 47, 168

Neves, Tancredo, 58

Nietzsche, Friedrich, 20, 92, 96, 101, 136–38, 156, 161–62, 168, 192, 230, 251 n.17, 254 n.10, 260 n.30, 265–66 n.13, 268 n.8

Noll, João Gilberto, 11, 16, 20, 37, 189–209, 266 n.22

Ocampo, Silvina, 50

O'Donnell, Guillermo, 54, 245 n.36

Olea, Raquel, 263 n.22

Onganía, Juan Carlos, 212

Ortega, Julio, 263 n.22

Ortiz, Renato, 243 n.9

Ortiz, Scalabrini, 102

Orwell, George, 129

Osorio, Nelson, 44

Oyarzún, Pablo, 166, 243 n.20, 255 n.22, 261 n.10

Parmenides, 101, 109–10

Parra, Catalina, 165

Parra, Nicanor, 168

Parra, Violeta, 47

Partnoy, Alicia, 63

Paz, Octavio, 11, 26, 139, 238 n.3

Pellettieri, Osvaldo, 52

Pérez V., Carlos, 261 n.11, 262 n.17

Perón, Juan Domingo, 39, 48, 51, 114

Phelan, Peggy, 253–54 n.8

Phrynichus, 253 n.5

Piglia, Ricardo, 9, 16–20, 37, 50, 53, 86–135, 163, 186–89, 202–3, 250 n.15, 254 n.11; on Roberto Arlt, 91–97; on Borges, 86–91; *La ciudad ausente*, 107–35; on Macedonio Fernández, 101–6; *Prisión perpetua*, 94–96; on Manuel Puig, 186–89; *Respiración artificial*, 90, 92, 98–99, 104–5, 109–10, 131–33, 250 n.15; on Rodolfo Walsh, 186–89

Pinochet, Augusto, 15, 44–46, 71, 164, 178, 181

Plato, 107, 111–14, 120

Poe, Edgar Allan, 16, 98–99, 107–8, 117, 121, 192, 252–53 n.1

Portantiero, Juan Carlos, 54

postdictatorship, 1–4, 10–11, 19–21, 115–16, 135, 163, 215–17; and postmodernity, 77–80, 187–88, 230–33

Prieto, Adolfo, 83, 244 n.25

Proust, Marcel, 26–27

Puenzo, Luis, 53

Puig, Manuel, 187

Pynchon, Thomas, 187–88, 203

Quevedo, Francisco de, 173

Rama, Angel, 28, 238 n.2

Ramos, Graciliano, 17, 140–63 passim, 256 n.12, 257 n.14

Ramos, Julio, 29, 238 n.2

Reati, Fernando, 52

Reed, John, 62

Rego, José Lins do, 140, 147–51

restitution, 2–3, 110–11, 117–19, 123–
    24, 135, 144, 163, 168–70, 177, 185,
    194, 210–11, 217, 220–22, 226, 268
    n.13
Reyes, Alfonso, 83
Ribeiro, João Ubaldo, 209
Richard, Nelly, 165–66, 169, 243 n.20,
    261 n.11, 263 n.22
Rivera, Eustasio, 27
Robbe-Grillet, 27
Rocha, Gláuber, 40
Rodó, Enrique, 81
Rodríguez Monegal, Emir, 11–12,
    24–28
Rojas, Ricardo, 81
Rolling Stones, The, 196
romance-reportagem, 61–63
Rosa, Guimarães, 26
Rosas, 98, 133
Rosenfeld, Lotty, 166–67
Rousseau, Jean-Jacques, 100
Rowe, William, 242 n.37, 259 n.25
Rozitchner, León, 48, 53
Rulfo, Juan, 26, 207

Saer, Juan José, 53–54, 186–87
Santiago, Silviano, 16–20, 37, 136–
    63, 202; *Em Liberdade*, 140–63; on
    Graciliano Ramos, 140–63; on the
    Inconfidência Mineira, 143–45, 152–
    63; on modernism, 138–40; on the
    northeastern social novel, 140–42,
    146–50
Saramago, José, 249 n.5
Sarduy, Severo, 173
Sarlo, Beatriz, 28, 49, 53, 82, 239 n.21
Sarmiento, Domingo, 24, 29, 86–88,
    90, 97
Sarney, José, 58
Sarraute, Nathalie, 27

Sartre, Jean Paul, 26, 48
Schelling, Friedrich, 77
Schelling, Vivian, 259 n.25
Schiesari, Juliana, 269 n.19
Schleiermacher, Friedrich, 77
Schopf, Federico, 44
Schubert, Franz, 123
Schwarz, Roberto, 33, 40, 151, 258–59
    n.25
Sebreli, Juan José, 48, 83
Sigal, Silvia, 49, 244 n.25
signature, 16–17, 143–45, 151–53, 202–
    3, 257 n.17, 264 n.30
Silva, Aguinaldo, 245 n.48
Skármeta, Antonio, 44
Socrates, 96, 104–5, 111
Sodré, Nélson Werneck, 242 n.1, 258
    n.24
Solanas, Fernando, 53
Sommer, Doris, 240 n.26
Sophocles, 130, 253 n.8, 255 n.17
Soriano, Osvaldo, 246 n.64
Spinoza, Baruch, 237 n.1
Steinbeck, John, 26
storytelling, 20–21, 121–24, 132–35
Subiela, Eliseo, 53
Süssekind, Flora, 62, 202, 243 n.9,
    245 n.48, 247 n.70, 258 n.24
Swift, Jonathan, 193

Taussig, Michael, 256 n.10
Terán, Oscar, 54, 244 n.25
testimonio, 23–24, 61–68, 246 n.57
Thales, 101
Thayer, Willy, 58, 248 n.76
Timerman, Jacobo, 63–65
Tiradentes, 154–56
Tocqueville, Alexis de, 197
Torok, Maria, 7–8, 240 n.25
transference, 268 n.10, 269 n.20

translation, 126–32, 254–55 n.14, 255 n.17, 255–56 n.22, 258–59 n.25, 268 n.8
Trotsky, Leon, 219–20
Truman, Harry, 94
Twain, Mark, 45

untimely, the, 20–21, 128–32, 155–57, 160–63, 236–37 n.25

Valdés, Hernán, 63
Vale, João do, 40
Valente, Ignacio, 44, 168
Vargas, Getúlio, 138, 141, 148–50, 153, 257 n.14
Vargas Llosa, Mario, 11–12, 24, 27–28, 31, 34, 36
Vega, Garcilaso de la, 237 n.2
Veiga, J. J., 15, 68, 72–73, 75
Velázquez, Diego, 169
Veloso, Caetano, 40

Velvet Underground, The, 196
Veríssimo, Érico, 246 n.64
Vezzetti, Hugo, 53
Vianna Filho, Oduvaldo, 40
Videla, Rafael, 65
Viñas, David, 48, 53, 83
Viñas, Ismael, 48, 83
Viola, Roberto, 65

Walsh, Rodolfo, 86, 187
Wenders, Wim, 19, 197, 201, 266 n.22
Wilde, Oscar, 111
William of Malmesbury, 122
Williams, Raymond, 53

Yrigoyen, Hipólito, 81
Yúdice, George, 23–24, 238 n.3

Žižek, Slavoj, 266 n.26
Zurita, Raúl, 166–69, 174, 262 n.17, 263 n.22

Idelber Avelar is Associate Professor of Latin American Literatures and Critical Theory at Tulane University.

Library of Congress Cataloging-in-Publication Data
Avelar, Idelber
The untimely present : postdictatorial Latin American fiction
and the task of mourning / Idelber Avelar.
p.   cm. — (Post-Contemporary Interventions)
Includes bibliographical references and index.
ISBN 0-8223-2381-8 (alk. paper). — ISBN 0-8223-2415-6
(pbk. : alk. paper)
1. Latin American fiction—20th century—History and criticism.
2. Politics and literature—Southern Cone of South America.
3. Dictatorship—Southern Cone of South America—History—
20th century.   I. Title.
PQ7082.N7A87   1999
863—dc21   99-14157   CIP